LECTURES ON THE
HISTORY OF JOSEPH

LECTURES ON THE
HISTORY OF JOSEPH

GEORGE LAWSON

THE BANNER OF TRUTH TRUST

THE BANNER OF TRUTH TRUST
78b *Chiltern Street London* WIM IPS

*

First published 1807
First Banner of Truth Trust edition 1972

*

Printed in Great Britain by
W & J Mackay Limited, Chatham

CONTENTS

CONTENTS.

CONTENTS.

PREFATORY NOTE.

———❖———

THE Author of the volume now republished was
Professor of Divinity to the Associate or Burgher
branch of the Secession Church from 1787 to 1820. He
succeeded in that chair the well-known John Brown of
Haddington. Dr. Lawson enjoyed in the highest degree
the confidence of the Church and the esteem of all his
contemporaries. By his students he was loved and venerated as few Professors of any Church have ever been.
They were accustomed to speak of him with unbounded
enthusiasm, both as a man and as a teacher of theology.

His qualities both of head and heart gave him an ample
title to such a peculiar measure of affectionate regard. He
was a man of the most guileless and childlike simplicity
of character, and notwithstanding the remarkable gifts
with which he was endowed, and his vast erudition, his
humility was ·most conspicuous. Few have exemplified
more than he the meekness of wisdom. In short, there
was an admirable consistency between his whole manner
of life and his profession as a Christian minister.

Dr. Lawson was born at West Linton in 1749, and was ordained in 1771 to the pastoral charge of the Associate Burgher congregation of Selkirk. This office he held along with his professorship. His ministry extended over the long period of forty-nine years. His profound knowledge of the Scriptures, wisdom, and piety rendered his pulpit instructions singularly valuable. He was especially esteemed for his uncommon powers as an expositor of the Word of God. It is said that in the course of his long ministry he lectured through the entire volume of inspiration, and on some parts of it twice. His fertility of illustration, remarkable power of moral reflection, and spiritual ingenuity lent an interest to his exposition even of what might at first view seem bare and barren portions of the sacred oracles.

During his lifetime Dr. Lawson published several volumes of his lectures; one on the Book of Esther, one on the Book of Ruth, and two on the History of Joseph. Three posthumous volumes, containing lectures on the Book of Proverbs, and discourses on the history of David, were issued by his friends. All these works, together with some volumes of discourses, some fugitive sermons, and a pamphlet of great value, entitled "Considerations on the Overture lying before the Associate Synod on the Power of the Civil Magistrate in Matters of Religion," are now out of print, and often asked for—copies are rarely to be had. This applies more especially to the Lectures on the History of Joseph, which were printed in 1807, and much relished by the religious public. An attestation to their excellence was given by an eminent American writer in a way not to be commended. Professor Bush, of New York, has borrowed large portions of them, without acknowledgment, and inserted them in his Notes on Genesis, a work otherwise of considerable merit, and enjoying a large circulation in this country, as well as on the other side of the Atlantic.

We do not claim for Dr. Lawson's writings brilliant eloquence. There is no attempt in them at anything sensational or striking. Neither is there a *display* of learning : we say *display* of this quality ; for the results of it are there. But any parade of his acquisitions was foreign to his truthful, sincere, unostentatious nature, and, indeed, must have been unsuitable to the character of the Lectures themselves, which were addressed to a plain, popular audience, and simply designed for practical use. Any competent Biblical scholar will soon discern the extensive and deep knowledge that underlies his plain, direct, and often beautiful illustrations. With the original text Dr. Lawson was well acquainted ; and so wonderful was his memory, that it is said he could nearly have reproduced the English Bible, on which he habitually lectured to his congregation with the book shut. He had also by heart large portions of the Hebrew and Greek Scriptures, as well as of the Classics. With all the stores of English exegetical and theological learning he was familiar; to Continental sacred literature there was little access for Scottish students at the time when Dr. Lawson lived.

Intelligent readers of these Lectures cannot fail to be struck with the original thinking discovered in them, the author's knowledge of human nature, and his singular talent for generalising moral instruction. Mr. Spurgeon has said of him: "Dr. Lawson had a fertile mind, and a heart alive both to the human and Divine side of truth. He writes with a pleasing simplicity of style."

The history of Joseph being so favourite a subject both for lectures from the pulpit and for exercises in Bible classes, ministers and teachers will find this volume a valuable aid in their work.

A memoir of Dr. Lawson was written by Dr. Henry Belfrage, of Falkirk, and prefixed to the first volume of "Discourses on the History of David," which he edited. A much larger and very interesting life of Dr. Lawson was published in 1861 by Dr. John M'Farlane, of Clapham, containing many letters and anecdotes of this great and good man, as well as of his contemporaries. His memory is still cherished with affectionate reverence by a few survivors of those who enjoyed the benefit of his ministry or of his prelections. He died as he lived—in peace. The last words which he uttered on his death-bed were— "Take me to Paradise."

W. P.

1st *February*, 1878.

THE
PREFACE

———◦◇◦———

"BLESSED is the man that walketh not in the counsel of the ungodly, nor standeth in the way of sinners, nor sitteth in the seat of the scornful: But his delight is in the law of the Lord, and in His law doth he meditate day and night."

A man of this description will abhor those books, however well written, which have a tendency the reverse of that which is the great design of the Spirit of God in the Scriptures. He who truly desires to be sanctified through the faith will cease to hear the instruction that causeth to err from the words of knowledge.

He may allow himself the pleasure of amusement from books, as well as from other sources, as far as amusement can consist with the more serious business of life. But he certainly will not waste the greatest number of his reading hours on those books that afford little else but amusement.

The Bible will, undoubtedly, be valued far above the best books of human composition, by every lover of the name of God. He will not only read it, but meditate upon it, and endeavour to know what is that good, and perfect, and acceptable will of God, which it discovers unto men. When God has been pleased in His great mercy to write to us the great things of His law, they will not be accounted by us a strange thing, if we are not children of the night and of darkness. It is, however, to be feared that too often the Bible itself is read with little profit. If we run over a chapter, and throw aside the book, without endeavouring to understand what the mind of God in it is, and to improve it as the rule of our faith and practice, what will it profit us? We cannot expect that the Scriptures will operate on us as a charm.

The following Discourses are designed as a help to meditation on a very interesting portion of the Sacred History. We are all acquainted from our earliest years with the history of Joseph; and we may all derive much benefit from the thoughts which it will suggest to every pious mind, without the assistance of a commentator. Yet ordinary readers, it is to be hoped, will receive some advantage from the meditations of men of more leisure than themselves, who are called to be helpers of the faith and joy of Christians.

Christian parents are still under the obligation of that precept which Moses addressed to the Israelites—"The word which I command thee this day, shall be in thine heart, and thou shalt teach it diligently unto thy children,

and shalt talk of it when thou sittest in thine house, and
when thou walkest by the way." The history of Joseph
is one of those portions of Scripture concerning which
parents may hope to speak to their children with advantage, before they are fit to receive much instruction
concerning the doctrines and duties of religion. May not
this book assist parents in speaking of it to their. little
ones, in a manner fitted to insinuate into their minds some
of the most important lessons of religion ?

THE
HISTORY OF JOSEPH

LECTURE 1

Joseph is hated by his brethren, who form a resolution to destroy him.

xxxvii 1–17

OSES, having finished what he had to say concerning the Edomites, returns to his principal subject, and goes on with his history of Jacob's family. The patriarch Joseph must now be the chief object of our consideration. Nothing can be more interesting than the history of Joseph; and it affords us a rich variety of the most useful instruction. What sublime and generous virtues were displayed in his conduct! Where shall we find a nobler illustration of this important truth, that "the Lord of hosts is wonderful in counsel, and excellent in working;" than in the incidents of his life? We ought, no doubt, to except from this remark the history of our Lord Jesus Christ; and there is a very remarkable similarity between the character of Joseph and that of Christ, as well as between the events of their lives—only an allowance must be made for the incomparable excellency of our great Redeemer above all the sons of men. As the shadow is to the body, so were all the types and figures of our Lord Jesus Christ to Him, whom they represented.

B

VER. 1. *And Jacob dwelt in the land wherein his father was a stranger, in the land of Canaan.*

Esau did not grudge him his dwelling in that land where he and his father before him were but strangers and sojourners. Jacob had indeed bought a small piece of ground in this country, but still he was, and he thought himself, a stranger in the land of Canaan. Heaven was the country which he considered as his own personal inheritance. He pleased himself with the prospect of the settlement of his seed in the earthly Canaan, and his joy in the prospect was not greatly damped by the present circumstances of his family, or by the prospect of those afflictions which they were to endure in "a land that was not theirs," before the time of the promise should come, Gen. xv. 13. He knew that it would be accomplished when it pleased God, and that his seed, whatever afflictions they might suffer, would be safe under the protecting care of the God of their fathers.

VER. 2. *These are the generations of Jacob. Joseph, being seventeen years old, was feeding the flock with his brethren; and the lad was with the sons of Bilhah, and with the sons of Zilpah, his father's wives: and Joseph brought unto his father their evil report.*

We had an account of the generations of Esau in the last chapter. Moses, returning to his history of Jacob's family, proposes to give us an account of the generations of Jacob; but he does not give us a barren account of their names. He relates the most remarkable incidents in the lives of Jacob's sons, very little to the honour of the greater part of them. But it was his purpose to relate facts as they stood. Had he intended, as infidels allege, to aggrandise his own nation, without regard to truth, he would have certainly given us a very different account of the advancement of Joseph from that which is now before us. But every man who reads the writings of Moses with the least degree of impartiality, must see an inviolable regard to truth clearly displayed in every part of them.

Joseph, though his father's favourite, was not kept in idleness about his father's house while he was a boy. When he was but seventeen years of age, he was employed with his brethren in keeping his father's flock. Idleness in young persons is the nurse of every vice, and the beginning of a wicked and miserable life. If you love your children, inure them betimes to honest and useful labour.

Joseph, in his youth, associated himself chiefly with the sons of Bilhah and Zilpah. It is probable they were not so high-minded as the sons of Leah, who reckoned themselves superior in dignity to all the rest of Jacob's children, because they were his sons by the first of his wives. Pride is very natural to our race, and soon begins to discover itself in the children of Adam. Better to be of mean birth, and humble, than to be of royal extraction, and high-minded. Joseph was the son of a woman who had a right to have been Jacob's first wife, and he was the best-beloved son of his father; yet he did not reckon it below his dignity to associate with the sons of the handmaids.

And Joseph brought unto his father their evil report.—We have no reason to think that he took any pleasure in carrying bad tidings to his father concerning the behaviour of his brethren. Their conduct, in some instances, it seems, was shameful; and Joseph had it not in his power to reform them. Grieved at their sins, he made his complaints to his father; and in doing so he performed a charitable and brotherly office. When we see any man's children disgracing and hurting themselves, if we cannot by our own influence persuade them to reform their conduct, we will deserve the thanks of their parents by letting them know how much they are dishonoured, and what grief is likely to be brought upon them by their children if they are not checked. If parents are to admonish or to correct their children for bad behaviour, it is necessary for them to inspect their conduct; but they cannot be always under their own eyes, and therefore they ought to reckon themselves indebted to the persons who assist them by prudent and seasonable informations in this part of their duty. Yet great caution must be used in this office of love, that we may not bring upon ourselves the guilt and reproach of officious interference in other men's matters.

Ver. 3. *Now Israel loved Joseph more than all his children,*

*because he was the son of his old age; and he made him a coat
of many colours.*

Joseph was the best-beloved of all Jacob's children, not only
because he was the first-born son of his best-beloved wife, and
the child of many prayers, but because he was the son of his
old age. There is, however, a difficulty in understanding this
reason of Jacob's love to his son. Benjamin was much more
the son of his old age than Joseph; and it cannot well be supposed that Joseph was younger than Zebulun and Dinah. The
word in the original for old age properly signifies " old men,"
or " senators." And when it is said that Joseph was " a son of
old men," or " senators," the meaning is (as some learned men
have understood it), that Joseph, even in his early years, had
the wisdom of a sage. This was a reason for loving him, more
worthy of Jacob than the time of his birth. The time of birth
would probably have ingratiated the eldest son, rather than the
youngest but one or two, with his father, if Reuben had not
been utterly unworthy of Jacob's fondness. But it is certain
that Joseph was very wise in his early years; and it is no less
certain that " a wise son makes a glad " and a fond " father."

Jacob, to testify his love to his son Joseph, " made him a coat
of many colours," fit to be worn by the sons of princes. But
whether Jacob acted wisely in distinguishing Joseph from his
brethren by this mark of his regard, may admit of a doubt. It
seems as if Jacob had already taken the birthright from Reuben
for his sin, and given it to the first-born of his beloved wife.
The birthright was indeed to be Joseph's; and it was due to
him as the eldest son of Rachel, when the first-born son of Leah
had forfeited it. But Joseph was exposed to great envy by
this mark of his father's fondness; and the effects of that envy
cost the good old man many years of grief. Parents ought to
love most affectionately those children who best deserve their
love, but they ought not to hurt, instead of benefiting, the
children whom they love by imprudent testimonies of their
regard. Joseph might have lived happily in his father's house
without a garment of divers colours; but he could not wear it
without encountering the hatred of all his brethren.

We must not, however, blame Joseph for accepting this testimony of his father's goodness. It was not his province to affect wisdom superior to that of his father; nor would it have become him to suspect all the evil that was in the hearts of his brethren. Only the bad are ready to suspect that others are bad, till experience give them information of the corruption that abounds in the world.

VER. 4. *And when his brethren saw that their father loved him more than all his brethren, they hated him, and could not speak peaceably unto him.*

Joseph's brethren were far from thinking that he was wiser, or that he deserved his father's love better than themselves. They grudged his father's kindness to the boy, and could not afford him a kind word. The happiness of other men is poison to the envious man. The odious passion of envy torments and destroys one's self, while it seeks the ruin of its object.

Beware of envy; you know not to what it tends. Beware of all its fruits; you will find them to be deadly, when they have time and opportunity to ripen. Joseph's brethren did not proceed to extremes of cruelty when they were first seized with this baleful passion. They "could not speak peaceably to him," but they entertained no thoughts of killing him, till their envy had by indulgence acquired a greater degree of strength. Their "lust conceived and brought forth sin; and when their sin was finished, it brought forth death" to Joseph in their intentions. They contracted the guilt of his blood, although they did not shed it. They were chargeable with intended murder in the sight of men when they cast Joseph into the pit; but in the sight of God they were chargeable with this crime as soon as they began to hate Joseph; for "he that hateth his brother in his heart is.a murderer."

You see that the best of men have been hated by those from whom they had reason to expect kindness. Jesus Himself was hated by His brethren, and became "an alien to His mother's children." Why should we think it strange to find the same afflictions accomplished in us that have in every age been accomplished in our fathers, whilst they were in the world?

Is it not enough for the disciples of Christ that they be as their Master, and for His servants that they be as their Lord?

Joseph might seem unhappy in the envy of his brethren; but this unhappiness was in a great measure counterbalanced by the kindness of his father; and it was more than counterbalanced by the love of God, who watched over him, and who brought much good out of it, both to Joseph himself, and to all his father's house.

VER. 5-8. *And Joseph dreamed a dream, and he told it to his brethren; and they hated him yet the more. And he said unto them, Hear, I pray you, this dream which I have dreamed: for, behold, we were binding sheaves in the field, and, lo, my sheaf arose, and also stood upright; and, behold, your sheaves stood round about, and made obeisance to my sheaf. And his brethren said to him, Shalt thou indeed reign over us? or shalt thou indeed have dominion over us? and they hated him yet the more for his dreams, and for his words.*

Joseph was predestinated to high honours before he came into the world; and while he was yet a boy he was favoured with a presage of his exaltation, by a dream that made a deep impression on his mind. There is certainly a great difference between those dreams that came from God to announce future events, and such dreams as are the mere illusions of fancy. When God spoke to men in dreams of the night, He made His voice known to be His own divine voice, and not the wild reveries of a wandering imagination.

Joseph told his dream to his brethren. Whether he acted wisely in telling it or not may be questioned. But it is certain that the dream was suggested by God, and that Joseph was directed by an overruling Providence, at least, when he made his dream known. For, although his brethren made a very bad use of it, that bad improvement of what was told them tended, without their knowledge, and against their inclination, to the completion of it. God makes use, not only of the imprudence, but of the worst vices of men, to the accomplishment of His own pleasure.

" Hear, I pray you," said Joseph, " this dream which I have

dreamed : for, behold, we were binding sheaves in the field, and, lo, my sheaf arose, and also stood upright ; and, behold, your sheaves stood round about, and made obeisance to my sheaf."

The images used in this dream to represent Joseph's future advancement were not taken from that kind of substance with which Jacob's sons were most conversant, but from the precious fruits of the earth. Joseph himself did not yet know that his exaltation was to be procured by the interpretation of another dream concerning the fruits of the earth, and that his brethren were to bow down to him for a supply of that precious commodity. The propriety and beauty of the images which God uses to represent future things, in the language of prophecy, is best understood when prophecies are accomplished.

The general signification of this dream was very obvious. Joseph's brethren perceived it at once, as clearly as Joseph himself. "What!" said they, "do you imagine that all of us will ever bow down to you? Shall we be subject to our own younger brother? Has he the presumption to hope that we ever will?" Thus we find David's elder brother jealous of his advancement, and upbraiding him with his alleged pride. Thus the Jews, in our Lord's time, imagined that a citizen of Nazareth was very unfit to be acknowledged as their king. Such is our pride, and the stoutness of our spirits, that we cannot bear the thought of being subject to men who have been our equals, or our inferiors. But let us remember that "promotion cometh not from the south, nor from the east, nor from the west : it is the Lord that puts down one, and sets up another ; and who shall stay his hand, or say unto him, What dost thou?"

VER. 9-11. *And he dreamed yet another dream, and told it his brethren, and said, Behold, I have dreamed a dream more ; and, behold, the sun and the moon and the eleven stars made obeisance to me. And he told it to his father, and to his brethren : and his father rebuked him, and said unto him, What is this dream that thou hast dreamed? Shall I and thy mother and thy brethren indeed come to bow down ourselves to thee to the earth? And his brethren envied him ; but his father observed the saying.*

This dream represented his exaltation by brighter images than the former ; and if his brethren envied him when they heard the former dream, it was to be expected that their spirits would be kindled into rage when they heard this also. The thing seemed to be certain, and the interpretation sure, when the vision was doubled. Joseph seemed incorrigible in his pride when he repeated it.

"God speaketh once, yea, twice unto men ; but man perceiveth it not." Here we find men so far from perceiving what God said, when they heard it twice, that they were filled with the blackest malice against the child who told them what God had spoken to him. Hatred and envy turn good into evil, and fill the minds of many with an irreconcilable aversion to the Word and to the providence of God. If Joseph's dreams had been the mere rovings of the fancy in sleep, they were not worth the minding, although Joseph might have deserved a reproof for his folly and vanity in telling them. But if they were indeed from God, and signified the future advancement of Joseph, his brethren sinned not only against the lad, but against the Lord Himself, when they were displeased with them. What were they that they should direct the Most High? If God had been pleased to make one of their own slaves head and prince over them all, what right had they to complain? To be discontented with our own situation, or with the elevation of our neighbours above ourselves, is rebellion against that Providence by which all our affairs, and the affairs of all mankind, are conducted.

But Jacob himself had very different views from his sons concerning Joseph's dreams, although he affected to treat them with contempt. "His father rebuked him, and said unto him, What is this dream that thou hast dreamed? Shall I and thy mother and thy brethren indeed come to bow down ourselves to thee to the earth?" A very natural exposition is here given of the dream, in such a manner as to suggest that it could not be accomplished. The head of a nation is often, in figurative language, signified by the sun ; and the same emblem might be applied to a family, which, making a part of no other nation, might be considered as a nation by itself, especially considering how large and powerful it was, chap. xxvi. 29 ; xxxvi. 6. For the same reason, the mother and mistress of a family might be represented by the moon, aud the children of the family by the stars. But according to this interpretation, the dream had the appearance of absurdity. Joseph would not wish nor expect that his father should do him obeisance. It would be strange if his brethren, who were all, or most of them, older than himself, should all bow down to him ; and it was impossible that his mother could bow down to him, for she was already in her grave.

But if this be the true interpretation of the dream, was not Jacob right in reproving Joseph for telling it ? It is not necessary to the accomplishment of a dream that every object which presented itself to the fancy should have something correspondent to it in the event, but only that the general idea should agree with what was afterwards to happen. Thus, in parables, it would be unreasonable to seek a distinct meaning to every circumstance that may be proper in the narration for connecting its parts, or for adorning it. It is certain that Rachel could not bow down to Joseph, and it is not certain that any of Jacob's wives went down with him to Egypt ; but it is certain that Jacob himself paid homage to Joseph, before he knew that he was alive ; and that after he knew that Joseph was alive, he depended upon him for support. If the words of God are rightly understood, they will be found faithful and true ; but we are not to think that God is under any obligation to verify the comments which we may put upon them. Groundless comments upon the Word of God are attended with this dangerous consequence, that they often tend to bring the oracles of truth under suspicion. They have not that stamp of divine majesty upon them which distinguishes the Word of God from human compositions ; nor is there that correspondency between our comments and the providence of God that there is between His Word and His works. If we entertain a just reverence for the Word of God, let us never mingle the truths of it with our own false conceptions, nor imagine that it can fail to be accomplished, because it would be unreasonable to think that it will be accomplished according to our own views of its meaning.

Jacob meant his reproof of Joseph, not so much to check the ambition or vanity of Joseph himself, as to dissipate the bad humour of his other children, who were disgusted with the young man's conduct. Jacob did not take the fairest, and perhaps he did not take the wisest, method to allay the fierce passions that threatened the repose and safety of Joseph. He gave too much countenance to their ill-nature, and furnished them with a fair pretence for alleging that Joseph's dreams were the fruits of his own pride, and not the dictates of the Spirit of God.

Yet Jacob laid up Joseph's dreams in his heart. He thought it probable, if not certain, that they came from God; and if they came from God, they merited the closest attention; for he says nothing that is false, and nothing that is of small consequence. When God, by His Word, gives us reason to expect any extraordinary events, it would be a mark of stupidity to be inattentive to the voice of the great Ruler of heaven and earth. His works and His words reflect light upon one another; and whoso is wise, and will observe their harmony, shall understand the loving-kindness, and see the glory of the Lord.

VER. 12-14. *And his brethren went to feed their father's flock in Shechem. And Israel said unto Joseph, Do not thy brethren feed the flock in Shechem? come, and I will send thee unto them. And he said unto him, Here am I. And he said to him, Go, I pray thee, see whether it be well with thy brethren, and well with the flocks. So he sent him out of the vale of Hebron, and he came to Shechem.*

His brethren, after this time, went to feed their father's flock in Shechem. We are not sure that Moses relates the story of the murder of the Shechemites in the exact order of time wherein it happened. We have already met with an account of Isaac's death, which did not happen till Joseph had been many years sold into Egypt. But if the Shechemites were, before the time here referred to, murdered by Simeon and Levi, the sons of Jacob discovered great boldness in going to Shechem to feed their flocks. Although the men of Shechem were all destroyed, yet surely they had neighbours around them who would entertain no good-will to their murderers. On this supposition, too, we may see a good reason why Jacob was so solicitous for the welfare of his sons, who had made both themselves and their father odious by their conduct. None of Jacob's sons were trained up to be idle, although Jacob had, by his industry, made a large provision for them all. They were careful of the state of their flocks, and attended them in person. But in these ages of simplicity, even the daughters of princes did not think it honourable to be idle; nor did they reckon it below their dignity to feed the flocks of their fathers.

Joseph was ever ready to comply with his father's wishes, as soon as they were intimated to him. Jacob, deeply concerned for the welfare of all his children, although he entertained a peculiar regard to the best of his sons, sends Joseph to Shechem, to bring him intelligence whether all his brethren were safe and well. As soon as Joseph was called by his father, he said, Here am I. Our Lord, in a parable, speaks of two sons commanded by their father to go and labour in the vineyard, one of whom said to his father, I go, sir, but went not; the other said, I go not, but went. The last was, without question, the best of the two; but Joseph was better than either. He said, I go; and he went. He loved and honoured his father, and would have gladly gone anywhere to please and serve him. He loved his brethren, and was happy to receive a commission to go and inquire after their welfare.

VER. 15 17. *And a certain man found him, and, behold, he was wandering in the field: and the man asked him, saying, What seekest thou? And he said, I seek my brethren: tell me, I pray thee, where they feed their flocks. And the man said, They are departed hence; for I heard them say, Let us go to Dothan.*

Joseph did not find it so easy as he supposed to gain the intelligence which his father desired. His brethren were not in Shechem; but he did not return to tell his father that they could not be found. He knew his father's anxiety, and felt himself interested in the welfare of his brethren. He wandered in the field to try what information he could obtain; and he succeeded to his wish. A man met him, who was acquainted with the family, and told him that his brethren must be gone to Dothan.   Thither Joseph went without delay; and there he met with his brethren, but found too much reason, for the present, to lament his success.   Disappointments in men's pursuits may arise from the interposition of Providence, by means which men cannot resist.   But they very often, too, arise from carelessness and sloth.   "The slothful man putteth his hand in his bosom; he grudges to bring it to his mouth," or he fancies that there are a thousand insurmountable difficulties and dangers in his way, so that he can never obtain the object of his wishes, or may lose his life in attempting it.   Joseph was a man of a very different spirit.   He might have supposed, with great probability, that there were lions in the way; and there were savage beasts, worse than lions, at the end of it, in the shape of men.   But he pursued his purpose of obeying his father.   He was ill rewarded by his brethren; but God turned their evil into good.

LECTURE 2
Joseph is sold by his brethren.
xxxvii 18–36

VER. 18-20. *And when they saw him afar off, even before he came near unto them, they conspired against him to slay him. And they said one to another, Behold, this dreamer cometh. Come now therefore, and let us slay him, and cast him into some pit, and we will say, Some evil beast hath devoured him: and we shall see what will become of his dreams.*

WE read of very cruel actions performed by the degenerate sons of Adam; but it is not easy to find a parallel in history to the cruel intentions, and to the cruel conduct of Joseph's brethren. Cain was of that wicked one, and slew his brother, and has left a name of infamy to all the generations of mankind. But where shall we find nine men conspiring at once to kill a brother? a brother whose amiable qualities deserved their warmest love? a brother who tenderly loved them, and was in the very act of showing his love to them at the time when their fury broke loose upon him?

Joseph put himself to much trouble to find out his brethren, that he might inform himself and his father of their welfare; but they took advantage from his love to wreak their hatred upon him, as if they had been devils in flesh and blood, rather than patriarchs in the Church. It is too common with discontented men to say that none were ever so ill-used as themselves. But let us consider how Joseph was used, how David was used, how Christ Himself was used, by those men from whom they

had most reason to expect kindness. Joseph had too good
reason, as David afterwards had, to say in the person of Christ,
" For my love they are mine adversaries."

The very sight of Joseph roused the fury of his unnatural
brethren. When he came within sight of them, they said one
to another, " Behold, this dreamer cometh. Come now therefore,
and let us slay him." Little did Joseph now think what was
to befall him; little did he suspect the plot that was framing
against him. He was happy at the sight of his brethren : he
was happy in the prospect of carrying glad tidings concerning
them to his father ; he no doubt thought they would be happy
too in seeing him, and in hearing from their venerable father.
How cruelly were his hopes disappointed! What pangs,
sharper than those of a woman in travail, must he have felt,
when he looked for a kind reception from brothers ; and, behold,
he was attacked by assassins in the persons of brothers !

" Behold, this dreamer cometh ; let us kill him, and we
will see what will become of his dreams." They insulted
the Sovereign of the world, while they persecuted their poor
brother. They intended to frustrate the word of the Lord, and
hoped that they would bring to nothing the counsels of the
Most High. Presumptuous creatures ! Did they think that
they were stronger than the Almighty ? If they had cut Joseph
into a thousand pieces, the word of the Lord would have stood
firm and sure. It would be far easier to arrest the sun in his
course, than to hinder the performance of any promise that God
has made to His people. " His counsel shall stand for ever : the
thoughts of his heart to all generations."

They might, no doubt, imagine that they were fighting, not
against God, but against a presumptuous boy, who fondly
dreamed of rising into honours above his equals or superiors,
and that Joseph's arrogance well deserved to be humbled. They
did not, perhaps, think that Joseph's dreams were from God ;
but why, then, were they so much piqued with his dreams?
Might they not have suffered them to pass away from their
memories like other vanities, which pass away the moment in
which they make their appearance ? Must a man be hunted

day after day, till he is chased out of the world, for a silly dream? But if their spirits had not been blinded by envy, they might have either seen that there was something more than ordinary in Joseph's dreams, or at least have seen good reason to suspend their judgment. It was not a good excuse that they did not know the dreams to be from God. They ought to have known with certainty that they did not come from God before they ventured to turn them into derision. The bonds of those who mock the messengers or the prophets of the Lord "shall be made strong;" and it will not exempt them from punishment to allege that they did not know the divine original of what they despised.

How were Joseph's brethren to secure themselves from the reproach of the world, and the indignation of their father? They would cast Joseph's body into some pit after they had killed him. But where were they to find a pit deep enough to hide him from the view of God? It was right not to disoblige their father; but was their God less to be regarded than their father? Many heathens will rise up in judgment against those professors of the true religion, who behave in such a manner, as if it were a matter of indifference what sins they commit, if they can preserve their characters from suspicion. A certain Indian, trained up in the strictest sect of the religion of his country, had macerated his body to such a degree, that his life was in imminent danger. A Christian physician, who went to see him with the governor of the town, begged him to swallow. an infusion of the Jesuits' bark in wine, which he thought might preserve his life. The religion of the Indian prohibited this cure. The physician promised that none should hear of it. But the poor Indian answered, that he could not hide it from himself, and chose to die rather than violate his conscience.

"Let us slay him, and cast him into some pit; and we will say, Some evil beast hath devoured him." Lying uses to attend upon other sins. Those who can commit any gross crime will not scruple a hundred lies to protect themselves from the shame to which their conduct exposes them. But they do not consider that by their lies they are exposing themselves to greater shame than they would otherwise incur. The righteous man hates and abhors lying; but the wicked man who trusts in lies is loathsome, and cometh to shame.

Beware of lying; for "lying lips are an abomination to the Lord." Beware of other sins, if you wish to keep yourselves from temptations to lying. One sin needs another to guard it from detection; and when men enter on the evil way, they know not where or when they will stop.

VER. 21, 22. *And Reuben heard it, and he delivered him out of their hands; and said, Let us not kill him. And Reuben said unto them, Shed no blood, but cast him into this pit that is in the wilderness, and lay no hands upon him; that he might rid him out of their hands, to deliver him to his father again.*

We have heard already of Reuben's great wickedness, in defiling his father's bed, and have conceived so bad a notion of him, that we expect him to appear foremost in all wickedness that may be projected by the sons of Jacob. But let not the worst of men be held worse than they really are. He took no active part in the assassination of the Shechemites; and he abhors the project of killing Joseph. He was not a bloody-minded man. The lust of uncleanness seems to have been his predominant iniquity, as the lust of blood or of revenge seems to have reigned in some of his brethren. All men have their own particular ways of sin, to which they turn when they are left to themselves. Let us watch and pray that we enter not into temptation, and that we may be kept from our own iniquities.

Reuben greatly wished to restore Joseph to his father, whose life he knew was bound up in the lad's life. He had formerly pierced the heart of his father with a wound which could never be healed. Charity obliges us to think that he repented of his wickedness; and now he wishes to make to his father all the compensation in his power. He could not undo what he had done, but he would have certainly done an eminent service to his father, if he could have saved the life of his best-beloved son. If we have done evil to any man, let us endeavour to do him as much good as we have done him evil. This will be the best evidence that we can give of the truth of our repentance. We must repent of our sins against God or men, not in word only and in tongue, but in deed and in truth. As every man is to be judged according to his works, so all our professions are to be tried by our works. How can we have the face to say that we are heartily sorry for having wronged our neighbour, unless we at last do him justice to the utmost of our power? If we cannot pay him in that coin of which we robbed him, let us pay him, if possible, equal value in a different coin.

Reuben knew that it would be to no purpose to protest with a loud voice against the crime. He takes a more effectual way to prevent it. He pretends not to dissent from his brethren in their resolution to destroy their brother, but alleges that it would be unnatural to lay hands on him, and proposes to put him into a pit, whence he might be prevented from making his escape till he died.

One would not think it likely that Reuben could have prevailed on them to adopt his plan of murder. It was evidently worse to kill him with hunger in a pit by a lingering death than to despatch him at once. Without renouncing common sense, they could not think their guilt would be diminished by this barbarous method of perpetrating the crime. But wickedness blinds men's eyes to the plainest truths, and Reuben prevails to obtain a respite for Joseph.

VER. 23. *And it came to pass, when Joseph was come unto his brethren, that they stripped Joseph out of his coat, his coat of many colours that was on him.*

As soon as Joseph came to his brethren, they too plainly discovered to him the black passions which poisoned their hearts. They stripped him of his coat, of his coat of divers colours, which his father had given him. How dearly did he purchase the honour bestowed on him by his father! What agonizing thoughts now distracted his soul! He was amazed and confounded to find such unnatural behaviour in brothers, in the sons of Jacob. It would now be almost impossible for him to think that his dreams were anything better than illusions of

C

his fancy. How bitter were the pangs which prepared the way for his advancement to the throne of glory !

It was an aggravation of the guilt of Joseph's brethren that he came to them adorned with his coat of many colours, although they might suppose it an extenuation or a justification of their offence. They no doubt considered it an insult to themselves that he came to them decked with this trophy of his superiority in their father's regard. But if they had any reason to be offended, why was not their father the object of their resentment? Besides, this coat, the evidence of his father's dear regard, might have reminded them that to murder Joseph was the same thing with murdering their father. If it would not deprive him of life, it would deprive him of the comfort of life, and fill up all the rest of his days with bitterness and sorrow.

VER. 24. *And they took him, and cast him into a pit; and the pit was empty, there was no water in it.*

Having stripped Joseph of his coat, they cast him into a pit; and the pit was empty, there was no water in it. Joseph's agitation of mind and his lamentable cries would parch his throat to an uncommon degree; but there was no water to cool his tongue. He was there left to perish by a death far more dreadful than if he had been killed by the sword; and yet the barbarians thought they were showing him mercy, because they did not stretch out their hands against him. Their tender-mercies were the extreme of cruelty.

To be brought out of a pit wherein there is no water is in Scripture represented as a great deliverance. Joseph would learn in this pit to bear those other sufferings that were allotted to him. He was sold to foreign merchants. He was carried into a strange land, to be again sold as a slave. He was cast into a prison, where he lay for several years. But the remembrance of the pit wherein was no water, and of his fruitless cries for relief, would make him think that his condition, under all these circumstances of distress, was not so bad as it might have been, and as it once actually was.

VER. 25-28. *And they sat down to eat bread; and they lifted up their eyes and looked, and, behold, a company of Ishmeelites came from Gilead with their camels bearing spicery and balm and myrrh, going to carry it down to Egypt. And Judah said unto his brethren, What profit is it if we slay our brother, and conceal his blood? Come, and let us sell him to the Ishmeelites, and let not our hand be upon him; for he is our brother and our flesh. And his brethren were content. Then there passed by Midianites merchantmen; and they drew and lifted up Joseph out of the pit, and sold Joseph to the Ishmeelites for twenty pieces of silver; and they brought Joseph into Egypt.*

Joseph's brethren sat down to take their repast. They did eat and drink as if nothing had happened, and cared not for the affliction of Joseph. They heard his cries, and pitied not the anguish of his soul. Their hearts were hardened like a piece of the nether-millstone. Their own consciences, if they had not been stupified, would have cried louder than Joseph, and have spoiled their relish for meat and drink; but the devil at this time appears to have taken them captive at his will.

Yet God, who rules amidst the raging of the seas, and stills the tumult of the people, controlled their rage, and restrained its remainder. It was of God that Reuben interposed to preserve Joseph from present death, and proposed to cast him into a pit. It was of God that Reuben's brethren complied with the proposal. It was of God that a caravan of Ishmeelitish merchants passed along in view of the sons of Jacob, before Joseph perished in the pit; and the same divine Providence inspired Judah with the proposal of selling him to these Ishmeelites, and disposed the hearts of his brethren to approve of the thought. How wonderful is the Lord in counsel! how seasonable are the interpositions of His providence in behalf of His people! What strange turns can He easily make in the thoughts and purposes of men!

The Ishmeelites by this time had increased greatly in number, and carried on a trade with Egypt. So early did the promise made to Abraham concerning Ishmael begin to receive its accomplishment: "I will make him," said God, "a great nation." He was already a little nation, when the seed of Jacob was but a family. But in this caravan there appears to have been so many Midianites, that it might with equal truth be called a company of Ishmeelites, or a company of Midianites. It seems that the seed of Abraham by the concubines cultivated mutual harmony at this time better than the seed of the free-woman, to whom the promises were made—"The children of this world are often wiser in their generation than the children of light."

We do not read that Judah at first opposed the motion for killing Joseph. It may be reasonably presumed; however, that all the sons of Jacob were not equally wicked. If any of them at first were averse to such a sanguinary method of gratifying their malice, they might think it needless, or even dangerous, to interpose. Simeon may reasonably be suspected as the ring-leader. Judah appears soon to have relented, and wisely seizes the opportunity which was afforded by the appearance of the Ishmeelites, and proposes to have the sentence of death exchanged for a sentence of perpetual slavery. We can almost forgive Judah his share in the guilt, for the wisdom and moderation, and happy event, of his proposal to sell Joseph, instead of killing him—"What profit is it if we slay our brother, and conceal his blood? Come, and let us sell him to the Ishmeelites, and let not our hands be upon him, for he is our brother and our flesh."

If he was their brother and their flesh, they ought not to have sold him. They ought rather to have defended him against any man that would have done him an injury. It was well, however, that this consideration had some degree of influence upon their hard hearts. Their consciences and their feelings told them that they ought not to kill Joseph. Their envy told them that they must at least sell him, that they might remove him to a distance from themselves and their father's house. Their consciences had leave to dictate as far as their envy would permit, and no farther.

We cannot but reprobate the conduct of these men, who remembered that Joseph was their brother, and yet resolved to sell him. Let us beware lest we behave in a manner equally reprehensible to any of our brethren; and let us remember that our fellow-men, without exception, are our brethren and our flesh, and that our fellow-Christians are doubly our brethren. They are our brethren both in the flesh and in the Lord. We cannot do them any wrong without violating the most sacred obligations.*

Judah's brethren were content to comply with his advice. As "one sinner destroyeth much good," so one wise man may prevent much evil.

Joseph was drawn out of the pit, and sold to the company of Midianites, or Ishmeelites. These men, too, were Joseph's brethren, for they were children of Abraham. But one does not wonder that the Midianites would buy a son of Abraham for gain, when his brethren, by a nearer relation, sold him from a worse motive. The Midianites did a real and an eminent service to Joseph, although they did it only to serve themselves. Their regard to their own interest was made, by the wise providence of God, instrumental in saving the life of Joseph, and of all the family of Jacob.

They bought him for twenty pieces of silver. A goodly price that he was valued at by his brethren! How many thousand pieces of silver would Jacob have given for his redemption, had he known that his beloved son was become a slave. But Joseph's brethren cared little what they had for him, if they could be rid of him, and never see him more.

Joseph was greatly dishonoured when he was sold for twenty pieces of silver, amounting in our coin only to fifty shillings. But we cannot forget that He who was infinitely greater than Joseph was sold by one of His brethren, and of His disciples, for a price not much greater.

VER. 29, 30. *And Reuben returned unto the pit; and, behold, Joseph was not in the pit; and he rent his clothes, and he returned unto his brethren, and said, The child is not; and I, whither shall I go?*

Reuben was not present when Joseph was sold. He had

* Eph. iv. 25.

gone apart from his brethren, that he might, without their
knowledge, take him out of the pit, and send him home in
safety to his father. His intentions were good, and his plan
seemed to be wise, but it was not successful. It was not by
Reuben that Joseph was to be delivered. He must yet go
through a sea of afflictions before he obtain that glory for which
he was designed. God often blasts those designs that are
formed for the good of His people, not because He hates them,
but because the whole work is not yet accomplished that He
intends to accomplish by their afflictions. They must not only
be.brought into distress, but kept in it as long as he sees fit;
they must not only meet with one trouble, but they must fall
into many temptations, that they may be made meet for those
honours and felicities that God has in view for them.

Reuben mourns bitterly when he finds his plan disconcerted.
Joseph, he thinks, is for ever lost to his father. " He rent his
clothes, and returned to his brethren, and said, The child is not;
and I, whither shall I go?" He appears to have loved, and he
sincerely pitied the child. He loved his father, and could not
bear to think of the new affliction that was falling upon him
after the severe griefs which he had already sustained from his
own misbehaviour, and that of his brethren. He pours out his
bitter complaints to his hard-hearted brethren, but it was to
little purpose. They could not well undo what was done, and
they had no wish to undo it. Reuben at another time will be
better heard by them, when their consciences are awakened to
take a just and a painful review of what they had done.

We may be afflicted with disappointment in the prosecution
of the best and wisest schemes. To prevent or mollify the
sorrows of disappointment, let us acknowledge the Lord in all
our ways. Then shall we have good success, or, if God sees
meet to deny us success, we shall have strong consolation to
balance all our disappointments, Prov. xvi. 3.

VER. 31-33. *And they took Joseph's coat, and killed a kid of*
the goats, and dipt the coat in the blood: and they sent the coat
of many colours, and they brought it to their father; and said,
This have we found: know now whether it be thy son's coat or

no. And he knew it, and said, It is my son's coat; an evil beast hath devoured him; Joseph is without doubt rent in pieces.

Sin is so ugly and so dangerous, that it must be concealed, if possible. Whatever darkness the pleasure of gratifying envy might spread over the minds of Jacob's sons whilst they were executing their purpose upon Joseph, they could not but condemn themselves when they reflected on their conduct, and they could not hope that their father would forgive them. If they could not forgive Joseph his many-coloured coat, and his innocent dreams, they could not well expect that their father would forgive them the atrocious injuries which they had done to his well-beloved son. How, then, shall they escape his resentment? They make lies their refuge. They dipped Joseph's coat in the blood of a kid, and sent it to their father, with this message, "Know now whether this be thy son's coat or no." They pretended not to know with certainty what they knew too well, and insult their father with a question which one would almost think was designed to upbraid him with the envied mark of his partiality to Joseph.

How cruel were these men to their own venerable father, who loved them all much better than they deserved! With what anguish did they rend his soul! He knew too well the coat of his beloved Joseph, and said—

"It is my son's coat; some evil beast hath devoured him; Joseph is without doubt rent in pieces." Nothing could be more like to truth than this conjecture. There appeared to be no reason for calling it in question. It would have been a flagrant breach of charity to suspect the truth, while there was no evidence of it. You see that sometimes the things which are so probable as to appear morally certain, are untrue, and that things may be true that have scarcely the most distant appearance of truth. We ought, therefore, in matters of importance, to examine well before we fix our judgment. "The simple believeth every word; but the prudent man looketh well to his goings."

The sorest griefs of God's people are sometimes founded in gross mistakes. Jacob was never penetrated with deeper

grief than he felt on this occasion, from his mistaken apprehension concerning the deplorable fate of Joseph.

VER. 34, 35. *And Jacob rent his clothes, and put sackcloth*
upon his loins, and mourned for his son many days. And all
his sons and all his daughters rose up to comfort him; but he
refused to be comforted; and he said, For I will go down into
the grave unto my son mourning. Thus his father wept for him.

" Jacob rent his clothes, and mourned for his son many days,
and refused to be comforted, saying, I will go down to the
grave mourning for my son." Jacob did not, on this occasion,
behave like himself. He had borne many afflictions of the
most grievous kind with unshaken fortitude. He mourns for
Joseph almost like a man that had no hope. Did he not
consider that Joseph was yet alive to God, though he might be
dead to men? "I shall go to him," said David, on a like
occasion, " but he shall not return to me." But Jacob speaks
of going to the grave mourning and weeping through the
whole remainder of his life. Even eminent saints may be
sometimes overwhelmed with sorrow, but they do not behave
like saints when they speak of their afflictions as if they were
insupportable. David felt himself almost overloaded with his
afflictions; but he did not voluntarily give place to the
inquietudes of his heart. " Why art thou cast down," he said,
"O my soul? and why art thou disquieted within me? hope
thou in God; for I shall yet praise him."

There were, however, some circumstances in Jacob's present
trouble which may serve to excuse, though not to justify, his
immoderate sorrow. Joseph was by far the best of his sons;
the son, we may suppose, of many prayers; a son of Rachel;
the son that gave him comfort amidst all the distress which his
brethren made him to suffer by their bad behaviour; the son,
of whose future greatness he had probably formed hopes that
seemed to be founded on a divine revelation; and, besides all
these recommendations of Joseph, he might think that he had
great reason to reflect with bitter remorse upon his own conduct
in sending him away without attendance, to travel through
places where he might be exposed to wild beasts. "The heart

knoweth its own bitterness;" a stranger cannot enter into all
its feelings, and ought therefore to judge without severity, even
where he cannot approve.

All Jacob's sons and his daughters (Dinah and his sons' wives)
came to administer to him such comfort as they were able to
give; but all was of little avail. It is our duty to comfort those
that are in any trouble, and especially our distressed relatives—
" For heaviness in the heart of a man maketh it stoop; and a
good word maketh it glad." But we cannot effectually relieve
those hearts that are broken with sorrow. The Father of
mercies, and He alone, can dispel every grief; and therefore,
when we undertake the charitable office of administering
comfort, we must direct our eyes to Him to make our words
effectual.

Jacob's sons acted very hypocritically when they endeavoured
to comfort him. They were themselves the wild beasts that
had devoured Joseph. Had they been sincere, they ought to
have tried every possible means to find out their brother, that
they might redeem him from slavery. Their father did not
know what they had done against Joseph; but he was not
ignorant of their ill-will to him; and this, probably, was a chief
reason why he turned a deaf ear to all they could say for his
comfort.

" I will go down to the grave " (or to the world of departed
spirits) " mourning for my son." Jacob did not hope to see any
more good in this world, when his choicest comfort in life was
taken from him. He had the prospect of no days of gladness,
when Joseph, the joy of his heart, was torn in pieces by wild
beasts. But he did not know what joys were yet before him
in the recovery of his long-lost son. We know not what joys
or what sorrows may be before us in the course of our lives.
Let us never despond while God's throne continues firm and
stable in heaven.

Jacob had the prospect of sorrow whilst he lived in the world.
He knew, and he ought to have rejoiced in the knowledge, that
his sorrows would last only during his present life. The saints
of God will indeed be in heaviness through manifold temptations

whilst they continue in this bad world ; but they have good reason (if they had hearts) to rejoice with joy unspeakable and full of glory in the prospect of the unknown joys that lie beyond the grave. The present life is but a single night to their future life ; and although sorrow may endure through the whole night, yet joy cometh in the morning ; and that joy shall no man take from them.

"Thus his father wept for him." Some have alleged that Jacob's father is here meant. Certain it is that Isaac was yet alive ; and though it seems best to understand this expression of Joseph's father, yet no doubt Isaac likewise deplored his grandson. Who that knew Joseph would not have wept for him ? Isaac had now lived long in the world ; and the longer men live they may expect the more griefs, as long as the lives of men are so frail and uncertain, and corruption so powerful in their hearts.

VER. 36. *And the Midianites sold him into Egypt, unto Potiphar, an officer of Pharaoh's, and captain of the guard.*

Joseph was brought into Egypt. Thus the Saviour of our race, long after, was forced, in infancy, to take shelter in that country from the rage of the king of the Jews. Little did the Egyptians know that their future lord was come to be sold in their country, when the Midianites brought down Joseph to be exposed to sale. Still less did they know the dignity and glory of our Lord Jesus Christ, when He was brought into their country by another Joseph, and by Mary his wife. Time brings the real characters and dignity of some men to light. There are still more whose real glory will remain unknown till the last day.

Joseph was sold to Potiphar, " an officer of Pharaoh's, and a captain of the guard," as we render these expressions. Some make the original expression to signify, that he was president of the sacrifices, or of the king's table ; or, that he had the charge of the criminals that were condemned to die. Whatever his office was, he now became the master of one that was one day to become his lord. Joseph was sold for a servant, although he was destined to great honour. What he now thought of his own dreams, we cannot say : but he was under great temptation to think that God's word failed for evermore.

Let us not judge of God's word by His providence, but rather judge of His providence by His word. We must not think that the promise of crowns and of rivers of pleasures is made void because at present we are subjected to the cross. Many promises have seemed to be forgotten by the Promiser, and yet have been exactly fulfilled in their season. God's word is established in the heavens, although it may seem, to our narrow views, to be buried under the earth. Joseph no doubt lived, like his fathers, in faith, and died in faith ; and his faith supported him under every trial, however severe. " He that believeth shall not make haste."

LECTURE 3

Joseph obtains his master's favour, but meets with dangerous temptations from his mistress, which he nobly withstands.

xxxix 1–9

VER. 1. *And Joseph was brought down to Egypt; and Potiphar, an officer of Pharaoh, captain of the guard, an Egyptian, bought him of the hands of the Ishmeelites, which had brought him down thither.*

JOSEPH was sold and bought as if he had been a beast, or a captive taken in war. How improbable was it that ever he should be the lord of his brethren, or the lord of Egypt! But God provided a master for him, in whose house he was to enjoy a respite from his sufferings. All the ways of a good man are ordered by the Lord, and His eyes are upon His people for good at the very times when they seem to be forgotten.

VER. 2. *And the Lord was with Joseph, and he was a prosperous man; and he was in the house of his master the Egyptian.*

"The Lord was with Joseph;" and if the Lord was with him he was a happy man, although his fond father was not with him. He was a stranger in a strange land; he was also dependent on the caprice of a haughty master, and yet he was blessed; for he enjoyed the presence, the protection, the favour of the Lord.

We are too ready to doubt of God's favour if we meet with unprosperous accidents, or if we are not speedily delivered from afflictions ; as if outward prosperity were a sign of God's favour, and adversity a sure sign of His hatred. But do not the Scriptures declare that "whom the Lord loveth he chasteneth, even as a father the son in whom he delighteth?" The Lord was with Joseph, and could have easily restored him at once to his father's bosom, yet He did it not, but left him many years in a state of slavery. Cease, then, to judge of God's ways by man's ways—"For as the heavens are higher than the earth, so God's ways are higher than man's ways." He shows His love, and manages His affairs according to His own infinite wisdom, and not according to the plans which our weak understandings could prescribe. Shall we presume to teach wisdom to "the Father of lights?" If Joseph had been at this time raised to all that dignity which he afterwards possessed, where would the glory have been which he obtained by his unequalled continence and meekness, his extraordinary wisdom, his constant patience? The crown of Egypt would not have been so bright an ornament to Joseph's head as the glorious virtues which God enabled him to show forth in a suffering condition, and which his sufferings fitted him to display in his exaltation.

But Joseph was not left in his servile condition without manifest tokens of the love of God ; for the Lord made him to prosper in all his undertakings and labours, so that he soon obtained the esteem, the love, and the confidence of his master. Prosperity is not always a sign of God's special favour, yet prosperity undoubtedly comes from God, and is a fruit of God's love to His own people, when He sees that prosperity is better for them than adversity. But how did God show that He was present with Joseph by making him to prosper? Was not Joseph's prosperity more properly his master's than his own, when all the business which he transacted was his master's and the profit redounded to him? It is true that Joseph's prosperity was, to outward appearance, his master's advantage rather than his own. But as "the little that a righteous man hath is better than the riches of many wicked," so the benefit which Joseph derived from God's kindness to him was far greater than his master's. He saw the love of God mitigating and sweetening his sorrows, and recommending him to his master's favour, that he might spend even the days of his banishment and humiliation with comfort. The more clearly we can discern the love of God in any prosperous incidents, the more pleasure we can take in them. A breathing in bondage with the love of God is worth more than all the prosperity which godless men can enjoy.

VER. 3-5. *And his master saw that the Lord was with him, and that the Lord made all that he did to prosper in his hand. And Joseph found grace in his sight, and he served him; and he made him overseer over his house, and all that he had he put into his hand. And it came to pass from the time that he had made him overseer in his house, and over all that he had, that the Lord blessed the Egyptian's house for Joseph's sake; and the blessing of the Lord was upon all that he had in the house, and in the field.*

The blessing of God upon Joseph's labours was so conspicuous, that his master himself observed and acknowledged it. Great was the honour that God put upon a poor servant, when a great man in the court of Egypt honoured him with his attention and respect, and acknowledged him to be the blessed of the Lord. When men are precious in God's sight they are honourable, whatever be their station in life. If they are at present despised by men, they are honoured by angels; and when God makes it known that He loves them by signal proofs of his favour, He will make them honourable in the eyes of those who formerly despised them. When Laban saw that the Lord was with Jacob, he courted him to abide in his service. When Potiphar saw plainly that the Lord was with Joseph, he made the young man the overseer of his house, and the manager of all his business. It is good to have those for our friends and for our servants who are beloved by the Lord. His kindness towards His people overflows to all with whom they are connected. Pious stewards, or pious servants of any kind, are a blessing to their masters, because they are faithful, and manage all their affairs in the fear of the Lord. But they are a blessing likewise on another account, because the Lord makes all they do to prosper, Ps. i. 4; and we are sure that no skill or industry will be of any use to men without the blessing of God.

The blessing of the Lord was upon everything that belonged to Potiphar, as far as Joseph was concerned in it, before he was advanced to the stewardship; but after Joseph became Potiphar's steward, the blessing of the Lord was upon everything that he had, whether in the house or in the field, for Joseph's sake. Great was the favour that was now conceived for the young slave, and an entire confidence was reposed in him. Potiphar saw that he had no more occasion to trouble himself with anxious cares about anything that belonged to him. He was sure not only that every business would be managed with care and fidelity, but that good success would attend all his affairs. Potiphar now knew nothing of all that he had, save the bread which he did eat; all was left in the hands of Joseph, who never betrayed his master's confidence.

The ancient patriarchs were rich and great men; yet, through the wise providence of God, they were placed in circumstances which furnished them with opportunities for setting an example to men of the lowest station. Joseph, like his father Jacob, is an example of contentment, industry, and fidelity to servants. It is true, servants cannot command success, and God does not bind Himself by an absolute promise to grant success to the best conducted affairs. But it is undoubtedly the duty of servants to take the most likely means to promote the prosperity of their masters, and to seek the divine blessing upon those affairs that are committed to them. By such behaviour, they are likely to prove blessings to their masters, and to attain that favour and confidence which they take pains to deserve. But if they should be ungratefully treated by their masters according to the flesh, they have a Master in heaven who will by no means suffer them to want their due reward.

Masters may likewise learn from this passage what treatment is due to faithful servants. They ought to trust, to honour, and to love them. Potiphar was a stranger to the family of Israel, and yet he loved Joseph for his fidelity, and honoured him as the instrument of God's providential blessings to himself. Christian masters have far stronger motives to honour Christian servants, whom they know to be not only servants, but above servants, brethren, partakers of the same heavenly blessings and dignities with themselves. Thus masters who do not honour faithful servants endeavour to make Solomon a liar, for he says that "as he who keepeth the fig-tree shall eat the fruit thereof, so he that waiteth on his master shall be honoured."

VER. 6, 7. *And he left all that he had in Joseph's hand ; and he knew not ought he had, save the bread which he did eat. And Joseph was a goodly person, and well favoured. And it came to pass after these things, that his master's wife cast her eyes upon Joseph ; and she said, Lie with me.*

Joseph spent his time comfortably in the house of his master, for the Lord made his yoke easy, and his burden light. He might now have waited patiently for his exaltation, which he was sure would come in due time ; but he needed other severe trials to prepare him for it, and to make way for its coming to him. God only knows what degree of trouble is necessary for His people, and how long it is proper they should continue under its pressure. It was Joseph's comfort that he was beloved by his master, but it was his misfortune that he was too well beloved by his mistress. He had a lovely face, which his mistress could not behold without conceiving a regard for him, which proved for a time prejudicial to Joseph, but infinitely more prejudicial to herself.

Beauty of person and face is a quality which gains love, and ought to make the possessor of it thankful ; yet let not the fair pride themselves in their lovely features, which may prove a snare to the beholders, or to themselves. Sarah's beauty pleased the eyes of Abraham, but cost him many anxious thoughts, and sometimes instigated him to use dishonourable methods for the preservation of his life. Joseph's beauty was a dangerous snare to his mistress, and procured him the misfortune of a tedious confinement. Hast thou beauty ? trust not in it, but be modest and cautious. Dost thou want beauty ? be content, and thankful that you are free from those snares which often attend it. Dost thou behold a beautiful face in the other sex ? beware of being too much charmed with the lovely aspect. Remember that "favour is deceitful, and beauty is vain." "Lust not after the beauty of the strange woman," says Solomon to his disciple, "neither let her take thee with her eyelids." That the other sex may stand in need of like admonitions is too plain from the story of Potiphar's wife.

She saw Joseph, she loved him, and said unto him, Lie with me. Her eyes ensnared her heart, and she lost her modesty, as well as every other virtue. She must have been lost to all sense of shame when she so barefacedly tempted Joseph to violate her chastity. Joseph was now in a dangerous situation. Few young men could have resisted the strong temptation which he was enabled to encounter. How easily did his brother Judah, in a more advanced period of life, fall before a temptation, which, in the comparison, was very small. We may say of Joseph, that there were few like him in all the earth. Sin spread out before him its strongest attractions—pleasure and profit. It drew up the most formidable terrors in battle array, but none of all these things moved Joseph. He held fast his integrity, and would not let it go, for his heart was mightily fortified by the fear of God, and he was powerfully supported by that grace "which is able to keep us from falling, and to present us faultless before the presence of the divine glory with exceeding joy."

VER. 8, 9. *But he refused, and said unto his master's wife, Behold, my master wotteth not what is with me in the house, and he hath committed all that he hath to my hand ; there is none greater in this house than I ; neither hath he kept back any thing from me but thee, because thou art his wife : how then can I do this great wickedness, and sin against God ?*

He not only refused to comply with his mistress, but gave her his reasons for refusing ; and these reasons were well adapted to cure her of her madness, if it had not been incurable. "Behold," said he, "my master wotteth not what is with me in the house, and he hath committed all that he hath into my hand : there is none greater in this house than I ; neither hath he kept back any thing but thee, because thou art his wife : how then can I do this great wickedness, and sin against God ?"

D

If a man has not a lively sense of important benefits conferred upon him, he is worse than a brute. Even lions, we are told, have testified a grateful disposition for benefits conferred on them; and we know that the dog and the horse, and even the stupid ass, are very far from being insensible to kindness. Joseph, we find, was penetrated with a sense of the favours heaped upon him, and would not behave in a manner unworthy of them. And if Joseph, a poor slave, had such a grateful sense of Potiphar's favours, how monstrously ungrateful was the wife of his bosom, who wished to repay his love with the blackest stain to his honour!

Confidence will always beget in a well-disposed mind a disposition to repay it with fidelity; and one who betrays trust is regarded as an enormous transgressor of the laws of society. Joseph was trusted with everything by his master, and therefore he resolved to observe inviolable fidelity. Such motives to honest behaviour were strong, though not the strongest that governed his soul. He proposes them, however, at greatest length, because the force of them would be best understood, and perhaps felt by his mistress. How base was her conduct, when she tempted his favourite servant to betray him in the most cruel manner, and to repay the greatest favours with an irreparable shame.

"He hath withheld nothing from me but thee, because thou art his wife." These words ought to have pierced her heart like daggers. She was his wife, and a man's wife ought to be his alone, and not another's with him. The servants that have everything else put into their hands, the friend that is to a man like his own soul, must consider the wife of their master or friend as his exclusive property. The more favoured they are in other respects, the more careful must they be to maintain this property inviolable. A man's wife is a part of his own flesh. To separate between a man's soul and body is not a much greater injury than to separate a man's wife from himself.

"How then can I do this great wickedness?" Joseph speaks as if it had been impossible for him to bring himself under the guilt of such atrocious ingratitude, injustice, and impurity. It would have been impossible for him to commit a crime so black and complicated, without divesting himself of humanity as well as piety. He found an unconquerable reluctance in his heart to such baseness, and endeavoured to convey his own way of thinking into the heart of his tempter, by setting before her eyes in few words the complicated horrors of that iniquity to which she wished to seduce him. Adultery is not only a sin, but a great wickedness. It is perjury and impurity in their highest degree. It is, in any circumstances, a great wickedness, abhorred by heathens as well as Christians, and judged by many nations to deserve a painful and ignominious death.

When Joseph was tempted to this sin, he placed before his own eyes, and endeavoured to place before his tempter's eyes, its extreme malignity. It is one great misery, that in a time of temptation, we lose the benefit of our knowledge, by a temporary forgetfulness that seizes upon our hearts, and renders us an easy prey to the devil. We are often surprised that men and women should make themselves, in one fatal moment, miserable for life, with their eyes open. But their eyes were not open at the time when they gave such a fatal stab to their fame and peace. The God of this world found means to shut their eyes till they had done his work, and then their eyes were opened to see the shame of their nakedness. Whenever you find yourselves dangerously tempted to any iniquity, beware of forgetting what reason, what experience, what the Scriptures tell you concerning it. Pray to God that you may be enabled to retain just apprehensions of its malignity in the hour of darkness. When your corrupt hearts would fix your eyes upon present pleasures, turn your thoughts to the vileness of the sin, to the intolerable misery which it brings, and to those mighty arguments which ought to steel us with unshaken resolutions to keep ourselves pure.

Turn your thoughts to God the great Lawgiver, who is able to save and to destroy. "How shall I do this great wickedness," says the holy patriarch, "and sin against God?" If the excellencies of God, the relations in which we stand to Him, the account we must give to Him, the sure vengeance denounced by

Him against the workers of iniquity, were always present to our minds, temptations to rebellion against Him would lose much of their strength. "I have kept thy precepts, and thy testimonies," says David, "for all my ways are before thee."

"How shall I do this great wickedness, and sin against God?" The offence against Potiphar would have been very inexcusable, but it was a small thing compared with the offence which would have been given to God. God is our Maker, and our Judge. He is infinitely glorious, and His laws are worthy of Himself. To sin against Him is to sin against our own souls, for He can kill both soul and body.

Under the Gospel, we see in the light of the cross of Christ what it is to sin against God. He would not suffer the least sin to escape unpunished. For all sins that have been, or shall be pardoned, full satisfaction was made by Christ. He endured all the horrors of the curse of God, that all rational creatures might know how evil and how bitter a thing it is to sin against the Most High. If, in the most ancient times, those who knew the Lord said, "How can we sin against God?" how much more will those, before whose eyes Jesus Christ hath been evidently set forth crucified, tremble at the thought of transgressing His commandments, unless they are under the bewitching influence of the devil!

Beware of sinning against men, because in doing so you sin against God. Our fellow-men are entitled to our regard, and we ought to render unto all their due; but let us ever remember that our chief regard is due to God, and that we ought to discharge our duty to men in the fear of God, and under deep impressions of His authority. The transgression of the wicked said in David's heart, that the fear of God was not before his eyes. By the fear of the Lord, men depart from evil. If we felt upon our spirits past transgressions of His majesty and glory, what manner of persons would we be in all holy conversation and godliness!

LECTURE 4
Joseph is falsely accused by his mistress, and cast into prison.
xxxix 10–23

VER. 10. *And it came to pass, as she spake to Joseph day by day, that he hearkened not unto her, to lie by her, or to be with her.*

IT is not enough for us to resist one, or two, or twenty temptations to any sin. We ought to continue steadfast and unmoved amidst all the terrors and all the allurements that are spread out before our eyes. God is ever the same, His love is ever the same, and our duty is ever the same, whatever Satan may suggest, whatever bad men may say to us, and whatever corrupt motions we may feel in our own spirits. Samson refused for a long time to satisfy Delilah's insidious questions concerning his great strength, but at last the mighty man was conquered by the tears and importunities of a fair woman. He revealed the fatal secret, and his indiscretion cost him his eyes and his life. Thus sinners startle at the first proposal of a temptation. They refuse for a time to comply with the great enemy of their souls, but at last, tired of resistance, they yield to the destroyer, and bring that guilt and misery upon themselves which the devil, with all his wiles, could not have brought upon them without their own consent. They forget the important words of our Lord: "He that endureth to the end, the same shall be saved ; and he that overcometh, and keepeth my works unto the end, to him will I give power over the nations."

Joseph was a good soldier of that God whom he served. He was far from yielding to the most insinuating and most urgent temptations. " And it came to pass, as she spake to Joseph day by day, that he hearkened not unto her, to lie by her, or to be with her." He regarded neither her caresses nor her frowns, her threatenings nor her promises. None of her arts could induce him to do that great wickedness to which she solicited him, and to sin against God. If she could have given him all the treasures of Egypt as the price of his virtue, he would have despised them. She might threaten him with death; but he knew that the God whom he served was able to save him from her power and her wiles; and, besides, a thousand deaths were less dreadful to him than the loss of his innocence, and the loss of that divine favour which had hitherto moderated and sweetened all his distresses. "Count it all joy," says James, "when ye fall into divers temptations." But the temptations of which James speaks were of a different kind from those by which Joseph was assaulted. When we meet with frequent solicitations to a sweet or profitable sin, we have great reason to be alarmed. But let us take to ourselves the whole armour of God, and we shall be able to stand in the evil day. In this armour Joseph was arrayed, and he was a glorious conqueror. In a thousand assaults he remained unhurt, for he was supported by the mighty power of God. Let young men learn from him how they may escape the edge of that sharp sword, the mouth of a strange woman, the flattery of the tongue of a strange woman; and let us all learn how to keep our ground when we are assaulted by the fiery darts of the wicked one.

Ver. 11-15. *And it came to pass about this time, that Joseph went into the house to do his business; and there was none of the men of the house there within. And she caught him by his garment, saying, Lie with me: and he left his garment in her hand, and fled, and got him out. And it came to pass, when she saw that he had left his garment in her hand, and was fled forth, that she called unto the men of her house, and spake unto them, saying, See, he hath brought in an Hebrew unto us to mock us; he came in unto me to lie with me, and I cried with a loud voice: and it came to pass, when he heard that I lifted up my voice and cried, that he left his garment with me, and fled, and got him out.*

Secrecy is favourable to temptation. There was a day after Joseph had resisted many assaults of his mistress, that he happened, in the course of his business, to be alone with her in the house. She did not suffer this opportunity to pass neglected. She did not consider, perhaps she did not know, that the eye of God was upon her. No human eyes saw her but those of Joseph, and now she thought that she might almost compel him to gratify her licentious desires. What an indignity is this to the Most High, that men and women will venture to do those things in His presence which they would not venture to do before the eyes of the meanest of their fellow-creatures. Are we more afraid of the eyes of our own servants, or of our own children, than of those eyes which " behold the hearts and try the reins of the children of men, to give to every one according to his ways, and according to the fruit of his doings."

Joseph's mistress saw that words were vain. She now takes another way of dealing with him. She caught him by his garment, saying, " Lie with me." How dreadfully was her heart hardened by the deceitfulness of sin ! How odious does such a woman make herself ! Beware of giving way, in any degree, to the allurements of sin, lest it obtain a complete dominion over you. Beware of rejecting admonitions, lest God punish you with judicial hardness of heart. Many remonstrances had been disregarded by Potiphar's wife. The bright example of Joseph's virtue had no other effect but to inflame her licentious desires ; and now behold what a vile woman she is become. Is she ashamed of her abominable desires? No, she is not at all ashamed, neither can she blush.

Joseph is now in a critical situation. By his superior strength or swiftness, it was possible for him to escape from the presence of the wicked woman ; but how will it be possible for him to escape the effects of her fierce resentment? Joseph at this time did not think of her resentment. More important cares engrossed his mind. Her presence was more abhorred by him than death in any of its forms. " He left his garment in her hand, and fled, and got him out." The danger incurred by leaving his garment in her hands was very obvious. Her resentment might improve it as the instrument of his destruction; or if she endeavoured, for her own sake, to conceal it, an accident might very probably discover it, and raise cruel suspicions against him; but Joseph acted upon this principle—that of two evils the least is to be chosen; and that sin is an infinitely worse evil than disgrace or death.

Joseph flies, that he might be a conqueror. "Flee youthful lusts," says the apostle; and again he says, "Abstain from all appearance of evil." "Avoid the tempter's house," says the wise man, "pass not by it, turn from it, and pass away." We cannot keep ourselves too far from an evil matter. Those who have manfully resisted temptation at one time, have, through unwatchfulness, or self-confidence, fallen at another time. But happy is the man that feareth always, and that flees to the utmost distance from the place of danger.

Potiphar's wife was grievously disappointed when she found Joseph so resolute against complying with her wicked solicitations. She had long waited, and used all means; and she now saw that all the means she could use were vain. How, then, does she behave? Hope defeated makes her heart sick, not with dejection, but with wrath. Her love was turned into the blackest hatred. She could not ruin Joseph's soul, but she will, if possible, ruin his body, and will spare no lies nor hypocrisy to attain her purpose. Joseph himself, in his haste to get away, had furnished her with the means: and her genius is fruitful in expedients to improve them.

She first called her servants, and made bitter complaints of the young Hebrew servant, as if her lord had intended to affront her by bringing him into the house; and in proof of what she said, she showed Joseph's garment, which, she pretended, he had left in her hands, that he might run and escape detection in an attempt upon her honour. By her own account, Joseph was a monster of wickedness, and herself a pattern of purity. "What shall be done unto thee, or what shall be given thee, O deceitful tongue? Burning coals of juniper, sharp arrows of the mighty."

If we were amazed, in reading the foregoing part of the

history, to find this woman so brazen-faced, we are now astonished at her infernal artifices. She was as wise to do evil, as if the old serpent had brought her all his lying arts, and " deceivableness of unrighteousness."

She scrupled at nothing that was wicked. She not only dissembles and lies, but she plots the destruction of the best of men, for no other reason but his incomparable virtues. Murder was in her heart and tongue. She now becomes as wicked as Satan could make her, " the enemy of all righteousness," a miserable slave to the devil, who carried her captive at his pleasure. No depth of wickedness is too shocking for those who are lost to shame, and left in the power of their own lusts.

VER. 16-18. *And she laid up his garment by her, until his lord came home. And she spake unto him according to these words, saying, The Hebrew servant, which thou hast brought unto us, came in unto me to mock me: and it came to pass, as I lifted up my voice, and cried, that he left his garment with me, and fled out.*

Potiphar's wicked wife drew her husband, by her vile arts, into a partnership of her guilt, by her lying speeches. She represented the matter to him in such a light, that he might think himself bound, by the laws of marriage, to inflict the most exemplary punishment upon his poor servant. "The Hebrew servant, which thou hast brought unto us, came in unto me to mock (or to insult) me." She seemed too modest to speak in plain terms of Joseph's crime. But she does not leave any room to doubt of the nature of the insult. "And it came to pass, as I lifted up my voice and cried, that he left his garment with me, and fled out." The accusations at first view might seem to be proved beyond a doubt by the garment which was found in the house, for she had laid it up to be showed to her lord when he came home.

Believe not every word that is spoken; for there are many liars, many artful deceivers in the world. If a man must be held guilty because some circumstances seem to establish the charges brought against him, what innocence would be safe? Jesus Christ Himself must have been justly condemned; for if

He did not speak the very words produced by the witnesses that bare testimony against Him, He spake words that had almost the same sound; and it is very probable that Naboth had spoken words that might be, with great plausibility, twisted into blasphemy against God and the king, yet his death was severely avenged upon the house of Ahab.

VER. 19, 20. *And it came to pass, when his master heard the words of his wife, which she spake unto him, saying, After this manner did thy servant to me; that his wrath was kindled. And Joseph's master took him, and put him into the prison, a place where the king's prisoners were bound: and he was there in the prison.*

A sagacious and penetrating mind may often detect the vile arts of deceivers, and discern the truth through the mist by which their dissimulation covers it. The story of Potiphar's wife might well have been suspected. Joseph was not likely to have left his garment in the hands of his mistress to be a witness against him, if he had really insulted her. His strength was superior to hers, otherwise it is not probable that he would have thought of the insult which was pretended to be given her; and therefore no good account but the true one could be reasonably believed concerning the garment which was found in the house. The first appearances, however, were against Joseph. If he had told his own story, it is not likely he would have gained credit. Who could have believed that a young man would exhibit such a rare instance of virtue? His own testimony would be insufficient to procure belief from Potiphar; and it would be almost impossible for him to believe that his own wife was so utterly abandoned as her behaviour showed her to be. When the truth was known, an indifferent person might, perhaps, have pronounced sentence, on the whole, in Joseph's favour. But Potiphar was partial, and his wife's complaints raised a storm of passion in his breast, which would render him incapable of hearing truth and reason. If you would behave like rational creatures, let not anger run away with your judgment. Nothing more effectually blinds the mind. It is a short madness; and the judgment which we form of persons and things under its influence ought to be reversed when we come to ourselves. "Wrath is cruel, and anger is outrageous." Joseph exposed himself, by his unconquerable virtue, to the fierce wrath of his mistress; and his pretended crime exposed him to the wrath of his master, which would have proved fatal to him if God's eye had not been upon him for good.

Potiphar paid too much deference to his wife. He ought not to have believed her words against Joseph without examining into the truth of them. A man ought to love his wife as a part of himself; but however dear she may be to him, truth and justice ought to be still dearer. We are not acting dutifully when our deference to one class of relations makes us unjust to relations of another class. Men ought to love their wives above their servants; but their fondness for their wives ought not to make them unjust to their servants, by adopting, without examination, every quarrel of their mistress. Our tenderest and most amiable affections must be kept within the bounds of reason and religion, that we may act like honest men.

"Doth our law judge any man before it hear him?" said a Jewish ruler to the enemies of Jesus. Justice says the same thing, and yet we find nothing more common among men than judging their neighbours without hearing them. We may very warrantably condemn Potiphar's injustice in dooming Joseph to a prison without a fair trial. But let us beware, lest in condemning Potiphar we condemn ourselves. We have, indeed, no prisons at command for those men against whom we may conceive a causeless resentment; but is it not manifest injustice to do what lies in our power to deprive them of their good name, when, for aught we know, our displeasure against them originates in ignorance and error?

"Joseph's master took him, and put him into the prison, a place where the king's prisoners were bound: and he was there in the prison." This situation was sufficiently dreary for a young man who had been so much caressed in his father's house. But we are further told, by a writer who could not be mistaken, "that he was laid in irons, and that his feet were hurt with fetters." We cannot but sympathise with Joseph, whose virtues were so transcendent, and who was so ill rewarded by the man to whom he had been so inviolably faithful. What, then, shall we think of the treatment which our Lord received from a people whom He came to save? Upon a false accusation, the great pattern of all virtue was cast into the prison of the grave, after He had been made to endure such ignominy and such pain as were never allotted to freemen of Rome for the blackest crimes.

But why did not Joseph represent his own innocence, and obtain a milder sentence? It does not appear that he said anything in his own defence; and it would have been to no purpose to have pleaded his own cause before a tribunal so prejudiced as that where he was judged. Christ Himself, at His trial before the chief priest, before Herod, and before Pilate, said nothing, except when He saw that to speak might tend to a good end.

But if Joseph was deemed guilty of an attempt so audacious upon his mistress, why did his master, who had so much power in his hands, satisfy himself with the punishment of imprisonment. We know that "jealousy is the rage of a man, and that he will not spare in the day of vengeance;" but we know, also, that jealousy, and every other passion, is under the control of the Most High, who mightily restrains them, so that they cannot interfere with His counsels, and binds them into a compliance with the divine purposes of His will.

Potiphar's former love to Joseph might, at this time, operate upon his mind, and prevent his rage from inflicting death on Joseph, or perhaps he might entertain some faint doubts of his wife's veracity. But whatever motives hindered him from proceeding to extremities, it is certain that he was under the overruling influence of God, whose set time for Joseph's dissolution was not yet come. He had much to do in this world before he obtained his dismission to another. He was to become "the shepherd and the stone of Israel." He was to become the father of two mighty tribes in Israel. He was to be the lord of Pharaoh's house, according to the dreams which came to him from heaven. He was to see good and glorious days on earth;

and he will not perish whilst the promises which he received from above were yet unaccomplished. All the devils of hell combining their powers would find themselves unable to put one of God's servants to death, whilst any part of their work on earth remains unperformed. It was not Joseph's death, but his imprisonment, that was to be the means of his elevation ; and Potiphar, and even Potiphar's wife, served Providence in all the evil which they did to Joseph; whilst they were most egregiously violating His commandments, they were fulfilling His counsels. Let not God's people be afraid of the violence of their enemies. What can man do against God? Not only the righteous and the wise, and their works, but the unrighteous, the unwise, and the worst of their works, are in the hand of God.

VER. 21-23. *But the Lord was with Joseph, and shewed him mercy, and gave him favour in the sight of the keeper of the prison. And the keeper of the prison committed to Joseph's hand all the prisoners that were in the prison; and whatsoever they did there, he was the doer of it. The keeper of the prison looked not to any thing that was under his hand ; because the Lord was with him, and that which he did, the Lord made it to prosper.*

Joseph was indeed cast into prison, but still the Lord was with Joseph. "The goodness and mercy of the Lord followed him all the days of his life," and through every condition of life. It followed him to a strange land, and attended him in the house where he was a bondman. It followed him to the dungeon ; and when the irons entered into his soul, it preserved him from sinking under his calamities. It did not indeed bring him out of the dungeon as soon as he was cast into it, but it soon lightened his yoke. The jailor behaved kindly to him ; and there is reason to think that Potiphar's rage was succeeded by emotions of compassion ; for the jailor could not have treated Joseph with so much humanity without Potiphar's leave. Upon calm reflection, he might see reason to think that the accusation laid against Joseph did not deserve belief, and yet he might think it imprudent to liberate him from his confinement.

The Lord was with Joseph, and showed him mercy. It was divine mercy that lightened the burdens of the good man.

Joseph himself could not claim the favour which was showed him in prison as the reward of merit. If any man on earth could have advanced such a claim, it was Joseph; but the rewards of the best works that ever Joseph or any of his fathers before him performed were rewards of grace, and not of debt.

Think not that the presence of God with His people is limited to palaces or to churches. It has been often manifestly seen that He was with them in prisons, in caves or dens, on gibbets, in fiery furnaces. Ask not, why He does not snatch away His people from such dreary places, if He is present with them! Why should you think yourselves wiser than God? He can tell why Christ, though he was the Son of God, did not come down from the cross, that His enemies might believe in Him. The sufferings of Christ were necessary for our salvation. The sufferings of the saints are necessary for their own salvation, though in another sense.

The keeper of the prison soon saw that the Lord was with Joseph, and made him his assistant in the management of the prisoners. It is strange that a poor prisoner, condemned to a dungeon for the worst of crimes, should find such favour with his keeper. Keepers of prisons are not the men from whom mercy is expected. But the hearts of keepers of prisons are in the hands of the Lord, as well as the hearts of other men. Paul had much favour shown him in bonds and imprisonments, for which Christians in every age ought to be thankful to God. He was in prisons oft, but his keepers allowed him paper and ink, with which those epistles were written, which will be read with pleasure and edification while the world stands. Onesimus, and probably many other men and women now with Christ, were begotten by Paul in his bonds.

Let those who are unjustly shut up in prisons, and all who suffer for righteousness' sake, remember Paul and Joseph, and let them "be followers of those who through faith and patience inherit the promises," Ps. cvii. 10-16.

LECTURE 5

Joseph interprets the dreams of the chief butler and baker of the king of Egypt.

xl 1–15

VER. 1. *And it came to pass after these things, that the butler of the king of Egypt and his baker had offended their lord the king of Egypt.*

WE are not informed either of the names or of the fault of these two servants of the king of Egypt. We have not any wish to know either the one or the other. We feel not any interest in their concerns. We would have heard nothing about them if their story had not been connected with that of Joseph ; and we wish to know nothing more concerning them than what relates to this amiable youth. One of them came to an untimely end, and perhaps deserved it. The other deserved not to have his name recorded. He escaped the sword of Pharaoh, but his name, if it had been known, would never have been mentioned with honour, for he could receive favours without returning them when it was in his power, and could suffer an innocent youth to languish in prison, without endeavouring to procure his release, although he could have told a story that would probably have gained him his liberty. He told, indeed, this story to the king, a long time after his own deliverance, but at a season when he hoped to recommend himself by doing what he ought long before to have done in gratitude to Joseph.

All that we know of the fault of these men is, that it was conducive by its remote consequences to Joseph's deliverance and aggrandisement. The Lord knows how to overrule everything in a subserviency to His own purpose. No crimes are permitted by Him without a design worthy of His infinite wisdom, although it is but a very small portion of His ways that we can understand.

VER. 2. *And Pharaoh was wroth against two of his officers, against the chief of the butlers, and against the chief of the bakers.*

"The king's wrath is as a roaring lion, and the man who sins against him wrongs his own soul." Yet there is no comparison between the wrath of an earthly king and the wrath of God. "Fear not him," says our Lord, "who has power to kill only the body, but fear him who is able to cast both soul and body into hell-fire." The king of Egypt committed his two offending servants to a prison, and condemned one of them to death, but after that could do no more to testify his resentment. Yet no wise man would expose himself when his conscience does not require him to such calamities. How much less will a man who loves his own soul expose himself wilfully to that wrath which never ends !

VER. 3. *And he put them in ward in the house of the captain of the guard, into the prison, the place where Joseph was bound.*

Too often it happens to the righteous according to the wish of the wicked. Here we find two men who had sinned against their lord, the king of Egypt, confined in the same prison with Joseph. Yet the same prison is not the same to a good and to a bad man. The two offenders trembled in anxious dread of some severe punishment ; and the consciousness of their demerit, if they were really guilty, was more painful to them than the irons were to Joseph, although they entered into his soul. Joseph had the testimony of his conscience to cheer him. He not only suffered without cause, but suffered for righteousness' sake, and trusted that God would bring his sufferings to a comfortable conclusion. In the world you may meet with much distress. But keep conscience void of offence towards God and man, and you shall be preserved from the sting and venom of those troubles that Providence allots you.   " Let no man suffer as a thief, as an evildoer, as a busybody in other men's matters.   But if any man suffer as a Christian" (or without deserving to suffer) " let him not be ashamed ; but let him glorify God, who executes righteousness and judgment for all that are oppressed."

VER. 4. *And the captain of the guard charged Joseph with them, and he served them : and they continued a season in ward.*

The captain of the guard had the command of the royal prison.   He appears now to have been convinced of Joseph's innocence, and to have loosed his fetters, although he did not dismiss him from confinement.   But why did he not release Joseph entirely from the prison, if he thought him fit to be trusted with the care of other prisoners?   He seems to have condemned himself in that which he allowed.   If Joseph was guilty of the crime imputed to him, the closest imprisonment was too good for him ; and it is not likely that his master would have showed him any favour, if he had not now thought the accusations of his mistress unjust ; " for jealousy is the rage of a man, he will not spare in the day of vengeance."

But if the accusation was false, Joseph ought to have been brought forth with honour, and to have received a compensation for the injury done to him by his master and mistress.   But private reasons, from a mistaken sense of honour in the matter, or a too partial regard to the mistress, appear to have overbalanced the consideration of justice at the very time when the force of conviction procured to Joseph such mild treatment, as none would have experienced who was judged guilty of the crime with which he was charged.   How few were found amongst the heathen whose sentiments and practice exactly corresponded to that eternal rule of righteousness, " Do not that to another which thou wouldst not have another man do to thyself."

Unjustly as Joseph was treated, he was no doubt thankful that his affliction was lightened.   He would remember the time when the irons entered into his soul, and bless God that, though still in prison, he enjoyed a reviving in his bondage.   Let not

E

those who are in some degree recovered from sickness, though
not restored to perfect health, repine that it is not with them
as in former times. They perhaps taste more sweetness in that
measure of health which they enjoy, than they formerly enjoyed
when their health was entire. Troubles are greatly alleviated
by the remembrance of greater troubles.

"And he served them." "Do all thy works in meekness,"
said an ancient sage, "so shalt thou be beloved of Him that is
accepted." Joseph had been unjustly enslaved, unjustly imprisoned, unjustly detained in his prison, and yet he declined
not the work enjoined by that master, who confessed, by the
trust reposed in him, that he deserved very different treatment.
He was a better man than the men whom he served. He
was sprung from noble ancestors, and knew that he would
one day be exalted above them, but at this time he cheerfully
performed to them every service in his power. Let us always
cheerfully accommodate ourselves to those circumstances in which
Divine Providence is pleased to place us. They are unworthy
to be exalted who cannot bear to be humbled. "The Son of
man himself came not to be ministered unto, but to minister,
and to give his life a ransom for many." But thus said the
Lord (and He hath now accomplished His word), "To him whom
man despiseth, to him whom the nation abhorreth, to a servant
of rulers, kings shall see, and arise, princes also shall worship
because of the Lord thy God."

"And they continued a season in ward." A year, as some
suppose. But it was not necessary for us to know how long.

VER. 5. *And they dreamed both of them, each man his dream
in one night, each man according to the interpretation of his
dream, the butler and the baker of the king of Egypt, which were
bound in the prison.*

Dreams, for the most part, are worthy of little regard on any
other account than as they indicate the present state of the
body or mind. Yet sometimes God has given unto men intima-
tions of His will concerning themselves or others in the season
of the night, when dead sleep had fallen upon them. God used
this method of communicating His mind more frequently to men,

before there was a written revelation of His will than at present. "God speaketh once, yea twice," said a holy man of ancient times, "yet man perceiveth it not. In a dream, in a vision of the night, when deep sleep falleth upon man, in slumberings upon the bed ; then he openeth the ears of men, and sealeth their instruction." God communicated His mind to whom He pleased, and in what manner He pleased. He spake in divers manners to the fathers by the prophets. But He spoke to other men, when He pleased, besides the prophets, by dreams or visions. We read in the following chapter of a prophetical dream presented to the imagination of Pharaoh, king of Egypt. Here we have an account of a prophetical dream sent to two of Pharaoh's servants, men who probably did not know the Lord. But the fancies and hearts of those who know not God are as much under the divine government as the hearts of the saints, and He makes what impressions on them He pleases.

The chief butler and the chief baker both dreamed in the same night, and neither of their dreams were the idle vagaries of fancy. Each of them dreamed according to the interpretation of his dream. Both of their dreams were significant. There was something so uncommon in their dreams, or in the impressions which they left, that the poor men were sore grieved for the want of an interpreter. They had often dreamed upon their beds, but none of their former dreams had taken such hold upon their minds as these. By a secret suggestion of the Divine Spirit, they were convinced that their dreams were supernatural, and portended something that should befall them in the after-part of their life, although what it was they were as ignorant of as before their dreams.

VER. 6. *And Joseph came in unto them in the morning, and looked upon them, and, behold, they were sad.*

Was it to be wondered at that men were sad, when they were bound in a prison, and knew not what their fate would be ? But the custom had in some degree reconciled them to confinement, and yet they appeared more dejected than ever they had been since the time when they were committed to custody. You see what access God hath to the spirits of men and how easily He can arm their imaginations against their own peace. We have heard of many besides Job who have been scared with dreams, whose days and nights have been filled with anxiety and terror by presages and forebodings of uncertain evils. Let us endeavour to preserve a clear judgment, and a pure conscience, that we may neither fear where no fear is, nor be shaken in our minds by the apprehension of those evils that cannot be avoided. Happy are those men who can hope and wait quietly for the salvation of the Lord. " In the fear of the Lord is strong confidence, and his children shall have a place of refuge."

VER. 7. *And he asked Pharaoh's officers that were with him in the ward of his lord's house, saying, Wherefore look ye so sadly to-day?*

It was not from an impertinent wish to know secrets that Joseph asked these men what ailed them. He wished to administer to them all the comfort in his power. Thus our Lord, meeting two of His disciples in the way to Emmaus, said unto them, " What manner of communications are these that ye have one to another, as ye walk, and are sad?" He wished to have an account from their own mouth of the causes of their dejection, that he might apply the proper remedies.

In our moments of dejection, it would be good for us to ask the question at ourselves, why we give way to discouraging thoughts? Are we warranted by the circumstances of our condition to indulge ourselves in sorrows that are so inimical to the happiness and duties of life? "Why art thou cast down, O my soul? and why art thou disquieted in me?"

Some might have asked Joseph, why he was not himself as sad in heart as the two servants of Pharaoh? He had long been an exile from the house of his venerable and affectionate father. He had long been dwelling with strangers, with heathens. He had not only been a stranger in a strange land, but a slave to an imperious mistress and a cruel lord, who kept him in prison, although he now in effect confessed his innocence. Yet was this patient youth so far from sinking under the weight of his calamities, that he kindly attempted to console his fellow-prisoners, and inquired into the cause of their grief, that he might, if possible, remove it.

Ver. 8. *And they said unto him, We have dreamed a dream, and there is no interpreter of it. And Joseph said unto them, Do not interpretations belong to God ? tell me them, I pray you.*

They told him that they dreamed dreams, which they firmly believed portended something that should befall them. What made their apprehensions more worthy of credit was, that they had both been troubled with their dreams in the same night ; but that which above everything else disquieted them was the want of an interpreter. Had they enjoyed their liberty, they would have been at no loss. They would have called the magicians, or interpreters of dreams, and would have known the worst of the matter. But they were shut out from all manner of information concerning what they were so anxious to know.

It is a miserable thing to stand in dread of uncertain evils. When men know the worst of what they have to fear, they will make up their minds, and fortify their spirits to bear the expected shock. But when they apprehend themselves exposed to some dreadful evils, without being able to form a conjecture of the nature or extent of them, wherewith shall they comfort their hearts against sorrow ? What if the consolations or remedies which they employ should prove quite insufficient ? This is one proof of the excellency of our religion, that it furnishes us with effectual antidotes against every sorrow and every fear. We know not what may befall us in life. We could still less know what is to befall us at the end of life, if the Gospel had not given us the knowledge of an immortal life, and of the path that leads to it. But whatever may befall us in this, or in another world, we know in whom we have believed, and that He is able to keep that which we have committed unto Him against that day.

The butler and baker would have thought themselves happy if they could have procured an interpreter to set their minds at rest about their dreams. But alas ! what could they reasonably expect from such interpreters of dreams as Egypt afforded ?

Were they sure that the interpreters would not impose upon them some groundless imaginations of their own hearts? Or if their dreams portended some great evils, had the interpreters any power to avert them, or to furnish them with sufficient supports under those evils that were unavoidable? How vain are the wishes and hopes of minds unenlightened by divine revelation!

"Do not interpretations belong to God?" said Joseph. He wished to turn their thoughts from man to God, that they might place their hope in Him who alone knows what is to befall any of His creatures, who alone can avert the evils which we dread, or turn them to our comfort. This ought to be our consolation, that God knows what we know not; that He has given us the living oracles, in which we have all the information necessary for us concerning the things that are to come to pass hereafter.

God was pleased, from the earliest ages, to make known to some of His servants a portion of His designs concerning themselves, or concerning their fellow-men. Joseph was honoured with some of these discoveries. He was at this time assured, by the inward inspiration of the Spirit, that the dreams of Pharaoh's two officers were truly prophetic, and that he should be enabled to explain them when they were made known to him. God could have saved Joseph the trouble of learning from the men what they had dreamed. The same Spirit that taught him to interpret could have made known to him the dreams. Daniel learned from the Spirit what thoughts had passed through the mind of Nebuchadnezzar in the visions of his head on his bed. But Joseph needed no supernatural information concerning the dreams themselves, which were well enough remembered by the dreamers. It was sufficient for him to know the meaning of the dreams when he was told what they were.

VER. 9-11. *And the chief butler told his dream to Joseph, and said to him, In my dream, behold, a vine was before me; and in the vine were three branches; and it was as though it budded, and her blossoms shot forth; and the clusters thereof brought forth ripe grapes: and Pharaoh's cup was in my hand; and I took the grapes, and pressed them into Pharaoh's cup, and I gave the cup into Pharaoh's hand.*

It were not strange that a butler, deprived of his post and of his liberty, should dream of wine, and grapes, and cups, and of putting a cup into his master's hand. If Joseph had been left solely to the direction of his own good sense, he would have told the butler that his dream was the pure effect of his waking thoughts, that he had often anxiously wished for restoration to his former office, and that his fancy, in the time of sleep, had gratified him with the enjoyment of his desires. But Joseph was left at no uncertainty about the matter.

VER. 12, 13. *And Joseph said unto him, This is the interpretation of it: The three branches are three days: yet within three days shall Pharaoh lift up thine head, and restore thee unto thy place: and thou shalt deliver Pharaoh's cup into his hand, after the former manner when thou wast his butler.*

"He shall lift up thy head." The expression seems to signify that the king would exalt the chief butler. So a like expression concerning Christ is to be understood, Ps. cx. 7.

"He shall lift up thy head, and restore thee unto thy place: and thou shalt deliver Pharaoh's cup into his hand, after the former manner, when thou wast his butler." All this was a very obvious exposition of the dream. Thus far the only difficulty was to know whether the dream wanted an interpretation. If it had been merely the effect of the butler's waking thoughts, all that could have been reasonably inferred from it was, that he was very desirous of restoration to his office. Nothing but divine inspiration could assure Joseph that the dream was to be realised. But there was another circumstance which left no room to doubt whether the interpretation was only a favourable conjecture or a divine discovery. The time was specified. The three branches were three days. What human sagacity could have discerned that the branches of the vine had any reference to time; or if certain portions of time were signified by them; whether three days, or three months, or three or thirty years were meant; and whether the time specified was to pass before the butler was restored, or after his restoration to his office. Anacharis, the Scythian, said that a vine had three branches, the first of which produced pleasure, the second intoxication, the third remorse. Might not some such interpretation of the three branches have appeared as natural as that which Joseph gave? But it was wisely ordered that one part of the dream should require a divinely inspired interpreter. It was God's design to assure the butler that Joseph learned his wisdom, not from man, but by revelation from above.

God hath determined the times before appointed. In many cases He confirmed the mission of His messengers, by specifying the time when their words were to be accomplished, and fulfilling them exactly in their season. Who could doubt whether Jeremiah was a messenger from God, when he foretold the death of Hananiah within the year? What reasonable man can doubt whether Jesus of Nazareth was the Messiah of whom the prophet Daniel heard these words from the mouth of Gabriel, "Seventy weeks are determined upon thy people, and upon thy holy city, to finish transgression, and to make an end of sin, and to make reconciliation for iniquity?" For Joseph's sake, and not for the sake of Pharaoh's officers, were dreams of a prophetical kind sent to them. For his sake was the time of their accomplishment specified, that it might be known with certainty whether Joseph was favoured with divine revelation or not. He would have been a fool if he had explained the three branches to signify three days to pass before the fulfilment of the dream, unless he had been well assured that God spake by his mouth.

That he was well assured of the truth of his prediction appears still more clearly from the request which he made to the chief butler. This request must have exposed him to contempt, as a fool, if his prediction had not been verified by the event.

VER. 14. *But think on me when it shall be well with thee, and show kindness, I pray thee, unto me, and make mention of me unto Pharaoh, and bring me out of his house.*

Although Joseph patiently bore his confinement, yet he earnestly desired deliverance, and thought it his wisdom and his duty to use means for obtaining it. Jesus Himself, the all-perfect model of our behaviour, prayed earnestly for deliverance from those troubles which He endured for our sake.

"Think on me when it shall be well with thee." God required His people to show kindness to a stranger, because they knew the heart of a stranger, for themselves had been strangers in the land of Egypt. One of the reasons why God brings us into trouble is, that we may know the feelings of those who are in trouble, and may learn to "weep with those who weep," and to dry up their tears by offices of kindness. Paul teaches us, in our troubles, to draw strong consolation from that compassion which Jesus learned by the things which He suffered—" We have not an high priest, who is not touched with the feeling of our infirmities, but one who was in all points tempted like as we are, yet without sin."

"And make mention of me unto Pharaoh." Although the butler could not, by his own authority, bring Joseph out of prison, he might, by his influence with Pharaoh, obtain his release. We may do much good by the hands of other men, and then we make two persons at once our debtors, him to whom the benefit is done, and him who is excited by us to perform the benefit. The last is more indebted to us than the first; for " it is more blessed to give than to receive."

Kings ought to perform acts of justice and mercy ; and those who have the ear of kings perform an eminent service to them and to their subjects by giving them such information as will direct their attention towards suitable objects. " The king that faithfully judgeth the poor, his throne shall be upholden by mercy."

" Make mention of me unto Pharaoh." Let him know that I foretold thy advancement, by giving thee a just interpretation of thy dream. Such a proof of wisdom, more than human, must at once have gained the favour of the king as soon as it was represented to him. " Righteous lips are the delight of kings, and they love him that speaketh right." Pharaoh might have his dreams as well as his servants, and he would be glad to have a man in his court, and indebted to his favour, who might one day perform to him the most useful and the most desirable service in return.

VER. 15. *For indeed I was stolen away out of the land of the Hebrews: and here also have I done nothing that they should put me into the dungeon.*

The butler, perhaps, might have been afraid to recommend Joseph to the favour of Pharaoh, because he might think that his imprisonment was probably the just punishment of his crimes. Joseph, to obviate this suspicion, tells him, that neither his slavery nor his imprisonment were the just reward of his own conduct. He had been a Hebrew, and was stolen away from their land. He does not tell by whom. Deeply as his brethren had injured him, he does not choose to publish their fault. He only wished to justify himself. When he became a slave, he had done nothing to merit imprisonment. He did not choose to tell by what wicked arts of his mistress his imprisonment had been procured. It would not have been prudent, nor was it necessary. The chief butler could not but know that slander was too often believed. And within three days Joseph was to receive a testimonial of his character from Divine Providence. If Joseph had been the man his mistress represented him to be, was it supposable that God, who hates all wickedness, would have given him the knowledge of those secrets that were hidden from other men.

Joseph was an innocent man, and therefore he had a right to expect compassion, both from the butler and the king, when he should be informed of his condition. Nature itself teaches the great to defend the poor and fatherless, to do justice to the poor and needy. All men are bound to help, when it is in their power, the poor victims of oppression. We ourselves are in the body. We may fall into afflictions that demand the sympathy of other men ; "but they shall have judgment without mercy, who have not learned to shew mercy."

It is a melancholy truth, that the innocent do not always find that compassion which they need in the day of distress. "So

I returned," says Solomon, " and considered all the oppressions that are done under the sun ; and beheld the tears of such as were oppressed, and they had no comforter ; and on the side of their oppressors there was power, but they had no comforter." But whatever mortifications we may feel in the day of trouble, from the want or the coldness of earthly friends, there is a God in the heavens who will execute judgment and righteousness for the oppressed. " He will be a refuge in the time of trouble to the distressed ; and they that know his name will put their trust in him ; for he has never forsaken them that seek his face."

LECTURE 6
The same subject continued.
xl 16–23

VER. 16. *When the chief baker saw that the interpretation was good, he said unto Joseph, I also was in my dream.*

THE chief butler was now a happy man. It is true, he might still be in some doubt what credit was due to the young man who gave him such hopes. But men are strongly disposed to believe what they wish to be true. The exposition of the dream was at least very plausible. The young man spoke like one assured of the truth of what he said ; and his countenance helped to procure credit to his words. At any rate, the terrors raised by the dream were now at an end. If anything was portended by it, it was good, and not evil. The countenance of the butler was brightened, as if a warrant had been already issued from court for his liberation ; and his companion in misery strongly wished to participate his pleasures.

The chief baker saw that the interpretation was good ; and hoped that his own dream might receive as good an interpretation. We naturally wish to be as happy as our neighbours, and when we see others enjoying prosperity, whose prospects were a little ago no better than our own, we see no good reason why we may not share in their good fortune. There are few who can rejoice like Paul, when their brethren are strong, and themselves weak. But let us remember, that Divine Providence is under no obligation to be equally kind to us all, and that prosperity and adversity, life and death, are distributed to men by one who has a right to do what He will with His own.

Hope of receiving a favourable interpretation induced the chief baker to tell his dream. Hope is good. It is the great sweetener of the miseries of life. Yet it will be our wisdom to suppress those elevations of hope that may terminate in cruel disappointment. Whilst we hope the best, let us fear the worst, and be prepared for any event that may fall out, for any tidings that we may hear. If we are not prepared for everything that may befall mortals, our happiness " is like a house built upon the sand."

VER. 16, 17. *I also was in my dream, and, behold, I had three white baskets on my head : and in the uppermost basket there was of all manner of bakemeats for Pharaoh ; and the birds did eat them out of the basket upon my head.*

The chief baker had very little reason to hope for a favourable interpretation to this dream. It was a very different one from that of the butler. The butler pressed the grapes into the king's cup, and put it into his hand, but the bakemeats which the chief baker carried in his basket never went to the king's table. They were eaten from off his head by the hungry birds. Yet the poor man hoped that his dream might have as favourable a meaning given to it as his neighbour's. We have no reason to be surprised at his vain expectation, the fruit of his fond wishes for life and prosperity. How often do we see sick persons promising themselves life, when their physicians see nothing but symptoms of approaching death !

VER. 18. *And Joseph answered and said, This is the interpretation thereof: The three baskets are three days.*

So far the interpretation agreed with the interpretation of the butler's dream. How anxiously did the poor baker wait for the next words of the interpreter ! How fondly did he hope that the third day might bring the same happy change of circumstances to himself, which was already promised to his companion ! but soon was his hope changed into despair.

VER. 19. *Yet within three days shall Pharaoh lift up thy head from off thee, and shall hang thee on a tree; and the birds shall eat thy flesh from off thee.*

Pharaoh was not to lift up the head of the chief butler in

the same sense as that of his companion. The expression has a very different meaning. "He shall lift up thine head from off thee," by depriving thee of life. "He shall hang thee on a tree." The flesh with which the birds are to be fed is not that of thy bakemeats, but of thine own body.

"Hope deferred maketh the heart sick." But how dreadful is it to have hope entirely extinguished, and changed into despair? Such was the melancholy case of the wretched baker, when he heard the interpretation of his dream. Although he did not know what was meant by it till this moment, yet the words of Joseph must have carried conviction with them to a man already possessed with the firm belief that his dream was significant of what was to befall him.

Men are ordinarily desirous to know what shall befall them. They are fools if they indulge this desire. Who could bear the assurance, that in a few days he shall die, or meet with some trouble that shall embitter his life? Had the baker known what interpretation was to be given of his dream, would he not rather have continued willingly ignorant of its meaning? What would he not have given for a draught of the waters of oblivion, if they had existed? He died three days before his time. The thoughts of the fatal moment, and of the birds feeding on his carcass, took possession of his soul. Sleeping or waking his heart was dead within him.

But why did Joseph so expressly inform him beforehand of his fatal end? "Sufficient unto the day was the evil thereof." Might he not have left it to the day to declare that misery which no means could prevent?

Joseph was laid under a necessity to interpret the dream. He had in effect promised to do it. If he had now refused to satisfy the baker's ardent desire, his silence would have been little better than the words in which the fatal sentence was pronounced. It is not to be supposed that the pious youth would speak lies in the name of the Lord. He professed to have his knowledge from above, and faithfully delivered to the two prisoners what he had received from the Lord.

But there was another reason why Joseph declared plainly

what he had learned from God. He wished to have it known amongst the Egyptians that interpretations belonged to the God of the Hebrews, and that He alone could show things that were to come to pass. Joseph afterwards received the name of Zaphnath-paaneah, the revealer of secrets ; but it was his desire to have it known, that his God was the fountain of all his knowledge, and that confidence in any other God, or in any other way of coming to the knowledge of futurity, but by revelation from Him, was vanity, and the work of error.

It was hard for the poor baker to be told that in three days his head was to be taken from him. But Joseph could not but speak what was made known to him by God, to be communicated to his companions ; and the unfortunate person must have heard, within three days, his sentence, although Joseph had been silent. If he made the proper use of his present privilege, it was of infinite use for him to be now told that in three days he should die. Some space was allowed him of preparation for the awful event ; and he had an instructor in the prison to assist him in his preparations. He might have seen that Joseph had his knowledge from heaven. If he was wise for himself, he would request Joseph to inform him what he knew of the state of man after death, and of the best preparation for it. Whether he availed himself of his opportunities or not, we cannot say. If he did not, the fault was his own. Those men must be hardened in wickedness to an extraordinary degree whom the near prospect of death does not awaken to a serious consideration of that eternal state on which they must soon enter.

It is certainly unwise to strike a damp upon the spirits of men, by pronouncing abrupt and unguarded sentences of death upon them when they are sick. Some could not bear it. They will be left for the most part in a better condition of mind for thinking about the necessary preparations for death, by being reminded that the event of their trouble is uncertain, or that it may probably terminate in death, than by being roundly told that no hope is left them of a recovery. But it is inhuman and improper to feed men with the hopes of life, that will in all appearance deceive them. Is it not far better to lead men

gradually to the expectation of that awful event, whilst some
time of preparation is left them, than to suffer them all at once
to be overwhelmed with the tremendous prospect when their
last struggle is approaching, and when the severity of pain
must disqualify the mind for thinking with composure on the
subjects that relate to men's eternal welfare?

We cannot but pity those who are told that they must die in
a few hours, or who are compelled, by the racking pains which
they feel, to see that they are fast approaching to the grave.
What if the case should in a short time be our own? That it
will one day be our own, we have little reason to doubt. If we
are not prepared to meet our last enemy, we have made a bad
use of our precious opportunities. We are not fit to live with
comfort, if we are not prepared to hear with composure the
sentence of death, for already we are appointed to die. The
day is fixed, although we do not yet know it. We are not sure
that it will be so much as three days hence.

"In three days," said Joseph to the chief butler, "thy head
shall be lifted up by the king." "In three days," he said to
the chief baker, "thy head shall be lifted off from thee, and
given for a prey to the fowls of the air." It does not appear
from the history that the chief butler was more innocent than
the chief baker. They had both offended their Lord. If one
of them was pardoned, why not both? Such would be the
thoughts of this unhappy man. His own misery would be
aggravated by the good fortune of his companion in sin and
danger. In our Lord's parable of the labourers in the vineyard,
we find some of them who received the full reward promised to
their work, grudging that others received as much as themselves.
Much more might this poor man feel the stings of envy when
life and honour were granted to his companion in evil, whilst
himself was doomed to an ignominious death. But if the man
deserved to die, he had no reason to find fault with his judge
for refusing that pardon to himself which he gave to another.
Kings must have a power of pardoning some offenders, but their
authority would be at an end if others were not punished. How
much more must the Sovereign of the world have power to

pardon or punish offenders, according to the counsel of His own will? Let us not dare to dispute His sovereignty, but let us tremble at the thought of being found in the unhappy number of those who shall be left when others are taken. How wretched will be the condition of those children of the kingdom who see many coming from every region of the world to take their seat in the kingdom of heaven, when themselves are cast out!

"And the birds shall eat thy flesh from off thee." The terror of approaching death would be aggravated to the poor man by the prospect of the indignity with which his body was to be treated. Our religion furnishes us with effectual consolation, not only against the fear of death, but against all that the wrath of man has power to do against either our bodies or our names, after the stroke of death is past. We read of the bodies of saints that have been cast out to the wild beasts of the earth, and to the fowls of heaven. But were the bodies of Christians swallowed up by the most abhorred of God's creatures, they sleep in Jesus, and God will bring them with Him at the day of His appearance and His kingdom.

VER. 20. *And it came to pass the third day, which was Pharaoh's birthday, that he made a feast unto all his servants: and he lifted up the head of the chief butler and of the chief baker among his servants.*

It has been customary with kings, and with many other great men, to celebrate their birthdays with feasts and gladness. And we have all reason to rejoice at the remembrance of our birth into the world, if our lives have been employed for the purposes for which they were given. We ought to bless God for the gift of existence, and for making us rational creatures. We ought to bless Him for that goodness and mercy which have hitherto followed us all the days of our life. The most patient of men was at a certain period of his life overwhelmed with such dreadful calamities, that he cursed the day of his birth, and the night in which it was said, There is a man-child brought into the world. Let us endeavour so to live that we may always rejoice in our existence. There are too many for whom it would have been good that they had never been born.

F

Pharaoh made a feast for all his servants, that they might rejoice with him ; and on this happy day, it is probable, he wished to perform some acts of grace, that all his people might rejoice in the clemency of his government. With this view he lifted up the head of the chief butler, by raising him again to his former station. But, at the same time, to warn his servants against provoking his displeasure, he lifted up the head of the chief baker in a very different sense, by depriving him of life. What reason he had to make this difference between his two servants, we cannot say ; but we know that he fulfilled the will of God, and verified the prediction of His servant Joseph.

Ver. 21. *And he restored the chief butler unto his butlership again ; and he gave the cup into Pharaoh's hand.*

"The desire accomplished is sweet to the soul." The chief butler had found that the king's wrath was like messengers of death. He now found that the king's favour was like dew upon the grass. His former fears would heighten his joy, and make him cautious of his future behaviour, that he might not expose himself to new danger. His deliverance would give him double pleasure, when he considered that his fate might have been the same with that of his unhappy companion. Pain and fear are the objects of great aversion, whilst they are present, but some of the sweetest pleasures of life would be wanting if they were never felt.

Ver. 22. *But he hanged the chief baker, as Joseph had interpreted to them.*

If both these men's dreams had portended pardon, the interpretation of the dreams might have been considered as a lucky conjecture. It might have appeared reasonable to think that on the approaching festivity of the king's birthday he would signalise his clemency by acts of grace to offenders. But who could have foreseen that he would make one of his servants to feel the severity of his displeasure on this happy day, whilst he pardoned the other, or that he would execute his displeasure by hanging him on a tree, and exposing his dead body to the fowls of heaven ? Every circumstance concurred to establish the credit of Joseph as a man that enjoyed intercourse with heaven.

All who heard of the verification of Joseph's words ought to have learned and been assured that the word of the Lord was with him. How much more ought we to be established in the faith of the Bible after the many proofs given us by the accomplishment of prophecies that the holy men who wrote it spoke by inspiration of the Divine Spirit. Who of all the gods of the nations was ever able to give such proofs that they were entitled to the veneration of their worshippers? "Remember the former things of old," says God by Isaiah, "for I am God, and there is none else; I am God, and there is none like me. Declaring the end from the beginning, and from ancient times, all things that are not yet done, saying, My counsel shall stand, and I will do all my pleasure."

VER. 23. *Yet did not the chief butler remember Joseph, but forgat him.*

The chief butler could not drop from his memory the high obligations under which he lay to the man who had, by interpreting his dreams, relieved his mind from the tormenting apprehensions which had taken possession of it. Every thought of his former unhappy condition, and of its happy reverse must have called up Joseph to his mind. Yet he did not remember Joseph, to recompense his goodness, but shamefully forgot one of the most wonderful services which had been ever done him; for certainly he gained two days' happiness from misery, when his dream was interpreted so much to his joy.

If the butler had owed nothing to Joseph, it was certainly a duty imposed by the laws of humanity, to do what he could for his relief, when he knew him to be unjustly enslaved and imprisoned; but he was utterly inexcusable, after what Joseph had done for him, when he did not so much as open his mouth to Pharaoh on his behalf. Interpretations of dreams were highly esteemed in Egypt, and yet none of their interpretations was ever so well confirmed as Joseph's. Many stories were doubtless told of other interpreters of dreams, which, if they had been true, would have been sufficient proofs of their skill.

But the story which the chief butler could have told the king concerning Joseph was probably the only one which could admit of no doubt.

The chief butler, in the first transports of his joy, doubtless intended to show his gratitude to the Hebrew youth, but he was soon swallowed up in his own concerns, and thought but little of that man who had changed his desperate sorrow into joy and gladness. Potiphar was a powerful man at the court of Pharaoh. Commendations of Joseph might have been offensive to the man who had imprisoned him, and the chief butler would not risk his own safety in support of an oppressed stranger. Inordinate self-love is the bane of every virtuous emotion. " The fear of man bringeth a snare, but whoso putteth his trust in the Lord shall be safe." He will be more afraid of displeasing God by the neglect of duty, than of displeasing any man on earth by performing it.

The ungrateful man cares for nothing but his own welfare ; but he disappoints himself. The chief butler might have advanced his own interest if he had remembered Joseph, and procured his release from prison. After Joseph was advanced to honour, he would have accounted the instrument of his advancement one of his best friends, and loaded him with new favours. But when it was so evident that the chief butler was wholly under the influence of a selfish spirit, even when he spoke favourably of Joseph to the king, a man of Joseph's sagacity, though he could forgive his ingratitude, must have considered him as a man not worthy to be esteemed or trusted. Joseph's own generous feelings must have taught him how base and contemptible those men are who in the time of their own prosperity forget the distresses of their benefactors.

We all reprobate the conduct of the chief butler. His memory will be held in detestation while the world lasts. The Word of God hath recorded his infamy, that other men may be warned to show proper returns of gratitude to their benefactors. We can, indeed, be under no apprehensions that the book of God will transmit our character to future ages. The chief butler felt as little fear of that perpetual dishonour to which his memory was to be subjected by a book that should be read to the end of the world. But do we not know that there is another book of God, which contains the records of every individual's life—a book which shall be opened before the assembled world? What confusion will then cover the faces of those who are found to have been insensible to the favours done them, either by their fellow-men or by their Maker! The unthankful and the unkind are kindred characters, 2 Tim. iii. Those who are unthankful to benefactors of their own race are likewise unthankful to their Maker and Preserver. If they were duly sensible of the blessings conferred upon them by God, they would not be ungrateful to those whom He is pleased to employ as the instruments of His benefactions.

If all men abhor those who return not good for good when it is in the power of their hands to do it; if they are justly accounted no better than publicans or heathens who love only them who love themselves, how black is our ingratitude if we are not penetrated with grateful love to Him who not only pitied us in our low estate, but wrought redemption for us by a life of sorrow, and by an accursed death!

When the chief butler was put into his former place, Joseph, doubtless, hoped to be remembered by him, and felt bitterly the disappointment of his hopes. The chief butler would not be slack in making promises, and Joseph would not be less ready to believe his words. We are not told how he behaved when he saw that he had hoped in vain. He was a man, and felt as a man; but he was a wise man, and a saint, and knew how to bear and how to improve his disappointment. After the treatment he received from his brethren, the sons of the best of men, he would not think it a strange thing to be treated with ingratitude by a stranger, the slave of an Egyptian prince. He had already learned, and now he was taught by a new lesson of experience, to trust not in man, but in God, who knows how to bring the greatest good out of the greatest evil. The discovery that God had made to him of the meaning of the two dreams was a token for good to him from God. It could not be for the sake of the ungrateful butler that God made known the secrets of His providence.   What method God would use to turn the gift bestowed upon him to his own advantage, Joseph could not yet know.   The God who told him that in three days his companions should be taken out of prison, had not yet told him how long himself was to continue in his confinement.   But he could not be miserable when God was with him.   Although one man treated him with cold neglect, and another man treated him with unmerited cruelty, he was well assured that God would not leave him nor forsake him till he had done all that he had spoken to him of.   He had no doubt heard of the promises made to his father Jacob (Gen. xxviii.), and knew that neither the ingratitude of Laban nor the hatred of Esau had made them of no effect. His father's God was his God, and although the time was not yet come for his deliverance and exaltation, he knew that it would certainly come at last, and would furnish him with materials of joy and power, more than sufficient to compensate all his sufferings and sorrows.   " Why art thou cast down, O my soul ? and why art thou disquieted within me ? hope thou in God : for I shall yet praise him for the help of his countenance.   Surely men of low degree are vanity, and men of high degree are a lie.   To be laid in the balance, they are altogether lighter than vanity.   But power belongeth unto God.   Also unto thee, O Lord, belongeth mercy, for thou renderest to every man according to his work.

LECTURE 7
Pharaoh's dream.
xli 1–16

VER. 1. *And it came to pass at the end of two full years, that Pharaoh dreamed : and, behold, he stood by the river.*

WHETHER we are to date the two full years from the time that Joseph was put into the prison, or rather from the time that the butler was taken out of it, which was the event last spoken of, the mention of the time is designed to point out the length of Joseph's confinement. Two years of imprisonment will appear like twenty years to one who has not learned to bear the evils of life with an uncommon degree of patience. Two years of disappointed hope of deliverance are still more intolerable, "for hope deferred maketh the heart sick."

Even those who have been taught of God are strongly tempted, under long-continued afflictions, to weary of the Lord's correction. Few men were more patient under trouble than David, and yet we find him sometimes saying, "How long wilt thou forget me, O Lord? for ever? how long wilt thou hide thy face from me? How long shall I take counsel in my soul, having sorrow in my heart daily? how long shall mine enemy be exalted over me?" Job was more famous than David for his patience, and yet we hear him saying, "My soul is weary of my life. I am made to possess months of vanity; wearisome nights are appointed unto me."

Joseph was now in that period of life which, to men in health and ease, is the most pleasant of all others, for he was thirty years old when his troubles came to their period. He might think it a hard matter to live all the best of his days in a prison, when he had done nothing to deserve it ; and his prison would be the more wearisome to him, that his hopes of deliverance, founded on God's own word, confirmed by His providence, seemed to fail for evermore. What could God intend by the strange dreams of his fellow-prisoners, and by the gift of interpretation bestowed on him ?˙ He had surely good reason to think that it was in favour to himself, rather than to the ungrateful butler, that God had made known what should happen to him some days before it happened ; and yet both the dream and the interpretation seemed to be forgotten. Joseph had begged the butler, and the butler, as we have reason to believe, had promised to speak of him to Pharaoh, that he might be released from his dungeon ; and yet he was suffered to languish in it week after week, month after month, and probably one year after another. Had God suffered His gracious intentions to be frustrated by the mean selfishness of a man who never thought of his companion and benefactor, when he had obtained what he desired for himself? No great wonder that "the chief butler remembered not Joseph, but forgat him." It is too common for men in prosperity to forget the friends of their adversity ; but had the Lord also forgotten to be gracious to His poor afflicted servant? Had He in anger shut up His tender mercies, and did His promise fail for evermore ? By no means ; Joseph never thought that the promise of God could fail for evermore ; or if such a thought ever entered into his mind, he knew that it was his infirmity.

Let us be patient under the trials of our faith. Surely God knows better than we what is the fittest season to interpose for our help. We may wait days and years for the performance of God's word ; but let us bless Him for that word which He gave us for the ground of our hope, that we may be preserved from fainting till the time of deliverance come, even the time that He hath set. "It is a good thing both to hope and quietly to wait for the salvation of the Lord."

The chief butler forgot the kind interpreter of his dream, but the Lord took care that both Joseph and the butler's dream should again come into remembrance. Pharaoh himself now dreamed, and, behold, he stood by the river Nile.

VER. 2-7. *And, behold, there came up out of the river seven well favoured kine and fatfleshed; and they fed in a meadow. And, behold, seven other kine came up after them out of the river, ill favoured and leanfleshed, and stood by the other kine upon the brink of the river. And the ill favoured and leanfleshed kine did eat up the seven well favoured and fat kine. So Pharaoh awoke. And he slept and dreamed the second time: and, behold, seven ears of corn came up upon one stalk, rank and good. And, behold, seven thin ears and blasted with the east wind sprung up after them. And the seven thin ears devoured the seven rank and full ears. And Pharaoh awoke, and, behold, it was a dream.*

This dream will appear to many but a jumble of incoherent ideas, which no wise man would retain in his memory. What other man ever thought, even in a dream, of kine, or of ears of corn, eating one another? Yet it is certain that this dream came from God, and that it was an intimation of future events, of exceedingly important consequence, both to the Egyptian nation and to all the neighbouring nations, and even to the Church of God. "God's ways are not as our ways," nor ought we to measure His providential administration by our own rules. He discovers His mind in the manner best fitted to serve His purpose. It was not the will of God that Pharaoh should understand his own dream till it was explained by a heaven-taught interpreter. If the meaning had been so plain that it could have been explained by the wise men of Egypt, the design for which it was sent to Pharaoh would not have been gained. It was for Joseph's sake, and for the sake of his father's house, that Pharaoh dreamed, and that his dream required such an interpreter as Joseph. There are dreams and visions recorded in many places of the Bible that appear to our narrow minds as dark as this dream of Pharaoh. God hath His reasons for choosing to deliver many parts of His mind in dark figures, which we would need a Joseph to interpret. But to allege that any part of Scripture ought to have been plainer than it is would be daringly presumptuous. Every part of it was dictated to the holy men of God by that wisdom which cannot err. Every censure of the divine wisdom must be folly and blasphemy. The darkest portion of Scripture was not written in vain.

VER. 8. *And it came to pass in the morning that his spirit was troubled ; and he sent and called for all the magicians of Egypt, and all the wise men thereof: and Pharaoh told them his dream ; but there was none that could interpret them unto Pharaoh.*

Why was Pharaoh's spirit troubled by a dream? Might not his princely education have set him above the credulous fears of the vulgar, who are often tormented by the illusions of their own ungoverned fancies, as the tales that pass current among men who have not sense to discover their absurdity? We deny not that the princes, as well as the common people in Egypt, were, like the men of Athens in later times, "in all things too superstitious." It was their common custom to pay a senseless regard to dreams, and to other things as unmeaning as dreams generally are. But at this time the trouble of the king had a just foundation. His dream was from God ; God imprinted on his mind a firm conviction that it was from above, and that it contained an intimation of some very important events, although what these events were he could not guess. God has the spirits of the wisest, the greatest, the bravest, and most daring of mankind under His control ; and can fix what convictions and terrors He pleases in the minds even of those who reckon themselves superior to the rest of mankind. "He cutteth off the spirits of princes, and appeareth terrible to the kings of the earth." Was there ever a more undaunted courage than Nebuchadnezzar possessed? and yet God could make him afraid like a grasshopper, by the visions of his head upon his bed. He that made the proud leviathans of the world can make His sword to approach unto them, and to pierce them with deadly wounds, which none but Himself can heal.

Pharaoh, to relieve his spirit from the terror of some unknown calamity, sent in haste for the magicians and wise men of Egypt, to explain his dreams. Egypt was famous in the earliest times for its wisdom. If there was a man in the world who could explain riddles, or interpret dreams, Pharaoh doubted not but he must be found amongst his wise men. And if his opinion of them had been just, he was wise in seeking information from them of what it so much concerned him to know. If God is pleased to speak to us, it is our duty to seek the knowledge of what He says, and to borrow that wisdom from others which we have not in ourselves. If there are any that may be reasonably believed to know the mind of God better than ourselves, we sin against our own souls if we do not avail ourselves of their superior light. " The manifestation of the Spirit is given to every man to profit withal."

But it was the unhappiness of the king of Egypt that his magicians knew as little as he did of God and of His will. Their high reputation was founded on ignorance and imposture. It is our happiness that we enjoy such clear revelations of the will of God, as to enable us to judge for ourselves upon sufficient evidence who those interpreters of the divine oracles are whom we ought to regard as the faithful servants of God. We need men qualified to instruct us concerning our duty, but we are authorised and furnished with sufficient means of judging for ourselves what those instructions are which accord to the words of knowledge, or cause to err from them. " The entrance of God's word giveth light, it giveth understanding to the simple."

Pharaoh sent for all the wise men of Egypt, and told them his dream, which he perfectly recollected, and yet none of them could explain it to him. When Nebuchadnezzar, on a like occasion, sent for the wise men of Babylon, he requested them to tell, not the interpretation of the dream only, but the dream itself, which he had forgotten. These wise men were so confident, either of their skill in dreams, or of their power of invention to conceal their ignorance, that they promised to interpret the king's dream as soon as it was made known to them. The magicians of Egypt were not so conceited of their knowledge. Although Pharaoh's dream was rehearsed in their ears, they did not pretend to know the meaning of it. All their combined wisdom durst not pretend to penetrate the secrets of Divine Providence, to which it referred. How dim-sighted is human wisdom ! " The things of a man knoweth no man, but the spirit of a man that is in him ; and the things of God are known only to the Spirit of God, and to him to whom the Spirit will reveal them."

When we consider the antiquity of the symbolical manner of instruction in Egypt, it appears strange to us that the magicians did not so much as pretend to understand the king's dream. Oxen or ears of corn are very natural emblems of fertility, since corn is produced from corn by the labours of oxen. Kine and ears of corn, on the brink of the river, might very naturally have been supposed to denote the increase of the fruits of the earth, for which the Egyptians are indebted to the overflowings of the river.

If fat kine and full ears of corn, on the banks of the Nile, were fit emblems of an abundant harvest, lean cattle and thin ears of corn might have been justly considered as emblems of a very scanty produce. But it appears either that such thoughts did not come into the minds of the wise men, or that they did not know what to think of the number of the kine, and of the ears of the corn.

It was well ordered by God that the butler was permitted to behave so ungratefully to Joseph, that he never told the king of the interpretation which he gave of the two dreams of the king's officers. That interpretation, had it been known, might have been a key to the wise men to open Pharaoh's dream, and then the honour of expounding it would not have been reserved for Joseph. The three branches in the vine, and the three baskets on the head of the baker, were three days. By a parity of reasoning, the seven kine and the seven ears might denote, not seven days, but seven years. There could not be merely seven days of plenty or famine, either from the labours of the kine, or from the abundance or scarcity of water in the Nile. But the plenty or scarcity of the years can be known beforehand with certainty from the rise of its waters in the season when it overflows its banks.

As it is not probable that the magicians and wise men of Egypt would have scrupled a lie to advance or to preserve their credit, it may still appear wonderful that they did not agree to give some pretended interpretation of the king's dream, although they could not satisfy their own minds about it. All that we can certainly say is, that God, by His overruling influence upon their minds, constrained them to acknowledge their ignorance. It is possible that they were little less troubled in mind than the king himself about the uncertain event so directly pointed out. If they had pretended to foretell from the dream what was to happen, the event might have made them liars, and it might appear wiser to confess their ignorance for once, than to undergo the risk of a confutation from facts, which would have covered their pretended art with perpetual infamy. Even liars, if they are not infatuated, will be cautious to avoid those falsehoods which may soon be detected. " A lying tongue " at the best " is but for a moment," yet a well contrived lie may keep its credit longer than others.

Ver. 9. *Then spake the chief butler unto Pharaoh, saying, I do remember my faults this day.*

The chief butler at last remembers Joseph. When he thinks he may advance his own credit with the king, by commending his comforter, he faithfully relates what he knew to his advantage. Joseph was not indebted to the man, but to that Providence which opened his mouth in praise of Joseph, when the time set by God was come.

" I do this day remember my faults." He ought to have remembered his fault against Joseph, and against God, whose goodness he concealed when he ought to have published it, that the glory of the God whom Joseph served might be made known to the Egyptians. But this fault made no impression on his mind. The fault of which he spoke was that offence to the king of Egypt which was the cause of his imprisonment. This fault he acknowledged in deference to the king. If he had not confessed that he was guilty of that crime, which was the cause of his imprisonment, he would have seemed to call in question the king's justice in imprisoning, and his mercy in sparing him.

"It is not fit to be said unto a king, Thou art wicked, or to princes, Ye are unrighteous;" far less to Him that respecteth not the rich more than the poor. We ought, therefore, when we mention our chastisements, to confess those sins by which we have deserved them. God does not afflict willingly, nor lay upon man more than is meet, that he should enter into judgment with God.

"I do remember my faults this day."

Ver. 10-13. *Pharaoh was wroth with his servants, and put me in ward in the captain of the guard's house, both me and the chief baker: and we dreamed a dream in one night, I and he; we dreamed each man according to the interpretation of his dream. And there was there with us a young man, an Hebrew, servant to the captain of the guard; and we told him, and he interpreted to us our dreams; to each man according to his dream he did interpret. And it came to pass, as he interpreted to us, so it was; me he restored unto mine office, and him he hanged.*

In common language, as well as in the language of Scripture, it is not unusual to speak of things as if they were done by those persons who only say that they are done, or shall be done. In this sense, God says (Rev. xi. 5), that if any man will hurt His two witnesses, fire proceedeth out of their mouth, and devoureth their enemies, and that they have power to shut heaven, that it rain not during the days of their prophecy.

The chief butler now told Pharaoh what he ought to have told him, probably two years before this time. Yet if he had then given the account which he now gave of Joseph, the event might have been very different. The king might have taken Joseph out of prison, but not to reign. He would have been numbered with the other wise men of Egypt, who were reputed skilful magicians, or interpreters of dreams. Perhaps he might have been preferred to them, and called upon to interpret Pharaoh's dream before any other of them, and then the excellency of his wisdom above that of the magicians would have been unknown, or unacknowledged. They might have pretended that they could have interpreted the dream as well as the young Hebrew, if Pharaoh had done them the honour to make use of their skill. As matters stood, they were under a necessity of confessing that Joseph and Joseph's God were above them.

"What thou knowest not now, thou shalt know hereafter," said Jesus to Peter. Often are believers in God filled with amazement at those dispensations of Providence, which they will one day call back to their minds with wonder and praise. Many and many a time, during the course of two years, Joseph wondered why the God of his fathers and his own God left him so long in the dungeon; but the joyful day was now come when this part of the mystery of Providence was to be cleared up.

VER. 14. *Then Pharaoh sent and called Joseph, and they brought him hastily out of the dungeon : and he shaved himself, and changed his raiment, and came in unto Pharaoh.*

"Where the word of a king is there is power." Neither the hatred of an imperious mistress, nor the wrath or policy of Potiphar, could detain Joseph in prison when the word of the king came to set him free. Now was the patience of the pious youth well rewarded. The sorrows and perplexities of his imprisonment gave place to joy and praise. He forgot his misery, or remembered it as waters that pass away.

"They brought him hastily out of the dungeon." Perhaps the word *dungeon,* in this place, is not strictly to be understood; for he seems, long before this time, to have been set free from the horrors of that close confinement in the dungeon of the prison to which he was at first doomed by the rage of his uxorious master. His situation, however, till this time, had been very unpleasant. He was not suffered to leave the walls of his prison. Long was his patience tried by unworthy treatment, but now he was "brought up out of the deep pit and miry clay, his feet were set upon a rock, and his goings were established, and a new song was put into his mouth, to magnify the Lord."

It is said of Mephibosheth, that he had not washed his clothes, nor washed his feet, nor trimmed his beard, from the time that David left Jerusalem because of Absalom, till he returned again in peace to his house. By these signs of grief he expressed his deep concern for the afflictions of his royal benefactor. Joseph expressed, by like signs, his humiliation of spirit under those afflictions which Divine Providence laid upon himself. But when he was called into the presence of the king of Egypt, he laid aside his mourning apparel, and shaved himself, that he might appear with decency and due respect in the presence of the king. Doubtless, when he exchanged his prison-garments for such as are worn in king's palaces, his heart rejoiced less in the change of his circumstances than in the favours of God, who had "put off his sackcloth, and girded him with gladness, to the end that his glory might sing praise to the Lord."

VER. 15. *And Pharaoh said unto Joseph, I have dreamed a dream, and there is none that can interpret it : and I have heard say of thee that thou canst understand a dream to interpret it.*

When Nebuchadnezzar heard that his wise men could not tell him the dream which he had forgotten, he issued out orders to put them all to death, without inquiring whether any other man could be found out to do what the magicians could not do. The king of Egypt behaved very differently. He did not talk of putting the magicians to death. All that he did against them was, to publish their incapacity to perform what they were understood to profess, and to seek that information elsewhere which they confessed themselves unable to give.

Joseph had now an opportunity, which he did not suffer to pass unimproved, of showing forth the superiority of his own God to the gods of Egypt, and of that wisdom that comes from Him to that wisdom of which the magicians boasted.

VER. 16. *And Joseph answered Pharaoh, saying, It is not in me, God shall give Pharaoh an answer of peace.*

It is not in me to interpret dreams, said Joseph to Pharaoh, but in God, who by my mouth will give Pharaoh an answer of peace. "The secret which the king hath demanded," said Daniel to Nebuchadnezzar on a like occasion, " cannot the wise men, the astrologers, the magicians, the soothsayers, shew unto the king ; but there is a God in heaven who revealeth secrets, and maketh known to the king Nebuchadnezzar what shall be in the latter days. But as for me, this secret is not revealed to me for any wisdom that I have more than any living." Humility has been in every age a distinguishing ornament of all God's faithful servants. Never were their hearts haughty or their eyes lofty, nor did they deal in great matters, as in things too high for them. What good things were in them they have always acknowledged to be the gifts of divine mercy. "I can do all things," says Paul, but how? "through Christ strengthening me." Without Christ he neither could act nor think. He laboured more abundantly than all the apostles, but it was not he, it was the grace of God that was with him. It was Christ that wrought by him when he preached among the Gentiles the unsearchable riches of Christ, and turned thousands of them from darkness unto light, and from the power of Satan unto God, Rom. xv. 19 ; 1 Cor. xv. 11.

No man is fit to declare the counsels of God who is not deeply sensible of his own unfitness without receiving light and help from the Spirit of God, the only Author of all useful gifts, as well as of every saving grace. Those who take the praise to themselves of what they do in the service of God are worthy, like Herod, to be eaten up of worms.

Although Joseph was conscious that it was not in himself to interpret the king's dream, he was fully persuaded that God by him would give the king an answer to his demand. Humility and faith are kindred and inseparable graces. We cannot trust both to ourselves and in God, any more than we can serve two masters. We should learn to distrust ourselves, that we may trust in God, the Father of lights, from whom every good and perfect gift comes.

"God shall give Pharaoh an answer of peace." These words are expressive of the wishes and expectations of Joseph. Pharaoh was disquieted through the apprehension of some calamity, portended by a dream which had taken hold of his mind. Joseph hoped that there was no ground for his apprehensions. He had reason to believe that the dream was sent to Pharaoh in mercy to himself, and that the interpretation would be such as to gain for him the favour of that prince; and therefore, before he knew what the dream was, he soothes the mind of Pharaoh, by giving him hope that he would not find the interpretation so unpleasing as he feared it might be. The interpreters of God's mind must, like Micaiah, say nothing to please man without warrant from God—"If I yet pleased men," says Paul, "I should not be the servant of Christ;" yet they will be glad when they give comfort to the disquieted. Messages of peace, and not of evil, are most pleasing to themselves. Joseph rejoiced in the hope that he would have it in his power to give Pharaoh an answer of peace from God, with respect to those things of the present life that were most interesting to him. It is the joy of the ministers of the Gospel of Christ that they are commissioned to bear to men the tidings of that "peace which passeth all understanding"— "How beautiful upon the mountains are the feet of him that bringeth good tidings, that publisheth salvation, that bringeth good tidings of good things, that saith unto Zion, Thy God reigneth!"

LECTURE 8
The interpretation of Pharaoh's dream.
xli 17–36

VER. 17-24. *And Pharaoh said unto Joseph, In my dream, behold, I stood upon the bank of the river: and, behold, there came up out of the river seven kine, fatfleshed and well favoured; and they fed in a meadow: and, behold, seven other kine came up after them, poor and very ill favoured and leanfleshed, such as I never saw in all the land of Egypt for badness: and the lean and the ill favoured kine did eat up the first seven fat kine: and when they had eaten them up, it could not be known that they had eaten them; but they were still ill favoured, as at the beginning. So I awoke. And I saw in my dream, and, behold, seven ears came up in one stalk, full and good: and, behold, seven ears, withered, thin, and blasted with the east wind, sprung up after them: and the thin ears devoured the seven good ears; and I told this unto the magicians; but there was none that could declare it to me.*

PHARAOH had not forgot one word of his dream. It had taken firm hold of his mind, and made impressions of terror on his fancy. The language in which he expresses the unsightly appearance of the ill-favoured kine is stronger than that which Moses had used in giving an account of the dream at the beginning of the chapter. Nor was their appearance altered for the better, says Pharaoh, "after they had eaten up the well favoured kine." Something very bad, he was afraid, must have been portended by the unpleasant vision of the night, especially when it was followed by another that appeared equally ominous of mischief. But that which disquieted him most was, that none of all the magicians was able to afford him one ray of light about its meaning—" I told this unto the magicians, but there was none that could declare it to me."

It was happy for Pharaoh that the magicians confessed their incapacity to interpret this dream. Had they pretended to give some meaning to it out of the imaginations of their own hearts, it is probable that he would have sought no farther; the abundance of the seven years of plenty might have been spent in dissipation, and no provision made against the long and terrible famine. But when he was convinced that the mind of God was not with the magicians, he was forced to seek for light where he could find it. Happy will we be if we are thoroughly convinced that we must have recourse to the great Prophet for that instruction in the mind of God which we so greatly need for the prevention of infinitely greater evils than a famine of seven years could produce. When we are deeply convinced that it is not in man that walketh to direct his steps, and that Christ alone can give us the light of life, we will seek the true wisdom where it is to be found, and will not be disappointed.

VER. 25. *And Joseph said unto Pharaoh, The dream of Pharaoh is one: God hath shewed Pharaoh what he is about to do.*

Pharaoh had two dreams. He awoke from the dream about the seven kine before he dreamed about the ears of corn. But both the dreams were in effect one, for they both meant the same thing. It is a mercy to such inattentive creatures as we are that God speaketh not once only, but twice. He must often speak more than twice before we can find ears to hear.

"God hath shewed Pharaoh." The first thing to be considered about the dream was, whether it had any meaning, or was a mere vagary of the king's fancy, like a thousand other wanderings of fancy in the time of sleep which had formerly passed through his mind, and been forgotten when he awoke.

Pharaoh was already firmly persuaded that his dream had an important meaning, and Joseph assures him that he was not mistaken.

"God hath shewed Pharaoh what he is about to do." Joseph seizes the happy opportunity to speak of his own God, the Governor of the world, to Pharaoh. "I will speak of thy testimonies to kings," says David, "and I will not be ashamed." Joseph here speaks to Pharaoh of the providence and foreknowledge of God. He knew that events would soon confirm his doctrine, and that Pharaoh's mind was already prepared by his fears and his disappointment to receive it. It was certainly a point of infinite importance, when different gods were worshipped by different nations of the world, to know what proofs of godhead any of them had given. The God who governs the world, and who is able to foretell things to come to pass hereafter, must be the true God. The God of Israel, therefore, calls upon the worshippers of false gods to know and consider, whether their own gods were ever able to foretell future events; and, in opposition to their pretensions, published many predictions which were in due season to be accomplished. "Produce your cause, saith the Lord, bring forth your strong reasons, saith the King of Jacob. Let them bring them forth and shew us what shall happen : let them show the former things what they be, that we may consider them, and know the latter end of them, or declare us things for to come. Shew the things that are to come hereafter, that we may know that ye are gods, yea, do good or do evil, that we may be dismayed, and behold it together. Behold ye are of nothing, and your work of nought; an abomination is he that chooseth you. I have raised up one from the north, and he shall come, from the rising of the sun shall he call upon my name."

"God hath shewed Pharaoh what he is about to do." If the Lord governs all things by His providence, none but He can declare the end from the beginning. If any man can foretell those events which depend on the sovereign pleasure of God, he must derive his information from God Himself. When Joseph, therefore, professes to declare from God Himself what he was about to do, and when everything happened according to the prediction, it was undeniably evident that the God whom Joseph worshipped was the Ruler of the universe, and that Joseph received from Him that wisdom in which he so far excelled all the magicians and wise men of Egypt. Thus the true God left not Himself without a witness in the most famous kingdom of the world, at the time when the nations were all revolting, or had revolted, from His service to the worship of those gods that were no gods. All the Gentiles were inexcusable, because when the works of nature manifested to their eyes the things of their Maker, "they did not glorify him as God, neither were thankful." The Egyptians were doubly inexcusable for persisting in their idolatry when the living God manifested His glory amongst them by prophecies fulfilled, and by many works which none but God could do.

VER. 26, 27. *The seven good kine are seven years ; and the seven good ears are seven years : the dream is one. And the seven thin and ill favoured kine that came after them are seven years ; and the seven empty years blasted with the east wind shall be seven years of famine.*

It is probable that Pharaoh had before this time heard the particulars of the two dreams which Joseph had interpreted to his officers in prison. He had heard what meaning Joseph had assigned to the three baskets and to the three vine-branches, and how exactly the interpretation of them corresponded to the time in which himself had released the butler, and hanged the baker. He would, therefore, be fully satisfied that the interpretation now given of the seven kine and of the seven ears of corn was just. Whatever doubts might have been entertained of the truth of Joseph's predictions by the officers of Pharaoh before this accomplishment, their master would see good reason, from experience, to believe that the mind of the God of heaven was in his mouth.

VER. 28. *This is the thing which I have spoken unto Pharaoh : what God is about to do he sheweth unto Pharaoh.*

Again Joseph tells Pharaoh that God was both the revealer and the doer of those things that were presignified by his dream.

We need often to be put in mind that God is both the speaker of His word, and the doer of His works. When we hear the Word of God spoken by the mouth of men, we are ready to confine our attention to the visible speaker. ' When we behold the earth abounding with the bounties of Heaven, or feel the distresses of famine, we are too ready to forget that our prosperity or adversity is the allotment of Heaven.

If Pharaoh had heard Joseph interpret his dream without remembering that God revealed His intentions by him, he could not have made the proper improvement of what was said to him. He was disposed to believe what was said, but he would have given that praise unto Joseph which was due to God, and, instead of admiring and adoring that infinite knowledge to which future things are present, would have given that honour to a man which was due to God alone. Thus the heathen nations, by the excessive admiration of the authors of useful inventions, were drawn into abominable idolatries, and gave that worship to creatures which is due only to Him who is over all, blessed for ever.

It was no less necessary to attend to the agency of God in the events predicted. We can never make the proper use of what befalls us, or of what we see around us, unless we remember that all things are under the direction of Divine Providence. When God predicted by Isaiah the great events to be accomplished by Cyrus, He called upon that prince to observe and acknowledge the divine hand that conducted him in all his undertakings, and crowned them with success. " I form the light, and create darkness : I make peace, and create evil : I the Lord do all these things," Isa. xlv. 1-7.

Pharaoh was told that the following years of plenty or famine, in which his dream was to be accomplished, were from God, who gives and who withholds good things according to His pleasure.

" What God is about to do he sheweth unto Pharaoh."

VER. 29, 30. *Behold, there come seven years of great plenty throughout all the land of Egypt: and there shall arise after them seven years of famine.*

In Egypt, plenty or scarcity were supposed to depend upon the River Nile. When in the season of its inundation it rose only twelve cubits, a famine was the consequence; scarcity, if it rose only thirteen; a competency, if it rose fourteen or fifteen; great plenty, if it rose still higher. The Egyptians idolised their river, as if it could have afforded them a plentiful crop without the agency of God. They alleged that other nations might perish with hunger if their gods should forget to send them rain. When the people of Israel were brought out of the land of Egypt, Moses told them that in the land to which they were going they would see every day before their eyes visible proofs of their absolute dependence on God for the blessings of life—" For the land whither thou goest in to possess it is not as the land of Egypt, from whence ye came out, where thou sowedst thy seed, and wateredst it with thy foot as a garden of herbs. But the land whither ye go in to possess it is a land of hills and valleys, and drinketh water of the rain of heaven : a land which the Lord thy God careth for ; the eyes of the Lord thy God are always upon it, from the beginning of the year even unto the end of the year."

From Pharaoh's dream, and the interpretation of it, compared with the accomplishment, it was plain that Egypt depended as much as other countries upon God. The seven years of great plenty were to be the accomplishment of the word of God, and the work of His providence. All the waters of the river were His, as well as the rains of heaven. As no hand but His could collect the vapours from the sea, and distil them upon the earth in fertilising showers, so none but He could raise the waters of the Nile to that height which could give them the prospect of plenty. Perhaps the Egyptians did not at this time know that the annual increase of their river was caused by the impetuous rains that descended in another country, but it was fit they should know that the fertility of their land was the fruit of divine goodness, and that God dispenses His bounties to all men according to His own will.

" Behold, there come seven years of great plenty." Egypt, in ordinary years, produced great abundance of all things necessary for men, but during these seven years it was to exceed itself in fertility, as much as at other times it exceeded other countries. This extraordinary fertility was not to be confined to a few districts, but to extend through all the provinces of the land of Egypt. God can give plenty to one part of a country, whilst He afflicts another part of it with famine, Amos iv. He is to be praised for every instance of His goodness to a land. He is greatly to be praised when He blesses every part of it with those good things which are most useful to man. Gold and silver are far from being so valuable as corn and grass. When God provides abundant supplies for the ever-returning necessities of men and beasts, let us not forget, when we enjoy and see others enjoying the fruits of His goodness, to bless the name of the Lord who deals wondrously with us, Joel ii; Ps. lxv.

VER. 30, 31. *And there shall arise after them seven years of famine; and all the plenty shall be forgotten in the land of Egypt; and the famine shall consume the land; and the plenty shall not be known in the land by reason of that famine following; for it shall be very grievous.*

Think not in the day of prosperity that you shall never see adversity, or in the day of fulness that you never can feel the pressure of poverty. "If a man live many years and rejoice in them all, yet let him remember the days of darkness, for they shall be many."

There was less fear of famine in the land of Egypt than in any other country under heaven. When there was a famine in the land of milk and honey, in the days of Abraham, the patriarch hoped, and he was not disappointed, that he would find bread in the land of Egypt. When there was a sore famine in the same land, in the days of Isaac, that patriarch would have gone down to Egypt for supply to his necessities, if God had not forbidden him. When God threatened those nations with famine that did not come to Jerusalem to worship the King, the Lord of hosts, and to keep the feast of tabernacles, He thought it necessary to insert a clause to obviate the hopes of the Egyptians, that they could not feel this calamity, Zech. xiv. 16-18.

Yet Joseph here foretells that there should not only be a grievous famine in Egypt, but a famine so terrible, that it should consume the land, unless by good management, under the direction of a kind Providence, the miserable effects of it were prevented. It was to be so grievous, that all the luxuriant plenty of the former fruitful years should be forgotten as if it had never been; and it was to continue, not for one or two, but for seven years. What prospect could be more dreadful? We had seven years of great scarcity in Scotland at the end of the seventeenth century, and many died with hunger. But this scarcity was not to be compared to the famine of Egypt. The product of these seven years in Egypt was almost nothing, and the people were numerous in proportion to the ordinary fertility of the country. Probably the population increased to a great degree in the seven years of famine; but the earth did not yield food for the tenth part of its former inhabitants.

God did what He spake, when He brought this famine upon the land of Egypt. We have little reason to doubt but the plenty of the good years was abused. The Egyptians were not better than other people; and nothing is more common in days of plenty than to spend on men's lusts what God has given them, and to turn His creatures into instruments of rebellion against Himself. If you wish not to be bereaved of those good things which are most desirable in your eyes, beware of ingratitude to the Giver of them. "Jeshurun waxed fat and kicked, when he was fed with butter of kine, and milk of sheep, with fat of lambs, and rams of the breed of Bashan, and goats. Then he waxed fat, and grew thick, and was covered with fatness, and forsook the God that formed him, and lightly esteemed the rock of his salvation." What was the consequence? Among other calamities which fell upon him, he was pierced with the evil arrows of famine; he was burnt with hunger, and devoured with burning heat, and with bitter destruction.

Ver. 32. *And for that the dream was doubled unto Pharaoh twice; it is because the thing is established by God, and God will shortly bring it to pass.*

When God speaks but once, He certainly deserves credit, for

He cannot lie; but knowing how slow of heart we are to believe, He often repeats the same important truths. It is impious to disbelieve any of His words. It is more than double impiety to disbelieve Him when He speaks not once, but twice. What excuse, then, can we make for our conduct, if we refuse to believe when He speaks not once nor twice, but a hundred and a thousand times? How often did Moses repeat the same necessary truths in the ears of the children of Israel! How often did Christ and His apostles explain and enforce the most important doctrines of the Gospel, and duties of the Law! Shall we never find ears to hear the voice of Him that cries so loud and so constantly, in the chief places of concourse, to the sons of Adam, to turn them out of the paths of destruction and misery into the way of life and peace? Would not Pharaoh have been inexcusable if he had disbelieved or disregarded the double admonition given him in his sleep when it was explained to him by Joseph? Will not our folly be a thousand times less worthy of excuse if we disregard the many admonitions of the Bible so often sounded in our ears by the ministers of the Word?

The doubling of the vision signified, not only the certainty, but the nearness of the perdicted event. When a man sees his neighbour in imminent danger of destruction, he will cry out again and again to make him sensible of the need of speedy exertions to prevent the approaching mischief. God saw the Egyptians in danger of perishing by famine, if speedy methods were not used to secure the people against that calamity. Several years were yet to pass away before the famine came; but when it came very near, means of preventing its fatal effects would have been too late.

When we hear God foretelling those evils, to avert which we are called to use the means which He hath presented, we are too much disposed to say, like Felix, "When we have a more convenient season we will attend to these matters." We put far away the evil day, as if God's prophets spoke only of remote events. If we believed that the days were at hand in which the wrath of God will be executed on the impenitent, it would appear to us high time to awake out of sleep ; and who knows how near the day of vengeance may be to any individual who refuses to turn from his iniquity? Thou fool, this night thy soul may be required from thee, and then what will become of all thy purposes to attend to the voice of God at another time? What is thy life? A vapour—a wind, that passes away and never returns.

VER. 33. *Now therefore let Pharaoh look out a man discreet and wise, and set him over the land of Egypt.*

"God will give Pharaoh an answer of peace," said Joseph. If it had been impracticable to obviate the bad effects of a seven-years' famine, the answer would have been a message of evil, and not of peace. Seven years of prosperity cannot compensate seven years of adversity but by furnishing the means of providing against the time of evil before it comes. The good advice that Joseph adds to the interpretation of the dream makes the answer of God an answer of peace, and not of evil, to give him an end better than his expectation.

It is foolish to desire to know the things which are to come to pass hereafter, for the mere gratification of curiosity. That is a mischievous curiosity which burdens men with the weight of future evils before their time—"Sufficient unto the day is the evil thereof;" yet that foresight of evils which may prevent or mitigate them is useful—"The prudent man foreseeth the evil, and hideth himself, but the simple pass on, and are punished."

It is a question whether Pharaoh would have made any good improvement of his dreams, if Joseph had only interpreted them, without subjoining the use that ought to be made of the divine discovery. God reveals nothing before it happens without some good end in view. The intention of the prophecies concerning judgments was to excite the persons who were threatened with them to take proper measures for averting them. The design of the prophecies concerning Christ was to beget and to increase faith in those who lived before His coming. The intention of God in Pharaoh's dreams was to procure deliverance and honour to Joseph, and to preserve Egypt, and the family of Jacob, and the countries around, from destruction. Joseph advises Pharaoh to look out a man discreet and wise, and set him over the land of Egypt.

VER. 34. *Let Pharaoh do this, and let him appoint officers over the land, and take up the fifth part of the land of Egypt in the seven plenteous years.*

Joseph's advice proceeds on the principle, that kings are bound to use their power for the welfare of their people. They are to their people what shepherds are to their flocks.

When a famine was foreseen at the end of seven years of plenty, it was not a sufficient discharge of the royal duty to forewarn the people, that they might lay up store of food against the calamitous period. Not one, perhaps, of ten, or of a hundred, would have made a proper use of the warning. Many would have turned into money the superfluous product of the year to gratify their avarice, and left the days of famine to provide for themselves. The greater part would have abused the bounties of Providence to gratify their prevailing desires; and the whole nation must have been exposed to extreme misery, if the king did not take effectual measures of prevention.

To this purpose, he was advised to choose a wise and able minister, who should employ officers under him to collect a fifth part of the crop during all the years of plenty, to be reserved for the years of famine. It is probable that a tenth part of the produce of the ground was the acknowledged due of the king. Joseph, doubtless, intended that the remainder of the fifth part should be bought at the current price, which in years of such plenty would be very small. It is computed that in ordinary years the price of necessaries was, in ancient times, so small in the land of Egypt, that parents could rear up their children to maturity for a sum equal to fourteen or sixteen pence of the money current among us.

When the land yields an abundant increase, the bounty of Providence is not to be wasted in riotous living. It would be better to throw it into the sea than to pamper a luxurious appetite with what God gives us for very different ends. It might have appeared needless in Egypt to lay it up seven years beforehand for a time of famine, unless God Himself had warned the king of the necessity of doing it. A prudent frugality is at all times laudable. But let us not, on pretence of providing for what may never happen, withhold from the service of God, and from the poor, that portion of our substance which the laws of piety and humanity require. "Give a portion to seven, and also to eight, for thou knowest not what evil shall be upon the earth."

VER. 35, 36. *And let them gather all the food of those good years that come, and lay up corn under the hand of Pharaoh, and let them keep food in the cities. And that food shall be for store to the land against the seven years of famine, which shall be in the land of Egypt; that the land perish not through the famine.*

"Lay not up for yourselves treasure on earth," says our Lord, "where moth and rust do corrupt, and where thieves break through and steal." But this rule is not intended to prohibit us from providing in the time of plenty for a time of scarcity, as far as it can be done without neglecting the necessary duties of charity and piety, according to our circumstances. The poor ought not to want what their present necessities demand; but a provident care, in public governors, to guard against the mischiefs of famine, is requisite, chiefly for the sake of the lower ranks in society. If the superfluous produce of the earth has been given to the poor in the years of plenty, they must have been starved in the time of famine. No liberality to the poor ever deserved greater praise than Joseph's, even to secure needful supplies both to the poor and rich.

It was well ordered by the providence of God, for the safety of the people, that the years of famine were preceded by the years of plenty. If the seven years of famine had come before the years of plenty, few men would have been left to enjoy them. But from the years of plenty a sufficiency could be reserved to maintain life with comfort in the years of famine. "Let them gather all the food of those good years that come, and lay up corn under the hand of Pharaoh, and let them keep food in the cities; and that food shall be for store to the land against the seven years of famine ; that the land perish not through the famine." How great is the goodness of God, who provides so liberally for man and beast, and who tempers those calamities that are allotted to mankind with such undeserved mercy, that even in days of famine few perish with hunger ! When the earth does not bring forth her usual increase, He finds out means to mitigate or to relieve the distress of His creatures, and especially of His own people. He had a special view to the preservation of the house of Jacob, in providing beforehand abundance of corn for the years of famine, and in suggesting to Joseph the good advice which he gave to Pharaoh, and in disposing Pharaoh to follow it. " O taste and see that the Lord is good ! There shall be no want to them that fear him. The young lions may lack and suffer hunger, but they that seek the Lord shall not want any good thing."

We have seen scarcity in our times, but we cannot say that we have ever seen famine ; and we ought to be thankful, when the land does not bring forth its usual product, that there are remains of the product of former years to supply the deficiency, that supplies can be brought from foreign countries, and that there are seldom many years of scarcity in uninterrupted succession. A second year of famine would be far more dreadful than the first ; a third year of famine would be more awful than a pestilence. So David thought, when he rather chose three days of pestilence than a three-years' famine. But who could have lived in want of all good things ? which would have been the consequence of the seven years of famine in Egypt, if Joseph had not been raised up to preserve the lives of the people.

The Spirit of God, by Joseph, warned Pharaoh and the Egyptians to store up the means of natural life against the time of need. But what provision shall we make for that period in our existence which will at once deprive us of everything that this world affords, by dissolving our connection with present things ? It is our wisdom to provide against those evils that may happen to us in the course of our life. It is still more necessary to be provided with resources for the time when the possession of the whole world will not avail us. A greater than Joseph, whose name is Wonderful, Counsellor, calls upon us to lay up treasure in another world, to lay up in store a good foundation for the time to come, by providing for ourselves bags that wax not old—"Labour not for the meat which perisheth, but for that meat which endureth unto everlasting life, which the Son of man shall give unto you ; for him hath God the Father sealed."

LECTURE 9

Joseph's exaltation, and his care to lay up supplies of corn against the famine.

xli 37–45

VER. 37. *And the thing was good in the eyes of Pharaoh, and in the eyes of all his servants.*

SOME great men will not thank their inferiors for advice when it is not asked. They think that they have a sufficiency of wisdom to direct their own conduct, or if they need any addition to it, that they can ask the advice of whom they please for the management of their affairs. But Pharaoh was not too great to take advice kindly from a poor prisoner, from the slave of one of his servants. There is no man so wise as not to need counsel. "In the multitude of counsellors there is safety;" but sometimes one wise counsellor is better than a thousand; and happy is the man who has wisdom and humility to avail himself of the good counsels that are offered him, from whomsoever they come. A poor wise man, or wise woman, may deliver a city, or preserve a kingdom, if due respect is given to their wise counsels. A wise woman of Abel-beth-maachah delivered the city besieged by Joab, when all the wise men in it behaved like children. She went to the people in her wisdom, and persuaded them to do what they ought to have seen of themselves the need of doing. Joseph, by his wisdom, preserved many countries from the horrors of famine. But some part of the praise is due to Pharaoh and his servants. It is a sign of great wisdom to be

H

able to give the best counsel, but it is a sign of wisdom also to know good counsel when it is given, and to be ready to follow it.

VER. 38. *And Pharaoh said unto his servants, Can we find such a one as this is, a man in whom the Spirit of God is ?*

The advice of Joseph was so evidently good, and the measures he proposed so evidently necessary for the public safety, that we do not wonder at Pharaoh's intention of complying with it. But we are surprised to find that Joseph himself should be the man employed to execute his own proposal, and to hear the high commendations bestowed on him by the king. He was only that day taken from a prison in which he had been long shut up, as if he had been an evil-doer; and yet now he must be raised to the highest office in the kingdom, as a man who has not an equal in the whole earth, and in whom was the Spirit of the Holy God.

It is not necessary for us to know what ideas Pharaoh affixed to his own words, when he said that the Spirit of God was in Joseph. When the queen-mother of Babylon commended Daniel as the wisest of men, she said, that "the spirit of the holy gods was in him, and, therefore, light, and understanding, and wisdom were found in him above all other wise men in Babylon." Pharaoh, too, was sensible that God must be Joseph's teacher, and that He communicated to him extraordinary measures of knowledge. Whether Pharaoh understood by this spirit a divine person, or divine influence, it is plain that he could not have discovered the dream by his own sagacity. Joseph himself had confessed it to the glory of God in the ears of Pharaoh, and Pharaoh did not esteem Joseph the less, but the more, that he had modestly refused praise to himself, that it might be given to God. If Joseph was the favourite of Heaven, he shall be Pharaoh's favourite too. His affairs are most likely to prosper in the hands of a man whom God loved and taught.

Does any man appear plainly to have the Spirit of God enlightening his mind and sanctifying his heart? He is entitled to our warm regard as a member of that body of which Christ is the Head. Is a man furnished by the Spirit of God with endowments that eminently qualify him for service to his fellow-men, whether in the Church or state? He is entitled to a degree of respect proportioned to the gifts which he hath received. Office-bearers in the Church are to be chosen out of those whom the Spirit of God hath qualified for public usefulness. No man is called to fill any office in the house of God for which he is not fitted by the Divine Spirit. And none are fit to serve their generation by public offices in the state, unless the Spirit of God has adorned them with endowments suited to the stations which they are called to occupy. Although Cyrus was a heathen, he received from the Spirit of God those extraordinary qualifications by which he was enabled to accomplish the subversion of Babylon, that he might let go God's captives, and build His temple. That great prince was the Lord's anointed, at a time when he did not know the Lord, Isa. xlv. 1, 5.

"Can we find such a man as this, a man in whom the Spirit of God is?" What had Joseph that he had not received? There was none like him in the land, because the Spirit of God had communicated to him an uncommon measure of wisdom.

VER. 39. *And Pharaoh said unto Joseph, Forasmuch as God hath shewed thee all this, there is none so discreet and wise as thou art.*

"Those that honour me," says God, "I will honour." Joseph honoured God before Pharaoh, and God honoured Joseph in the sight of Pharaoh. The king bestows upon him the highest commendations and the highest honours. A little time ago he was traduced as one of the vilest of men. Now the king honours him as a man of incomparable wisdom. Let us not be greatly dejected by reproach, nor puffed up with praise. The best of men have passed through good report and bad report. Jesus Himself was one day a great Prophet, and another day a friend of Beelzebub. This, however, may be a comfort to the followers of Jesus, that after enduring reproach and ignominy, He was crowned with glory and honour; and as He was, so they shall be, either in this world or in the next. The reproach of Joseph was fully wiped away when he appeared so great in the sight of Pharaoh and of all his servants. And God has promised that He "will wipe away the reproach of His people from the face of all the earth."

Joseph was never greatly dejected by reproach, and he was not swelled with vanity by commendations even from the mouth of a king. "As the fining-pot for silver, and the furnace for gold, so is a man to his praise." A man whose heart is lifted up by praise never deserved it.

VER. 40. *Thou shalt be over my house, and according unto thy word shall all my people be ruled: only in the throne will I be greater than thou.*

"Let a wise man be set over the land of Egypt," said Joseph to Pharaoh. "Thou art the wisest man whom I know," said Pharaoh, "and therefore thou shalt rule over both my house and my kingdom." Joseph himself was the first man who reaped the fruit of these wise instructions which he had given to Pharaoh. Wise advice is highly useful to those who can receive it, and the honour and advantage return in part to the giver. All men will honour them by whom, under God, they are made wiser and better.

Those who have the distribution of honours and offices ought to consider to whom they give them. "As he who bindeth a stone in a sling, so is he that giveth honour to a fool." He is in some degree accountable for all the mischief that follows his choice when it is unwise. When Omar II. Caliph of Bagdad, resigned the Caliphat, under impressions of his own unfitness to reign, he absolutely refused to nominate his successor, that he might not be accountable for another man's actions. Although Pharaoh had not the advantages that we derive from the Bible, yet he saw the necessity of choosing only a wise man to the government of his house and kingdom. It is to be feared that there are Christian kings who have not learned so much wisdom from all the admonitions of the Bible on this head, as Pharaoh learned from a few words of Joseph.

"Only in the throne will I be greater than thou." In this, too, Pharaoh complied with the advice of Joseph. "Let the

52498

officers lay up corn under the hand of Pharaoh," in ver. 34. Every prince, and every man in every station of life, ought to know and keep his place. If he does not maintain the authority which belongs to it, how shall he discharge the duties of it?

Ministers of state must maintain the respect which they owe to their masters. Great as they are, they are but subjects. In inferior departments, too, men ought to consider who are above them, as well as who are below them. How can we expect that deference from our inferiors which is due to our station, if we do not set them the example in our own conduct?

Pharaoh did not think it necessary to put Joseph in mind of his inferiority to himself, when he says : "Only in the throne will I be greater than thou." His intention is not to caution Joseph against aspiring to an equality with himself, but to authorise him to claim a superiority to every other subject, however noble in birth, or high in office. And it was for the good of his subjects that he wished them to acknowledge the superiority of Joseph, that they might learn some portion of that wisdom in which he excelled, and might all concur with him, according to their respective places and stations, in promoting the general good. Pharaoh made him lord of his house and ruler of all his substance, "to bind his princes at his pleasure, and teach his senators wisdom," Ps. cv.

VER. 41. *And Pharaoh said unto Joseph, See, I have set thee over all the land of Egypt.*

Alexander Severus made a law in the Roman empire, that before a man, chosen to office in the state, was invested with the power of his office, public intimation should be given, that any person who could produce any valid objection to the appointment might have an opportunity of being heard. The hint of this law was taken from the custom observed by Christians in the choice and ordination of bishops and deacons. It was certainly a good law, and yet Pharaoh acted wisely in investing Joseph with the powers of government as soon as he had formed his resolution. Not only Pharaoh, but his servants, were filled with admiration, when they heard Joseph's interpretation of Pharaoh's dream, and his own advice founded upon it. But if a few days or weeks had been suffered to pass before Joseph was put in possession of his power, the king might have found it less easy to execute his intentions without exciting discontent among his native subjects. "This man Joseph," they might say, "is a stranger and an exile, and was recently a slave and a prisoner. Why should he be exalted above all the great men, above all the wise men of Egypt? Is our country, formerly so renowned for its wisdom, now sunk in so deep degeneracy, that a young man brought by merchants from a distant country, to be sold as a slave, must be our governor?"

At present, the people and even the princes were willing to submit to his authority, and it was to be hoped that all complaints for the time to come would be obviated by his wise government, and by the manifold benefits derived from it. The king, therefore, acted wisely in doing without any further deliberation what was evidently so fit to be done. Precipitancy in affairs of importance is dangerous, but delays in many cases are not less dangerous. "A wise man's heart discerneth both time and judgment."

It is, however, to be ascribed to God's kindness to Joseph that Pharaoh acted so wisely on the present occasion. The time was now come, the time that God had set for exalting Joseph to that dignity and power which a long time before he had been made to expect. Pharaoh was the minister of Divine Providence for placing him in a condition so glorious to himself, and so useful to his father's house, as well as to the nation of Egypt. The heart of kings is in the hand of the Lord, as the rills of water, to turn them whithersoever He pleases. "Whilst all men seek every one the ruler's favour, their judgment cometh from the Lord."

VER. 42, 43. *And Pharaoh took off his ring from his hand, and put it upon Joseph's hand, and arrayed him in vestures of fine linen, and put a gold chain about his neck; and he made him to ride in the second chariot which he had; and they cried before him, Bow the knee: and he made him ruler over all the land of Egypt.*

Joseph, when he left the prison, had dressed himself in a manner fit for those that stand before kings; but now his dress must be again changed. Ornaments almost royal suited his present station, and the favour in which he was. held by the king. The royal ring is put upon his finger. He is arrayed in vestures of fine linen, or perhaps of richer stuff, if such were to be found in Egypt, which was famous among the nations for its manufactures. A gold chain is put about his neck. He rides in the most splendid chariot of Egypt, except the king's chariot of state. A proclamation is heard as he advances along in his chariot, Bow the knee. How strangely is his condition changed in one day! His prison exchanged for a palace, his fetters for a golden chain, his prison-garments for robes of state. For a course of wearisome years he was confined within the walls of a prison, and could not enjoy the cheerful light of day. Now he traverses all the land of Egypt at his pleasure, in a chariot drawn by the swiftest of horses. Formerly he was pitied or despised, or forgotten by all who once knew him. Now he is admired and received as the man whom the king and whom God Himself delighteth to honour.

The constant changes that take place in the world are an admonition to us not to set our affections on things below. If we are great and rich, and admired by all to-day, we know not what a sad reverse may take place to-morrow : and we know, certainly, that all those things on which the lovers of the present world value themselves will soon come to an end. But there are pleasant as well as comfortable changes. The man who at present wears rags may one day be clothed in scarlet. The city of Shushan was astonished to see the alteration in Mordecai's circumstances, when he exchanged his garments of sackcloth for robes of state—" Mordecai went out from the presence of the king in royal apparel of blue and white, and with a great crown of gold, and with a garment of fine linen and purple : and the city of Shushan rejoiced and was glad," Esther viii.

Such wonderful changes as those which took place in the condition of Joseph or Mordecai are so rare, that few can indulge the hope of the like happy reverse in their outward estate. But a change of infinitely greater consequence in the state of the soul passes upon all the redeemed of the Lord. Our natural condition under the power of sin is incomparably more wretched than Joseph's when the irons entered his soul. The garments of praise and salvation with which every believer in Jesus is arrayed infinitely excel in beauty those perishing ornaments with which the kings of the East were accustomed to deck their favourites. When Christ gives liberty to the captives, He bestows upon them beauty for ashes, the oil of joy for mourning, the garment of praise for the spirit of heaviness. Joseph, doubtless, felt lively emotions of gratitude to Pharaoh, when his prison-garments were exchanged for royal vestments. "We will greatly rejoice in the Lord, our souls shall be joyful in our God; for He hath clothed us with the garments of salvation, He hath covered us with the robes of righteousness, as a bridegroom decketh himself with his ornaments, and as a bride adorneth herself with her jewels."

VER. 44. *And Pharaoh said unto Joseph, I am Pharaoh, and without thee shall no man lift up his hand or foot in all the land of Egypt.*

We are not to suppose that the inspired historian records every word that passed between the king and his new minister. The high honours heaped upon Joseph, with an unsparing hand, far exceeded his hopes, and probably exceeded his wishes. He might be assured that the king's goodness to him would expose him to envy, and the king himself to reproach, and on this account he might express some reluctance to accept of all that honour and power which the king wished to confer. But Pharaoh was firm to his purpose. He was persuaded that he was consulting the best interests of his kingdom, and his own best interests, in Joseph's advancement, and required him by his royal authority to accept and to use that power to which he was so well entitled by his merits and by the king's favour.

"I am Pharaoh," and where the word of such a great king is there is power. "I have a right to appoint ministers of state, and to require the obedience of my people to those whom I am pleased to invest with authority. Why, then, should you be

afraid or unwilling to enter upon your new office? Do you
think that the great men in my kingdom will refuse obedience
to any man invested with my authority? In small, as well as
great matters, every man in all the land of Egypt shall submit
to your power."

If any man in Egypt had resisted the authority of Joseph, he
would at the same time have disobeyed Pharaoh. It would
have been no excuse for him to have said, that he would not
degrade himself to be the subject of an upstart slave. This man,
whom they might call by any degrading name they pleased, was
invested by Pharaoh with his own authority. The ring from
Pharaoh's finger, and the robes of state bestowed on him, as
well as the proclamation to bow the knee before him, were
public testimonies of the king's will. A rebel against a king
will not be exempted from the punishment due to his offences,
because the king did not give his orders in person, but by a
substitute.

If earthly kings claim respect and obedience to themselves
in the persons of those to whom they depute their power, and
account themselves insulted when their servants meet not with
due respect, may we not justly dread the vengeance of the
everlasting King, if we do not obey those whom He commands
us to obey?—Children, obey your parents in the Lord. Subjects, obey lawful magistrates set over you by Divine Providence.
Christians, obey those church-officers that have the rule over
you. If Christ has given them their authority, disobedience to
them, as far as they have a right from Him to command, is
disobedience to their Lord and yours. Let all of us yield
obedience to the Lord Jesus, whom God hath set to be His
King upon His holy hill of Zion.

VER. 45. *And Pharaoh called Joseph's name Zaphnath-paaneah;
and he gave him to wife Asenath the daughter of Poti-pherah priest
of On. And Joseph went out over all the land of Egypt.*

"They cried before him, Bow the knee." Some suppose
that the original word which we translate, Bow the knee, is
not an Hebrew, but an Egyptian word, denoting the king's
father; and it must be confessed, that as a son honours his

father, Pharaoh honoured Joseph. But, from the verse before us, it appears that the new name given by Pharaoh to Joseph was not Abrael (the word which we render, Bow the knee), but Zaphnath-paaneah, which seems to signify, The comfortable revealer of secrets.

It was not unusual in ancient times (as we find in several places of Scripture) to give new names to persons on particular occasions. Abraham and Jacob received new names from God Himself. Daniel, Hananiah, Mishael, and Azariah received new names from the king of Babylon. The new name given by Pharaoh to Joseph was a token of the high esteem in which he was held by the king, and a just expression of the great obligations under which he had laid the whole nation, by revealing for their benefit and safety the intentions of Providence, which could not be discovered by all the wisdom of Egypt.

There are secrets which we should not desire to know— there are secrets which it would be hurtful for us to know; but it was of high importance to the people of Egypt to know that their seven years of plenty were to be succeeded by seven years of famine. Their life depended upon it. The man who revealed this gave them solid comfort in the evil day, and saved them from destruction. Pharaoh wished them to know, and to give deserved honour to their benefactor. "A good name is better than precious ointment." Seldom has a name of praise and honour been more justly acquired by a mere man. Every name of glory belongs to that great Revealer of the will of God, who came from the Father's bosom to give us the knowledge of salvation through the redemption of our sins, "and to direct our feet in the way of peace."

When we explain the word *Zaphnath-paaneah* to signify *a revealer of secrets*, that gives rest or comfort, we suppose it to be compounded of certain Hebrew words, which afford the meaning. But learned men tell us that in the ancient Egyptian language it signified *the deliverer of the world*. He was the deliverer of the people from one of the most terrible of deaths, by providing against the most terrible famine of which history gives us an account. Joseph was the deliverer only of a small part of the world, and its deliverer from a death not to be compared with that from which we are saved by Him whom the Spirit of God declares to be the Saviour of the world. We reprobate the ingratitude of that king that rose up in Egypt who knew not Joseph, the saviour of his nation. What shall we say of those who forget what Jesus has done for the salvation of men? What must we think of ourselves if we are found amongst the unhappy number?

" And he gave him to wife Asenath the daughter of Poti-pherah priest of On."

We know nothing more than we are here told of Asenath, or of Poti-pherah her father. But it is plain that Pharaoh highly honoured him by giving him this lady for his wife, and strengthened his interest by connecting it with that of one of the greatest families in the kingdom.

We have no reason to find fault with Joseph for forming a connection with the family of the priest, by marrying his daughter. We cannot say how far religion had at this time degenerated in Egypt. Jethro's daughter was not rejected by Moses because Jethro was the priest of Midian; and Jethro appears, from what follows in his history, to have been either a fearer of the true God, or a man at least who was open to conviction when it presented itself to him.

If Poti-pherah was as bad as heathen priests often were, his daughter might, nevertheless, be a woman well disposed to receive the truth from Joseph. We have no evidence that she was a worse woman than Joseph's own mother, who was not free from a tincture of idolatry at the time when Jacob was sent by his pious father to seek a wife in the family to which he belonged. Suppose Joseph to have married a wife trained up in superstition, or idolatry, when it was perhaps not in his power to obtain a better, his example will be no excuse to those Christians who yoke themselves with an infidel or a graceless woman, when many better women are to be found. We have reason to believe that the pious youth, who acknowledged the Lord in all his ways, did not neglect to acknowledge Him in the important article of marriage; and though we ought not to be wise above what is written, may we not reasonably suppose that Asenath was far more indebted to God for giving her to Joseph, than Joseph for his exaltation from the prison to the chair of state? If Joseph had died in his dungeon, he would have been happy, for heaven would have been his eternal habitation; but it is probable that Asenath's union to Joseph brought her to the knowledge of the living and true God. Happy is that woman that marries a man who excels in wisdom and in piety! If she was a stranger to Christ, she is favoured with blessed opportunities of attaining the knowledge and love of Him. If she was a lover of Christ, she will be happy in the opportunities she enjoys of speaking and hearing of His blessed name. Husbands and wives must be happy in one another when, like Abraham and Sarah, they both live by the faith of the promises of God, and cheer one another with the blissful prospects of an everlasting union in a better world.

You that are unmarried have the advantage above Joseph, that you may choose the partner of your lives; and it is to be hoped that if you are unequally yoked with women destitute of the fear of God, the fault is your own. You live not under a king who claims a right to dispose of his subjects in marriage. You live not in a land of idolaters, but in a Christian country, where, degenerate as our days are, there are still many who love the Lord Jesus Christ, both of men and women. Solomon will give you all needful directions in the choice of a wife, and the throne of grace is accessible to those who wish to acknowledge God in all their ways, that He may direct their steps.

LECTURE 10
The interpretation of Pharaoh's dream.
xli 46–57

VER. 45, 46. *And Joseph went out over all the land of Egypt. And Joseph was thirty years old when he stood before Pharaoh king of Egypt. And Joseph went out from the presence of Pharaoh, and went throughout all the land of Egypt.*

THE life of different men presents not greater varieties to our observation than the life of the same men has sometimes done. How different is a king's grandson, a shepherd, a lawgiver, from one another! and yet Moses sustained all these characters in different periods of the same life. Joseph was in early days the favourite son of a venerable patriarch, cherished with fondness in the tents of his father. He was, in the next period of his life, a slave, and then a prisoner, held in long confinement under the imputation of one of the worst and basest of crimes; but in the best and longest period of his eventful life, he was the lord of all the land of Egypt, trusted with all the power of the king, and honoured by the people as their saviour from destruction. Let us not be greatly dejected by adversity, let us not trust in prosperity. It is a storm and tempest to-day; it may be sunshine to-morrow. If it should, storms may again disturb our tranquillity. Nothing is permanent in this world of changes. Nothing is more foolish than the presumption that to-morrow shall be as this day. They may be as unlike to one another, for aught we can say, as darkness is to light.

When Joseph was sold into captivity, he was seventeen years of age; and he was thirty when he stood before Pharaoh. Thirteen years were spent by him in slavery, and some of these years in the prison. It is very probable that Joseph hoped to be much sooner delivered from all his afflictions, and restored to the arms of his affectionate father. His prophetical dreams were perhaps not so well understood by him as the dreams of Pharaoh, and his butler and baker; but they were as plain in themselves, and their obvious meaning was suggested in his father's rebuke for telling them. Understanding them to be prophetical, he certainly expected a favourable event to his afflictions, and probably expected it in less than thirteen years. But it was good for him that he did not know beforehand when God should be pleased to give him the expected end of his sorrows. Thirteen years of suffering would have been an awful prospect. But the retrospect was pleasant when there was no dread of their return. The remembrance of grief turned into joy gives a rich compensation for its bitterness. Light is at all times pleasant, but it is doubly so after darkness.

Joseph spent that time of life which amongst us is usually the most delightful part of it, in slavery and in imprisonment; and yet we have no reason to think that God was unkind to him. If he was deprived of the pleasures which other young persons enjoy in that time of life, he was cheered with the prospect of pleasures in reserve at another time of life. He could not be unhappy when God was with him, and cheered him with tokens of His favour, and with the sweet hope of richer tokens of His favour in a more advanced period of life. Let not young persons who are restricted by affliction, or by narrow circumstances, from those enjoyments which are desired by persons of their time of life, murmur at the disposal of Divine Providence. It is difficult to believe, but it is certainly true, "that it is good for a man to bear the yoke in his youth;" or if it is not good for him, the fault is his own. Let him bear his afflictions as Joseph did, or as Jesus taught us by His example to bear them, and they will tend to his honour and his comfort. We will never have the honour of standing before such a prince as Pharaoh. We have been favoured with no dreams to give us the hope of a high fortune for us in this world. But we have the sure word of promise to give us the hope of what is infinitely better than crowns and sceptres. "Blessed is the man that endureth temptation; for when he is tried, he shall receive of the Lord the crown of life which he hath promised to them that love him."

Why should we seek great things for ourselves in a world which we must speedily leave? Let us mind our business, Whatever that is, our honour will consist in performing the duties of it. It was Joseph's honour that he stood before kings, and not before mean men. It was a greater honour to him, when he stood before the king, that he gave him every reason to be satisfied with his conduct. He did not spend his days in pleasure, or in receiving the compliments of the many friends which his prosperity procured. He did not contrive plans of revenge against his former master and mistress, or against the ungrateful butler. He was exalted to power for the good and safety of the people; and he went through all the land of Egypt to see with his own eyes what was fit to be done, to issue out proper orders, and to superintend the execution of them.

His high advancement was so far from exciting him to spend his time in ease, or in licentious mirth, that it roused him to unwearied activity, that he might not prove unworthy of the trust which the king had reposed in him. The kindness of his former master had been a powerful motive with him to resist the solicitations of his abandoned mistress. The still greater favours received from Pharaoh were a sufficient motive, if he had needed a motive, to be faithful and diligent in securing the country against the threatened famine.

VER. 47. *And in the seven plenteous years the earth brought forth by handfuls.*

The Lord is abundant in truth. He had told Pharaoh that there should be seven years of plenty, and the plenty was great beyond the example of any former years, for the earth brought forth by handfuls.

How glad would the lovers of corn and wine be if the earth

would every year bring forth by handfuls! and undoubtedly God could give us as rich crops at any time as He ever gave to any nation in their best years. But are we sure that it would be an advantage to us to be exempted from the necessity laid on our race, of procuring our bread by the sweat of our faces? God is infinitely good. But years of plenty are not always good for us. It is very probable that they were not good for many of the Egyptians. Some, we have reason to think, who heard of the approaching years of famine, would lay up some part of their stock for future provision. But there were others, to a far greater number, who either wasted, by their carelessness, the bounties of Providence, or expended them in sensual gratifications, to the great damage both of their souls and bodies. Joseph might have been saved a great part of his troubles, if there had not been too good reason to fear that the greater part of the Egyptians wanted the wisdom necessary to provide sufficient supplies for themselves against the approaching famine, although they had the means of doing it in abundance.

VER. 48. *And he gathered up all the food of the seven years, which were in the land of Egypt, and laid up the food in the cities: the food of the field which was round about every city, laid he up in the same.*

The account of Pharaoh's dream, and of the interpretation, must have spread through all the land of Egypt, with the account of Joseph's advancement; and the people might easily have seen that it was their own interest to be frugal and provident. Although Joseph was appointed by the king to make sufficient provision for the security of the kingdom against the miserable effects of famine, yet it was evident that corn, either in his hands or in any other hands, must be sold at a very high price in the days of famine; and those persons would have a great advantage over their neighbours who were careful to lay up a stock of provision for themselves in the days of plenty. But the years of plenty were not soon to come to an end. It was not necessary, they might think, to be in haste to make provision for days of famine that were yet at a considerable distance. Thus they would defer their preparations till it was too late to lay up a sufficiency of what was necessary. Joseph knew human nature. He foresaw that a great part of the inhabitants of the land must perish, unless he prevented the danger by his own care. Accordingly, he gathered up all the food of the seven years, and laid it up in the cities. He left great abundance for present use. That food which was laid up was the fifth part which was brought to him, in compliance with the royal mandate; and it was laid up and carefully preserved in the store-houses which he had caused to be prepared for its reception.

It is the duty of those who are invested with power to use it for the advantage of those over whom they rule. "Those who rule over the nations," says our Lord, "are called benefactors;" and they ought to deserve the honourable appellation. Whatever the Egyptians might think of Joseph during the years of plenty, they were sensible of the value of his services when they were at an end.

VER. 49. *And Joseph gathered corn as the sand of the sea, very much, until he left numbering; for it was without number.*

To what purpose, some might say, was all this endless care to store up heaps of corn that seemed to be almost inexhaustible? But Joseph was assured that all would be necessary, either for the Egyptians themselves, or for their neighbours, who, not having the premonitions which were granted to him, would take no care to lay up provision against the days of famine.

"Take no anxious thought for to-morrow," said our Lord, "what ye shall eat, or what ye shall drink." Did Joseph transgress this rule by taking thought what the people should eat seven years afterwards? By no means. Although this precept had then been published, Joseph would not have been prohibited by it to heap up his rich stores of corn through all the land of Egypt. He was Pharaoh's steward for the whole people, and "it is required in stewards that a man be found faithful." Fathers ought to provide for the necessities of their children, and God had made Joseph a father to Pharaoh, and to his people.

Our Lord's precept against anxious care is so far from prohibiting a prudent care for the time to come, that it requires us to take all proper measures to prevent temptations to anxiety about our subsistence. Every commandment requires us to avoid everything that may tempt us to break it. Those who are tempted to immoderate cares about their subsistence are chiefly the slothful and the careless, who will not be at the trouble of managing their affairs with discretion. In the seven years of famine, those who had nothing laid up in store were the men whose hearts were rent with anxious thoughts. Joseph knew that he had no reason to tremble, either for himself or for the people that were placed under his care.

VER. 50. *And unto Joseph were born two sons before the years of famine came, which Asenath the daughter of Poti-pherah priest of On bare unto him.*

" Drink waters out of thine own cistern, and running waters out of thine own well. Let them be only thine own, and not strangers with thee. Let thy fountain be blessed, and rejoice with the wife of thy youth." Thus did Joseph, and he was blessed in the fruit of his body. If he had complied with the licentious desires of the wife of Potiphar, children by her would not have been a blessing, but a curse to him. He would not have known or acknowledged them as his own. The sight of them must have been a torment, for they would have brought his sin to remembrance, and they would not have been written in the writing of the house of Israel.

He firmly kept his ground on the day of temptation, and God blessed him with a noble wife and an honourable seed. Two children were born to him, whom Jacob blessed with the choicest of his blessings—" In them Israel blessed, saying, God make thee as Ephraim and as Manasseh."

VER. 51. *And Joseph called the name of the first-born Manasseh: For God, said he, hath made me forget all my toil, and all my father's house.*

We too commonly look no farther than the instruments employed by Providence in conferring upon us the benefits which we enjoy, or in inflicting the evils we suffer. But Joseph saw that all his adversities and all his prosperity came from God. He was grateful to Pharaoh, but he was grateful chiefly to God, for the happy change in his condition. " God hath made me forget all my toil, and all my father's house." It was God that brought him into Egypt. It was by divine permission that he was for many years confined within the walls of a prison. It was God that brought him out of it, and advanced him to the dignity and power which he now possessed. All things are of God. If we do not refer the happy changes in our condition to His good providence, we lose the benefit and pleasure of them, and cannot be sensible of the duties which our benefactor requires, to testify our gratitude.

Names in ancient times were often imposed as memorials of events. Eve called the name of one of her first-born sons Cain, saying, " I have gotten a man from the Lord." Abel, the name of the second, was probably given him to signify the vanity which our fallen parents found in their earthly enjoyments. Another of their sons was called Seth, because the Lord had appointed them another seed instead of Abel, whom Cain slew. Joseph called his first-born son Manasseh, because God had made him to forget all his toil. He did not mean that the remembrance of his toil was obliterated from his mind. His mention of it when he gave a name to his son was a proof that in one sense he still remembered it. It was his duty to remember it. How could he have retained just impressions of the divine goodness, if he had forgotten the evils from which he was delivered? If we must forget none of God's benefits, we must forget none of those evils from which we have been relieved by His gracious providence. But Joseph, in another sense, forgot his misery. He remembered it as waters that pass away, and leave no trace behind. There is a bitter remembrance of our affliction and misery, and of the wormwood and the gall of our affliction. This is banished by Divine Providence, which saves us from all distresses; but it gives place to a pleasant remembrance of them, in a contrast to that happiness by which they are succeeded.

" God hath made me forget all my toil, and all my father's house." What! was old Jacob banished out of Joseph's memory? Did not thoughts now enter into his mind of his father's kindness to him in the days of his childhood? Certainly he would not have forgotten his father, and his father's house, although he had been advanced to a throne greater than Pharaoh's. Joseph's kind remembrance of his father's house appeared very evident when his brethren and when his father came into Egypt. But the painful remembrance of his father's house was expelled from his mind when his adversity was changed into prosperity. He tenderly remembered his father's love, and would have been happy if he could have been restored to his father's arms. But God did better things for him than if he had been suffered to continue with his father all his days, enjoying the smiles of his brethren, along with parental endearments.

But was grandeur such a charming object with Joseph, that he preferred it to all the endearments of the love of such a father as Jacob? By no means. But Joseph rejoiced in what was of incomparably higher value than grandeur—in extensive opportunities and power of being useful to men, and in the glorious testimonies which he had received of the loving-kindness of the Lord. Those are the happiest of men who have even the least evidence that they are beloved of the Lord, and the best opportunities and dispositions to do good to their fellow-creatures.

VER. 52. *And the name of the second called he Ephraim: For God hath caused me to be fruitful in the land of my affliction.*

He had formerly been like the heath in the desert, but now he was like a tree planted by the rivers of water, which brings forth abundance of fruit, and whose leaf does not wither. This happy change he ascribes to the divine goodness. When changes and war are against us, we must be dumb, not opening our mouths, for it is God that does it. When changes are in our favour, our mouths ought to be opened to the praises of Him who turns the shadow of death into the morning, and makes the desert to rejoice and blossom as the rose.

Joseph was fruitful in comfort, in good works, in children. He had, indeed, at this time only two children, but might expect that a troop was coming; and although that hope was uncertain, he was thankful for what God had already given him. Perhaps it was by a divine suggestion that the name Ephraim was given to Joseph's second son, rather than his first. Joseph, as far as we know, had no more children of his own body, but he was fruitful in his remote progeny, especially by Ephraim. " Joseph was a fruitful bough, even a fruitful bough by a well, whose branches run over the wall." Manasseh was great, but truly Ephraim was greater than he; for the horns of Joseph were like the horns of a unicorn, and they were the ten thousands of Ephraim, and they were the thousands of Manasseh.

Where was it that Joseph became fruitful? Not in the land of his nativity, but in the land of his affliction. And all his afflictions wrought together, under the all-wise providence of God, to bring about his exaltation. We must leave it to God to choose for us the place of our habitation; and if our dwelling is assigned us in places where we never wished to be, let us acquiesce in the will of " Him who is wonderful in counsel, and excellent in working." He can make the valley of Achor a door of hope, and turn the wilderness into a paradise.

VER. 53. *And the seven years of plenteousness that was in the land of Egypt, were ended.*

When the people heard that the days of plenteousness were to be seven years, they might say to their souls, Eat, drink, and be merry; to-morrow shall be as this day, and so shall the next day, and many following days and years be, and much more abundantly. But the end of all the changeable things in this varying scene will come. And then the beginning of them will appear like yesterday when it is past. "A perpetuity of bliss is bliss."

VER. 54. *And the seven years of dearth began to come, according as Joseph had said : and the dearth was in all lands; but in all the land of Egypt there was bread.*

Why should you put the evil days far from you? The time to come will at last be the time present; and the evils determined by God will fall heavy upon those that would not use the means graciously afforded by God for safety and comfort. Joseph could look forward with a steady eye, and without terror, to the days of famine. When they came, he knew that his wisdom would be acknowledged by all the land of Egypt, and by all the people of the surrounding countries.

They began to come, as he had said. They came at the time specified, and they were as grievous as he said they would be. The works and the word of God exactly correspond. "Hath He said, and will He not do it?" and will He not do it exactly as He hath said? "And the dearth was in all lands; but in all the land of Egypt there was bread." Why was there a difference between all other lands and the land of Egypt? The reason was plain: Joseph, the revealer of secrets, was in the land of Egypt, and was lord of the whole land. Of what importance is it to have a good governor, beloved of the Lord, and attentive to his duty!

The value of the sure word of prophecy may be illustrated from the great and happy difference between the land of Egypt and other lands. One prophecy filled it with plenty, when other countries must have perished with famine, had they not received supplies from it. What a treasure, then, do we possess in numberless prophecies of the Bible, equally sure, and of far greater importance—prophecies not relating to years of famine or plenty, but to the power and coming of the Lord Jesus Christ!

The prophecy concerning the famine would have been of no use, if it had not been improved as an excitement to lay up stores of provisions against the time of scarcity. Joseph's advice was no less important than his prediction. The reason why we derive so little advantage from the prophecies of Scripture is, that we do not consider what use is to be made of them in our practice, although God usually joins directions with them, that we may know how to act in the prospect of what God is about to do in the world. "Blessed is he that readeth, and they that hear the words of this prophecy, and keep those things that are written therein, for the time is at hand. Behold, I come as a thief. Blessed is he that watcheth, and keepeth his garments, lest he walk naked, and they see his shame," Rev. i. 3, 22; ii. 15, 25.

VER. 55. *And when all the land of Egypt was famished, the people cried to Pharaoh for bread: and Pharaoh said unto all the Egyptians, Go unto Joseph; what he saith to you, do.*

Although there was abundance of corn in the land of Egypt, the people of the country were ready to perish for want. What was the reason of this? Had they not been forewarned that the terrible famine was coming? Although Joseph had gathered up the fifth of the corn, enough was left not only to supply the present wants of the people, but to lay up for themselves against the famine. But they wanted Joseph's prudence. The ant prepares her food in the summer and the harvest, and she enjoys ease and plenty in the days of winter. The butterfly, that only amuses herself and gratifies her appetite in the pleasant days of summer, has nothing in reserve for the days of storm and tempest. God has not given her the wisdom of the ant, or rather has suited her instinct to her condition, for it was not intended that she should live through the winter. But why should rational creatures be fools, when the meanest insects discover all that instinctive understanding which can be of any use to them. Thou sluggard, consider the ant and the butterfly. If thou art destined for as short an existence as the butterfly, spend all thy days in amusement and pleasure. If a winter is before thee as well as a summer, prepare for the days of winter whilst the summer continues. If thou art to live for ever in another world, lay up treasures in heaven.

The Egyptians came in their distress, and cried to Pharaoh for bread. Whither should they go but to Pharaoh, who had enough in his store-houses, and to spare in abundance? Whither should those who are oppressed with poverty go for relief but to the rich? Whither should we all go in those distresses in which God alone can help us, but to the Fountain of all good, whose stores can never be exhausted, who gives liberally, and upbraids not?

"Go unto Joseph; what he says unto you, do." Joseph had showed his great wisdom in collecting and keeping all the rich stores, from which the necessities of the people were to be supplied, and he was the fittest person to be intrusted with the care of distributing them. The king had given him all the requisite power, and with him the people were to treat. If any of the people of Egypt had refused to go to Joseph, they would have despised not Joseph only, but the king, and would have deserved to want that sustenance which he only could give them. And are not the despisers of our great Redeemer in like manner despisers of His Father, who set Him as His King upon the holy hill of Zion? If we need food for our souls, we must have recourse to Jesus, for Him hath God the Father appointed to be the dispenser of that bread which nourisheth to life eternal. Those who will not come to Him, that they may have the bread of life, are despisers of their own mercies. They must perish, and their blood shall be upon their own heads.

VER. 56. *And the famine was over all the face of the earth: and Joseph opened all the store-houses, and sold unto the Egyptians; and the famine waxed sore in the land of Egypt.*

When there is great scarcity amongst us, we expect relief from other countries by sea. Great are the advantages which we derive from the improvements of modern times in the art of navigation. Unless a famine should pervade the whole globe, we hope to obtain a lesser or greater measure of the precious fruits of the earth. In the days of Joseph, when the famine was sore through the countries bordering on Egypt, the people, ready to perish with hunger, were under the necessity of travelling to Egypt to procure corn. The Egyptians themselves were exempted from the labour of travelling to a distant land, for there were store-houses scattered through all the country; but they were under a necessity of parting with their money for corn. They had themselves only to blame. Joseph did not compel them to sell any more corn than they were all willing to sell, and would probably have suffered to perish, or have wasted in riot, if they had not sold it. And now he demanded no greater price than, in the present circumstances, he had a right to claim. It was not necessary to inform us that Joseph did not oppress the people in his dealings with them. The people themselves attested his uprightness, when they afterwards said, "Let us find favour in the sight of our lord, for thou hast saved our lives."

If Joseph had thrown open his store-houses before the Egyptians felt the pressure of hunger, they might soon have wasted the fruits of his prudent care. They would have consumed those precious fruits of the earth that would afterwards be necessary for themselves. We are too little disposed to set a value upon our blessings till we have felt the want of them. Hunger, though very unpleasant, is often more useful than fulness of bread. They were very willing to give the price demanded for their food, as long as their money lasted. What will a hungry man give for bread? It is more precious than thousands of gold and silver. How precious, then, is the food of our souls! What is the reason why so many are unwilling to come and receive that wine and milk which they are called to come and buy without money and without price? They feel no appetite for it. They are not sensible of their need of it. They are in their own eyes rich and increased with goods, when they are in reality poor and ready to perish.

VER. 57. *And all countries came into Egypt to Joseph for to buy corn; because that the famine was so sore in all lands.*

All that a man hath will he give for his life, and for those things that are necessary to preserve life. He will travel into the most distant regions rather than perish with hunger in the land of his nativity. He will brave the perils of the sea. He will not esteem any trial too great to be endured, any danger too dreadful to be encountered, for the precious fruits of the earth. Why, then, do men grudge a little labour, or a little expense, for what is no less necessary for our souls than the bread that perisheth is for our bodies?

"The famine was sore in all lands," but the land of Egypt afforded its stores to the purchasers from every country. Why should not one nation derive advantage from the superfluities of another? God has made us to serve one another in love, as the offspring of the same ancestors, as the creatures of the same God, furnished alike by Him with the powers of the mind, and standing in need of the things which His bounty has provided to satisfy the desire of every living thing. Joseph would have been very unworthy of his place, and of the favours bestowed on him by the providence of God, if he had refused to sell his corn to the people of distant countries. He was raised up to be the common benefactor of mankind.

Happy are the men who are made blessings to all around them. Happy are all those men who are taught by God to love their neighbours, although they cannot give such proofs of their charity as men in high stations. "What doth the Lord our God require from us, but to do justly, to love mercy, and to walk humbly with our God!"

LECTURE 11

Joseph's brethren are sent to Egypt by their father to buy corn.

xlii 1–8

VER. 1. *Now when Jacob saw that there was corn in Egypt, Jacob said unto his sons, Why do ye look one upon another ?*

THE famine was sore in the land of Canaan, the land of promise, the land where milk and honey used to abound. There were famines in the land, not only in those days of degeneracy, when the people of Israel forsook the God of their fathers, but in the days of the holy patriarchs themselves. Abraham, Isaac, and Jacob saw days of famine in that land which they were taught by promise to expect as the inheritance of their seed. The faith of those eminent believers was tried by those famines, and it was found unto praise. Other good purposes, with which we are unacquainted, might be served by this calamity. May we not reasonably suppose that the distresses occasioned by the famine contributed to bring down the high spirit of Jacob's sons? It forced them, at least, to come down to Egypt, where they were to meet with treatment that drew expressions from their mouths and their hearts of bitter regret for their sins.

"Jacob saw that there was corn in Egypt." He received information of the supplies that others had found in Egypt, and wished to share in the common benefit. But why did not God tell him beforehand of the famine, as well as his son Joseph, who was not a greater favourite of Heaven? or why, without any premonition, did he not store up corn in the good years to satisfy himself and his family in the years of famine?

These are questions that scarcely require an answer. They are like many others which an impertinent curiosity has proposed about matters with which we have very little concern. " God giveth not account of any of His matters;" and the holy men of ancient times had very good reasons for many parts of their conduct, of which we could not reasonably expect information. We may learn, however, from the history before us, a very good reason why matters were so ordered by Divine Providence, that Jacob should feel the scarcity of famine, and that he should have no supplies at home to prevent his needing them from Egypt. It was the will of God that Jacob should go down with his whole family to the land of Egypt, where his seed was to be oppressed till the time of their glorious deliverance. It was the will of God, likewise, that Joseph should be made the " shepherd and the stone of Israel," and that his brethren should be made to bow down before him. The Lord is holy and wise in all His works, although we can see only a small part of their wisdom and beauty.

Jacob could not be blamed for wanting supplies of grain for his family from the increase of his own fields. He was but a stranger and a sojourner in the land, and his riches consisted not in corn but in cattle. No man is to be blamed for not foreseeing what is known only to God, and to those to whom God is pleased to reveal it. Nor was God bound to give His own prophets a previous knowledge of all that He intended to do on the earth. What He made known to one, He did not always make known to another equally favoured by Him. Jacob was not less dear to God than his son Joseph; but he had not been in prison, and did not need those special favours which led the way to Joseph's liberation and advancement. He was to be satisfied, as well as Joseph, in the days of famine; and all the paths of the Lord were mercy and truth to him, as well as to his son. The discoveries made to Joseph were mercies to his father as much as to himself.

Jacob saw that there was corn in Egypt to be sold, and he no doubt rejoiced and praised God for His goodness to the children of men. He would, probably, be more deeply affected with that goodness which provided supplies for himself and his neighbours in another country than he had formerly been with that mercy which gave them abundance at home. Even good men are generally most sensible of the mercy that appears in blessings unexpectedly bestowed, or in those needful blessings, of which a slight alteration in circumstances might have left them destitute. It was to be lamented, indeed, that the famine was sore in the land; but what a signal mercy was it that corn had been reserved in Egypt for supply of the neighbouring nations! It was not wonderful that in ordinary years Egypt could afford a considerable portion of its corn to other countries; but that when the famine was as sore in Egypt as in Canaan, it should have enough to spare to all its neighbours, was very strange. It was the doing of the Lord, and it was wonderful in the eyes of Jacob; but he did not yet know how deeply he was interested in this wonderful instance of God's goodness to His creatures.

"Why do ye look one upon another?" They spent that time in painful anxiety which might have been better employed. None of them proposed an effectual method for relieving them from their present distress. They all looked at one another, as if each of them expected that another would propose something for their common benefit. But they were equally at a loss what to say or do.

VER. 2. *And he said, Behold, I have heard that there is corn in Egypt: get you down thither, and buy for us from thence; that we may live, and not die.*

How had Jacob heard that there was corn to be sold in Egypt? From the common report of the country. But why had he not heard from Joseph himself? Why did this favourite son delay a moment to inform his mourning father of the happy change in his circumstances? When he was a slave or a prisoner, it is probable that he could send no messengers to his father. But when he was lord of Egypt, he certainly had it in his power to send as many as he pleased. Surely, it will be said by some, he showed little regard to his father's comfort, when he left him for seven years ignorant of the fate of his best-beloved son.

But far be it from us to form a rash judgment, to the disadvantage of such a man as Joseph. He doubtless often thought of his beloved father, and would have been very happy to communicate any pleasure to a parent whom he so dearly loved. But there is a time for everything. What if the news of Joseph's exaltation would have given more pain than pleasure to the good man, when he was informed of the circumstances that prepared the way for it? The highest earthly grandeur of one son would not have compensated the grief which he would feel for the wickedness of his other sons. The time might come when Joseph would be enabled to inform his father of his glory to more advantage, and with less risk of making him unhappy.

It is plain that Joseph was directed in all his steps by the good providence of God. And how do we know that he had not a revelation of the mind of God about the way and time of conveying that information which he certainly wished to communicate to his father?

What has been said on this subject renders it unnecessary to answer another question, Why Joseph suffered his poor father to be reduced to straits before he sent him supply? He knew, or might easily have known or supposed, that there was little bread at that time in his father's house. No son amongst us, who is not void of natural affection, would suffer his father to be in want when he can prevent it; yet Joseph suffered his father to feel the distress of anxiety, if not of hunger, before he sent him any supply of corn. The happy consequences of that distress to which Joseph's brethren were reduced when they came into Egypt may account for this seeming neglect. Joseph either saw or conjectured what would happen. If he had no particular revelation on the subject, be might conjecture, partly from what he heard of the famine in Canaan, and partly from his dreams concerning his own advancement, that his brethren would come to Egypt, and bow down before him, as the lord of the country.

"I have heard that there is corn in Egypt ; get down thither, and buy for us from thence." It may seem strange that he sent his sons to buy his corn. He had men-servants in abundance. Might he not have spared the travel and peril to his sons ? He no doubt had his reasons. He might think that his sons were more to be trusted, in a matter of such consequence, than servants, and that the perils of delay in the business were greater than the perils of the journey. His sons were not trained up to idleness or cowardice.

"Buy for us from thence, that we may live." Bread is the staff of life. Man does not live by bread alone ; and yet the want of bread, in ordinary cases, would prove fatal to our lives. Jacob and his sons had flocks and herds in abundance. Their flesh and milk had hitherto been very useful to them, when bread was scarcely to be found. But "the Lord had called for a drought upon the land, and upon the mountains, and upon the corn, and upon the new wine, and upon the oil, and upon that which the ground brought forth, and upon men, and upon cattle, and upon all the labours of the hand. The beasts groaned, the herds of cattle were perplexed, because they had no pasture ; yea, the flocks of sheep were made desolate."

"That we may live, and not die." The patriarch uses strong language to show his sons the necessity of getting down to Egypt to buy food. He sets life and death before them ; not their own life or death only, but the life or death of the whole family. The Lord was the God of their life ; but they could not trust God for their life in a manner agreeable to His will, without using the necessary means of life. God has promised His blessings, not to sluggards, but to those who trust in the Lord, and do good, Ps. xxxvii. 3.

"That we may live, and that we may not die." The sons of Jacob might set their faces with cheerfulness to all the evils of a long journey, to all the risks of it, to all the pains of a long separation from their father, their wives, and their children, when they remembered that their travel was necessary for preserving the lives of persons so dear to them. That man deserves not the gift of life who would not put himself to expense, who would not toil, who would not even risk his life when necessity requires it, for those to whom he is indebted, or who are indebted to him for life.

Ver. 3. *And Joseph's ten brethren went down to buy corn in Egypt.*

It is probable that they would have gone more cheerfully to a remote country than to Egypt, although it was in the neighbourhood of Canaan. What if Joseph should meet them in the land of Egypt, to bring to remembrance their sin in selling him into that strange land! But their father's authority, and the reasons by which his command was enforced, were sufficient to overcome their aversion. They sat looking on one another till this time, although they had no doubt heard, as well as their father, that there was corn in Egypt. But where the word of a father is there is power, if his sons and his daughters are worthy of being called his children. The sons of Jacob were unnatural in their conduct towards Joseph, but nature maintained its rights in their behaviour to their father. Those who are bad in one respect may be good in another.

Be it our care to stand perfect and complete in the performance of the duties of all relations, and in all the will of God. He who commands us "to honour our father," commands us "to love our brother also." Are we not, then, partial in the law, whatever reverence we yield to our father, if other relatives are treated with rigour or unkindness?

Ver. 4. *But Benjamin, Joseph's brother, Jacob sent not with his brethren ; for he said, Lest peradventure mischief befall him.*

Benjamin is called Joseph's brother in a stricter sense than the rest of his brethren. One mother brought them both into the world. Jacob's fond attachment to Benjamin was in part the effect of his grief for the loss of Joseph. He loved that son of his old age, not merely as his own son, and the son of his beloved Rachel, but as the brother and heir of Joseph, whom he never again expected to see. Besides the natural propensity in parents to love the fruit of their own bodies, there are adventitious motives in many cases, which have a mighty influence in endearing some children more than others. But parents ought to be cautious against those family partialities, which have often engendered strife among brethren. Love your children as much as you please, provided that you put none of them in God's room, and do no injustice to one in your kindness to another.

Benjamin was not suffered to depart with his brethren, that he might not be exposed to those perils in the way to which all his brethren might expose themselves. Benjamin had done nothing, as far as we know, to merit this preference to his brethren.

But he was, what none others of them were, the son of Rachel, and the brother of Joseph by both parents. The brethren of Benjamin do not appear to have taken any exception against the preference of their younger brother to all the other members of the family. It is likely they already had felt so bitter remorse for their wrongs to Joseph, and the grief that they had given to their father, that he might have safely given to Benjamin a coat of divers colours, like that which excited their envy against Joseph. Let sinners consider the profit and loss of sins already committed before they involve themselves in the guilt of new crimes.

VER. 5. *And the sons of Israel came to buy corn among those that came : for the famine was in the land of Canaan.*

"The Lord knoweth the days of the upright : and their inheritance shall be for ever. They shall not be ashamed in the evil time : and in the days of famine they shall be satisfied," Ps. xxxvii. 18, 19. This is one of the faithful sayings of God, which has been often fully verified in the experience of believers, and yet God does not always make a sensible difference between His own people and His enemies in the days of famine. He provides food for all flesh. The sons of Israel came down to Egypt to buy corn, but they were not the only persons that came. They made a part of a caravan of Canaanites ; and the Canaanites that came with them found less difficulty and trouble than themselves in procuring what they wanted. But God designed something better than a supply of grain to the sons of

K

Jacob. He gave them what they wanted; but He gave it to them in such a way as was most conducive to their best interests.

" For the famine was sore in the land of Canaan." Wonder not that we have years of scarcity in our cold and variable climate. There have been seen famines of long continuance in the most fertile countries upon earth. Think not that you are secured against famine by the modern improvements of agriculture. Have the moderns discovered any method of forcing the earth to produce its fruits without rain ? or have they found out any method of bringing down rain from the clouds, or of causing the vapours to ascend from the ends of the earth ? " Therefore will we wait upon thee, O Lord, because thou dost all these things."

Think not that God is under any obligation to do for you what He has done for your fathers before you. There was a famine in the land of Canaan in Isaac's days, but Isaac had no occasion either to go down to Egypt, or to send for corn from it. He dwelt by divine direction in the land of Gerar, and sowed the fields adjoining to his tents, and the Lord gave him a hundredfold, and the Philistines saw that he was blessed of the Lord. Jacob seems not to have reaped better crops than his neighbours. He must send his sons to Egypt for corn with other Canaanites. But he afterwards saw that the Lord dealt well with him in leaving him under a necessity of sending his sons to that foreign country. Our straits and perplexities, under divine superintendence, will have a happy issue. God is good in what He withholds as well as in what He gives—in giving us what we procure with difficulty and danger, as well as what we procure with ease.

VER. 6. *And Joseph was the governor over the land, and he it was that sold to all the people of the land : and Joseph's brethren came, and bowed down themselves before him with their faces to the earth.*

The time was when Joseph's brethren were men of high respectability in the land of Canaan, whilst Joseph was a slave or a prisoner in the land of Egypt. Now Joseph was governor over all the land of Egypt, when they appeared before him as humble suppliants, almost craving, as an alms, those supplies of food for which they were both able and willing to give the price that should be demanded. If Joseph had thought, or pretended to think, that there was no more grain in Egypt than was likely to be necessary for the people of that country, the companies of the land of Canaan must have turned back with shame and grief to their own land.

We cannot suppose that Joseph, in person, sold all the corn that was carried out of the land Egypt; but it is probable that he gave more attention, in person, to the travellers from Canaan than to those from other countries, because the easiest entrance into Egypt, for an enemy, was from Canaan. It was so ordered, partly perhaps by Joseph's care, but chiefly by the providence of God, that he met with his brethren when they came into Egypt.

Let not great men think that they a right to take their ease, eat, drink, and be merry, and leave all the business of their office to be done by poorer persons, who must labour for their subsistence. If any office is committed to us, let us do the duties of it with diligence. Joseph would have been ungrateful to Pharaoh, to the Egyptians, but most of all to God, if he had indulged himself in ease and sloth when he was made lord of Egypt. He would have been very unwise if he had left all his business to be managed by inferior officers, without superintending their conduct. Let all masters treat their servants with confidence, if it is deserved, but let them still remember their own station, and practise its duties.

"Joseph's brethren came, and bowed down themselves before him with their faces to the earth." Where was now their mouth with which they said to him, after he had told them one of his dreams, "Shalt thou indeed reign over us, or shalt thou have dominion over us?" "Come now, therefore," said they on another occasion, "and let us slay him, and cast him into some pit, and we will say some wild beast hath devoured him, and we will see what will become of his dreams." They did not indeed slay him, but they took a method which they hoped would be no less effectual to hinder the accomplishment of his dreams. They cast him into a pit, and sold him into Egypt. The consequence of his subjection to the will of a capricious master was, that he was cast into a dungeon. And yet the remote consequence of their measures was the very thing which they hoped to prevent. They did not know that the Lord of hosts, " who is wonderful in counsel, and excellent in working," can accomplish His purposes by the means which are used to prevent their accomplishment. The imprisonment of Joseph was the preparation for his glory, and now his brethren, without knowing him, bow down before him, and must, if he pleases, not only be left destitute of provisions for themselves and their families, but consigned to a prison. Let us never attempt evident impossibilities. You will not endeavour to pull down the sun from the firmament when his beams dazzle your eyes. You will not attempt to dry up the waters of the sea when they obstruct your path. It is still more impossible to change the counsels of God, or to prevent their accomplishment, for He hath prepared His throne in the heavens, and His kingdom ruleth over all. Follow the providence of God, but never think of forcing it to follow you. " The Lord bringeth the counsels of the heathen to nought, he maketh the desires of the people of none effect. The counsel of the Lord standeth for ever, the thoughts of his heart to all generations."

VER. 7. *And Joseph saw his brethren, and he knew them, but made himself strange unto them, and spake roughly unto them; and he said unto them, Whence come ye? And they said, From the land of Canaan to buy food.*

Joseph dearly loved his brethren and his father, and did not forget the form of their countenance when he was banished from them. The loved idea of his father daily presented itself to him, and brought with it the ideas of his brethren, who had so unmercifully expelled him from his father's house.

Although Joseph knew his brethren, he affected not to know them. Although he still loved them, he dealt roughly with them. It would be an injury to Joseph's memory to suppose, that his rough treatment of them was the effect of a revengeful spirit. He never thought of revenging himself on any of the persons who had dealt unkindly or unjustly with him in his low estate. We will afterwards find that even when his heart melted for the distress of his brethren, he continued to deal roughly with them. He turned himself about from them, and wept, when they were expressing their remorse for their cruel treatment of himself, and yet he took from them Simeon, and bound him before their eyes.

Why, then, did he deal roughly with them? Partly to obtain a much-desired information from them about his father, and the condition of his father's family, without making himself known to them before the proper time was come for making himself known; partly to humble them by affliction, and bring them to a sense of the evil of dealing unjustly and harshly with himself. He was like a wise father, who thinks it necessary to correct his son, although he feels in his own bowels more distress than his child, that folly may be driven out of his heart.

"Judge not according to the appearance, but judge righteous judgment." Kindness must sometimes put on an angry aspect, as hatred too often wears smiles on its countenance.

Ver. 8. *And Joseph knew his brethren, but they knew not him.*

Some men remember countenances far better than others, but it is easy to see how Joseph's brethren might not have known him, although he knew them. Joseph conjectured that his brethren, like others in the land of Canaan, would be compelled to come down to Egypt to buy food. But his brethren never imagined that Joseph was to be the lord of Egypt. Besides, it was now a long time since they had seen him. It is probable that the years of plenty did not begin for some few years after Joseph's advancement. God had showed Pharaoh what was soon to happen, but it does not appear that what he had reason from his dreams to expect came to pass immediately. Now, Joseph, in the interval between the time when he was sold, and the time when his brethren first came to Egypt, had endured much affliction, by which his countenance would in some degree be altered, and his habits and dress must have been greatly changed by his exaltation, whilst his brethren retained the manners and dress to which they had been accustomed in their early years. If one who has been twenty years absent from his father's house, and had left it in poor circumstances, should return with a splendid equipage, he would find no difficulty in knowing his father, but his father would scarcely believe his own eyes when he beheld the features of his son.

Joseph had often thought about his brethren, and called the features of their countenances to his mind, but he was probably banished from their remembrance like one that was dead of old. It would have been very unpleasant to them to think of one whom they had treated with such unnatural cruelty. They willingly forgot the features of a man of whom they could not think without pangs of sorrow. Yet though they did not remember his face, they could not forget their guilt. We will soon hear, that in a day of distress they remembered it with horror. Joseph, in the meantime, remembered his prophetical dreams.

VER. 9. *And Joseph remembered the dreams which he dreamed of them.*

No doubt Joseph had all along remembered his dreams after he came into a state of bondage, and the remembrance of them would be attended with very different workings of his mind at different times. Sometimes he would say to himself, " ' Doth God's word fail for evermore ? ' I believed that my dreams were from heaven. Have I been deceived ? This could not be the case. They had all the characters which have usually distinguished prophetical dreams. I knew by a heavenly inspiration that the dreams of the king's butler were from above. And why should I think I was mistaken about my own dreams ? And yet, instead of being elevated to power, I am bowed down under oppression, and my hopes of deliverance are so long deferred, that my heart is sick with disappointment."

At other times, the remembrance of his dreams would cheer the gloom of his prison-house, and fill him with joy in the prospect that the days of his mourning were drawing to their end. The end at last came of his days of mourning. Still his dreams promised him the submission of his first enemies, the men of his father's house, when they bowed down before him with their faces to the earth. He remembered his dreams, and felt his heart enlarged in praise and gratitude. His faith was confirmed, his hope was realised. He saw, that as for his God, " His work was perfect," that "the word of the Lord was tried, and that He is a buckler to all them that trust in Him."

" Destroy this temple," said Jesus to the Jews, " and in three days I will build it up." When He was risen from the dead, His disciples " remembered that He had said this unto them, and they believed the scripture and the word which Jesus had said." They certainly believed the Scripture and the word that Jesus had said before the time when He was raised from the dead. But new acts of faith in the Scriptures and the words of Jesus were drawn forth by their remembrance of His words, when they saw them accomplished. Who is wise, and will observe the doings of the Lord, and compare them with the Scriptures? he shall understand the loving-kindness and faithfulness of the Lord, and his mouth will be filled with the praises of that mercy and truth which follow them all the days of their life, not excepting those days in which they are too ready to think that the Lord hath forgotten to be gracious, according to His word unto His servants.

LECTURE 12

Joseph treats his brethren as spies, and confines them to a prison, where they are seized with deep remorse for their cruel treatment of their brother.

xlii 9–20

VER. 9. *And Joseph remembered the dreams which he had dreamed of them, and said unto them, Ye are spies ; to see the nakedness of the land ye are come.*

FAR be it from us to say that Joseph had attained absolute perfection when he was on earth, although his virtues were far beyond those of most other men. It will not be easy, or rather it will be impossible, to exempt him from the charge of dissimulation, when he alleged that his brethren were spies. His words are not to be considered as an assertion, but they express a suspicion, which certainly did not enter his mind. His design was good. He meant to humble them for their good, but good intentions will not excuse a departure from truth. He knew that they were not spies come to see the nakedness of the land, but he wished, without discovering himself to them, to be informed of the welfare of his father, and of his father's house. It is to be remembered that Joseph lived before the law was given. The light which discovers sin and duty shone less brightly in his days than in ours, and therefore the limits between what is lawful and what is unlawful would not be so easily discerned. It is likewise to be feared that Joseph's station, as prime minister in the court of Pharaoh, led him into connections, and placed him in circumstances, unfavourable to progress in virtue. He held fast his integrity, and would not let it go amidst great temptations, but human infirmity discovered itself in some parts of his conduct.

Canaan was the country from which Egypt would have been invaded with most hope of success. This gave Joseph (whose office obliged him to watch for the safety of Egypt) a pretence for saying that his brethren were come to spy out the nakedness of the land, and what prospect there might be of invading it with advantage, in the distress which might be supposed to be occasioned by the famine.

Ver. 10. *And they said unto him, Nay, my lord, but to buy food are thy servants come.*

The high-spirited men, who would not suffer the prince who had dishonoured their sister to live above the ground, and who thought the extermination of a whole city a proper revenge for an affront given to their father's family, behaved humbly and submissively to the man who endeavoured to fix upon them a dangerous imputation, for which they had given no reason. They were not filled with resentment at the imputation; or if they were angry, their pride was swallowed up by fear, for the man with whom they had to do was the lord of the country.

Ver. 11. *We are all one man's sons; we are true men, thy servants are no spies.*

It could not be supposed that one man would suffer ten of his sons to engage at once in a business so full of perils as that of spies, or that so many brethren should risk the almost total extirpation of their father's house at one blow. It requires a very daring spirit for a man to venture his own life in an office so desperate; but who would venture at once his own life, and the life of almost all that are dear to him, along with his own? Clear proof, at least, is requisite before belief can be given to an accusation so improbable as this which was laid against Joseph's brethren, when it was known that they all belonged to the same house, and that there was only one brother left at home with father sinking under the burden of age.

"We are true men, we are no spies." "We are what we

pretend to be, and have assumed no false character." The business of a spy is not in all cases unlawful. Moses, by divine direction, sent men to spy out the promised land; Joshua sent men to spy out Jericho, who appear to have been worthy of his confidence. It is a business, however, so full of temptations to falsehood, that an honest man will not rashly undertake it. If Joseph's brethren had really been spies, they would have lied when they pretended to come and buy corn. But from the charge they could clear themselves with a good conscience.

VER. 12. *And he said unto them, Nay, but to see the nakedness of the land ye are come.*

When a man once says what is not consistent with strict truth, he is on dangerous ground. He will be tempted to say again what he perhaps designed to say only once, or to invent some new falsehood to give plausibility to the former. May the Lord remove far from us the way of lying. If even a Joseph or a David stumble into this way, he will find difficulty in getting out of it.

VER. 13. *And they said, Thy servants are twelve brethren, the sons of one man in the land of Canaan; and, behold, the youngest is this day with our father, and one is not.*

Joseph gains his end by insisting on his charge against his brethren. He has the satisfaction to learn that his father is yet alive—that Benjamin, his brother, was his father's favourite, as himself had been. That his brethren treated their father with the respect which he so well deserved might be inferred from the manner in which they spoke of him, and from their leaving Benjamin to comfort him in their absence.

They did not, indeed, speak truth when they said, "One is not;" but it is probable that they said what they thought likely to be true. That Joseph had been torn by wild beasts must have been the common opinion in the country where they dwelt. His brethren knew that this was false, but they did not think it prudent to contradict it, lest their own wickedness should be suspected; and they had so often spoken of Joseph's death, that they now almost believed their own lie. If we wish to be kept out of the way of lying, let us beware of everything that needs concealment.

" One is not." Think not that Joseph's brethren were ignorant of the immortality of the soul. This important doctrine they had doubtless learned from their father and grandfather. Moses himself says of Enoch that " he was not," and yet in the same sentence he lets us know that Enoch was still alive in a better world.

Yet when they said, " One is not," they were not wholly free from the blame of falsehood. A man lies, not only when he says what he knows to be false, but when he says what he does not know to be true. We may, indeed, tell what seems to us only probable, but let us tell it in language expressive of uncertainty ; the words *possibly* or *probably* may be spoken without any great loss of time, and they are useful words when they preserve truth in a sentence, which without them would be a lie.

It is sometimes amusing to observe how liars, in attempting to deceive others, deceive themselves. Joseph's brethren little thought that they were telling the governor of Egypt that himself was dead. But his brotherly affection would plead their apology. It was not to be expected that they would inform him of their own cruelty to one of their brethren. A liar is not easily believed when he speaks truth. Yet we may believe a man who on some occasions will say what is not true. A man, if he is not lost to all sense of virtue, will not lie without a temptation. Joseph knew that his brethren said what they did not know to be true concerning himself, but he entertained no doubt of what they said concerning his father and his younger brother.

VER. 14. *And Joseph said unto them, That is it that I spake unto you, saying, Ye are spies.*

He then knew that they had yet said nothing that gave him any sufficient reason to alter his opinion. They had, indeed, said something in their own defence that might be true, but he wished to have better evidence of the truth of it. Let them bring that younger brother of whom they spake, and he will believe that they were what they called themselves, and that they were not spies come to see the nakedness of the land.

VER. 15, 16. *Hereby ye shall be proved : by the life of Pharaoh, ye shall not go forth hence, except your youngest brother come hither. Send one of you, and let him fetch your brother, and ye shall be kept in prison, that your words may be proved, whether there be any truth in you : or else by the life of Pharaoh surely ye are spies.*

It was not, indeed, probable that one man would send all his sons into a foreign country on the perilous business of spies. This Joseph allows. The only question, then, about which Joseph pretended to desire satisfaction was, Whether they were really the sons of one man ? Let them bring that other brother of whom they spake, and he will believe them.

It was not easy to see how the sight of their youngest brother could have removed all doubts about their veracity, if doubts had been really entertained. If the governor had sent some of his own people to that place in Canaan where their father dwelt he might have been assured, upon better grounds, that they were speaking truth. But the business was not of such importance as to require him to take so much trouble about it. If they were spies, he could easily secure the land against any danger from the intrigues of their employers.

Joseph's conduct must have appeared harsh and unreasonable to his brethren. What reason had he to take them for spies? What reason had he to suspect the truth of the account which they gave of themselves? He would not have much better reason to believe the truth of their account when their younger brother was brought down by one of themselves, than he had at present. Did he not appear like a tyrant, when he threatened them with a gaol upon surmises that appeared so groundless, and promised to release them on a condition so frivolous? It looks as if Joseph sought no more than a thin pretence for his conduct, and that he had no aversion, for the present, to expose his character in their eyes, which he knew he would soon be able to retrieve. In the meantime, he hoped, by conduct which would appear capricious and unjust, to bring them to repentance for their own injustice and cruelty to himself.

But there is one part of Joseph's behaviour on this occasion which does not appear defensible. Does he not swear by the life of Pharaoh? What occasion was there to swear at all, or how can his words be reconciled with strict truth? If they had refused to comply with his proposal, were they to be accounted liars and spies? He knew very well that they were true men, whether they complied with his terms or not.

We must not justify the righteous themselves in what is not right. If Joseph swore without reason, if he swore by a creature, or if he swore to confirm what was not strictly true, he was to be blamed; but still it must be said, that his sin was his infirmity, and affords no excuse for those who can, on ordinary occasions, profane the ordinance of swearing. If a man slips with his foot into a ditch, is his neighbour, for that reason, to lie down willingly in the ditch, and continue in it, to the danger of his precious life? Every good man is liable to sin; he may mingle his best actions with sin, but he will not " walk after the flesh."

It may be questioned, however, whether the words that Joseph used on the present occasion amounted to an oath. There are two different senses in which they may be understood, and if the favourable sense is not less obvious than the worst, it ought to be preferred; for why should we hunt for occasions of reproach against one of the best of men, whilst he is performing one of his best of actions.

" May Pharaoh die unless ye are spies, if ye do not bring down your younger brother to this place."

If you take the words in this sense, they are an oath, and a curse very unworthy of the mouth of such a good man. " As sure as Pharaoh lives ye are spies, if you do not bring down your brother to this place." If you take the words in this sense, they are only a strong asseveration, like that expression, " *as thy soul liveth.*" Yet it must be confessed that this is not the most obvious sense, and that even in this view they are too like a needless oath. Joseph's example is not our rule. " Abstain from all appearance of evil." "Swear not at all" in ordinary converse, either by God or by the creatures, and beware of any kind of speech that entrenches upon the reverence due to God. "Let your speech be always with grace, seasoned with salt," that ye may neither bring guilt upon yourselves, nor upon others, who may be disposed to follow your example, or to go beyond it.

VER. 17. *And he put them all together into ward three days.*

It seems they did not consent to the terms proposed. None of them would consent to go and bring down Benjamin, if all his brethren were kept in prison. If Joseph thought he had any reason to account them spies, they thought they had better reason to distrust a man who seemed to seek an opportunity to get into his power all their father's family.

Doubtless it was with reluctance that Joseph threw into prison those men that had thrown himself into the pit, and sold him into Egypt. But he longed to see their repentance. He hoped that imprisonment by the governor of Egypt would awaken their consciences to a sense of the great iniquity of selling their brother into that country where God was now rendering their own sin into their bosom.

Whilst they were in prison, they did not enjoy those consolations which Joseph enjoyed when he was cast into the dungeon. Their brother did not confine them in a dungeon, nor make them fast with irons. Joseph had continued, perhaps, as many years as they continued days in their prison. But three years of hard imprisonment, with a good conscience, are far less grievous than three days of mild imprisonment, embittered by the consciousness of guilt.

"Three days did Joseph suffer his brethren to continue in prison." We may, perhaps, wonder that he suffered them to continue so long in prison, whilst his heart so deeply felt their affliction. But there is no inconsistency between goodness and wisdom. These excellent qualities ought always to be conjoined. If Joseph's goodness had not been regulated by wisdom, he would not have committed his brethren to prison. If his wisdom had not been sweetened with goodness and compassion, he might have left them in prison till their spirits failed, or were exasperated by harsh treatment, and till their poor father and his family were ready to perish with want.

He could not leave them many days in prison. His heart pleaded so powerfully for them, that before the end of the third day he restored them to liberty. Surely our Lord Jesus will not always contend with His people, "lest the spirit should fail before Him, and the souls which He hath redeemed." Joseph knew the heart of a prisoner. for he was held in a prison several years. Jesus is "touched with the feeling of our infirmities;" for all His lifelong "He was a man of sorrows." If He should slay us, let us trust in Him. "After two days will he revive us, in the third day he will raise us up, and we shall live in his sight."

VER. 18. *And Joseph said unto them the third day, This do, and live; for I fear God.*

Did Joseph repent of his harshness to his brethren, or did he still carry on the plan which he formed in his own mind from the beginning, when he changed his conduct, and treated his brethren with less asperity? It is not inconsistent with his character to suppose that he might see reason to make some alteration in his behaviour. He might think, that though he meant, from the first time that he saw his brethren, to treat them in the way best fitted to promote their best interests, he had not acted with all that circumspection which would have been proper. There is often a great difference between the behaviour of good and wise men on those sudden emergencies where there is no time for deliberation, and on those occasions when time is allowed to consider at leisure every step of their conduct. There are, indeed, principles of conduct from which a good man will not recede on any occasion, unless he is left by God to himself, to make known what is in him, even in his flesh. But whilst integrity is maintained, unallowed infirmities will cleave to the work of our hands, and these infirmities will be most evident in those trying circumstances when persons must act without much previous consideration. As a judicious hearer will observe more incorrect expressions in a discourse which a minister delivers without previous leisure for study, than in a discourse prepared by the same minister at his leisure; so it might be expected that Joseph would now, after due deliberation, be better fitted for transacting the delicate affair in which he was engaged with his brethren, than in the moment when he first saw them, and when, though he was prepared to expect them, he found his mind agitated with a variety of the most powerful passions, and perhaps at some loss about the most proper methods to accomplish one part of his design without frustrating another.

It was his wish to make his brethren know, and understand, and feel what an evil and a bitter thing it was to be guilty of inhuman conduct towards the innocent. But it was his wish also not to forfeit entirely the confidence of his brethren; for if they did not trust his word, they would not be induced to do what he desired. Perhaps he might think that the reason of their unwillingness to send up one of their number to bring down their younger brother, was the distrust which they had conceived of his designs from the severity with which he had treated them. He therefore told them on the third day, that he feared God, and would deal justly and truly with men. And therefore, instead of keeping them all confined within the walls of a prison, he would detain only one of them, till the rest went and brought down their younger brother, of whom they spake.

" This do, and live; for I fear God." There were such different sentiments in those days concerning God, that different speakers had very different meanings when the same language was used concerning Him. When it is said (2 Chron. xxxv.) that Josiah would not hearken unto Pharaoh speaking from the mouth of God, we must not imagine that the good prince wilfully disobeyed the commandment of the God of Israel, but he considered the god or gods of whom Pharaoh spake as the gods whom Pharaoh acknowledged. When that Pharaoh who reigned in the days of Jacob said that the Spirit of God was in Joseph, we cannot well tell what god or gods he meant. The same word in the original may signify either one god, or more gods than one. When Joseph said to his brethren, "I fear God," it is a question in what sense they would understand him. Unless they were informed that Joseph worshipped a different God from the people of Egypt, they would think that he either meant the gods of Egypt, or in general that God who was believed by the heathens to rule over all gods; for it can scarcely be supposed that the nations had yet forgotten the leading doctrine of Noah concerning one Supreme Being, to whom all visible as well as invisible things were subject. But it was certainly no secret in Egypt, or to Canaan, that Joseph's religion was different from the religion practised by the rest of the nation. He was never ashamed to confess his God, even before Pharaoh. And an event so uncommon as the exaltation of a foreigner, and a man of a different religion, to the station of prime minister, must have excited the attention of strangers who came into the country as well as of the natives.

Although Joseph had been of the same way of thinking as the Egyptians in matters of religion, his impressions of religion must have preserved him from acts of injustice towards men. The worship of false gods has a malignant influence on human practice, but atheism a much worse. There were virtues as well as vices, which the notions generally entertained of the gods of the heathen tended to cherish. They imagined that those beings, so far superior to men in power, were severe avengers of what they esteemed wickedness; and falsehood, inhumanity, and injustice were amongst most of the nations esteemed acts of wickedness, which would sooner or later bring down their displeasure.

Joseph's brethren might, therefore, be induced to place some confidence in him, although they did not know that he was of the same religion with themselves, when they understood that he was impressed with a reverence for the gods whom he worshipped. They would be still better disposed to trust his words if they had heard that he was a worshipper, not of the Egyptian gods, but of one only, the living and the true God, who hates every iniquity, and who will not suffer liars and bloody men to escape unpunished.

L

We are professed worshippers of this God. Let us not be heathens in our practice. It was enough for men to be like the God whom they worshipped. If worship was really due to such gods as were ordinarily worshipped in the heathen world, they were authorised to indulge themselves in those gratifications of lust, of revenge, and other unruly affections, by which their gods themselves were enslaved. Why call we Christ our Lord, and His Father our Father, if we are no better than heathens, who called Jupiter or Baal their gods? But many of the heathens will rise up against us in judgment if we can practise even the wickednesses which, according to the creed of heathens themselves, would be punished by those detestable gods whom they served. How dreadfully is the name of God profaned if we give occasion by our behaviour to the heathen, or to them who have no gods, to blaspheme! "This do, and live; for I fear God."

VER. 19. *If ye be true men, let one of your brethren be bound in the house of your prison : go ye, carry corn for the famine of your houses.*

At first Joseph proposed to confine them all but one in prison, now he proposes to bind only one of them. If he was sincere in his first proposal, he had not duly considered the consequences. The house of his father might have perished for want. It is likely that he had no serious intentions of holding them all in a state of confinement for such a long space of time as the journey might have occupied, although the distance was not very great. A few days are incalculably valuable to men pressed with hunger, and looking out earnestly for relief. But if Joseph appeared too severe, he was willing to retract his mistake. A fearer of the name of God may inadvertently err, but he will be ready to retract his error when it is pointed out, either by other men, or by the reflections of his own mind. "If I despised," says Job, "the cause of my man-servant, or of my maid-servant, when they contended with me, what shall I do when God riseth up? and when He visiteth me, what shall I answer Him?" Job xxxi. 13, 14.

"Go ye, carry corn for the food of your houses." Although

Joseph seemed to be set above the power of evil by the affluence attending his situation, he was far from being unmindful of the state of the poor. It is honourable in people of high rank to consider the necessities of the poor, and especially of those poor persons who have the care of families lying upon them. All wise governors will do what lies in their power for the comfort and relief of those who are burdened with families, which they find it difficult to support.

VER. 20. *But bring your youngest brother unto me; so shall your words be verified, and ye shall not die. And they did so.*

Joseph was not less desirous to see his father than to see the son of his beloved mother ; but it was not yet the proper time to desire his father to be brought to Egypt, nor to inform him that himself was alive, and lord of all the land of Egypt. Joseph's pretence was, that the ten brethren would give him satisfactory evidence of the truth of the account which they. gave of themselves, by bringing down their younger brother. His real view was not so much to be gratified with the sight of Benjamin, as to see in what manner his brethren were affected to him. If he found that they were truly penitent for their offence against himself, and that they entertained a friendly disposition towards Benjamin, he intended no longer to restrain those ardent longings which he felt to make his father, his brethren, and himself happy in the renewal of those tender domestic endearments which made a great part of the felicity of his first years of life.

" So shall your words be verified." Joseph affected to call in question the truth of their words, and at the same time to wish for a confirmation of them, that he might have it in his power, consistently with his public duty, to treat the ten brethren with that humanity to which innocent and unsuspected persons were entitled. We should not take it amiss to have our behaviour, or the truth of our words, called in question, when there are reasons for suspicion, especially by those whose duty it is to watch over the public safety, or the purity of the Church. In meekness we should vindicate our character from suspicions attached to it. We ought to remember that those who have the rule over us, as members of the Church and state, do not pretend to be omniscient, and must judge from evidence.

If no person were called to account till his guilt was certainly known, the discipline of the Church would be completely relaxed, and the nation might be ruined before the plotters of its destruction could be punished.

" And ye shall not die." Joseph had not only a right, but it was his indispensable duty, to punish them, if they were spies come to search out the nakedness of the land. But he feared God ; and therefore wished, as he pretended, to spare their lives. If we truly fear God, we will abhor the guilt of innocent blood, and of all unrighteousness. " By the fear of the Lord men depart from evil" of every kind. Of the man who can deliberately perform those actions which he knows to be offensive to the all-seeing eye, it may be justly said, that there is no fear of God before his eyes, no real impression on his heart of the abhorrence in which all sin is held by Him, who spared not His own Son, when He was loaded with the guilt of our iniquities. "If ye call on the Father, who, without respect of persons, judgeth every man according to his works, pass the time of your sojourning here in fear ; for ye were not redeemed with corruptible things, such as silver and gold, from your vain conversation received by tradition from your fathers, but with the precious blood of Christ, as of a lamb without blemish, and without spot."

" And they did so." They were under a necessity of doing it, and probably they were glad to find that great man, in whose power they were, willing to dismiss them upon such easy terms. One of them (they yet knew not which) must be left in pledge for their return, but it was in the governor's power to have kept them all in his prison, or to have suffered only one of them to depart.

When we cannot have what we wish, let us be content with what we can have. Why should we contend, when we know that we cannot overcome? We must often yield to men when we have right on our side, because our power is not equal to theirs. We are sure that God has both right and power on His side, whether He afflicts us by His own immediate agency, or by men who are His sword. " Let the potsherds strive with the potsherds of the earth; but let not man strive with his Maker, that he may not be broken in pieces."

LECTURE 13

Joseph's brethren in prison are struck with remorse for their cruelty to him, in refusing to comply with his piteous cries for mercy. They all return to their father, except Simeon, who is left in bonds.

xlii 21–24

VER. 21. *And they said one to another, We are verily guilty concerning our brother, in that we saw the anguish of his soul, when he besought us, and we would not hear; therefore is this distress come upon us.*

IT would be good for us if we could entertain the same views of sin in the time of temptation that we are likely to have after it is committed, or at the time when trouble brings it home to our consciences. When Joseph cried piteously to his brethren out of the pit, they thought only of the pleasure of gratifying their envy. They then wilfully overlooked the guilt they were contracting, and the sorrows they were preparing for their father, and for themselves; but when they were in trouble, they remembered their guilt in all its aggravating circumstances, and they would have given all they had in the world to recover that degree of innocence to which they might have pretended before Joseph came into their hands.

They were chargeable with many other sins. Simeon and Levi, in particular, were chargeable with a crime not less heinous than the murder of Joseph. Yet the affliction which they endured in prison brought to remembrance in a special manner this sin against their brother. This was an atrocious iniquity, of which the most of them were equally guilty. Simeon and Levi very probably thought with bitter remorse of their treachery and cruelty to the men of Shechem; but all of them thought and spoke of the crime against their brother. They had all shared in that guilt except Reuben, and they all suffered. They were unjustly put in prison, but they had with as little justice, and with less appearance of it, cast Joseph into a pit. The governor of Egypt suspected them to be spies, and treated them as such, when they were true men. They had hated Joseph, as if he had been a spy on their conduct, when he carried their evil report to his father for their good, and revenged his innocent behaviour, and his father's merited kindness, by threatening to take away his life, and by actually depriving him of a blessing almost as precious as life. They turned a deaf ear to the piteous cries of their poor brother; and the governor of Egypt turned a deaf ear to their apology for their own conduct, and to their supplications for liberty to return to their father, who would be ready to die with grief and fear if they continued many days longer in Egypt. They had already almost brought down his grey hairs with sorrow to the grave by what they had done, and now they were afraid that he would be actually brought to his grave, either by famine, or by grief for their misfortunes. Thus their sin seemed to be inscribed on their punishment, and the disgrace and hardships to which they were exposed were but a very inconsiderable part of the evils which they suffered. If the lord of Egypt had proceeded to the utmost extremity of what he seemed to intend against them, the sufferings he could inflict were not equal to those which a sense of guilt inflicted upon them. " The spirit of a man will sustain his infirmities, but a wounded spirit who can bear ? "

We are naturally averse to suffering of every kind, and yet nothing is more necessary than suffering when we have sinned. It is necessary for us to know and feel the bitterness of sin, that we may confess and forsake it. And the sufferings which our flesh endures are often necessary and useful to bring our sins

to our remembrance. No doubt Joseph's brethren had often
formerly thought with regret of the hatefulness of their conduct.
If they were not hardened to a very uncommon degree, their
hearts must have smitten them soon after the fact was committed. The sight of their father's anguish must have melted
their stubborn spirits. But they needed their afflictions in
Egypt likewise to awaken a new and more affecting sense of
their wickedness. Joseph, and God by Joseph, did them a
kindness in giving them an experimental knowledge of the
bitter sufferings of an oppressed man, when he pours out tears,
but finds no comforter. A great part of those who are
accounted happy are unhappy because they never felt unhappiness. They know not how to feel for others, because they
have not felt misery in their own persons. They know not the
heart of an afflicted person, and therefore they know not how
to show mercy, or how to bewail their own offences against the
law of mercy. How much better are those afflictions that
teach us repentance and humanity, than that prosperity which
hardens our hearts against our fellow-men !

Joseph's brethren at Dothan instigated one another to sin ;
now they add to one another's grief for sin. They formerly
thought their guilt was not great, because each of them thought
himself no worse than another, and found out abundance of
pretences to excuse himself and his brethren ; but now they all
join in a humble confession of their sin in its dreadful mag-
nitude and aggravations. We are not true penitents if we
endeavour to conceal from ourselves any part of our wickedness,
or from our neighbours any part of it that ought to be confessed
to our own shame and to the glory of God.

"We are verily guilty concerning our brother." Most of
them, it is likely, had some share in the guilt of massacring the
people of Shechem, and it is very probable that they thought
and spoke of it during the days and nights of their imprisonment. We do not expect an account of all that passed in their
minds, of all their prayers and confessions, in the time of their
imprisonment. We have only an account of their bitter reflections concerning their conduct towards Joseph, who is the

principal subject of this part of the sacred history. They now remembered that he was their brother, the son of the same venerable father, whose heart they rent with grief, by making him believe that his son Joseph was rent in pieces. That we may be duly affected with a sense of the evil of our sins against our neighbours, we ought to consider the relation in which they stand to us, either in the flesh or in the Lord. "Have we not all one Father? hath not one God created us? why do we deal treacherously every man against his brother?" When Paul requested Philemon to forgive the fault of Onesimus, and receive him again into friendship, he pleaded the cause of the poor penitent, by an argument whose force could not be resisted by so good a man as Philemon, and such a good woman as Apphia, that Onesimus was now more than a servant, a brother, entitled to the love of all the children of the same Heavenly Father.

All men are brethren according to the flesh, for God hath made of one blood all nations and generations of men. All Christians are brethren in the Lord, for they have all received Christ—"And as many as received Him, to them gave He power to become the sons of God." Are we not ashamed before our Father? Are not our hearts pierced with sorrows for the many injuries we have done to those who are connected with us by a relation so endearing? Joseph's brethren could not forgive themselves the wrong they had done to Jacob in their treatment of Joseph. Let us consider what injuries we have done to Christ in the violation of the law of love. When we sin against the brethren, we sin against Christ, their Redeemer, and their Head.

Although the Scripture gives us very impressive views of the evil of our offences against our neighbours, by speaking so much about the relations in which we stand to one another, yet it does not suffer us to forget that there is a more than common malignity in outrages committed against those who, in ordinary language, are our brethren. If we can forget for a moment that we are the children of Adam, or that we call ourselves the children of God, and the brethren of Christ, can we forget who that mother was that bare us, and gave us suck in infancy, or that father who begat us, and who trained us from our infant years in the way wherein we should go? Should we requite them in the persons of their children with injury and insult? Should Cain's example be followed by the children of Seth?

"We are verily guilty concerning our brother, in that we saw the anguish of his soul when he besought us, and we would not hear him." Not only the sin itself, but the circumstances attending it, were bitter to their remembrance. Murderers have often been haunted by the remembrance of the piteous appearance made by those whom they killed in their last moments. No ghost appearing to an innocent man could strike half the terror that the remembrance of the features of murdered children, or grown persons, has often struck into the hearts of their murderers. Joseph's brethren did not know his face at this time, but they could not forget the dismal appearance of his countenance, when he discovered that those whom he took for brethren were assassins. They could not forget his piteous supplications from the pit in which he was confined. "They sat down to eat and drink, and were not grieved for the affliction of Joseph," till it was too late to undo what they had done; but now they felt more bitter grief in the recollection than ever they had made their poor brother endure.

What will become of us when we are in trouble, if God refuse to hear our prayers, when all refuge fails us but God Himself? We are utterly lost if He turns a deaf ear to our cries; but can we hope that He will hear us if we refuse to listen to the requests of the miserable, especially of those who are made miserable by our injustice? God hath taken to Himself this gracious character, The Hearer of Prayer. "He will regard the prayer of the destitute, and He will not despise their prayer." This was written in ancient times, that the generations to come might praise the Lord; but it was also written for the warning of wicked men, that he who turneth away his ear from hearing the law, even his prayer shall be an abomination; and that "he who turneth away his ear from the cry of the poor shall cry himself, and shall not be delivered."

"Therefore is this distress come upon us." Jacob's sons did not think that the man who had treated them with such severity knew anything concerning their conduct to their poor brother, but they knew that there is a God in the heavens, who knoweth and judgeth all the actions of the children of men. In this knowledge they were trained up by their father. But although they had been the children of a man.who knew not God, this reflection might have occurred to them in the day of trouble. Adonibezek, king of Jerusalem, had his education amongst the most hardened sinners that ever lived in the world, and was himself one of the most hard-hearted tyrants that ever disgraced a throne; yet, when sore trouble came upon him, he acknowledged that it was the infliction of just punishment from God, Judges i. It is said of the virtuous Dion, the Syracusan, that when he was compelled to flee from his country, and knocked at some doors that did not open unto him as they would have done in former times, he meekly observed to his servant, that perhaps himself, in the time of his prosperity, had not always opened his door to the stranger.

When we meet from men with treatment which we did not deserve, it may be of use, for calming our spirits, to consider whether we have not been guilty of as bad, or even worse, conduct to some of our neighbours. What if God has commissioned these men who behave ill to us, as His messengers, to execute His anger for offences against some of their fellowmen?

Look forward, ye who have hitherto lived in ease and prosperity. The day of trouble will come. Plant not your dying pillow beforehand with thorns and briars. If no reverse of circumstances should come upon you till you die, yet you are sure that you must die; and a death-bed will be the very worst place for such reflections as an awakened conscience may produce. Bitter was the anguish of Joseph's brethren, but it would have been ten times more bitter if they had seen inevitable death before their eyes. They had little prospect of repairing the injury done to Joseph; but they might yet live to repair in some degree the wrong they had done to their father, and to seek with tears and supplications the forgiveness of their sins from God. Look back on your former conduct. Consider whether you have not done some injuries that may yet be repaired, or neglected some important duties that may yet be done, before you go to that place where there is no counsel, nor device, nor work. O death! how terrible are thy approaches to the man who is conscious that he hath shut his ears against the cry of the poor, or against the loud calls of the Son of God, urging him to improve the space given him for repentance! Those words which he often heard and disregarded in the days when he promised himself many years to come, may force themselves upon his attention. "Because I have called, and ye refused; I have stretched out my hand, and no man regarded; but ye have set at nought all my counsel, and would have none of my reproof: I also will laugh at your calamity; I will mock when your fear cometh; when your fear cometh as desolation, and your destruction cometh as a whirlwind: when distress and anguish cometh upon you."

VER. 22. *And Reuben answered them, saying, Spake I not unto you, saying, Do not sin against the child; and ye would not hear? therefore, behold, also his blood is required.*

"Miserable comforters are ye all," said Job to his friends, who pronounced him to be a wicked man. They came professedly to comfort him, and yet aggravated his distress by false accusations. Reuben did not pretend to be a comforter to his brethren, nor did he charge them with a crime of which he did not know them to be guilty. He was angry with them when they sold Joseph, and his anger was kindled afresh when he thought he was involved in the punishment of their guilt. If you wish to do no hurt to your friends and neighbours, give no offence to God, who might in His righteous providence involve them in the merited consequences of your iniquities. You would not willingly rob your neighbour of the least part of his property. What if, without knowing it, you should contribute to bring upon him some calamity more grievous than the loss of the whole? Reuben was held in prison, and put in great fear of something worse than imprisonment, because his brethren were guilty of a crying iniquity against Joseph.

Do not think that God is unrighteous, when He smites with the sword of His vengeance the righteous as well as the wicked. It is only in a limited sense that men can be called righteous. Jeremiah was a very holy man, and yet he suffered much when Judah was carried to Babylon; but Jeremiah was far from thinking that God was unrighteous, when the righteous suffered with the wicked, or when the wicked enjoyed prosperity, whilst the righteous groaned under oppression, Jer. xii. He knew that by the mercy of God he was truly righteous; but he knew also that he had in many things offended, and that it was only by God's long-suffering that he was preserved alive, Jer. xv.

Reuben had little reason to reflect with severity on the conduct of his brethren. He also had sinned, though in a different way from his brethren. If he had thought upon his own great offence against his father, he would have confessed that he deserved to be punished, as well his brethren who had sinned against Joseph. If he forgot his own sin at this time, he was put in mind of it long after, and found that it had drawn down upon his head, and upon the head of his posterity, more lasting evils than he or his brethren were now suffering. He lost his birth-right, because he had gone up to his father's bed, and defiled his couch, Gen. xlix. 3, 4.

We do not, however, blame him for helping forward the painful convictions of his brethren. Although his reflections were probably drawn forth by his displeasure at their conduct, and the consequences of it to himself, as well as to his brethren, it was fit that they should be made to feel the stings of conscience. It is not an easy matter to deal wisely and safely with a wounded conscience. An interpreter, who is one among a thousand, is to be desired for dealing with a sinner under trouble of body and mind, Job xxxiii. It is necessary to guard him against utter despondency, that he may not say, "There is no hope, why should I wait for the Lord any longer?" But it is necessary, at the same time, to let him know, and, if possible, to make him feel, the danger of his condition, and the malignity of his sins. It is dangerous slightly to heal dangerous wounds, or to say to sinners, Peace, peace, when there is no peace; but it is necessary to show them, that all manner of sin and blasphemy may be forgiven, and that the man who cometh to the blessed Jesus He will in nowise cast out. Convictions of sin cannot be too deep and permanent. But the terror that attends conviction may be very hurtful. The fear of God is very consistent with hope in His mercy, for with Him is plenteous redemption. Job's miserable comforters thought that he was one of the worst of men, but they were far from telling him that there was no help for him in the mercy of God. Eliphaz, in his last speech, told him that he was a merciless oppressor, and no better than an atheist, and that he had brought the awful judgments of God upon himself by his atrocious crimes: "Thou hast sent widows away empty, and the arms of the fatherless have been broken. Thou sayest, How doth God know? can he see through the dark cloud?" What must be the end of such a daring sinner? Surely there can be no succour for him with God? Yes, there is mercy for him in abundance, if he does not refuse it by holding fast his sins. "Acquaint now thyself with him, and be at peace; thereby good shall come unto thee. If thou return to the Almighty, thou shalt be built up, thou shalt put away iniquity far from thy tabernacle. Then shalt thou lay up gold as dust, and the gold of Ophir as the stones of the brook," Job xxii.

" We saw the anguish of his soul when he besought us, and we would not hear." All the intolerable anguish apparent in Joseph recurred to their minds, and harassed their consciences. But Reuben brings to their remembrance another circumstance of their sin, by which it was exceedingly aggravated. He had warned them against that wickedness. He referred it to their own consciences, whether he had not spoken to them, saying, "Do not sin against the child." When we are warned by friends or ministers against any sin, and yet refuse to desist, we add rebellion to iniquity. " He that hateth reproof is brutish." We must give an account for all the dealings of God with us. The admonitions which we have received through His providence will be like burning coals in our bosoms, when our consciences tell us that we have treated them with contempt.

"Do not sin against the child." Their crime was capable of no apology. Did they consider his telling of his dreams an insult? He was but a child. Had they a right to destroy a youth of seventeen years of age, because he had not all the wisdom and caution of a man of thirty? Those men ought never to be fathers who know not how to make allowance for the inexperience of youth.

"Therefore is this distress come upon us," said the nine guilty brethren. Reuben seconds the remonstrances of their own consciences. "Therefore, behold, also his blood is required." Conscience of itself will be a terrible witness against offenders when it is awakened; but its voice will be attended with the testimonies of other dreadful witnesses to verify its charge, and leave the sinner no possibility of opening his mouth to vindicate himself. If you have sinned with others, their society in guilt will not lessen your share in guilt and misery. Was it any consolation to Levi that Simeon had been equally guilty with himself in murdering the Shechemites? Your companions, whether they concurred with you, or refused to share in your rebellion against God, will be witnesses against you. The heavens and the earth will rise up against the workers of iniquity. But the most tremendous of all witnesses against them will be the Lord Himself, in whose book of remembrance every aggravating circumstance of iniquity is recorded.

"Therefore, behold, also his blood is required." Why does he say that his blood was required? They had shed no blood. Judah's remonstrances were more effectual than Reuben's. They would not lay hand upon Joseph, because he was their brother; yet they at first intended to kill Joseph, and their purpose was murder in the sight of God, though not of so black a kind as the actual shedding of his blood would have been. To form a wicked purpose, and to be induced to relinquish it, is less criminal than to hold it fast till it be accomplished; yet the purpose is marked in the book of God's remembrance, till it be pardoned through the great Atonement.   Repentance and atonement are two very different things; and persons may be dissuaded from the execution of a bad purpose without repenting of the sin which it involves.   If Joseph's brethren had altered their bloody purpose from a principle of true repentance, they would have sent him home to his father in peace, and endeavoured to compensate for their intended cruelty by kindness. But the reason, probably, why Reuben charges his brethren with the guilt of blood was, that he thought there were good reasons to believe that death was the consequence of their barbarous treatment of their brother.   In the space of more than twenty years he had not been heard of.   Was it likely that he would never have found means, during all that space of time, to inform his sorrowing father that he was alive? The ten brethren seem to have been all of opinion that he was dead— "One is not."   Had he continued with his father, he might have been still alive (so they might reasonably think).   He was as vigorous as any of his brethren, and younger than most of them ; but by their inhuman conduct they had exposed him to those hardships and sorrows which brought him to an untimely grave.

Although it was not certain that Joseph was dead, yet Reuben had too good reason to charge his brethren with blood-guiltiness. They were guilty of a bloody crime even in the eyes of men. No thanks were due to them for the care that Divine Providence took of him, any more than we owe thanks to the murderers of our Lord, because God brought Him again from the dead. We are accountable for those mischiefs that are the probable consequences of our wilful sins, as much as for the real consequences of them, if we had the same reason to dread them, When we repent of such sins, our grief on the whole will not be so·painful as it would have been if God had not prevented the fatal effects which we had reason to dread ; but the sin is the same, and the grief with which we ought to lament the sin is the same, only it is to be mingled with thankfulness and joy in that mercy which hath counteracted the natural effects of our misconduct.   Two pair of combatants go forth to fight a duel.

One kills his antagonist. Another fires his pistol with a view to kill his neighbour ; but Divine Providence mercifully prevents the shedding of blood. He is no less a murderer in the eye of God than the other, and has the same reason to deplore his bloody purposes. But the other has an additional reason for bitter grief, because God hath suffered him to execute his bloody purpose, and to send into the other world a fellow-creature, who died in an act of wickedness like his own.

You will all say, that whatever crimes are chargeable upon you, the guilt of blood is not in your skirts. Joseph's brethren might probably have said the same thing. They do not say, We are guilty of our brother's blood ; but, We are guilty of turning a deaf ear to his mournful cries. Reuben, however, does not hesitate to charge them in direct terms with the guilt of blood ; and we do not find that they had the courage to contradict him. They could not but see that their cruelty to Joseph had brought on, or might have brought on, his death. Isaiah tells the people of his own time that their hands were full of blood, Isa. i. 15. It is not to be supposed that the generality of the people were chargeable with that kind of murder which would have exposed them to an ignominious death by the laws of their country. But in the eyes of the great Judge, they were stained with blood in such a manner, that when they made many prayers, with hands stretched out to His throne of mercy, He turned away His eyes from beholding them, and His ears from hearing their supplications, Isa. i. 15. Consider what every commandment requires and forbids. " Your sins," by the commandment, if you understand it, " will become in your eyes exceeding sinful."

VER. 23. *And they knew not that Joseph understood them ; for he spake unto them by an interpreter.*

Joseph had been long in Egypt, but he had not forgotten the language which he was first taught to speak, and in which he had often heard his father, and sometimes his grandfather, speak of the glory, and covenant, and laws of God. These early instructions dwelt upon his memory, and were his songs in the land of bondage.

M

But Joseph, wishing to be unknown to his brethren, spake to them by an interpreter. We need not wonder that an Egyptian needed an interpreter to explain what was said by a Canaanite. Some in our island would need an interpreter to explain what is said by others who speak the same language in a different dialect. Time and other circumstances are constantly making changes in language, as in most other things under the sun.

Joseph's brethren would by no means have spoken so freely in his presence about their own wickedness if they had known that he understood their speech. The interpreter, it seems, was not now present, and they knew that they would not betray one another. But it will be our wisdom, not only to take heed to whom we say anything, but to say nothing in the presence of any person (without an urgent reason) that might prove hurtful to ourselves, or to any one else, if it should be published. " Birds of the air may carry the voice, and that which hath wings may tell the matter."

VER. 24. *And he turned himself about from them, and wept ; and returned to them again, and communed with them, and took from them Simeon, and bound him before their eyes.*

The hearing of the bitter reflections made by his brethren upon their barbarous treatment of himself brought rivers of waters from Joseph's eyes. Many passions, many unpleasant and many pleasant remembrances, struggled together in his mind. He tenderly sympathised with the distress of his brethren. He was grieved when he found it necessary to inflict such grief upon men so dear to him, after all they had done to ruin his comfort. He wept at the remembrance of that anguish which he had felt in the day of his calamity, and of the unavailing applications to his hard-hearted brethren, extorted by strong necessity and bitter anguish. He called to mind his afflictions and his misery, the wormwood and the gall ; but he remembered, also, how the Lord had sent from above, and taken and drawn him out of many waters, and set him in a large place, and established his goings.

Although Joseph was now exalted to glory and power, he was not in the place where all tears are wiped from every eye.

We must in this world weep often, even for ourselves; we must often weep for our friends; but "they that sow in tears shall reap in joy." He that "goeth forth and weepeth, bearing precious seed, shall doubtless come again with rejoicing, bringing his sheaves with him."

Joseph wished not that his brethren should see his tears. When he found he could not refrain, he turned himself from them, and wept. Tears shed in secret are the truest indication of the heart. Jeremiah wept in secret places for the calamities coming upon his people, when the Lord's flock was to be carried away captive.

He turned himself again to them as soon as he was able to dry up his tears; and, putting on an air of stern authority, he took Simeon from them, and bound him before their eyes. Simeon was the eldest of his brethren, except Reuben, who shared not in the guilt of what was done to Joseph. All that could be alleged against him in the black affair was, that he did not "resist unto blood, striving against" the sin of his brethren. But if Simeon had been as well inclined as Reuben, it is probable that they might have been able to dissuade all the rest from their cruel purpose. It is probable that Judah would have in that case taken part with them. But it is generally believed, not without plausible grounds, that the hands of Simeon were chief in the trespass. For, on a former occasion, he had given too good proof that, to gratify his passions, he was capable of the most atrocious wickedness. Simeon and Levi, brethren no less in mischief than in blood, in their pride and rage, slew the male inhabitants of a whole city, leaving only the women and children alive as a prey to themselves.

The former behaviour of Simeon and Levi, in whose guilt the other sons of Jacob had some share, concurs with the story of the early part of Joseph's life, to justify the behaviour of Joseph at this time in his treatment of his brethren. We are certainly bound freely to forgive our offending brethren their trespasses; and we justly despise those hypocrites who say that they forgive, but will not forget, the injuries which they have received. But it would be unjust and disingenuous in the highest degree to allege that Joseph acted in this manner, when, although he supplied his brethren with corn, he kept one of them bound in prison till they returned to Egypt. The circumstances of the case required such a behaviour from Joseph as ought not to be made a precedent, unless similar circumstances, or different circumstances of a very uncommon kind, render it advisable. It was not sufficient to satisfy Joseph that he heard his brethren sorely regret their conduct towards himself. In the judgment of charity, he hoped their repentance was sincere; but further proofs of their sincerity were requisite before he could place that confidence which he wished to do in any professions they might have made. Parents are not to be blamed when they forgive their offending but penitent children, although they watch over them with anxious jealousy, lest they should not " bring forth fruits meet for repentance." The surgeon is not to be blamed although he give great pain to his patient, by incisions deeper than appear to ordinary beholders to be necessary. Joseph had too good reason to know the stubborn spirit of some of his brethren, and in particular of Simeon; and who knows but he had particular directions from God about the proper means for taming it ? During the two or three days of his brethren's imprisonment, he had time to acknowledge the Lord in this important affair, and the Lord directed his steps.

You must not be rash in passing judgment on men's conduct. " A tree," says our Lord, " is known by its fruit." And yet there are cases in which the fruit is to be judged of from the tree. If a good man does actions that are certainly bad, that charity which rejoiceth not in iniquity, but rejoiceth in the truth, will not hinder you from assigning them that character which they deserve. But if actions are dubious, charity, which believeth all things, hopeth all things, forbids you to pronounce them bad till better evidence appear. If Joseph had, in any other instance of his conduct, given us reason to believe that he was a man of an unforgiving temper, we might have censured him as an imperious governor, or have at least thought that he did not excel other men in a meek and forgiving temper. But if he was eminent above most men, in any age or country, for wisdom and meekness, we are bound to ascribe the apparent harshness of his conduct to the best of motives. He bound Simeon in prison, but he did it to set him free from far worse chains, in which he had been held by his own fierce passions. Words of reproof were not sufficient. When his own father, the most venerable man at that time in the whole world, reproved him for an enormous crime, he answered him with words of rudeness and impiety.

If we must not judge hastily of the actions of men like ourselves, let us never presume to judge rashly of the ways of God, " whose judgments are past finding out." Was Jesus unkind to Lazarus, because He did not come to heal him at the moment when He heard of his sickness? Did He not show His love to His friend by suffering him to be bound with the cords of death, and to be laid in the place of corruption, before He interposed to deliver him? If men are often cruel because they are kind, is it fit to be said to Him who is love itself, Thou art become cruel to us, because He sees it necessary to bind us with the cords of affliction for our good? Simeon, it is to be hoped, is now praising God in a better world for putting it into the heart of Joseph to bind him in a prison, that he might learn that humility and sober-mindedness to which, in the days of his prosperity, he was a stranger.

" He bound Simeon before their eyes." This circumstance of Simeon's imprisonment puts us in mind of Nebuchadnezzar's cruelty to Zedekiah, king of Judah, whose sons he slew before their father's eyes, and then caused his eyes to be put out, that he might never behold another object. His intention was to double the calamities of the loss of sight, and of the murder of his children. But those actions may be not only different, but opposite in their nature, which present the same appearance when viewed with a careless eye. An enemy wounds that he may destroy, but " faithful are the wounds of a friend." All Joseph's brethren now with him, except Reuben, needed severe rebukes; and no reproofs of the tongue were so likely to subdue their haughty spirit as the sight of the distress of their brother and companion in iniquity. But it is probable that

Joseph's chief design in presenting this melancholy spectacle to their eyes was, that they might be excited to return more speedily with their younger brother, whom Joseph was impatient to see. The eye affects the heart. Envy hindered them from regarding the distress of Joseph in the pit; but it was to be hoped that they would compassionate the sufferings of that brother who had never offended them by his dreams, nor received from his father a coat of divers colours.

We cannot pretend either to the power or to the wisdom of Joseph. We do not enjoy such intercourse with Heaven by immediate revelation as he frequently enjoyed; and, therefore, it would be presumptuous in us to pretend to take such methods as he employed to humble the spirits of those who have offended us. We have never met with usage that can be compared to the treatment which he had received from his brethren. We must not, however, hope to pass through life without trials to our patience and meekness. "Who is a wise man, and endued with knowledge among us? let him show out of a good conversation his works with meekness of wisdom." If we praise Joseph for his kindness to those who sought his life, and deprived him of liberty, whilst we entertain rancorous dispositions towards those who have only wounded our pride by trivial offences, do we not condemn ourselves? Do we not make it too evident that we are not "followers of them who through faith and patience inherit the promises," or of Him who prayed upon the cross for the barbarians who murdered Him?

LECTURE 14

Joseph's brethren return to their father; they are all terrified at finding their money in the mouth of their sacks.

xlii 25–38

VER. 25. *Then Joseph commanded to fill their sacks with corn, and to restore every man's money into his sack, and to give them provision for the way: and thus did he unto them.*

IF a man find his enemy, will he let him go well away? It is not the ordinary manner of men; but it is the manner of such men as Joseph and David to do good to them who have done evil to themselves. Joseph had his enemies in his power, but those enemies were brethren, and servants to the God of his father, by whom Joseph had been helped and blessed. If he inflicted any pain upon his brethren when they came into his power, it was all meant for their good, and it all tended to their good.

If they had not given too good reason to distrust them, we cannot doubt but Joseph would have soon made himself known to them, and sent information to his father, without delay, of his life and glory. But if he had been as hasty in making known the welcome tidings to the good old man, as we might probably have been in like circumstances, what was likely to have been the consequence? Would the message have been faithfully delivered? Was there not reason to fear that Joseph's brethren, ashamed of their former conduct, would have sought to hide their confusion in some other corner of the world, rather than hold up their faces to their father, to inform him that they were murderers, that they had been the wild beasts that bereaved him of his beloved son ? They appeared to be greatly humbled; but better proofs than they had yet given were necessary to satisfy Joseph that he might trust them with the confidence and fondness of a brother.

He commanded to fill their sacks, and to put every man's money in his sack's mouth, and to give them provisions for the way. Thus did Joseph unto them, although they had sold him to be a slave. He heaped coals of fire upon their heads. He not only gave them provisions to be carried to their father, to their wives, and to their children, but provisions for the way, that there might be enough for all their families at their return, till a new supply might be conveniently procured.

He did not sell his benefits to them. He indeed took their money to prevent a suspicion from rising up in their minds that Zaphnath-paaneah was more nearly related to them than he was to others ; for it is likely that he was not yet known to them by the name of Joseph. But he caused their money to be secretly returned. His generosity could not bear the appearance of taking money from his father for the corn which he sold. What he thought it necessary to take with the one hand, he restored with the other. But was it generosity to give away the king's money ? or did he not know that the clandestine restoration of his brethren's money would rather give them pain than pleasure, by the fears which it would awaken in their minds ?

We need not spend many words in vindicating Joseph from the suspicion of dishonesty. He was not one of those corrupt ministers, who think they may do what they please with the money of a nation. He used no more discretionary power than his master authorised him to do. The corn put into his brethren's sacks might be his own private property ; or if it belonged to the king, the emoluments of his office would enable him to put the price into the king's treasury.

Nor have we the least reason to call into question the goodness of Joseph's intention, when he caused the money to be put into the mouths of the sacks. It is easy to see the probable effects of anything after they have taken place. We know what fear was struck into the minds of Jacob and of his sons when they saw the money, but Joseph might not conjecture, or might not at the moment consider, what was to happen. He might think it a doubtful matter whether his father's stock of money did not need a supply in the present famine. But if it occurred to him that his brethren might be uneasy at the sight of the money, his intention was not to make them unhappy by distressing fears. He had already found that his brethren derived much benefit from the fear struck into their minds by his harsh treatment ; and if new fears disquieted them, these also might be useful to their souls. Many strokes of the hammer are necessary to form hard iron into the shape intended by the workman.

VER. 26. *And they laded their asses with the corn, and departed thence.*

They were happy (although they were compelled to leave one of their number) that liberty was at last given them to leave the country, and that they had a good supply of corn to carry to their father, and to their wives and children, who were impatient for their return, and often looking out of their tents to discover them from a distance, as soon as they should make their appearance.

Men in respectable conditions of life were not ashamed in those days of simplicity either to ride on asses (Judges v.) or to use those animals which are despised amongst us in carrying their provisions or commodities. David, in his glory, was not ashamed to ride upon a mule. Our Lord rode into Jerusalem on a colt, the foal of an ass.

VER. 27. *And as one of them opened his sack to give his ass provender in the inn, he espied his money : for, behold, it was in his sack's mouth.*

It was not in an inn like those which are frequented by us, but in the house usually frequented by travellers, according to the custom of the country, that this son of Jacob happened to observe the money that had been put into the mouth of his sack. His joy and that of his brethren was damped at the sight of the money.

VER. 28. *And he said unto his brethren, My money is restored ; and, lo, it is even in my sack ; and their heart failed them, and they were afraid, saying one to another, What is this that God hath done unto us ?*

" Could we get clear away from the tyrant, who so causelessly takes us for spies, we would be happy." So they would think when he was charging them with bad designs, and confining them in his prison. Now they were in a hopeful condition. Simeon was left behind them when they were dismissed, yet they saw an easy method to regain his liberty. That austere man, the lord of the country, had compromised matters in such a manner, as gave them better presages than they at first could entertain. Yet, after all, they did not know what to think of him when one of them found his money in the mouth of his sack. In all appearance, the money was returned by his order for some bad purpose.

Yet, on the other side, they might have thought it very unlikely that he would have let them go well away if his intentions were bad. He had power given him by Pharaoh to bind his own subjects in chains at his pleasure. Surely he had power likewise to treat strangers as he thought fit. If he had meant to kill them, or to make them slaves, they were in his power.

But the minds of Jacob's sons were at this time liable to the impressions of fear. They had but lately escaped from imprisonment, and a slight appearance of danger was sufficient to awaken new terrors in their hearts. They were like a man newly recovered from a dangerous distemper. Every slight pain in his head alarms him.

They had, however, learned one good lesson, that all their troubles and dangers were the appointments of a righteous Providence. " What is this that God hath done to us ?" They do not think so much of the cruel governor of Egypt as of the God of heaven. He had been requiring the tears and blood of Joseph at their hands ; and although He had given them a respite, it appeared to them that He had not yet done with them. He had led them, and brought them into darkness, and not into light. And what might be the end of His present dispensations, no man could tell them.

It might have occurred to them, as the most proper measure on the present occasion, to search the other sacks, in order to find whether the same trick had been played with them all, and to contrive some method of sending back the money, if they were afraid to return with it in person. But when men are in distress, they are unwilling to make those inquiries that might add to their trouble, and wish to put sorrow to as great a distance as possible, although by that means they should make it incurable. Happy is the man who trusteth in God. He knows that God will do nothing to him inconsistent with His precious promises, and suffer no man to inflict any calamity that shall not be overruled to his good. Whilst others are troubled and perplexed by the evils which befall them, believers in God are kept in perfect peace, because their minds are stayed on Him.

"They said one to another, What is this that God hath done unto us?" They all spoke the same language of despondency. None of them, as far as we find, administered any comfort to his companions. It is an unhappy thing when in a company of men not one is found who can speak a word in season, for advice or consolation to his companions in trouble. It is reported that in a time of persecution some faithful ministers met together to deliberate about their duty. All of them for a time were silent, or if anything was said, it tended only to increase the general dejection. At last they all recovered their spirits at hearing one of their number say, "We are all immortal till our work is done." These few words gave effect to a truth which they already knew, that their days were numbered by a divine decree, and that it was not in the power of all the men on earth to cut them off from the land of the living a moment before the time appointed by the wisdom and love of that God whom they served.

VER. 29. *And they came unto Jacob their father unto the land of Canaan, and told him all that befell unto them; saying.*

When men return from a long journey to their parents and

friends, they ordinarily entertain them with an account of all that has befallen them, or of those remarkable things which they have seen. And such conversation may be useful as well as entertaining. At all times we have reason to bless God. When we are allowed to return again to our habitation without meeting with any bad accident, we see new reasons of thankfulness to Him who keeps our going out and our coming in, who suffers not the sun to smite us by day, nor the moon by night, who keepeth our feet from falling, who preserves us from all evil. "Thou shalt visit thy tabernacle, and shalt not sin." This is one of the advantages of true penitence which was promised to Job by his friends. Their error consisted, not so much in mistaken views of the happiness attending true religion, as in their misapplication of their doctrines to Job.

When we meet with troubles and dangers, if our parents are alive, to whom can we with more propriety utter our complaints, than to persons so tenderly solicitous about our welfare? Jacob's sons might reasonably expect counsel, direction, and comfort from their father when they told him how roughly they had been used by the man who was the lord of the country. If he could do nothing else for them, he was a prophet, and would pray for them. It was not in his power to redress their imagined wrongs, but "the effectual fervent prayer of a righteous man availeth much."

Some of you, perhaps, have no father alive, or no earthly friend to whom you can tell your grievances, with any hope of advantage from their sympathy. But have you not a Father in heaven? Does all refuge fail you? does no man care for your souls? Let God be your refuge and your portion in the land of the living. He will perfect that which concerns you. Jacob's sons could not inform their father of the hardships they had undergone till the danger was in a great measure over, and he could do little to help them. You can at all times make your requests known unto God, and He is a very present help in the time of trouble, Heb. iv. 16.

VER. 30-34. *The man, who is the lord of the land, spake roughly to us, and took us for spies of the country. And we said unto him, We are true men; we are no spies: we be twelve brethren, sons of our father; one is not, and the youngest is this day with our father in the land of Canaan. And the man, the lord of the country, said unto us, Hereby shall I know that ye are true men; leave one of your brethren here with me, and take food for the famine of your households, and be gone: and bring your youngest brother unto me: then shall I know that ye are no spies, but that ye are true men: so will I deliver you your brother, and ye shall traffick in the land.*

In this changeable world, we should be prepared for hearing evil as well as good tidings, for our condition is wisely made up of mercies and trials. It is said of the good man, that "he shall not be afraid of evil tidings, for his heart is fixed, trusting in the Lord." He is so far from thinking that his faith was vain when he hears of evil befalling him, that in such times, above all others, he finds it is no vain thing to trust in the Lord. And yet he sometimes finds it difficult to maintain his faith without wavering. Jacob anxiously waited for the return of his sons. When Simeon was not with them, his heart would misgive him. What if that fierce young man had, by some new daring enterprise, brought upon himself that vengeance which he had too well deserved on a former occasion. But he is informed by his sons that Simeon was unjustly held in bondage by the lord of Egypt, who had behaved to them all in an imperious manner, suspecting them to be spies, and had shut up Simeon in prison, to be there confined till they all returned with their younger brother Benjamin, as a proof that they were not spies, but true men. The good old man was grieved, yet perhaps he was glad to find matters no worse.

In this narrative, Jacob's sons gave their father a very bad idea of the lord of Egypt. They said nothing of him but the truth, and yet Jacob must have formed an opinion of him far remote from the truth. He appeared to be an insolent, overbearing tyrant, that made use of his power to crush poor men under his feet. We could not greatly blame either Jacob or his sons if they believed the man who treated them with such unmerited severity to be wholly destitute of the fear of God, and of humanity towards men. The appearance does not always correspond to the reality of things—"Judge not, that ye be not judged." If ye must needs judge, wait for evidence— "Better is the end of a thing than the beginning thereof." The man who was the lord of the country dealt hardly with the sons of Jacob, and pretended to hold them for spies, and kept Simeon by violence in a prison for a crime imputed to him without shadow of proof, and refused to liberate him till all his brethren should again put themselves in his power.

"Surely," might Jacob have said, "the fear of God is not before the eyes of this man, who shows so little regard to the comfort, the liberty, the lives of his fellow-men." Yet Joseph's conduct towards his brethren was full of wisdom and mercy. He dealt hardly with them, that he might do them good. He dealt most hardly with Simeon, and it is probable that he did more good to him than to any of them. The provisions and money that he gave to his nine brethren were not so useful to them as bonds and imprisonment to Simeon, if he made that use of his affliction which Joseph intended.

Joseph's brethren, in their younger years, suggested a very false account of his fate to their father. They gave him a true account of Simeon's condition, for they had no temptation to prevaricate concerning him. It was necessary to give a just statement of facts, that Jacob might be induced to send down Benjamin to Egypt, since they could on no other terms expect the liberation of Simeon. It is no evidence of integrity that a man speaks the truth when he has no temptation to lie. The upright man is he who at all times speaketh the truth in his heart.

Jacob was greatly distressed at the report of the condition on which Simeon was to gain his liberty. The sight of the money found in the mouth of the sacks added to his fear.

VER. 35. *And it came to pass, as they emptied their sacks, that, behold, every man's bundle of money was in his sack; and when both they and their father saw the bundles of money, they were afraid.*

Gold and silver are bright metals. They dazzle the eye of

the greater part of mankind. Achan saw a gold wedge, and, in defiance of an awful curse, took it to his tent. Yet when Jacob and his sons saw heaps of money in the mouths of their sacks, they were terrified as if they had seen a serpent. For what reason were they afraid at a sight so generally desired? They thought that this money was a snare laid for their lives. And have not many rich men still greater reason to tremble when they look at their gold and silver? All money unjustly got, or unrighteously or unmercifully kept, is a snare to the possessor, and will rise up to witness against him in the day of accounts. Such riches are corrupted and cankered, and the rust of them shall be a witness against the owners, and eat their flesh as it were fire.

But Jacob and his sons had no good reason to be afraid when they saw the money. It came not from an artful knave, but from a kind son and brother, who was tenderly solicitous about his father and brethren, that they should not come to poverty. Our fears often proceed from our ignorance and mistake. We are afraid of those evils that will never come, and stand in no fear of those that will come. Happy are they who can commit all their affairs to Him who knows everything that shall befall us.

Jacob's sons were afraid at the inn when they were told of money in one of their sacks. But the fears which they had endeavoured to forget were awakened anew at the opening of all their sacks. Every little circumstance heightens the distress of minds already dejected; and therefore, in dangerous circumstances, it is necessary to our peace and happiness to have our minds fortified with the consolations of God. "The wicked fleeth when no man pursueth, but the righteous is bold as a lion."

Yet even the righteous man may tremble through the weakness of his faith, or through the strength of his sensibilities. Jacob was not free from fear on account of his sons. There is a different expression used when his fear is spoken of from that which had been formerly used concerning his children. Their heart, it is said, failed them, and they were afraid. Here it is only said they were afraid.　The hearts of good men have some-times failed them; yet ordinarily their faith in God moderates their fears, as well as their other passions.　Jacob knew that God had spoken good concerning his house.　He knew by experience the faithfulness of the Promiser.　When he trembled exceedingly at the report of four hundred men coming against him, with his brother at their head, he prayed, and made supplication to God, who delivered him from the sword of Esau. Yet the promise of God did not secure the preservation of individual members of his family.　Joseph was lost, Simeon too, and Benjamin might be lost to him for ever.

VER. 36. *And Jacob their father said unto them, Me have ye bereaved of my children : Joseph is not, and Simeon is not, and ye will take Benjamin away : all these things are against me.*

We might have expected some better words from Jacob than those which we have here recorded; but we know not what more words he might speak on the present occasion, to teach his children how they ought to improve their distresses, and to seek help from God.　Certainly he was not negligent to put them in remembrance of the duty of humbling themselves under the mighty hand of God.

The words before us are the expressions of that peevishness and dejection which are ready to find place in the heart even of a good man in a day of darkness.　"Me have ye bereaved of my children : all these things are against me."　We ought, however, to remember, that words expressive of the passionate working of the mind ought always to be understood with a limitation of their import.　When Jacob says that he was bereaved of his children, the meaning is, that he was bereaved of two or three of them.　When he speaks of his sons then present, as if they had bereaved him of his children, he does not mean that they had murdered them, or sold them into a strange land.　He means, that by their unwise conduct they had some agency in bringing the calamity upon them. If they had not rambled about with their flocks from one place to another, Joseph might not have met with those wild beasts that tore him in pieces.　If they had not, by some imprudent conduct, excited suspicion in the mind of the hard-hearted governor of Egypt, Simeon would not have been kept in prison. If they had not spoken to the governor about their younger brother, he might still have been left with himself when they returned to buy more corn.

Jacob, however, spoke more truth than he knew in these words, "Me have ye bereaved of my children." They had sold Joseph into Egypt, and Simeon's imprisonment was the consequence of that criminal conduct. But as we have no reason to think that Jacob suspected them to be guilty, his words are to be considered as an angry reflection, which the distress of his mind drew from his lips rather than his heart. When your minds are disturbed, be watchful over your tongue. Beware of ill-natured reflections on your children, your servants, or any that are under your power. But, on the other side, let not children or servants be surprised or angry when unjust reflections are uttered or glanced at them by their parents or masters, when grief rather than reason has the direction of their tongues. We must all bear something from our fellow-mortals, and we all make some of our neighbours bear something from us that might be spared. There are few of whom it can be said, as it was of Charles VIII., King of France, that he was never in his whole life seen to be angry. In some instances he met with exceedingly bad usage, and yet he never lost possession of himself.

"Joseph is not." He was torn with beasts above twenty years before that time, as Jacob had reason to think; and he could never forget that beloved son. Jacob was not singular. Some of you who are parents think you have lost the best and most beloved of your children. Perhaps you are right, but it is as likely that you are wrong in thinking so. You probably felt no peculiar warmth of affection for them when you saw them in good health at the side of your table. Their sickness, the fears which tortured your minds in their days of life, the stroke that separated you from them, called forth your fondness, and you felt your love to them working more powerfully than the love you bore to other children, whom you would have found equally dear to you if their circumstances had required the same tenderness of affection.

N

But if you are conscious that those whom death has separated from you were the dearest to your hearts of all your family, remember Jacob. Joseph was dead to him for at least two and twenty years after he was sold into Egypt. He was indeed restored to his father after many days. So shall your favourite child be, if God blessed your endeavours to bring him up "in the nurture and admonition of the Lord." Mourn not like those who have no hope; "for if we believe that Jesus died and rose again, then them also who sleep in Jesus will God bring with him."

"Joseph is not, and Simeon is not." More is said than meant, and more was meant than what was true, in these words. The patriarch knew that Simeon was not dead, as far as this information reached, but he was almost given over as a dead man by his father. Yet he had not any strong reason to do it. Perhaps the money came by some oversight into the mouth of the sacks. Probably that hard man, who was lord of Egypt, did not intend to put Simeon to death; or if he did, his heart might yet be softened by the God of Jacob. We make our burdens heavier than they ought to be by adding to them the weight of our own gloomy apprehensions; or we represent them heavier than we feel them to be by words that convey more meaning than they ought. Surely the troubles laid upon us are heavy enough to be borne. Why should we court unhappiness, and yet complain of it?

"Joseph is not, and Simeon is not." A certain good woman, in a time of persecution, heard that one of her sons was killed in the field by the enemy. "Which of my sons?" said she. "The eldest," said the informer. "God be thanked," replied she, "he was the fittest to die. My other children will have some more time for preparation, and needed it more than their brother." Yet Jacob was more grieved for the loss of Joseph than for the loss of Simeon, although Joseph was sanctified in his early years; and Simeon, for anything we can learn, had yet given little evidence of piety. But it must be remembered that Jacob was only afraid that Simeon might die. Joseph was in his apprehension already dead. I believe that a good man, were it referred to his choice which of his children he must lose, would refer it to his Maker ; but it would be his deliberate wish that, if God pleased, He would remove to the other world that member of his family who was fittest for it, though much the dearest to himself.

"And ye will take Benjamin away." True ; they would take him away to Egypt, but not out of the world. To go a long journey was a very different thing from dying. He might be exposed to danger from the artifices of the unfeeling lord of Egypt. But will such a good man as Jacob make himself and his house miserable because a favourite son may be lost, when he was not exposed to greater danger than his brethren ? Even those who are eminent fearers of God are too often deprived of a great part of that happiness which they might enjoy by the infirmity of their faith.

"All these things are against me." How did Jacob know this ? Because his feelings, his affections, and the general sense of mankind told him that it was a great misery to lose a son, especially the best and most beloved of sons. But our feelings are often liars. The general voice of mankind is not always the voice of truth. But Jacob was more excusable than we would be, should we estimate our happiness or misery by our feelings, or by the sentiments of the world around us. Jacob never saw our Lord's Sermon on the Mount, in which He declares that mourners are blessed, because they shall be comforted. He never saw those holy writings which instruct Christians to call them happy which endure. Yet Jacob knew, from the revelations granted to himself, or to more ancient patriarchs, that God is good in what He withholds or takes away, as well as in what He gives. Job v.

As there is a great difference in the attainments even of the saints who are equally eminent, so is it likewise in the attainments of the same saints at different times. Job, it is likely, was not on the whole a greater proficient in holiness than Jacob, and yet when Job lost, not two or three sons, but all his sons and all his daughters, ten in number, all at one blow, he said, "Naked came I out of my mother's womb, and naked shall I

return thither.   The Lord gave, and the Lord hath taken away;
blessed be the name of the Lord."   Yet the same Job, at
another time, said, that the God whom he trusted was become
cruel unto him.

"All these things are against me."   The very reverse was
the case, as Jacob afterwards found.   Joseph was sent before
him into Egypt to provide sustenance for the family.   Simeon
was bound in prison to mortify his haughty spirit.   Benjamin
was to be taken away, that he might find Joseph alive and
happy.   We know that "all things work together for good to
them that love God, to them that are the called according to his
purpose."   Let us learn to apply this known truth to our particular cases; and that we may do it with ease and pleasure,
let us endeavour with diligence "to make our calling and
election sure," and to abound in the fruits of love to God.
"Blessed is the man that endureth temptation; for when he is
tried, he shall receive of the Lord the crown of life which he
hath promised to them that love him."

VER. 37.   *And Reuben spake unto his father, saying, Slay my
two sons, if I bring him not to thee : deliver him into my hand,
and I will bring him to thee again.*

I will give you leave to take away my life, unless I do this
or that.   Such modes of speaking as this do not become the
mouths of the disciples of our Redeemer.   How do we know
what we shall be able to do a day or an hour hence?   We ought
to say, If we live, and the Lord will, we shall do this or that;
"for a man's heart deviseth his way, but the Lord directeth his
steps."

When men use this language, their words are not to be
understood in their literal sense.   They are only strong asser-
tions, tinctured with a profane levity of mind.   Death ought
not to be made a by-word.   It will be found a serious thing
to die when death comes, if it is not habitually esteemed a
serious matter by us whilst we are living in prosperity and
health.

"By the life of Pharaoh, ye are spies," said Joseph to his
brethren.   Reuben engages, by the life of his two sons, that

he will bring Benjamin in safety to his father, if his father would trust the young man to his care.

Surely Reuben might have learned to avoid such strong asseverations about things of this sort. It was his wish to bring Joseph home to his father, and yet he could not persuade his brethren to comply with his intentions. It was his desire to bring Simeon safe to his father, and yet he was compelled to leave him in Egypt. He had reason to hope that his brethren would not treat Benjamin as they had treated Joseph. He had reason to hope that the lord of Egypt would keep his promise. But was he so sure of both these things, and of meeting with no bad accident in the course of his journeyings, that he could warrantably pledge the life of his two sons for Benjamin's happy return? He knew that Jacob would not take him at his word. But what if God should, by some untoward event, make him sensible that he had spoken amiss?

Jacob does not seem to have loved his children's children so dearly as his own children. When he spake of his family disasters, he made no mention of the fate of Er and Onan, which was much more dismal than Joseph's fate, although he had been really torn asunder by wild beasts. Perhaps he was less acquainted with Judah's children than with some others of his grandchildren. He certainly loved all the members of his family with all the fondness of the most affectionate of parents ; and Reuben might have drawn a much wiser argument from the consideration of his family to engage his father's compliance with their wishes. I have few children. My brethren have many children. For their sakes let Benjamin go with us. Is it not better to risk thy beloved son, than to suffer eleven sons, and more than fifty grandchildren, to perish by hunger? Jacob would have found no satisfaction for the loss of his son in the death of his grandchildren. But he would lay up stores of bitter reflections for himself, if his grandchildren were suffered to perish in his partial fondness for one son.

VER. 38. *And he said, My son shall not go down with you ; for his brother is dead, and he is left alone: if mischief befall him by the way in the which ye go, then shall ye bring down my gray hairs with sorrow to the grave.*

" My son shall not go down with you ; for his brother is dead." But had Jacob no more than two sons when Joseph was alive ? Had Benjamin no brothers yet alive ? Why does Jacob thus make such a distinction between the children of Rachel and his other children, as might kindle up envy among those who were equally related to himself ? It is well for us that we are so strictly prohibited from having more wives than one at the same time. It seems to have required more than all the wisdom of Abraham or Jacob to govern with impartiality a family born of different mothers. And let those fathers who have children by different wives in succession pray for wisdom to rule their houses in such a manner, that whilst they show their paternal fondness to the children of the one, they do no injustice, in word or deed, to the children of the other.

" His brother is dead." If mischief befalls this only son of her that bare him, I will be inconsolable ; ye shall bring my gray hairs with sorrow to the grave. Jacob speaks as a man of like ungoverned passions with his neighbours. His ardent affection to the son of Rachel and the brother of Joseph seems in the moment of anxiety to have overpowered his wisdom and his grace. Let Rachel's surviving son be fondly cherished by his father. Let all the love which Jacob bore to Rachel and Joseph be transferred to Benjamin. But was Leah nothing ? are all her sons nothing to Jacob ? They did not expect the same degree of affection ; but some degree of parental kindness might be expected by them. Benjamin, no doubt, might meet with mischief in the course of the journey, but was he in greater danger than his brethren ? His danger, in all appearance, was less. The stern governor's suspicions did not extend to Benjamin. He could not be suspected as a spy. He was sent for by the governor, who had promised to dismiss him in safety.

We can more easily justify or excuse Jacob's great fondness for Joseph, than his visible partiality to Benjamin. Yet we cannot tell what reasons he might have, from Benjamin's own conduct, to love him above his brethren. But he could scarcely have a good excuse (unless his great grief may excuse him) for publishing so loudly and so often his extreme partiality for his favoured son. One pleasing reflection we may make, that Jacob's sons were not now what they once had been. A coat of divers colours given to Joseph almost proved fatal to him, yet a partiality of a more grating kind did not alienate their hearts from Benjamin. If they had used the same freedom with their father that Joab could use with David, they might have said to him, "We perceive this day, that if Benjamin live, although we should all die, it will not greatly displease thee." But they respected their father's grief, they bore meekly with his reflections, and were as careful of Benjamin's life as of their own when it was in danger.

"If mischief befall him by the way in the which ye go, then shall ye bring down my gray hairs with sorrow to the grave." He puts them in mind of his gray hairs. Some graceless children despise their fathers and their mothers when they are old, and when their gray hairs claim reverence or compassion. If we must bow before the man of hoary hairs, although he is a stranger, what reverence do we owe to our own parents, when the respect due to age is added to the claims of parental relation! Those children that load the gray heads of their parents with crushing sorrows, are worse than common murderers. Yet let not parents, by their own frowardness, kill themselves with grief, and load their children with the blame due to themselves. The aged ought to remember that their infirmities may dispose them to make their burdens heavier than God or men have made them. And when we torment ourselves, we are too ready to transfer our own folly to the account of others.

Why should Jacob die with grief, if Benjamin should be lost? Is Benjamin his God, his life, his exceeding joy? "The Lord liveth, and blessed be the Rock of Israel." He is the Rock of Ages. God had made desolate all Job's company, and his hope had he removed like a tree; but Job knew that his Redeemer lived. "All flesh is grass, and all the goodliness thereof is as the flower of the grass; but the word of the Lord shall stand for ever." And whilst the word stands, those whose trust is placed on it are safe. They may, through the prevalence of unbelief and of earthly affections, speak unadvisedly with their lips; but the Lord will make them sensible of their folly, and enable them to commit their affairs into his hand, and to cast all their cares upon Him who cares for all His people. We shall soon hear Jacob saying, "If I am bereaved of my children, I am bereaved;" and on his death-bed he says, "I have waited for thy salvation, O Lord!"

LECTURE 15

Jacob sends his sons the second time into Egypt to buy corn.

xliii 1–14

VER. 1. *And the famine was sore in the land.*

FAMINE is, at the best, a very sore calamity; but a famine continuing year after year must be almost intolerable. What will a man not do for bread, when almost none is to be found in the country? Bless the Lord, who gives us rain from heaven, and fruitful seasons, filling our hearts with food and gladness.

VER. 2. *And it came to pass, when they had eaten up the corn which they had brought out of Egypt, their father said unto them, Go again, buy us a little food.*

Poor Simeon was left in the house of bondage. Although he was to continue there till the return of his brethren, yet they did not return till their own necessities compelled them. Who knows how long he might have been left to pine in his dismal prison if bread could have been procured any other way but by going down to Egypt? We do not, indeed, see why Jacob might not have procured corn by traders from Canaan, or by Midianitish caravans. Whether trade was ruined in those dismal days, or whether Jacob and his sons were struck with horror at the idea of procuring corn by other hands, whilst Simeon was left in captivity, Jacob, when the corn brought from Egypt was nearly spent, proposed that his sons should go in person, and fetch another cargo. They had indeed met with difficulties and danger in their former journey, but great difficulties and dangers must often be encountered to prevent worse.

Let it not be thought a hard matter that we may be called to encounter dangers, or to undertake difficult works, for the benefit of our souls, or in the service of Christ. The world requires as great sacrifices as Christ, and is less able to make us a recompence. In labouring for the meat that endureth to everlasting life, we seldom meet with such difficulties and perils as are often encountered in labouring for the meat that perisheth.

VER. 3. *And Judah spake unto him, saying, The man did solemnly protest unto us, saying, Ye shall not see my face, except your brother be with you.*

Reuben had tried to gain Jacob's consent to part with his Benjamin, and it was not to be wondered at that he was unsuccessful. Judah, a man much superior in prudence and activity to Reuben, attempts the difficult task, and gains his point. A man of good sense is a blessing to the societies with which he is connected, when he makes a good use of it.

Jacob was king, but not a tyrant, in his own house. His children obeyed him, but were not hindered from objecting to commands that appeared to them hard or impracticable. In the present case, there was an insurmountable difficulty in the way of obedience, which Jacob only could remove. "My son shall not go down with you," said Jacob; but Judah tells him that the man who ruled over Egypt did not merely say, but solemnly protest to them, that they should not again see his face, or traffic in the land, unless they brought with them their younger brother. Their father did not wish them to go in vain to Egypt. He did not desire them to confirm the unjust suspicions that had been entertained concerning them.

VER. 4, 5. *If thou wilt send our brother with us, we will go down and buy thee food: but if thou wilt not send him, we will not go down: for the man said unto us, Ye shall not see my face, except your brother be with you.*

"Children, obey your parents in the Lord, for this is right."

But let parents take heed that they provoke not their children to resist their commands, by enjoining that which is unjust, unreasonable, or impracticable. Judah was justifiable in making conditions with his own venerable father. But to object to the commands of a parent, without an urgent reason, is consistent neither with the law of Christ nor with the law of nature. The command of Jacob was not simply to go to Egypt, but to go and fetch corn from Egypt. This was impracticable, unless Benjamin went along with his brethren.

Every wise man will consider, when he undertakes a journey, or any great work, for what purpose it is designed, and how it may be executed so as to answer the end. What man would have travelled all the way from the place where Jacob sojourned in Canaan to Egypt, to buy corn in the time of famine, without the prospect of being able to obtain it? What man will plough or sow his land, without the prospect of a crop? What wise man will undertake any religious employment, without the prospect of obtaining the wished advantage to be found in the service of God? If those who call themselves the children of light were half as wise in their generation as the children of this world, when they wish to have the oil of grace, they would go to those who sell before the door is shut, and would not go without their Elder Brother, without whom no man can come to the Father with acceptance. It is said of the famous Themistocles, that when he fled for refuge to Admetus, King of Thessaly, he took the king's infant son in his arms, and obtained what he requested. He had been told that this was the law of the court of Admetus. And this is the law of God's house, that we cannot come with success to the throne of God's grace, but in the name of Christ, the only Mediator between God and sinful men.

VER. 6. *And Israel said, Wherefore dealt ye so ill with me, as to tell the man whether ye had yet a brother?*

Israel's mind was at present so intent upon one object, that he overlooked everything else. Everything that contributed to bring this great distress upon him, of parting with Benjamin, appeared an injury. It is true, the governor of Egypt would not have sent for Benjamin if he had not heard of him. But was it therefore a crime in Jacob's sons to speak of him? Beware of imputing blame in your passion where none can be attached. Think not that every man deals ill with you who is the innocent occasion of some distress, that neither he nor any other man could foresee. A man in pain will complain of the stone on which he happens to stumble, as if it had been capable of imagining his hurt; and of the friend that endeavours to serve him, as if he were an enemy, when his endeavours to do him good do not answer expectation.

Be not soon angry with men in grief, although they say some things that should not be said, or say them in the manner in which they ought not to be said. Children, bear with the infirmities of afflicted or of aged parents. When their words are not such as children may expect to hear from an affectionate father, let your own words be such as may be expected from a dutiful child. Hear with what meekness and respect Judah's brethren answer the sullen reflections of his father. They do not ask him, Where was the great calamity of telling any man that they had another brother? They do not tell him that he sought occasion to reproach them without any shadow of ground. But they calmly remind him that they were under a necessity of informing the man concerning their younger brother, and that it was impossible for them to foresee the use that would be made of the information.

VER. 7. *And they said, The man asked us straitly of our state, and of our kindred, saying, Is your father yet alive? have ye another brother? and we told him according to the tenor of these words: could we certainly know that he would say, Bring your brother down?*

To the good government of the tongue, it is necessary, not only that we say nothing that is not true to the best of our knowledge, but that we do not say even what is true, when the telling of it would serve no good purpose. Words that are not false may be vain, and even mischievous words, when they are not in season. David found it sometimes his duty to refrain his lips even from speaking good, and Doeg was rooted out of the land of the living for telling Saul what was true concerning the kind entertainment given by Ahimelech to David, Ps. lii.

Jacob's sons could clear themselves from the blame of publishing rashly the state of their father's house. The man asked them straitly concerning their state and their kindred, saying, " Is your father yet alive? have ye yet another brother?" What could they answer? They could not be silent, without strengthening the suspicion entertained of them. If they were under a necessity of answering these questions, they were bound to speak the truth. Interest as well as duty forbids men to lie, for a lie is always liable to detection. And men exposed to danger from suspicions unjustly conceived against them ought above all other men to avoid everything that may be found not strictly true. If one lie be found in their mouths, twenty more will probably be imputed to them.

Some have called in question the truth of what Jacob's sons said at this time to their father, because there is no account in what we have already been told by Moses of the close examination of Joseph's brethren. But we must not hold men for liars because we never formerly heard of what they tell us. Who ever thought that the sacred historian was under an obligation to tell us every particular that passed between Joseph and his brethren?

We are not accountable for the bad use that may be made of what we say, unless we could have foreseen the probability of it. Who could have imagined that the governor of Egypt would desire to see the young brother of those men whom he held to be spies? If we were answerable for consequences to which we give no just or probable occasion, we must cease from speaking or doing anything good or bad. The consequence of Christ's speaking to the Jews was, that the sin of many of them remained, and that their wickedness became enormous, John xv.; and yet He never spake a vain or ill-timed word.

VER. 8. *And Judah said unto Israel his father, Send the lad with me, and we will arise and go; that we may live, and not die, both we, and thou, and also our little ones.*

How forcible are right words! Jacob could not resist the

force of Judah's argument. He loved Benjamin dearly, but he loved all his other children, and all his little grandchildren; and surely he would not suffer them all to perish with hunger, that he might have the pleasure of enjoying the company of Benjamin. He stood in fear of Benjamin's life if he should go to Egypt. But the danger was greater on the other side. He was more likely to die if he did not go to Egypt; and it is more painful to die by hunger than by some fatal accident in a journey. But, indeed, the danger of perishing in the course of the journey appeared to Judah to be only imaginary.

VER. 9. *I will be surety for him; of my hand shalt thou require him: if I bring him not unto thee, and set him before thee, then let me bear the blame for ever.*

Judah must have known that his brethren were quite different men from what they once had been, when he became surety for Benjamin; nor did he entertain such a bad opinion of the governor of Egypt as his father seems to have done. It is not good to be rash, but neither is it good to be timorous. A proper mixture of fear and hope, in difficult and dangerous circumstances, is exceedingly useful. "The wise man feareth and departeth from evil. The prudent man looketh well to his goings, whilst the simple, who believes every word, passes on, and is punished." But although the prudent man will not pass on fearlessly, like the simple man, he will not stand still or go backward when he ought to go forward. The sluggard is a fool. He says, "There is a lion in the way, and I shall be slain in the streets." Who ever saw a lion in the streets, except those lions that are led about for spectacle? But if there should be a lion in the streets, will a man be in greater danger from the teeth of a lion than from the evil arrows of famine? Judah could not certainly say that either himself or Benjamin would return in safety from Egypt; but he saw that it was less unsafe to venture the journey than to tarry at home; and he trusted that the God who had fed Jacob all his lifelong, and the angel who had redeemed him from all trouble, would not leave the sons of Jacob unprotected when they went to procure food for their father and for his family.

" When ye intend to go into a city to buy or sell, say, If the Lord will, we shall live, and do this or that ;" but it is not necessary always to use these express words. Men may use them without a just impression of what they mean, and they are often to be understood when they are not expressed. Judah certainly knew that it depended entirely on the will of God, whether he or his brother should live another hour. When he became surety for Benjamin, he took it for granted that his father would attach no blame to him for what could neither be foreseen nor avoided.

VER. 10. *For except we had lingered, surely now we had returned the second time.*

Jacob's fondness for Benjamin was too great ; and in the consequence of it, we see how dangerous it is to suffer our affections to overbear our judgment. Simeon was detained much longer in prison than he might have been ; and the family of Jacob was reduced to a stinted allowance of provision, because Jacob would not suffer Benjamin to leave him. Besides, if he had suffered Benjamin to leave him some time before, when his other sons wished to go, Benjamin, along with Simeon, might, by this time, have both returned to their father's house. Men, blinded by affection, too often disappoint themselves. They lose that enjoyment of the objects of their affection which they might have if they were duly kept under the government of reason and religion.

" If we had not lingered, surely we might have returned this second time." Beware of needless and unwise delays. Surely we might all have enjoyed much more happiness than we do if we would always have observed this rule, to defer nothing till to-morrow that ought to have been done to-day. We hesitate when we ought to resolve. When our resolution is fixed, we linger, we stop short. Thus multitudes are miserable in this world, and likely to be miserable in the next, because they will not act like rational creatures. What comfort would it have been for Jacob if all had been over, if Benjamin had been already brought back from Egypt, and Simeon, and many assloads of corn with him ! What was the reason why the good man did not enjoy this comfort at that moment? The reason plainly was, that his aversion to part with Benjamin detained all his sons from going to buy corn. If Jacob was so unhappy when Benjamin was out of his sight, his best course was to send him away immediately, that he might return the sooner; for surely little pleasure would be taken in his company whilst the good old man was sensible that he must either soon part with him, or suffer him and all his family to pine away with hunger.

What must be done, do quickly. Is it not much better to feel the satisfaction of having done your duty than the pain of self-reflection for useless and dangerous delays?

VER. 11. *And their father Israel said unto them, If it must be so now, do this; take of the best fruits in the land in your vessels, and carry down the man a present, a little balm, and a little honey, spices, and myrrh, nuts, and almonds.*

"A fool rageth, and is confident;" but a wise man will yièld to reason, be it from a servant, from a son, from a wife, or from any other person, though inferior to himself in station, in good sense, or in holiness. "Ye younger, be subject to the elder; yea, all of you be subject one to another; and be clothed with humility, for God resisteth the proud, and giveth grace to the humble," 1 Pet. v. 3. Here you have an illustration of the apostle's precept, and the reason by which it is enforced. Jacob's sons submitted to their father in going down to Egypt, and their father complied with them in sending Benjamin along with them; and God crowned their designs with success, and gave them wonderful displays of His favour in the event of their journey.

How was Jacob persuaded to comply with a motion so adverse to his feelings? Not by Reuben's, but by Judah's solicitations. Judah addressed his father in words of wisdom and meekness. He set before him the absolute necessity of parting with Benjamin for a time, and the great comfort to be expected in the issue. Far was he from reproaching his father for his manifest partiality to his favourite son, but he gave him full assurance that his partiality should be gratified, if possible and necessary; for when Judah became surety for him, he, in effect, engaged to stand between him and every danger; and this promise he did not fail to perform.

Complain not, young persons, of tyranny in your parents, when the truth probably is, that you have not learned to treat with due reverence the fathers of your flesh. Do they refuse to comply with your wishes? Can you say with uprightness, that your desires were such as ought to have been granted? And if this has been the case, have you showed due respect to them in expressing your desires? and have you borne with a meek temper those eruptions of passion which disagreeable circumstances may sometimes produce even in the best men? You see in the instances before us, " that by much forbearing, a prince " and a father " may be persuaded, and that a soft answer breaketh the bone."

God inclined Jacob's heart, by Judah's argument, to send down Benjamin to Egypt; for " the steps of a good man are ordered by the Lord." By faith the good man was disposed to expose his son to the perils of the journey, for he trusted in that God who had blessed him with many gracious experiences of His favour; yet he did not neglect any prudent means he could think of to ingratiate himself with the lord of Egypt. He knew that " a gift maketh room for a man, and bringeth him before the great." Although the Lord was his stay in the day when he was terrified to hear that Esau was coming against him with an army, yet he tried what rich presents could do to appease his brother's anger. He had it not in his power, perhaps, or it was not convenient, to send so rich presents to the land of Egpyt. But what he had in his power, and what it was convenient to carry, he sent. " Take of the best fruits in the land in your vessels, and carry down the man a present, a little balm, and a little honey, spices, and myrrh, nuts, and almonds." It seems that even in these years of famine the land of Canaan still produced some precious commodities not to be found in Egypt, or not to be found there in such perfection. This is one instance of the kindness of Providence, that different countries are furnished with different products, which they can exchange to their mutual

o

benefit, and to the furtherance of that charity with which men ought to regard their fellow-creatures in different parts of the same earth. It was a mercy at this time to the poor people of Canaan that their land still afforded some precious things, which they could give in exchange for the more precious fruits of the earth, by which life is sustained.

Jacob could not conveniently send very rich presents to the governor; but he took care to send what he thought would be most acceptable to him. The hands of the righteous, as well as their lips, know what is acceptable. Presents of gold and incense are mentioned amongst those instances of respect by which the people of the East were to testify their submission to the King of Zion. Jacob sends presents of the most precious gums and spices to Joseph. Gold and silver were sent as a debt, and as a price for corn.

VER. 12. *And take double money in your hands; and the money that was brought again in the mouth of your sacks, carry it again in your hand; peradventure it was an oversight.*

It was to be expected that double money would now be necessary for buying corn, when the famine had been of long continuance, and there was no prospect of its coming to an end. High prices of corn in years of scarcity distress the poor; but let them be thankful that corn is to be had for any price, and that they are able, whether by their own labour, or by the charity of others, to afford the price required for what is so absolutely necessary for them.

"And the money that was brought in the mouth of your sacks, carry it back again; peradventure it was an oversight." It was difficult to say how it had come into the mouth of their sacks. Peradventure it was wilfully put in for some bad purpose. So Jacob feared when he first saw it. Perhaps it was an oversight; so he now thought, or wished to think. It is our wisdom, in dubious matters, to fix on those thoughts that will be most conducive to our peace. Possibly things may be worse than we think; and it will be good to arm ourselves with the consolations of God, that future evils may not overwhelm our spirits. Yet evils should not be voluntarily brought by us upon ourselves, by viewing everything in the most unfavourable light. "Sufficient unto the day," says Christ, "is the evil thereof." Present evils are as heavy as we can bear, and why should we double them by adding the evils of to-morrow? They may be but imaginary evils; but, by a timorous imagination, they are turned into real evils, heavier to be borne than those real evils which Providence brings upon us.

"Peradventure it was an oversight," and therefore carry back the money, says Jacob. He would take no advantage of the oversight of those with whom he dealt. No man of integrity will take an unrighteous advantage to himself of the mistakes of his neighbour. Nothing is more evidently inconsistent with the great rule of doing to other men what you would have other men to do unto you.

It would have been very unsafe for Jacob's sons to have taken advantage of an oversight in the present case. It might have confirmed the suspicions or awakened the resentment of the lord of Egypt. But it is never safe to do an injustice whilst God reigns in heaven, who will never suffer any man with impunity to go beyond or defraud his brother.

VER. 13. *Take also your brother, and arise, go again unto the man.*

The precious spices and gums that he sent were nothing. The double money that he sent was nothing. Benjamin was everything to Jacob. Could the good man have bought his security with all the substance of his house, he would have thought the purchase cheap. But Benjamin's presence with his brethren was indispensable. The man's face could not be seen, Simeon's liberty could not be recovered, corn could not be procured, without Benjamin. Jacob must lose him for a time, that he might afterwards receive him with pleasure, if it was the will of God. We must obey necessity, and ought to do it without repining. No harder necessity is laid upon us at any time than God has appointed in His wise decrees.

"Take my beloved Benjamin, and go with him to the man." At the first proposal Jacob would as soon have sent Benjamin to the lion's dens and the mountains of leopards. The wild beasts that tore Joseph did not appear more formidable to the dejected mind of Jacob than the man who had entertained such unjust suspicions concerning his sons, and who had probably put money into their sacks for no good purpose. But when we are under a necessity of making choice amongst evils, the least is to be chosen. The evil of sin is on no pretence to be chosen ; and this must be taken into the account when we must chose one of two evils. If there be one of them which we cannot choose without sin, the other must be the least, if we can choose it without sin. If neither can be chosen without sin, we cannot be under a necessity of choosing either of the two. It is not necessary for us to live. It is not necessary for us to escape an ignominious death. But it is necessary for us to " abstain from all appearance of evil." If Jacob had not sent Benjamin to Egypt, he would have been guilty of a great sin against God, and against his whole house, and even against Benjamin himself. The path of duty was now clear, and when that is clear, no room is left for further deliberation. " The ways of the Lord are right, and the just shall walk in them."

VER. 14. *And God Almighty give you mercy before the man, that he may send away your other brother, and Benjamin. If I be bereaved of my children, I am bereaved.*

" A good man will guide his affairs with discretion," but he will not trust to his own prudence. When he has done everything that he saw fit to be done, he will commit the event to God, and lift up his soul to Him in prayer for success to his designs. Jacob had once heard that an army of four hundred men was coming against him, when there were none with him but a few women, and children, and shepherds. But the Lord was his stay. To Him he prayed. " He wept and made supplications " to Him, and, with promises of safety to himself and his family, and of the best blessings, he obtained the glorious name of ISRAEL. To the same God he has recourse at this time. Thus David, when he had obtained great deliverance in answer to his prayers, resolved, that in every new time of trouble he would call on the name of the Lord. " I will call on the name of the Lord, who is worthy to be praised (for what

He has already done to me), so shall I be saved from mine enemy," 2 Sam. xxii. 4; Ps. xxviii. 3 ; cxvi. 2.

"God Almighty give you mercy before the man." He does not load the cruel man, who had treated his children so rigorously, with any railing accusations before the Lord. All that he asks is, not that the man's injustice should be turned upon his own head, or that the arm which had oppressed his family might be broken; but that his heart might be inclined to pity a poor distressed family, and let the oppressed go free. Jacob well knew that the hearts of kings and of ministers of state are in the hand of the Lord ; and that whatsoever a man devises, the Lord directs his steps. Were this truth written on our hearts, that every man's judgment cometh from the Lord, and that the mightiest men are but instruments in His hand to execute His pleasure, the fear of man would never rob us of the possession of our own souls.

"God Almighty give you mercy before the man." Oh! that we would make the same happy improvement of the revelation given us from God which the ancient patriarchs made of the revelation granted to them! He made himself known unto the fathers by the name of God Almighty. "I am God Almighty," He said to Abraham, "and I establish my covenant with thee." By this covenant Almighty God assured Abraham that he and his believing seed should ever be under the protection of His omnipotence. Isaac and Jacob, as well as Abraham, placed their confidence on that arm that was engaged for their help. They believed that what God had spoken he was able also to perform. "Trust ye in the Lord for ever, for in the Lord Jehovah is an everlasting rock."

Jacob prays to Almighty God for mercy and protection in the hearing of his sons. He expected that they would cordially join with him, and that when they were absent from him, they would follow his example. Let us all teach our children by example and doctrine to trust in the Lord, and pray to Him as the Rock of Ages.

"That he may send away your other brother." Simeon had given his father great sorrow ; and when he was reproved for what he had done, he returned a very unbecoming answer. Yet his father pitied him in his distress, and prayed for him, and greatly wished again to behold his face. When your children forget their duty, forget not your own. Undutiful children are still your children; and they need your prayers most when they deserve your favours least.

"And Benjamin." Why not Reuben, and Judah, and all the rest of the brethren, as well as Benjamin? Benjamin, in all appearance, was exposed to least danger. No suspicion could be entertained about the design of his journey to Egypt. But Jacob could not conceive what good design the governor could have in sending for him. He loved Benjamin most of them all, and therefore was most anxious about him. Love works fear where there is an appearance of danger. If you had a beloved son in the army when it is in the field of battle, you would be more afraid on his account than for any of his companions, although some of them were amongst the number of your acquaintances, because you do not love them as you love your own son.

Thus you will often hear the lovers of Christ perplexed with fears lest they should never see His face in heaven, whilst those who love Him not feel no anxiety about going to that place of blessedness. The reason is, that the love of the friends of Christ earnestly desires gratification in the sure hope of enjoying Christ in perfection. But the men whose love is set on present things, find in them the life of their hands; and therefore they are not grieved at the want of good evidence of their relation to Christ.

"That he may send away your other brother and Benjamin." It entirely depended on the will of God whether the man would send them away or not. Not only the end and measure of our days are determined by God, but every circumstance of our life is appointed by Him. Whether we are in a prison or a palace, in our own or in a foreign land, we are in the hand of God; and it is to be hoped that we do not wish to be at our own disposal, or at the disposal of our kindest friends on earth. Our friends can do nothing for us, our enemies can do nothing against us, without God. If our enemies boast of their power, we may say to them what our Lord said to Pilate, "Thou couldest have no power over me, except it were given thee from above." If they become our friends, God has wrought the agreeable change; and we may say to them as Jacob to Esau, "We have seen your face as though we had seen the face of God, and ye were pleased with us."

When Jacob committed his children to the care of Almighty God, one would think he might have confidently expected that he would not be bereaved of any of them. But when we pray for outward blessings, we must remember, that the promise of them is to be understood with a limitation. They are to be conferred upon us only as far as it is for God's glory and our own good. After all the promises which God had made to Jacob concerning his house, he had lost Joseph. He did not think that God's covenant was made void by the wild beasts that devoured him; and he would not have thought that God was unfaithful if Benjamin were likewise lost. He had made up his mind, that if this sore affliction should come upon him, and tear up afresh the wounds of former afflictions, he would submit to that will which could not be resisted. "If I am bereaved of my children, I am bereaved." "If I perish, I perish," said Esther; she determined to do the present duty if her life should go for it. "If I am bereaved," said Jacob, "I am bereaved." "I have already been bereaved of the dearest of my children. If I am bereaved of others of them, there is no remedy but patience." "The Lord gave, and the Lord taketh away."

When Abraham was called of God to offer up Isaac, he did not linger, but rose up early in the morning, and went to execute the commandment of the Lord.

Jacob's call to part with Benjamin was not so clear at first view as Abraham's call to offer up Isaac. Abraham was a strong believer, and was persuaded that God could raise Isaac from the dead. Jacob had not the same ground of persuasion that Benjamin would return to him alive. He was an eminent believer as well as Abraham. They both loved God far more than the dearest of their children, but neither the one nor the other were at all times equal to themselves. It is essential to real godliness, that in all things we resign ourselves to the divine will; but there is a lesser or greater measure of self-will to oppose this holy temper. "The flesh lusteth against the spirit." But the spirit will in due time obtain the victory, through the grace of Him that loved us, and gave Himself for us, to redeem us from all iniquity.

LECTURE 16

Joseph's brethren go down to Egypt, and find no complaints made against them on account of the money that was returned in their sacks.

xliii 15–23

VER. 15. *And the men took that present, and they took double money in their hand, and Benjamin ; and rose up, and went down to Eygpt, and stood before Joseph.*

OBSERVE how exactly they followed their father's directions. They took that present which Jacob commanded them to take, they took double money in their sacks, as he had advised. They did not take Benjamin till he had given them leave. We do not read that Benjamin said anything about his journey. He was unwilling to leave his father till he had obtained permission, and as soon as permission was obtained, he was ready for the journey. We may infer from his readiness to go, that no suspicion was as yet entertained of the cruel conduct of his brethren towards Joseph. It is strange that it could be so long concealed. But let it not be thought, that because sin is long hidden, it will never come to light. Within a few days, Benjamin was to know, and not long after their father was to know, the wickedness of their behaviour. Their own consciences knew it, and God knew it all along.

What servants, or whether any servants, attended the brethren on their journey, we are not informed. Jacob was left without one of his sons to cheer him in the absence of the rest. But their wives and their little ones, and what was far better, his God was with him. To Him he doubtless poured out his soul in many prayers for their safe return, and his prayers were heard.

They met with nothing to make them uneasy during the course of their journey. It may be presumed that they remembered their father's parting prayer, and that they seconded it with their own prayers. It was good for them that they were humbled by affliction and danger, if they learned to pray and make supplication to the God that could help them, and that had often answered their father in the days of his distress.

"They went down to Egypt, and stood before Joseph." Now was the crisis of their fate. They waited with anxious expectation to hear what he would say, and to see how he would act. Their safety and their father's happiness depended, under God, on his goodwill. What if he should still hold them for spies, after all that they had done to satisfy him? What if it should now be found a truth, that he had caused the money to be put into the mouth of their sacks, to find a pretence against them? Now it will be found whether he acted fairly and honestly with them or not, in requiring them to bring down their younger brother.

A state of suspense is very unpleasant. But Joseph's brethren must continue in it some time longer, for Joseph had not leisure, or behaved as if he had not leisure to talk with them at this time, although there was nothing that he more desired than to talk with Benjamin, and to make known his brotherly affection to all his father's sons. But all things, and every part of everything, ought to be done in its time and order.

VER. 16. *And when Joseph saw Benjamin with them, he said to the ruler of his house, Bring these men home, and slay, and make ready; for these men shall dine with me at noon.*

Would they not have been invited to his table if he had not seen Benjamin in their company? Doubtless, he would have given any of them a cordial reception, as far as it would suit his views. Yet the sight of Benjamin made him more desirous of seeing them at his table, that he might have the pleasure of conversing with his own brother, the son of his mother, with his father's Benjamin, and his mother's Benoni, whom he had not seen since the time of his childhood. The charities of father and mother, son and brother, afford some of the sweetest hours of life. We would taste much of the loving-kindness of the Lord in our relative connections, if our hearts were sufficiently warmed with the affections which they demand.

But the chief reason why Joseph wished to have his brethren at his table, when Benjamin was with them, seems to have been, that he might observe their behaviour to Benjamin, and discover whether peculiar honours conferred on him would excite that envy to which himself had owed so many days of grief. Joseph was not a man who would form an unreasonable suspicion of any person, but after what had already happened, it was desirable to obtain good proof of his brethren's reformation, for his own sake and theirs, and for the sake of his father, who was soon to hear how wickedly they had behaved, and would be greatly consoled if he heard that they now behaved in a very different way under like temptations.

"Slay, and make ready." Had Joseph no meat ready to entertain guests? The men of the East are more frugal in their meals than we. Flesh is not in common use amongst the greatest part of them. We sometimes find in scripture history that great men, and even kings, killed their beasts after guests came to their houses. We cannot suppose that such a great man as Joseph would at any time want stores of the best provisions for strangers that came to eat with him. But he would order a lesser or greater quantity to be prepared, according to the number of guests. Besides, meat cannot be kept any space of time in the warm regions of the earth, and therefore must be eaten very soon after it is killed.

VER. 17. *And the man did as Joseph bade; and the man brought the men into Joseph's house.*

"Slay, and make ready, for these men shall dine with me at noon." This was probably Joseph's ordinary time of dining.

The ruler of Joseph's house would no doubt be astonished to hear that these strangers, the brothers of Simeon the prisoner, were to have the honour of dining with his master, the lord of Egypt. If he had not known what deference servants owe to their masters, he would probably have desired to know why the governor made such a difference between these men, and the many thousands of other strangers that came to the country to buy corn. But it is the duty of servants to do what their masters command, without answering again, or inquiring the reason; and when they can see no reason for it, their masters may have a very good reason which they are not bound, and which perhaps it would not be proper, to tell them. Let us all do the duty of our own places, and leave other men to do theirs as they think fit, when we have no authority to control them.

Joseph's house was a magnificent palace. It was a very different kind of dwelling from that to which his fathers had been accustomed for more than 200 years. But Joseph was not happier in his palace than Abraham, and Isaac, and Jacob had been in their tents. The happiness of all these men consisted in hope. It was of no very great consequence to them whether they dwelt in palaces of cedar and marble, or in tents of rafters and goats' skins, for they knew that in this world they had no continuing city, but they sought one to come, whose builder and maker was God.

VER. 18. *And the men were afraid, because they were brought into Joseph's house; and they said, Because of the money that was returned in our sacks at the first time are we brought in; that he may seek occasion against us, and fall upon us, and take us for bondmen and our asses.*

The Arabians are the most revengeful people in the world; yet if you eat with them, you will be protected by them from all violence, and if you had done them the greatest injury, you need be under no apprehension from their resentment. One of them by accident offered a place of refuge to the murderer of his own son, not knowing the reason of his flight from justice. When he was informed of the truth, he furnished the murderer with the means of escaping the hands of the pursuer, for he accounted it the greatest of crimes to betray the man who had been received into his house, and shared in his victuals.

The Egyptians, though neighbours to the Arabians, have not been so much celebrated for their attention to the rights of hospitality. Yet it was incredible that such a man as the governor of Egypt, whose character for probity was very high, should invite men to his house with the intention of taking advantage against them, to rob them of a few asses, and to make them his slaves. A man so affluent, and so high in reputation, would never have blasted his own character for such a paltry consideration.

Why then did Jacob's sons conceive such base suspicions of the governor? The money found in the mouth of their sacks terrified them. Money is much too highly valued in this misjudging world. It is valuable when we obtain it righteously, and know how to use it according to the will of God who gives it. Yet all the silver and the gold that the sons of Jacob possessed through the whole course of their lives did not give them pleasure sufficient to counterbalance the vexation from that small quantity of money which they found in their sacks. If you wish to have pleasure in what you possess, follow Paul's example. He provided for things honest, not only in the sight of God, but in the sight of all men. Jacob's sons in the present case could have taken God to witness their honesty, but they were terrified on account of the suspicions which men might form of their behaviour.

Yet we do not know that their consciences were clear towards God in another point of view. When they first saw the unhappy parcels of silver, they saw the hand of God in the fraud that seemed to be intended—"What is this that God hath done unto us?" They knew that God would not punish them for stealing the money, but they were afraid that He might punish them for a crime of which they had been really guilty, by leaving them to suffer for another crime which they would have abhorred.

We have no reason to doubt that, when their consciences were awakened to the remembrance of what they had done against Joseph, and when they thought that divine vengeance was pursuing them, they would weep and make supplication to God for the pardon of their great iniquity. What hope of pardon they entertained we know not, but it is plain that fears of vengeance returned upon them, when there does not seem to have been any cause of fear. It is an unhappy thing to have guilt lying on the conscience—it deadens the enjoyments of life ; it embitters the sorrows of it ; it raises fearful apprehensions on every slight occasion. If you wish to be happy, seek the removal of that never-failing source of misery. Your comfort is very precarious when outward circumstances are most prosperous, if you have reason to think that God has a quarrel with you. And in change of circumstances to the worse, apprehensions of divine displeasure will be a far heavier burden than anything that men can do unto you. If Joseph's brethren had not been conscious of guilt before God, they would not have trembled at an invitation to a feast made for laughter. They would not at least have been afraid to lift up their faces to God for preservation, if they could have lifted them up without spot. What reason have we to be thankful for that atonement, through the faith of which we have peace with God, and are enabled to glory even in tribulation ? We may be corrected for sins that are pardoned, but those corrections will contribute to our best advantage.

Amongs, the other vexing thoughts that came into their mind, did it never occur to them, that their much-injured brother might be at this very time the slave of the governor of Egypt, or of some one of the inferior ministers ? They knew that the Ishmaelitish merchants who bought him for sale were travelling to Egypt, and probably to its capital. If he were still alive in any part of the city, he might, by his information concerning their bad conduct, have done them more prejudice than they had reason to dread from the silver in their sacks. But it is probable they really believed he was dead. If we truly repent of any crime, we will to the best of our power undo it. If we know not where to find the persons against whom we have sinned, we will endeavour to trace them out. The Lord told His people by Isaiah, that they might fast as much as they pleased, and bow down their heads like bulrushes, and spread sackcloth and ashes under them ; but all would be to no purpose, unless they undid the heavy burdens, and let the oppressed go free, and broke every yoke. But at present, however sincere the repentance of Joseph's brethren might be, it could not have been expected that they would seek out their injured brother, although they had not been possessed with the belief of his death. Their first business was to clear themselves from all suspicions, and to obtain Simeon's liberation from prison.

VER. 19. *And they came near to the steward of Joseph's house, and they communed with him at the door of the house.*

Joseph's brethren could not, in their younger days, bear the thought of bowing down before him, yet now they court the favour of Joseph's servant. Beware of pride. You know not by what changes in the affairs of this changeable world your loftiness may be bowed down. Some have been compelled by hard necessity to bow down before those whom they would once have disdained to set with the dogs of their flocks. That haughty spirit which sets itself in opposition to the will of God goes before a fall.

"They communed with him at the door of the house." They would not venture into the house till they had endeavoured to banish from his mind the suspicions which he might probably entertain of their behaviour. "If thou knowest," says our Lord, "that thy brother hath aught against thee, go and be reconciled to him quickly, and agree with thine adversary whilst thou art in the way." Delays may be very dangerous— "Thou mayest be delivered to the officer, and cast into prison." Joseph's brethren were afraid of sharing the fate of Simeon, or, what was little better, of being made slaves, to the ruin of the families which they had left at home, unless they could satisfy the ruler of Joseph's house concerning their innocence. They lost no time to explain their own behaviour, and to rectify misapprehensions, if any existed in the minds of Joseph and of his servants. They had no good reason to believe that these men were their adversaries, but they could not go into Joseph's house with pleasure till they were assured that neither he nor his people had anything to lay to their charge. The richest feast will give little pleasure to a troubled mind.

VER. 20, 21. *And said, O sir, we came indeed down at the first time to buy food: and it came to pass, when we came to the inn, that we opened our sacks, and, behold, every man's money was in the mouth of his sack, our money in full weight: and we have brought it again in our hand.*

We do not read that they opened any more sacks than one when they came to the inn. We cannot, however, say that they gave a false account of the matter. It is possible they might open more sacks than one at the inn, though we are not told of it; or the words may signify that they began the opening of their sacks at that place, although they did not finish it till they came to their father's house. It seems pretty clear that when Paul professed an account before Agrippa of the words that Jesus spoke to him in the way to Damascus, he recited not only what was spoken to him in the way, but likewise those words which Jesus spoke to him at Damascus, by the mouth of Ananias. Yet no man will say that Paul gave a wrong statement of facts. The words spoken at Damascus were a continuation and a full explication of what was said to him in the way, Acts xxvi. 3-18.

When your honesty comes into question, and you are called to vindicate your character from unjust suspicions, there is one rule from which, if you are wise, you will never depart: and that is, to speak truth, and nothing but the truth, whatever construction may be put upon it. If the fear of being reputed guilty should induce you to violate truth in a single instance, you have reason to fear that you will bring upon yourself the evil that you wish to avoid, and that you never will be able to remove it. Perhaps there are some at this moment in prison, who made use of prevarication to remove unjust suspicions from themselves. If they had spoken nothing but truth, they would not have been reputed guilty, but their miserable arts of evasion were considered as the effects of conscious guilt. "A lying tongue is but for a moment; but the lip of truth shall be established for ever."

Joseph's brethren gave a just and fair statement of facts, and suffered them to speak for themselves. They did not deny that they found their money in the mouths of their sacks, but they did not pretend to say how it came into them; and they had one good proof to produce that they had not knowingly and wilfully laid hands on that money, which was no longer their own. They had brought it down in their hands, with other money, to buy another lading of corn: "And we have brought again in our hands."

VER. 22. *And other money have we brought down in our hands to buy food: we cannot tell who put our money in our sacks.*

We have already mentioned a rule which ought above all others to be observed when we plead our own cause. We ought never to deviate one hair-breadth from the truth. Yet there is another maxim which ought to be almost as carefully observed— to say nothing but what is fit to be said. We are so far from being required to say all we think, that the truth imprudently uttered may be sometimes little better than a lie. He is a fool that utters all his mind. A wise man will keep it in till afterwards. There was a suspicion in the minds of the sons of Jacob that the money was put into their sacks by one of Joseph's servants, perhaps by the man himself to whom they were now speaking, but it would have been very foolish to express their suspicion. It might have kindled up resentment in his mind; and therefore they say they did not know who put the money into their sacks. It was true that they did not know. They only guessed the truth. All that they had to do was to restore the money when they found it in their hands; and their readiness to make restitution, when no man asked it from them, gave the steward reason to believe that they were honest men.

VER. 23. *And he said, Peace be to you, fear not: your God, and the God of your father, hath given you treasure in your sacks: I had your money. And he brought Simeon out unto them.*

Some have so little humanity that they can sport with the

P

uneasiness and fears of their neighbours. They would be pleased to see their fellow-mortals tossed with tempests, and held in terror for their lives, whilst themselves are safe on the shore. But the man in whom the love of God and of men dwells would be happy to see all other men happy, both in their outward circumstances and in the state of their minds. Joseph's steward appears to have learned much from his master. He saw Jacob's sons uneasy in their minds, and comforts them against their fears. Those who delight to terrify their neighbours (unless it be for their own good) are like the devil, whose pleasure lies in the misery of men. The followers of Jesus know that their Divine Master was anointed with the Spirit, to comfort all that mourn, and desire to imitate His goodness.

The ruler of Joseph's house seems to have learned the Hebrew salutation, "Peace be to you." The children of peace seek the peace of all around them. "Fear not." "You cannot be called to account for the money, for I had it; and what you have brought in place of it is your own." "The God whom you and your fathers serve hath given you this treasure in your sacks." The steward did not mean that God had put it into their sacks without the intervention of men; but that Divine Providence had given it to them by honourable means. He had learned a truth, the belief of which, followed up to its proper consequences, would put an end to the greatest part of the vexations and quarrels which have money for their object— "The silver is mine, and the gold is mine, saith the Lord of hosts." The devil was an egregious liar when he said to Jesus, "All the kingdoms and glories of this world are mine, and I give them to whomsoever I please." He cannot give a foot of land or a single penny to whomsoever he pleases. Millions of his servants are much poorer than he wishes them to be. If they had more money, they would perform better services to him. God is the absolute disposer of all things, great or little. He who gives us life and breath gives us all the other things we possess. We have neither less nor more of gold and silver than He is pleased to give us. When we lose any part of what we possess, we ought to say, "The Lord gave, and the Lord hath taken away." When treasure is given us, we ought thankfully to acknowledge the goodness of God, and to use it according to His will; and be ready to give it back when He demands it, either by His Word, or by His providence.

" Your God, the God of your father, hath given you treasure." This steward spoke like one who was informed of the history of the Hebrew patriarchs and their God. He very probably might have conversed frequently with Simeon; for it is not to be supposed that Simeon was held in such strict custody that none had access to him. From Simeon, or from his master, it is likely that he had heard some of those histories concerning the patriarchs which we learn from Moses. He might be informed, amongst other things, of the riches which God bestowed upon Jacob when he was a stranger in Mesopotamia. He had served fourteen years for two wives, and six years for cattle and sheep; and in the course of that time became rich in silver, and gold, and flocks, and herds, through the good hand of his God upon him. This God could give treasure to Jacob's sons by means which appeared to them inexplicable. Happy are the true children of the ancient patriarchs. The God of Abraham, Isaac, and Jacob is their God. The God who bestowed the treasures of temporal and spiritual blessings upon them, by which they were enriched in the land wherein they were strangers, is not now less abundant in goodness and liberality than He was in their days. He blesses us with all spiritual blessings in Christ Jesus; and He will bless us with all those temporal blessings also which He sees to be needful for us in the house of our pilgrimage.

From the good behaviour and religious discourse of the steward, we learn what care Joseph took to communicate his religious knowledge and impressions to his servants. Joseph was exalted by Pharaoh to teach wisdom to his senators, Ps. cv. Amongst other branches of wisdom which he taught, we have no reason to doubt that he taught them the most valuable wisdom, as far as it was in his power. His power was greatest in his own family, and there his instructions were likely to have most effect. If masters do not endeavour to promote the love and fear of God amongst their domestics, what will they do, or what account will they give, when God brings them before his judgment-seat, to give an account of all things done in the body?

Happy was the steward of Joseph's house. He enjoyed opportunities which few enjoyed, of obtaining religious knowledge. Joseph, no doubt, delighted to speak of his God, and the God of his fathers. His steward appears to have learned his sentiments and his language. Many have received their knowledge and impressions of religion in families where Divine Providence placed them as servants, and would not have exchanged the benefits derived from the servitude for a hundred kingdoms. Masters, behave in your families as you may reasonably suppose Joseph did. At the day of Christ's appearance and His kingdom, you shall have for your crown of rejoicing those whom you have been the happy instruments of turning to righteousness.

"And he brought out Simeon unto them." We have no account of the manner in which Simeon was treated whilst he was in prison; but we may be well enough assured that Joseph's servants would not be encouraged to insult his unfortunate brother. They were taught by their master to show compassion to the unhappy. Joseph doubtless treated Simeon with as much gentleness as was consistent with his design of remaining unknown to his brethren.

Simeon was at last released; and the pleasure of liberty, and of seeing his brethren, was a rich compensation for the pain of confinement. He received a still richer compensation for what he endured in prison, from the happy effects of the affliction, if he made that improvement of it which Joseph intended, and which reason and religion prescribed.

Joseph's steward was happy in executing his master's command for the liberation of Simeon. Good servants are happy when they have good masters, who employ them in good offices to their fellow-men. The steward shared in the pleasures felt by Simeon and by his brethren. Goodness carries along with it a part of its own reward.

Simeon's brethren were happy to find him restored to their society. They remembered their father's words, "Joseph is not, and Simeon is not, and ye will take Benjamin away." Although they had no hope of ever being able to restore Joseph, they pleased themselves with the hope that in a few days they would hear their father blessing God, and thanking themselves, for bringing Simeon and Benjamin again to his arms. The irretrievable loss of Joseph would be thought on by their father with the less regret, when two other sons were restored to his arms, about whose fate he was long in suspense.

"The morning cometh, and also the night." Fear had filled the hearts of Jacob's sons. It was now for the time dispelled, although it was soon to be succeeded by more disquieting apprehensions. But these too were to end in joy. It is good for us that we know not all the evils that are to meet us in life. Let us learn to commit all our ways to Him whose eye pierces through immensity, and through eternity. He will perfect everything that concerns all who put their trust in Him.

LECTURE 17

Joseph's brethren are entertained at his table.

xliii 24–34

Ver. 24. *And the man brought the men into Joseph's house, and gave them water, and they washed their feet; and he gave their asses provender.*

IT is probable that Jacob's sons had never seen a palace so magnificent as this into which they were now introduced. The houses of the petty princes of Canaan were not to be compared with the splendid palace of the prime minister of the King of Egypt. Yet all the magnificence of Joseph's palace, and all the provisions of his table, would have given them little pleasure, if their minds had not been set at rest about the money found in their sacks. They had reason to think that the governor intended them no hurt, but good; and that God was not now prosecuting His quarrel with them for the blood of their brother. "Go thy ways, eat thy bread with cheerfulness, and drink thy wine with a merry heart," when there is a well-grounded peace in thine own mind, "for God now accepteth thy works."

The exchange of a prison for a palace would be a great pleasure to Simeon, although he was only a stranger that was to tarry for part of a day. Little did he suspect that the lord of the palace came to it from a prison, to which he was brought in consequence of Simeon's own wickedness.

The ruler of Joseph's house gave them water to wash their feet. This was a usual and a necessary piece of respect to strangers in the countries of the East. Our Lord did not always meet with such respect from those who entertained Him as Jacob's sons met with from this steward. When He vindicated His own behaviour towards the woman that had been a sinner, He said to Simon the Pharisee, "Seest thou this woman? I entered into thine house, thou gavest me no water for my feet; but she has washed my feet with tears, and wiped them with the hairs of her head."

"And he gave their asses provender." He had learned from his master all the offices of a liberal hospitality. A good man is merciful to his own beast, and an hospitable man will attend to his neighbour's beast. Those animals that serve us have a title to what is necessary for their subsistence and comfort.

VER. 25. *And they made ready the present against Joseph came at noon: for they heard that they should eat bread there.*

Joseph longed to enjoy the company of his mother's son, but he did not neglect his important affairs to gratify his feelings. Diligence in business is commendable in all, especially in the servants of princes, who are entrusted with the affairs of a nation. None but a man diligent in business is fit to stand before great men. Yet those who are most active, must take time for the necessary refreshments of nature; and those who are most careful to do their duty will eat with most pleasure that bread which they have earned by their industry. After Joseph has despatched his necessary affairs, or the affairs of his master, he returns to dine at noon, and to enjoy the society of his brethren, who did not as yet know that they were in the palace of a brother to whom they were dear.

They were in a great measure relieved from their apprehensions by the humanity of the ruler of Joseph's house. But still they were anxious about the reception they should meet with from his lord. They could not yet understand for what reason they were singled out from all other strangers to the honour of dining with him. They had brought a present, which, they hoped, would recommend them to his favour. " A gift is like a precious stone in the eye of him who receives it; whithersoever it turneth, it prospereth." But that it may be acceptable with the great, it must be given with a good grace. Joseph's brethren drew from their baggage their balm and their honey, their precious fruits, and spices, and gums, and arranged them, and considered what posture would be proper for presenting them, and in what form of words they would beg his acceptance of them. It may be presumed that they lifted up their hearts to God, that He would make this present as acceptable to the great man in whose presence they were to appear, as their father's richer present was to Esau. But they knew not that the man whose favour they wished to enjoy was as nearly related to them (to one of them at least) as Esau was to their father.

If those who are to appear before kings, or the dispensers of their favours, are so solicitous to obtain favour in their eyes, how careful ought we to be to please God when we come before him! He invites us into His presence. He is so wonderful in grace and condescension that He accepts and requires presents from us. Let us consider what these offerings are with which He will be pleased, and how they are to be presented. Offer unto God thanksgiving. Give Him your hearts. Praise will please Him better when it comes from the heart, than bullocks, than any beast that hath horns and hoofs, than all the incense of Arabia. "We are a spiritual priesthood, ordained to offer spiritual sacrifices, acceptable to God by Jesus Christ."

VER. 26. *And when Joseph came home, they brought him the present which was in their hand into the house, and bowed themselves to him to the earth.*

Joseph knew that the present was an evidence rather of their fear than of their love. But he could excuse that fear of which his own behaviour had been the cause. He hoped soon to gain his brethren's love by discovering his own. It is probable, too, that the present would put him in mind of what he had heard his father tell concerning the rich presents by which he had, long before this time, endeavoured to melt the heart of his brother Esau. Joseph's heart would be melted at the thought that his anxious father was now, without knowing it, attempting to mollify his own heart by like methods; for it was obvious that the sons were acting with the concurrence and by the direction of their father.

The giving of handsome presents was a token of respect or homage to the great. As this present came from Jacob by the hands of his sons, Joseph's dream might now be considered as verified, that the sun, and the moon, and the eleven stars did obeisance to him : when his brethren bowed down themselves to the earth before him, they humbly solicited his favour to their father as well as to themselves. What the import of this gesture was we may learn from Isaiah's predictions concerning the homage that was to be paid by the Gentiles to Zion and to her King, Isa. xlv. 14 ; lx. 14 ; xlix. 22, 23.

VER. 27. *And he asked them of their welfare, and said, Is your father well, the old man of whom ye spake ? Is he yet alive ?*

It is not to be doubted that he sought and obtained information concerning the life and welfare of his father as soon as his brethren came to his house. But what men take pleasure to hear, they will desire to hear more than once.

One of the inconveniences that attend the separation of friends, when they live in places remote from one another, is, that they must often be solicitous about one another's life and health. The easy communication between distant countries in our times greatly lessens the inconveniency to those who love their parents and relations. Those children who go abroad, and neglect frequent correspondence by letters with their friends at home, discover little regard to their parents, if yet alive, or to those persons to whom they owe affection for the sake of their parents. How can we pray, or give thanks for our friends, if we have great reason to doubt whether they remain in the land of the living ? " Is your father well, the old man of whom ye spake ? Is he yet alive ?" The time was not very long since he had formerly heard them speak of him. But life is always uncertain. A young man that was alive and in health last year, or last month, or yesterday, may, for aught we know, be already numbered with the dead. Old men must die before many days pass over them. Old age of itself is a continual disease, which may terminate their existence of itself without any additional distemper. They ought always to remember that their life is now doubly uncertain ; and their children ought not to forget that if anything is to be done to please or comfort them, no time is to be lost.

VER. 28. *And they answered, Thy servant our father is in good health, he is yet alive. And they bowed down their heads, and made obeisance.*

Jacob might again be said to have done obeisance to Joseph, when his sons called him Joseph's servant, and did obeisance to him, whilst they informed him, in answer to his inquiries, of their father's life and health.

"Thy servant our father is in good health, he is yet alive." Considering his age, it was no small ground of thankfulness that he was yet alive. It was a double mercy that at his time of life he was in good health. Old men will see great reason to bless God when they consider what multitudes of their juniors are gone to the land of forgetfulness, and how few of them survive. They have reason to wonder at the goodness of God, when they enjoy some measure of health in those days of life which are for the most part evil days, of which men say that they have no pleasure in them. What am I better than my neighbour that God has so long borne with my manners, and still continues to load me with His blessings?

It is said of Epaminondas, the Theban general, that when he had gained the famous victory of Leuctra, he told his friends, when they congratulated him on the glory which he had acquired, that the greatest pleasure he felt in his victory arose from the consideration that his father and mother were yet alive to enjoy the pleasure of it. We may presume that Joseph was not less joyful to hear that his father was yet alive, to be informed of his life, and of all his glory in Egypt. His wealth and honours gave him much less pleasure than the prospect of again seeing his father, and being seen by him, to their mutual joy.

VER. 29. *And he lifted up his eyes, and saw his brother Benjamin, his mother's son, and said, Is this your younger brother of whom ye spake unto me ? And he said, God be gracious unto thee, my son.*

He saw his brother, his mother's son, and the remembrance of a fond mother, whom he lost in early years, powerfully attached his soul to the only child except himself whom she left behind her. " Is this," said he to his other brethren, "your younger brother, of whom ye spake unto me?" He probably knew him by his resemblance to others of the family, although his appearance must have been greatly altered since he had seen him in his father's house. But ignorance is not always the reason for inquiring. It was not yet fit that Joseph should seem to know another son of Jacob, without information.

" God be gracious to thee, my son." Next evening he would rather have said, " God be gracious to thee, my brother." At this time he called him his son, in token of his paternal affection. How happy would the world be if old men were treated by the younger as fathers, and young men by the old as sons !

Joseph still retained the language which he had learned in Canaan. His salutation to Benjamin was such a prayer as was often heard in the mouths of the venerable patriarchs. They were called to inherit a blessing, and they took pleasure in blessing the younger branches of their families. We ought to wish well to all, and to express our good wishes in prayer for grace and mercy from God.

Ver. 30. *And Joseph made haste ; for his bowels did yearn upon his brother : and he sought where to weep ; and he entered into his chamber, and wept there.*

The sight of Benjamin's beloved countenance brought to mind his mother, the kindness she showed to him in his youth, her death, and the name she had given to Benjamin, which was changed by his father. He remembered the attachment he felt to Benjamin in his infancy, and how dear both he and his maternal brother were to their afflicted father. Crowds of tender ideas rushed all at once into his mind. If he had not instantly retired, he must have discovered himself to his brethren before he had sufficiently proved their disposition towards his younger brother. Many were the bitter tears shed by Joseph when he was exiled from all that was dear to him on earth. But he now shed many tears of joy, far sweeter than the smiles or laughter of common life. He had now the pleasure of seeing all his brethren, and the hope of soon beholding his father's face with gladness. His grief for what had passed was swallowed up in joy for what was present and to come.

VER. 31. *And he washed his face, and went out, and refrained himself, and said, Set on bread.*

Tears, on proper occasions, are no dishonour to a man of spirit and sense. The passions are not to be extinguished, but governed. Joseph could not refrain from weeping at the sight of his mother's son. We love him for the warm sensibility of his heart. We esteem him as a man of sense, because he knew when and where to weep, and could refrain himself and appear cheerful when it was fit. He knew the "time to weep, and the time to laugh; the time to embrace, and the time to refrain from embracing." He who never felt an inclination to weep is a stone ! He whose tears are not in some measure under the government of his judgment is a child rather than a man.

At his table, Joseph had sufficient command of himself to do the honours of it. " He said, Set on bread."

VER. 32. *And they set on for him by himself, and for them by themselves, and for the Egyptians, which did eat with him, by themselves: because the Egyptians might not eat bread with the Hebrews ; for that is an abomination unto the Egyptians.*

It is not a sign of pride for men to know the dignity of their station, and to keep their inferiors at that distance from them which the law of decency requires. Joseph sat by himself, and the Egyptians that were honoured with a place at his table sat by themselves. Superiors ought to know that their inferiors have the honour to partake of the same human nature, and that they are on a level with themselves before God. Yet, by an unbecoming familiarity, they allow their inferiors to forget that deference which is due to their rank.

But why did the Egyptians abhor fellowship in eating with the Hebrews ? Some think the reason was, that the Hebrews were accustomed to eat the animals which the Egyptians worshipped as gods. But it is not certain that the Egyptians, in such ancient times, worshipped brutes, made to be eaten by men. And certainly none of the gods of the Egyptians were served up at that table where the Egyptians sat as guests. But it is probable that the Hebrews were reckoned impure by the Egyptians, because they did not observe those ceremonies in eating which made a part of the religion of Egypt. It is well known that the heathen nations in general were wont to honour their gods at their tables by certain observances, which they thought no religious person would neglect. We pity their blindness, but we cannot but lament that many Christians, at their entertainments, show less respect to that God who gives us all things richly to enjoy, than heathens showed to those vanities that could neither do good nor evil.

"The Egyptians might not eat bread with the Hebrews, for that is an abomination to the Egyptians." The Jews at this day will not eat the flesh of those beasts which have been killed by a Christian. It is our duty to glorify God in eating, and in all that we do, by avoiding all unhallowed communication with sinners. We must not pretend to a superior sanctity to those men who are perhaps better than ourselves. We must not place religion in superstitious observances in eating or drinking. But we ought not to be ashamed of acknowledging God at our tables. With a brother that walks disorderly, we ought not so much as to eat, that he may be ashamed; but if one who is not a brother walk disorderly, we are not bound to avoid fellowship in eating or drinking, so far as business, or good manners, or the hope of doing him good may require. Yet he must not be our chosen friend when he appears to be the enemy of God, 1 Cor. x. ; 2 Thess. iii.

VER. 33. *And they sat before him, the first-born according to his birth-right, and the youngest according to his youth : and the men marvelled one at another.*

Whether Joseph requested them to take their seats according to their time of life, or whether it had been their custom in their father's house to sit according to their seniority, we cannot certainly know. But it may very well be believed that the patriarchs taught their children to show a proper respect to seniority. The honour due to age was religiously paid in those ancient days by men of understanding, as we find in the Book of Job; and it may be presumed that such wise men as Jacob and Joseph would accustom their children from their tender years to this instance of good-breeding. It is of more importance than some parents seem to be aware of, that children should be early habituated to those decencies of behaviour which they ought through life to practise. And it would greatly lessen the burden of parental duties to give some share, or some shadow of authority, to the elder branches of the young families, as far as they are qualified to manage it. Let all things in families, as well as in churches and nations, be done decently and in order. And for this end, let the younger be brought to submit themselves to the older. When every one in a company knows his own place, there will be no confusion in arranging themselves.

"And they marvelled one at another." They looked with astonishment at one another's countenances, for they could not conceive what the governor's reasons were in admitting them to the honour of eating and drinking with him at his table. They were as much surprised as Mephibosheth afterwards was, when such a dead dog, as he called himself, was admitted to sit at the king's table as one of his children. May not Christians be filled with greater astonishment when they are called to partake of the fulness of God's house, even of His holy temple, and blessed with the joyful prospect of eating and drinking with Christ at His table in His celestial kingdom?

Ver. 34. *And he took and sent messes unto them from before him: but Benjamin's mess was five times so much as any of theirs. And they drank, and were merry with him.*

It was, and still is, the custom in the countries of the East, for the master of the house to testify his regard for his guests, by sending messes to them of that food which is served up to himself. Joseph sent messes to all his brethren, but Benjamin's mess was five times as large as the mess of the rest of his brethren. Thus Joseph pretended to testify a superior degree of regard to the youngest, although his real design was to try whether the superior honours given to Benjamin would kindle up envy in their breasts against him. Joseph had too good reason to know that men are naturally envious of the superior honours bestowed on those whom they are accustomed to consider as their equals, or their inferiors; and he would be persuaded that his brethren had subdued that envious disposition which wrought so powerfully in their breasts in former days, if they should still retain the warm affection of brothers to Benjamin, after he had been distinguished with peculiar honours by the lord of Egypt.

Joseph had a singular reason for making this experiment of his brethren's dispositions, and therefore his behaviour is not to be made a precedent in ordinary cases. It does not seem to be a wise custom in the men of the East to distinguish guests at their tables by marks of different degrees of respect, except where age or station entitle some to a preference which others have no pretence to dispute. We ought to give honour to whom honour is due, but we ought not, without good cause, to hurt the feelings, or to rouse the selfish affections, of any man. Let us, in the smaller as well as in the greater concerns of life, observe the royal law, "Thou shalt love thy neighbour as thyself." "Whatsoever you would that men should do to you, do even so to them."

"And they drank, and were merry with him." Joseph knew how to make his guests happy by his affability and agreeable conversation. "A feast is made for laughter," and therefore, when thou makest a feast, let thy behaviour be agreeable and pleasant. Yet we must not feast without fear. Intemperate mirth is not for accountable creatures. We must remember that we are under God's eye, no less when we are eating and drinking with our friends than when we are hearing the Word of God, or pouring out our hearts in prayer before the throne of His mercy. Job suffered his children to give feasts to one another. He wished them to enjoy all the reasonable pleasures of their age and station. He hoped that their frequent

convivial entertainments would promote their mutual friendship.
Yet he was careful that in their feasts they should never forget
the rule of temperance and piety.   They knew that, when the
days of their feasting were gone about, their father was jealous
over them with a paternal and godly jealousy, and offered
burnt-sacrifices according to the number of them all.

" And they drank, and were merry with him."   The marginal
readings of your Bibles will frequently help you to understand
the passages to which they refer.   But beware of misunderstanding the marginal reading in this place.   They *drank
largely*.   It is not meant that they drank more than enough.
The word which we render, "They were merry," or, "They
drank largely," is often used to signify that cheerful enjoyment
of God's good creatures which is perfectly consistent with the
laws of the strictest sobriety.   "Drink, yea, drink abundantly,
O beloved !"   Song of Sol., v. 1.   The two original words in this
passage are the very same that are used in the place before us,
and surely our blessed Lord will not borrow images from the
abominable debaucheries of revellers and drunkards to illustrate
His grace and kindness to the persons whom He loves.

" Every man at the beginning doth set forth good wine, and
when men have well drunk, that which is worse."   These were
the words of the governor of the marriage feast at Cana in
Galilee, where Jesus turned water into wine.   The word
which we render "have well drunk," answers in meaning to
the Hebrew word used in this place.   But it would be blasphemy
against Christ to allege that He turned water into wine to
supply the extravagant cravings of a licentious appetite.   And
it would be a violation of that respect which we owe Joseph's
memory to suppose that he either encouraged or allowed too
much liquor to be drunk at his table.   He would certainly
much rather have exposed himself to the censure or displeasure
of the noblest guests, by restraining debauchery, than to the
displeasure of the Most High God, by giving any countenance
to those fleshly indulgences which his law condemns.   Drunkenness excludes from the kingdom of God no less than whoredom
or murder; and therefore, he who tempts his neighbour to

exceed the bounds of temperance, must be an agent of the devil, by favouring his attempts to destroy the souls of men.

God is a gracious Master. He allows us a cheerful use of the good things of this life, but His goodness is abused and insulted if we take a pretence from His liberality to fulfil the lusts of the flesh. Shall we take the mercies of the Most High and turn them into instruments of unrighteousness, to provoke Him to anger? If we do, we turn His blessings into curses. Joseph had tasted too much of the goodness of God in the precious fruits of the earth to abuse them to purposes so offensive to the bounteous Giver.

We are not told what conversation passed at this cheerful feast between Joseph and his brethren. We scarcely needed to be told. We know what the subjects were on which he would desire information from his brethren. They had already told him that the old man their father was alive and in good health ; but he would find opportunity on this occasion to hear a thousand particulars about the history of the man whom he so dearly loved, although it is possible that he had found means before this time to learn from Simeon everything that he knew concerning him. No subject of discourse could gratify Joseph so much as the history of his fathers, Abraham, Isaac, and Jacob, which involved so many instances of the power and grace of God, and promises of good things to be bestowed on their posterity, and on all that should partake of the blessings to be bestowed on the nations through their seed. How far Joseph might think it expedient in the present company to discourse on these subjects, and to turn the conversation to them, we cannot say. But this we know, that out of the abundance of the heart the mouth speaketh, when opportunity is given. A good man, at a feast as well as at a funeral, will endeavour to have his speech always seasoned with salt, and will wish to hear discourse in which the useful is mingled with the agreeable. How tedious must a feast be, although royal dainties were the entertainment of the body, if chaff or poison is to be the only entertainment of the mind !

Q

LECTURE 18

Joseph's cup is put into Benjamin's sack, which affords a pretext for bringing him back to Joseph.

xliv 1–13

VER. 1, 2. *And he commanded the steward of his house, saying, Fill the men's sacks with food, as much as they can carry, and put every man's money in his sack's mouth. And put my cup, the silver cup, in the sack's mouth of the youngest, and his corn-money. And he did according to the word that Joseph had spoken.*

JOSEPH ordered his cup to be put into Benjamin's sack, that he might have a pretence for bringing him into slavery, and by this means make an experiment on his other brethren. If they discovered no concern for Benjamin's affliction, it would be too evident that they still lived under the influence of that selfish and envious temper which prompted them to sell himself into Egypt. But if they should discover a strong desire to preserve Benjamin, it might be presumed that they were very different in their dispositions from their former selves, and could entertain the affection of a brother to one whom their father loved above themselves.

We ought not to entertain sentiments of revenge against those who have done us an injury, but it is very desirable to see evidences of repentance in evil-doers. Although charity thinks no evil, it may assume the appearance of severity to work a salutary change, or to bring forth evidences of it.

" If thou wouldst get a friend," says an ancient sage, " prove
him first, and be not hasty to credit him." Joseph's brothers
ought to have been his friends from his earliest years, but had
proved his enemies. He ardently wished to have them for his
friends, but it was necessary to see some good evidences of a
complete change, that he might trust them and esteem them.
His conduct towards them will not justify us for like behaviour
when there is not the like occasion. We must not judge,
that we be not judged. We must not devise methods to explore
the secret principles by which our relations and friends are
actuated, when they have given us no good reason to form
suspicions concerning them. When they have sinned against
us, we ought to forgive them, so far as to be able to do them
good, even before they give us any proof of their repentance ;
but such proofs as discretion will admit are necessary before
we can restore to them that esteem and confidence which they
have justly forfeited. " Charity suffereth long, and is kind."
Charity bears all things, believes all things, hopes all things,
covers all things. But it is not one of the offices of charity to
suffer sin upon our neighbours, or to shut our own eyes against
clear light. Love your friends, bear much from them ; but that
your love may not wax cold, use means to make them sensible
of their sins, that by showing forth repentance, they may
recover a title to that esteem which they have forfeited. Doubtless Joseph would have given bread to all his father's house
during all the years of famine. He would not have suffered
their little ones to starve for the sin of their fathers. Yet he
could not have esteemed his brothers as true sons of Jacob and
Abraham if he had not seen their behaviour quite the reverse
of what it once was. Mutual esteem is necessary to the mutual
offices of friendship. And esteem which is lost must be re-
gained by evidences of returning virtue.

We can easily see why Joseph put the silver cup into
Benjamin's sack. But it is not so easy to guess for what reason
he ordered each man's money to be put in the mouth of his
sack. Joseph, no doubt, would have scorned the idea of
requiring the ordinary price, or any price, for that food with

which he wished to feed his father's household; but his generous
intentions do not account for a manner of restoring their corn-
money which he foresaw would fill them with terror and
amazement. The pain of such uneasiness as they felt was too
high a price for the money which Joseph restored. The reason,
probably, why he restored it was, that they might have no
reason to suspect Benjamin as the real thief of his cup. Whilst
he wished to have a pretence for detaining Benjamin, he did
not wish that his brethren should have reason to suspect that
he was really guilty. His desire was to find his brethren
disposed to defend Benjamin in a just cause from that oppression to which he seemed to be exposed. If there had been too
great appearance of guilt in their eyes, they might have been
excused if they had left him to the just punishment of his
crime.

Joseph gave his orders to the steward of his house, who did
according to the word which his master had spoken. This is
the excellency of a servant, to obey the commands of his master
without delay, and without gainsaying. Let us endeavour to
approve ourselves such servants to our Master who is in heaven.
Earthly masters may be unreasonable or unjust in their commands. Everlasting righteousness is in all the commandments
of the Lord.

VER. 3. *As soon as the morning was light, the men were sent
away, they and their asses.*

It is unwise to sleep in the morning, when you have a long
journey to go. Set off early, and you will have the pleasure at
every step to know that your journey will be completed before
the night comes, when you cannot walk without stumbling.
When strangers are travelling from your house, detain them not
by a cruel kindness till the best time for accomplishing their journey is lost. Always do in matters of small or great importance
not what is most pleasing at the moment, but what will please
you best on reflection. If you are men or women, and not
irrational creatures, you will prefer a lasting advantage to a
present gratification.

Joseph's brethren were early dismissed by Joseph, and set

out on their journey with cheerful spirits. They had corn in their sacks for their father and their little ones. They had met with unexpected kindness from that great man who had formerly treated them with such unmerited harshness. Simeon was restored to them, and no bad accident had befallen Benjamin. They would in a few days arrive at Hebron, and cheer the heart of their poor father with a sight of their younger brother and Simeon, for God had heard his prayer, and given them mercy in the sight of the man of whom they all stood in fear.

But the most beautiful morning may soon be overcast with dark clouds. Joseph was preparing for them grief and fear, although he intended them no hurt, but good. Let us never be too confident that to-morrow will be as this day, or that this day will continue serene and bright till the evening.

VER. 4. *And when they were gone out of the city, and not yet far off, Joseph said unto his steward, Up, follow after the men; and when thou dost overtake them, say unto them, Wherefore have ye rewarded evil for good?*

Although a great part of mankind are too chargeable with the guilt of ingratitude to some of their fellow-creatures, as well as to the Author of all good, yet there is scarcely a man breathing on the face of the earth who will not condemn ingratitude as one of the worst of evils. Oxen and asses, and even the wild beasts of the forest, feel the force of benefits, and love their benefactors.

"Wherefore have ye rewarded evil for good?" Thus Joseph commanded his steward to say to the sons of Jacob; but wherein were they chargeable with a crime so detestable?

VER. 5. *Is not this it in which my lord drinketh, and whereby indeed he divineth? ye have done evil in so doing.*

These words would not be at the first hearing of them understood by the sons of Jacob. It was not intended that they should be explicit. Their own consciences, it was to be supposed, would explain their meaning. If they had stolen the cup, they would understand what Joseph's steward had in his mind when he said, "Is not this it in which my lord drinketh, and whereby indeed he divineth?" The steward acted the part of a man whose passion was roused to such a degree by ill-usage that he omitted some words in his expostulation. An angry man is in too much haste to speak plainly. He is master neither of his tongue nor of his thoughts.

"Is not this it in which my lord drinketh?" Some great men use golden cups. A silver cup was sufficient for Joseph. He valued magnificence no farther than he thought it necessary to please his master, and command the respect due to his station.

"And whereby indeed he divineth." There are some among ourselves who pretend to foretell future things by means of cups or other utensils. No wonder that the Egyptians, who knew not God, believed that demons, by means of cups, might inform persons of hidden things. And yet it would scarcely consist with the veneration due to the memory of Joseph to suppose that he would rank himself, even in jest, with such worthless men as the pretenders to divination. He had plainly told Pharaoh that all his knowledge of future things was received from the God of heaven; and we have no reason to doubt of his constancy in bearing testimony to the exclusive right of his own God to be considered as the Father of lights. Besides, how could Joseph take it for granted, as a thing known to the sons of Jacob, that he made use of his drinking-cup for divination?

The word which we render "divine" is, in chap. xxx. 27, rendered "know by experience;" and some take the expression in this place to signify, "Would I not certainly come to the knowledge of it?"

"Is not this it in which my lord drinketh, and can he not divine concerning it?"—so others have rendered the words. The obvious meaning of them is, they might have certainly known that it would be impracticable to conceal their theft. What they had stolen was a utensil highly valued by the governor, who was well known to be at least a man of sagacity, and who was supposed to have an art of knowing secret things, which none else was acquainted with, for which reason his name was called by the king Zaphnath-paaneah.

Who would steal if he was persuaded that he could not conceal his theft? Who would expose his character and his best interests, by wilfully committing any wickedness, if he knew that it must in a short time be discovered? But do we believe that there is any truth in the discourses of our Lord Jesus Christ? Hath He not said, "There is nothing covered that shall not be revealed; neither hid that shall not be known?"

"Ye have done evil in so doing." To return evil for good is the worst thing that can be done. When you eat at a man's table, you profess friendship to him, and enjoy the fruits of his friendship towards him. Were you admitted to the table of a great man who never owed nor expected to owe any obligation to you, you would certainly be worthy of the gibbet if you should make use of his kindness to give you an opportunity for stealing some of the most valued furniture of his table or house. Were you permitted to eat and drink with the king himself, and returned injury and insult for his goodness, no punishment would be reckoned too severe for the crime. What, then, must we think of ourselves if, after admission to the table of the everlasting King, we have lifted up our heels against Him? Wherein are we better than Judas?

VER. 6. *And he overtook them, and he spake unto them these same words.*

But had not Joseph's steward good reason to suspect that some mischief was intended for the men, when they were charged with so black a crime upon false proof? Could he be justified for obeying his master when he was commanded first to lay snares for the innocent, and then to convict them by false evidence? I believe Joseph chose for the steward of his house a man too honest to have concurred even with his master in a villainous scheme. But the steward knew his master too well to think that he intended anything but good to the men who had done him no wrong. Men of known integrity enjoy this privilege, that their character ought to secure them against suspicions of dishonesty even when they behave in such a way as might expose other men to suspicion. The best of men may fall into sin; and yet there are some sins into which a good man will seldom be suffered to fall, and into which he ought not to be believed to have fallen without such evidence as cannot be resisted. Such a crime was that of David in the matter of Uriah.

What Joseph designed it was perhaps impossible for the steward to guess, but he was persuaded that what he knew not at present he would soon know. Relying on the justice and wisdom of his master, he dexterously seconded his designs, and appeared so much in earnest, that no doubt seems to have been entertained of his sincerity by Joseph's brethren. But they thought themselves able to give him satisfactory evidence of their integrity.

VER. 7. *And they said unto him, Wherefore saith my lord these words? God forbid that thy servants should do according to this thing.*

The sons of Jacob were chargeable in the sight of God with many evils. They were conscious of as great evils as this which was now laid to their charge, or rather of evils far greater in all reasonable estimation, and yet they were·struck with amazement at the accusation, and expressed a strong detestation of the crime. "God forbid," or, "Far be it from us, that thy servants should do according to this thing." Could they be so base and so wicked as to steal a favourite cup from the great man who had treated them with such distinction? Was it possible that they would abuse his goodness to an opportunity of pilfering the most precious furniture of that table where they had been honoured with a place? They certainly would have abhorred the thought of such a mean piece of wickedness, and yet they did not always abhor the thought of far greater wickedness.

It is strange that rational creatures should deceive themselves every day, by thinking themselves incapable of going to a certain extent of wickedness, when they make no scruple of going far beyond it. They would think that a man deserves to be cudgelled who should charge them with the least instance of theft, and yet they will not scruple to defraud a young woman of her virtue, and to deprive a whole family of peace and comfort, to gratify the desire of a moment.

Although you have repented of your great iniquities, you must not think that you are ill-used when you are believed to be capable of new acts of wickedness. Your corrupt nature is not extirpated. You have a right, indeed, to be displeased when guilt is imputed to you without proof, but there is a great difference between the imputation of guilt and the supposition that you may have sinned, or that you may sin. If Joseph's cup had been really lost, his brethren could not have reasonably complained that they were suspected, when circumstances seemed to point them out as the guilty persons. And yet they were sincere in expressing their detestation of theft and of ingratitude.

That we have the same corrupt nature with other men, we cannot deny. That we have too often done things as bad as those of which we are sometimes unjustly suspected, we will probably confess, if we know ourselves ; and therefore we must not say with Hazael, "Are we dogs, that we should do such things?" In meekness let us justify ourselves when we are wrongfully accused. Meekness, under great provocations, has seldom made things worse, but has ten thousand times made them better.

"God forbid that thy servants should do according to this thing."

VER. 8. *Behold, the money, which we found in our sacks' mouths, we brought again unto thee out of the land of Canaan : how then should we steal out of thy lord's house silver or gold ?*

This is the great advantage of those who have behaved irreproachably, that they can produce their own conduct as a witness in their favour, when they are falsely accused, or unjustly suspected. Their righteousness in times past answers for them. All that was known to Joseph or his steward concerning the behaviour of the sons of Jacob was honourable. Through some oversight, their money was restored to them, which they brought back, and returned when it was not sought. How, then, could it be believed that they would now seize upon what had never belonged to them, especially when it could not be expected that they would escape detection, disgrace, and punishment?

If you will not practise justice for God's sake, practise it for your own credit. "A good name is better than precious ointment." A good name, justly acquired, will repel false charges that might otherwise be dangerous to your fortune or your life.

VER. 9. *With whomsoever of thy servants it be found, both let him die, and we also will be my lord's bondmen.*

Jacob's sons could confide in one another. Although some of them had been chargeable with murder, and others of them with shameful impurities, yet they were all persuaded that none of them would degrade themselves so far as to pilfer what was not their own. They were so confident of one another's integrity, that they could risk their own liberty upon it. They unanimously doomed the thief to death, and themselves to slavery, if he was found among their number.

It was indeed true that none of Jacob's sons had stolen the cup, and it is probable that all of them had too much sense of honour to demean themselves to an action so ignominious. Yet they were too rash when they offered their liberty as the price not only of their fault, but of the fault of any one of their number. It was indeed brotherly conduct to express such a firm confidence in one another's innocence, but the money which they had formerly found in the mouths of their sacks might have taught them that the cup in question might have likewise been put into the sack of one of them, without any fault on his part. He that is hasty with his tongue often erreth. Our nearest friends may be left to fall into those sins of which we could not have believed them capable; or without falling into any sin, they may fall under unmerited reproach, which unexpected circumstances may disqualify them from wiping away. If God be not surety for us for good, we cannot be answerable for our own conduct; and when we are kept free from falling, we still need the protection of His providence to our good name. Some have been convicted and put to death without any fault in the jury or judge, who have afterwards been found guiltless of the crimes for which they suffered.

VER. 10. *And he said, Now also let it be according unto your words : he with whom it is found shall be my servant; and ye shall be blameless.*

The steward takes the sons of Jacob at their word, so far only as justice allowed. He will have the sacks searched, that it may be known whether any of them had taken the cup; but he will not, as they proposed, punish the innocent with the guilty, nor will he punish the guilty so rigorously as they proposed.

When our neighbours speak rashly, we ought not to take advantage of their error. We ourselves have too often come under engagements without due deliberation, from which we wished to be dispensed. We must not take those advantages of rashness in other men that we would not wish to be taken of rashness in ourselves.

" He with whom it is found shall be my servant." Adultery was thought, even by heathens, in those days, a more grievous crime than theft. Judah required the most dreadful of all punishments to be inflicted on his daughter-in-law for supposed adultery. Joseph's steward thought the stealing of his master's cup would be sufficiently punished by slavery.

" But all ye shall be guiltless." Why should an innocent man be punished because one of his brothers has committed a crime? The grief and shame which he feels for his guilty brother is a punishment more than sufficient for him, and he deserves pity because his punishment, if it can be called so, is unavoidable. Was Joseph worthy of reproach because Simeon and Levi, in their pride, destroyed the Shechemites?

VER. 11. *Then they speedily took down every man his sack to the ground, and opened every man his sack.*

" The righteous is bold as a lion." The sons of Jacob made no delay in exposing what was in their sacks. A few moments, they thought, would be sufficient for the full proof of their innocence. But their faces were covered with shame when they saw what they did not expect to find.

Ver. 12. *And he searched, and began at the eldest, and left at the youngest: and the cup was found in Benjamin's sack.*

Joseph's steward might have begun with the sack of the youngest, and saved himself the trouble of searching so many sacks in vain; but he thought it necessary still to put on the appearance of justice, although he knew that he could not deceive the brethren, nor is it likely that he wished them to be deceived. Artful men must always have pretences of justice in what they do, even when they know that they can impose on nobody.

All the brethren must have concluded that the cup was put into Benjamin's sack by the man, whoever he was, that put the money into their own sacks. The governor himself was, in all appearance, the author of this trick, that he might be furnished with a pretext for making their younger brother a slave. Although they durst not execrate him with their tongues, they certainly thought that he had basely and wickedly devised mischief against their unhappy brother. But they were deceived by appearances. He was laid under the suspicion of a black crime, that Joseph might find occasion to show the tenderness of his affection to him, as the dearest of his brothers, and might save him, if he found it necessary, from cruel hands. Possibly Joseph might be jealous over his brethren, lest they should resent the honours done to Benjamin, as they had resented the honours done to himself. At any rate, we are sure that he meant good, and not evil, to all his brethren, and most of all to Benjamin, when he seemed to be their worst enemy. The kisses of an enemy are deceitful, but the apparent cruelties of a friend may be full of kindness. The famous Frederick the Wise, Elector of Saxony, caused a company of horsemen to lie in wait for Luther, when he returned from bearing testimony to the Gospel at the Diet of Worms; but these horsemen conducted him to a strong castle, where he was kept in safety from enemies that thirsted for his blood.

Ver. 13. *Then they rent their clothes, and laded every man his ass, and returned to the city.*

How soon was their joy turned into mourning, and their cheerful hopes into dismal fears! Sudden changes daily happen in this uncertain world. But let us trust in that God who often makes the day dark with night, but who likewise turns the shadow of death into the morning.

Benjamin's brethren could not, without apparent danger, return into the city. Snares, it was too apparent, were laid for Benjamin. And what if all of them should be involved in these snares. No notice was yet taken of the money in their sacks, but they might all be reputed thieves as well as Benjamin, when the steward or the governor pleased. Was it not safest to leave Benjamin to his fate, and to secure themselves by a speedy departure? But their bowels yearned over their poor brother, and over their father, whose grief would be inconsolable if both the sons of his best-beloved wife were lost. Rather than see the misery of their father, they will return, and try what can be done to save Benjamin. Thus they might make some little compensation to their father for bereaving him of Joseph. They had sold him for a slave; and if they can preserve his brother from slavery, they will do all that can be now done, as far as they know, to repair their fault.

We never do ourselves more good than when we are most interested in doing good to our friends and brethren. If Jacob's sons had now returned to their father, and left Benjamin to his fate, they must have forfeited the esteem both of their father and of that brother who was raised up by God to be the shepherd and stone of Israel. By returning and interesting themselves so deeply in Benjamin's misfortunes, they dissipated Joseph's remaining doubts concerning them, compensated in his eyes for all the injuries they had done him, renewed in his bosom the kindness of his youth, and brought about a speedy eclaircissement of those perplexed circumstances which occasioned such anxiety to themselves and to their father.

Wait on the Lord in the path of duty. If it leads you through dangers and difficulties, stop not short, and turn not aside. Look to Jesus, who did not fail, nor was discouraged, amidst all the horrors of His state of abasement. Remember all the ancient believers, who kept the path of righteousness and mercy, till through many sufferings they came to the end of their course. " In the way of righteousness there is life, and in the pathway thereof there is no death." Danger is safety, and death is life, in the way wherein we ought to go.

LECTURE 19
Judah's speech to Joseph in favour of Benjamin.
xliv 14–34

VER. 14. *And Judah and his brethren came to Joseph's house ;
for he was yet there : and they fell before him on the ground.*

"JUDAH, thou art he whom thy brethren shall praise."
Thus spoke Jacob, in his last blessings to his children,
concerning the tribe of Judah. But the father of that
tribe seems before that time to have acquired great respect
among his brethren. It was Judah that persuaded Jacob to
send Benjamin into Egypt, and he returned at the head of his
brethren when they went back to Joseph's house to intercede
for the liberty of Benjamin. A man of sense and activity
ordinarily acquires that ascendant to which he is entitled
amongst his equals and companions, and frequently obtains
the favour of his superiors.

Judah and his brethren came to Joseph's house, which he had
not yet left, to transact the remaining business of the day, and
which he did not intend to leave till he had transacted one of
the most important businesses of his life. He was happy when
he saw all his brethren returning of their own accord. One of
the warmest wishes of his heart was fulfilled when he saw the
brotherly affection of all the sons of Jacob to his mother's son.
If he had not already forgiven, he would now from his heart
have forgiven, all the wrongs which they had ever done to
himself.

They all fell down before Joseph, and did him obeisance again in the. name of their father and their own. We may observe, however, that there is a very great difference between that outward respect which is due to great men and that inward veneration which is due to real worth. It was wise in Jacob's sons to bow down before the governor, who had them in his power; but it scarcely can be supposed that they now entertained either esteem or affection for a man whom they supposed capable of the blackest artifices to accomplish his designs.

Ver. 15. *And Joseph said unto them, What deed is this that ye have done? wot ye not that such a man as I can certainly divine?*

If we understand the word which is rendered "divine" in that sense in which our translators understand it, we may conclude that the Egyptians had not words to distinguish between the pretended arts of their diviners and the true gift of prophecy with which the Hebrew patriarchs were blessed. As the prophets of Baal and the prophets of Jehovah are called by the same general name of prophets, so the Egyptians would give to such a prophet as Joseph appeared to be the same appellation which they gave to their own pretended prophets. Joseph, therefore, when he laid claim to what was called divination in Egypt, did not mean that he was a diviner of the same kind with those of Egypt, but simply one that had the gift of discovering things hidden from other men. Was it not to be supposed that he who could foretell that seven years of plenty would be followed by seven years of famine, could also discover the pilferer of that cup out of which he drank?

But whether Joseph, by the use of the word, meant that he could discover the thief by his sagacity, or by some supernatural gift of intelligence, it is plain that for the present he designed to carry on the trial which he was making of the temper of his brethren. He had now good reason to hope that they would stand by his dear brother; and if they continued firm in his interest whilst he was exposed to danger, the result would be not only highly satisfactory to himself, but honourable to his brethren. Their bad behaviour to himself was likely soon to be known to their father, and to the world. But their generous interposition for Benjamin would tend to redeem their character, and to convince their father that they entertained still a warm regard to his comfort. It is thought by many that the discipline of the Church, strictly administered, is little better than tyranny. But what better thing can be done for those who are unjustly reproached, than to give them an opportunity of exculpating themselves? or what greater favour can be bestowed by men on those who have forfeited their character by sinning, than to give them an opportunity to recover it, by proper testimonies of repentance? Joseph did not tyrannise over his brethren when he furnished them with an opportunity of showing to their father and the world, that they now acted under the influence of tempers which were the reverse of those that once governed their behaviour.

He put on a stern aspect. He upbraided them with a pretended crime, but it was to give them occasion to show forth their innocency and their repentance.

VER. 16. *And Judah said, What shall we say unto my lord? what shall we speak? or how shall we clear ourselves? God hath found out the iniquity of thy servants: behold, we are my lord's servants, both we, and he also with whom the cup is found.*

No wonder that Judah was at a loss what to say. How could he justify or excuse Benjamin, without seeming to criminate the governor, whose favour it was so necessary to court? But if he confessed that his brother was guilty of the baseness imputed to him, how could he claim any favour for a wretch capable of the blackest ingratitude?

But when Judah seems uncertain what he should speak, his words are expressive of the perplexity to which he was reduced when he wished to obtain the liberty of a brother whose guilt seemed to be so manifest. Every appearance was against him. How, then, could his cause be pleaded with advantage? " What shall we say unto my lord? what shall we speak? or how shall we clear ourselves? God hath found out the iniquity of thy servants : behold, we are my lord's servants." " He may, without any impeachment to his justice, seize upon us all, and make

R

us his bondmen, since appearances are strong against us." So the last words of the verse may be understood, for there was ground of suspicion against them all, from the money that was found in their sacks. But the steward made no use of this circumstance against them. He had indeed found a quantity of silver in the mouth of every sack, but that silver might be their own, or God might again have given them money in the mouth of their sacks by some unknown means.

These last words, therefore, may be understood as a strong expression of their unwillingness to go up without Benjamin to their father. As when Jesus spoke to His disciples of going to Bethany, in the neighbourhood of that city where the Jews sought to slay Him, Thomas said, " Let us also go, that we may die with Him." Since Jesus would expose Himself to death, Thomas thought that his own life, and the lives of his brethren, would be of no more value to them. They might as well die with Jesus, as live a joyless life without Him. Thus Judah and his brethren thought their own liberty would lose all its value if their brother was made a slave, and their father's gray hairs brought down to the grave with sorrow for the loss of his favourite son. Joseph's steward had loosed them from the obligation they had voluntarily taken upon themselves to become his servants, if the cup was found in any one of their sacks. But they did not wish to be loosed from it, unless they could obtain liberty for their poor brother. They durst not say that he was innocent. But his punishment, if he was made a slave, must extend to many innocent persons.

When Judah said, " God hath found out the iniquity of thy servants," he does not confess that they were chargeable with any share of the guilt imputed to Benjamin, although his words might be understood as a confession of that guilt. It was not at present a time to plead their innocence, when by justifying their brother they must have accused their judge, who had them in his power. But Judah could with truth say, God hath found out their iniquity. They remembered other iniquities, for which God had a just right to punish them by the calamity which was likely to come upon them in the loss of their brother.

They had sold Joseph for a slave, and filled up many of the years of their father's life with bitter anguish. It would be a righteous thing with God to make them all slaves, or bring upon them the misery of seeing Joseph's brother reduced to the same state to which they had reduced Joseph, and to remove their father, loaded with new anguish, to a better world, where they should no longer give him any vexation.

Beware of sin. God knows all that you do, and may punish you for the injuries you do to one man, by permitting another man to deal no less unjustly with yourselves. Keep clear consciences, and in the day of evil you may lift up your faces without spot to God, who executes righteousness and judgment for the oppressed.

VER. 17. *And he said, God forbid that I should do so : but the man in whose hand the cup is found, he shall be my servant ; and as for you, get you up in peace unto your father.*

Joseph's steward appears to have obeyed his master's instructions with great exactness. He said the very same things to his brethren when he overtook them that Joseph himself now spoke. Both of them declared their detestation of extending punishments beyond the offence or the offender.

Joseph had no complaint against Benjamin's brethren, and therefore they might return in peace to their father. Why should any man of common sense speak or act as if men were to lose their good name for faults not their own—for faults which they probably lament in the bitterness of their souls— because they have been committed by their relations? Amaziah was not one of the best kings of Judah, and yet he would not put to death the children of his father's murderers, because the law of Moses had said, That the children should not be put to death for their fathers, nor fathers for their children, but that every man should die for his own sins, 2 Kings i. 4.

"Go ye up in peace to your father." This permission was intended for trial. It gave Joseph great pleasure to find that it was not accepted.

VER. 18. *Then Judah came near unto him, and said, Oh my lord, let thy servant, I pray thee, speak a word in my lord's ears, and let not thine anger burn against thy servant: for thou art even as Pharaoh.*

Judah had never attended the schools of the rhetoricians, and yet no orator ever pronounced a more moving oration. His good sense, and his affection for his venerable father, taught him eloquence. Let a speaker be deeply impressed with his subject, and words will follow of course.

He humbly begs leave to speak a few words in the governor's ears, without offending him. The poor useth entreaties, and the rich man betrays a mean pride when he answers him roughly.

" For thou art even as Pharaoh." Judah knew that great men ordinarily take pleasure in fair speeches, and that they are seldom averse to flattery. He no doubt had heard how his father had insinuated himself by well-chosen words into the good graces of Esau. Judah gave almost royal honours to his brother. As he spoke for all his brethren, they paid that homage by his mouth to Joseph which formerly to prevent they scrupled not to load themselves with the guilt of an enormous crime. Our sins can never prevent the execution of God's purposes, but they will bring upon us the judgments written in His Word.

VER. 19, 20. *My lord asked his servants, saying, Have ye a father, or a brother? And we said, We have a father, an old man, and a child of his old age, a little one; and his brother is dead, and he alone is left of his mother, and his father loveth him. Now therefore—(ver. 33.)—I pray thee, let thy servant abide instead of the lad a bondman to my lord; and let the lad go up with his brethren.*

This was Judah's petition to Joseph. To introduce and enforce it, he gives him a statement of facts sufficient to move a heart of stone. Some of these facts Joseph had already heard from the mouths of Judah or his brethren, when they had no purpose such as the present to serve by relating them. He had been informed by them that they had a younger brother, the only surviving son of a much-beloved mother, and therefore doubly dear to his gray-haired father. If Joseph had any regard for venerable age, any pity for an old man whose life was bound up in the life of his son, he would not bereave him of the solace of his declining days.

VER. 21-26. *And thou saidst unto thy servants, Bring him down unto me, that I may set mine eyes upon him. And we said unto my lord, The lad cannot leave his father: for if he should leave his father, his father would die. And thou saidst unto thy servants, Except your youngest brother come down with you, ye shall see my face no more. And it came to pass when we came up unto thy servant my father, we told him the words of my lord. And our father said, Go again, and buy us a little food. And we said, We cannot go down: if our youngest brother be with us, then will we go down: for we may not see the man's face, except our youngest brother be with us.*

We are sorry when we have been the innocent occasion of sin to others, and if it were in our power, would gladly prevent those calamities which the sin may bring upon them. Joseph had, without designing it, drawn Benjamin into that temptation which had proved fatal to his virtue, if he really stole the cup. He would not have thought of coming into Egypt, nor would his father have permitted him to come, if Joseph had not expressly declared that without their younger brother they should not again be permitted to see his face. He would at this time have been with his father, where his heart would not have been seduced by the sight of the precious cup, if the family had been permitted to purchase, without his presence, the sustenance necessary for their lives.

In consequence of that injunction which obliged Benjamin to come to Egypt, their father had already suffered by his absence greater afflictions than he was well able to bear. His life was endangered by it, and it was not to be expected that he would survive the shock if he found that a son so dear to him was detained as a slave in Egypt for theft. Joseph had declared his detestation of that rigour in punishment which ranks the innocent with the guilty. He had already, without intending it, loaded a venerable old man with sorrows. It was to be hoped that he would add as little as possible to his grief.

He certainly did not intend to kill a poor old man for the crime of his son.

VER. 27-29. *And thy servant my father said unto us, Ye know that my wife bare me two sons: and the one went out from me, and I said, Surely he is torn in pieces; and I saw him not since: and if ye take this also from me, and mischief befall him, ye shall bring down my gray hairs with sorrow to the grave.*

Sorrow is to be respected. Every person of humanity will be glad to alleviate the grief of him whom God has wounded by singular afflictions. That man must have the heart of a tiger who wilfully doubles those sorrows of an innocent man, which are already great. It is a dreadful affliction to have one of two favourite sons torn in pieces by wild beasts. The person who, without indispensable necessity, or the imperious demands of duty, bereaves him of the other, is more merciless than the beasts of prey which deprived him of the first.

Judah was far from thinking that the brother supposed by the father to be torn of wild beasts was the very man before whom he was pleading with such affectionate earnestness for the liberty of a brother on so many accounts dear to himself. Yet it is observable that he said nothing but what was true, although he did not tell all the truth. It was not to be expected that he would tell how Benjamin's brother was lost. He only told his father's opinion concerning it, and that was sufficient to melt any man's heart into compassion for the father bereaved in such a cruel manner, as he thought, of one son, and trembling at this time with the apprehension of losing his brother by some means not less fatal to his peace. He had indeed many other sons left, but none of them by the best-beloved of his wives. When he lost the son who was believed by him to be torn of wild beasts, his body was not enfeebled by extremity of age. In his present state of weakness, it was impossible, to all appearance, that he could survive a second shock more grievous than the first.

VER. 30, 31. *Now therefore when I come to thy servant my father, and the lad be not with us; seeing that his life is bound up in the lad's life; it shall come to pass, when he seeth that the lad is not with us, that he will die: and thy servants shall bring down the gray hairs of thy servant our father with sorrow to the grave.*

Beware of immoderate attachment to any created object, if you love your lives, or if you regard that commandment which requires you to use all lawful endeavours to preserve them. If your lives are bound up in any created enjoyment in this changeable world, you commit not only your peace and comfort, but your life, to a great hazard. Jacob's life was bound up in the life of Benjamin, and therefore there was great danger, if any mischief had befallen the young man, that his father's precious life would have been cut off by inconsolable griefs. Many parents have, without intending it, shortened their days by giving an unbounded license to parental tenderness. We pity them, but we cannot commend them. David deserved the severe reproof which Joab gave him when he would not restrain the clamours of his grief for the loss of Absalom. When God is our exceeeding joy, we know that whatsoever we lose, our happiness is secure; yet even this consideration will be insufficient to support the heart of a saint if he is not careful to mortify his inordinate affections to earthly objects. Jacob, without all controversy, trusted in the God of Abraham as his shield and his exceeding great reward; and yet the excess of his parental affection to Joseph and to Benjamin filled many of his days with the bitterness of anguish. Judah had authority from himself to say that he would not long survive the loss of Benjamin, chap. xliii. 38.

It was to be hoped that the governor of the land of Egypt would not be so rigorous in executing deserved punishment as to bring down with sorrow to the grave a venerable old man, who had already drunk deep in the cup of woe, and that he would not turn an excess of an amiable affection into an instrument of misery and destruction.

" Oh my lord," said Judah (ver. 18), "let thy servant, I pray thee, speak a word in my lord's ears, and let not thine anger burn against thy servant." In the conclusion of his speech, he shows that he was under a necessity of using such freedom with

his lord. He had become surety for Benjamin, and therefore
he hoped the governor would bear with his importunity in
pleading a cause in which he had solemnly bound himself to
exert all his powers.

Ver. 32. *For thy servant became surety for the lad unto my
father, saying, If I bring him not unto thee, then I shall bear the
blame to my father for ever.*

He that is surety for a debt must look upon the debt as his
own. He that is surety for the accomplishment of any business
must use all his influence, and exert all his powers, to procure
the accomplishment of it. Truth is the bond of society, and
we behave as enemies of mankind if we set an example of
infidelity to our fellow-creatures. If all around us should
follow the example, mutual trust must be at an end ; and men
will find it necessary to guard against their fellow-men, as if
they were briers and thorns, that cannot be taken with the
hand, but must be thrust away with an instrument of wood or
iron, 2 Sam. xxiii. 6.

Joseph knew how necessary it was to maintain truth in
families and nations. All wise statesman will abhor everything that tends to destroy the confidence of man in man, and
will esteem persons who are faithful to those engagements that
expose them to hardships and dangers.

Ver. 33. *Now therefore, I pray thee, let thy servant abide
instead of the lad a bondman to my lord ; and let the lad go up
with his brethren.*

He that sweareth to his own hurt, and changeth not, is a
man of tried integrity. Who will thank the man that fulfils
his promises when he has no temptation to break them ? A
man may be sufficiently wicked, although he does not commit
iniquity for the sake of iniquity. But that man is a lover of
truth and righteousness who prefers a pure conscience, not only
to gold and silver, but to his pleasure, his family, his liberty,
and life. Judah became bound to restore Benjamin to his
father, and wishes to perform his word, although by his
fidelity he should make himself a slave for life. Judah had
not at this time a wife, otherwise it would not have been his

duty to come under engagements that might separate him from her. He had three children, but these he might safely leave to the care of his father and of his brethren, especially his younger brother, whose liberty he wished to redeem with his own. There was no duty that imperiously prohibited him from taking the place of his unfortunate brother. His children, and even his wife, if he had been in the married state, might have been sent to Egypt. He was so far master of his own liberty, that he could warrantably put himself in Benjamin's room, if the governor gave his consent.

We think that a great deal more of charity is required from us than human nature can supply when we are commanded to love our neighbours as ourselves. We are disposed by our selfish passions to put a forced interpretation upon that precept which enjoins us to lay down our lives for the brethren. " John must surely mean something far short of the natural import of his words when he says that there are cases in which we must prefer our brethren's safety to our own"—such is the comment of a heart which is sensual, not having the Spirit. But here we find Judah laying down his liberty for his brother ; and a man of Judah's noble spirit would not reckon liberty much less precious than life. Yet Judah had not heard charity enforced by such powerful arguments as those on which John so warmly and so frequently insists. Jesus the Son of God had not then taken upon Him the form of a servant, and become obedient to death, even to the death of the cross for us.

Love to his father, as well as to his brother, disposed him to redeem Benjamin's liberty with his own.

VER. 34. *For how shall I go up to my father, and the lad be not with me? lest peradventure I see the evil that shall come on my father.*

Liberty was dear to Judah, but his father's comfort was dearer. Much rather would he have chosen to continue in Egypt a slave, excluded from the society of his father, his brethren, his children, his friend Hirah the Adullamite, than return to his father without Benjamin, and see the grief that would soon put an end to his father's life. Attend to this example of filial affection. Let children who have the pleasure of seeing as yet their fathers in the land of the living learn to put a just value on this blessing, and what attention they ought to pay to the happiness of those who brought them into the world. Will you not do what you can to make the lives of those men pleasant, without whom yourselves would not have tasted the pleasure of living? Are there any amongst us who, by undutiful carriage or bad behaviour, are bringing down the gray hairs of their parents to the grave? Repent, before your unnatural wickedness is sealed up by the consummation of it. The first commandment with promise was not published from Sinai when Judah discovered such tender and self-denying regard to his father. Nature and its law taught him that children could seldom do or suffer too much for a father, and especially for such a father as Jacob. Do you say, that if you had such a father as Judah had, you would not grudge him the warmest and most self-denying expressions of regard? But if you had such a disposition as Judah, you would render to the father by whom God gave you life, that honour and duty which the law of God requires. Your father is not so holy a man as Jacob; but the same God who made it his duty to honour his father makes it your duty to honour yours.

"Your father," you will say, "has not treated you with that kindness which he shows to some of your brothers or sisters. He has his favourites in the family. It is their business to requite the partiality of their parents with returns of tender affection. But a very moderate degree of filial love is all that can be expected from me." If you speak thus, you are far from wishing to copy that beautiful example which is set before you in this passage. Judah saw plainly that Benjamin was loved far above himself, or any of his brethren by the same mother; Jacob made no secret of his partial tenderness for Benjamin. Yet Judah is so far from repining at the superiority of his father's regard to Benjamin, that he was willing to become a slave for him, because his father would be less hurt by his misfortunes than by Benjamin's. How different was the spirit which he now discovered from that which appeared in the sons of Jacob when they sold Joseph into Egypt, because their father loved him better than themselves! Now Judah is willing himself to be a slave in Egypt for Benjamin, because his father loved Benjamin better than himself. It is not absurd to suppose that Judah had proposed the selling of Joseph, not because he hated him, but because he loved him, and thought that the surest way to obtain his life would be to gratify the envy of his other brethren by reducing him to the condition of a slave and exile. But the brethren of Judah were certainly much changed in their dispositions, for they all concurred with him in his efforts to obtain the liberty of their younger brother. Blessed be God, that though the thing that has been done cannot be undone, yet the persons who have done bad things may be made as though they had not sinned. " If any man be in Christ, he is a new creature : old things are passed away ; behold, all things are become new."

Let not penitents be upbraided with their old sins. They are not what they once were, and when their iniquities are sought for, they shall not be found. We admire the generous love of Judah to his younger brother and to his aged father. Such noble examples of disinterestedness are rare amongst men. But can we ever sufficiently admire the grace of our Lord Jesus Christ, who became surety for millions of transgressors, and for their salvation took upon Himself the form of a servant, and became obedient unto death, even to the death of the cross ? His own honour and ease were nothing to him when His Father's glory was to be advanced by His sufferings. " Now is my soul troubled, and what shall I say ? (Shall I say ?) Father save me from this hour : but for this cause came I unto this hour." When Judah desired to be made a slave to preserve his brother from slavery, he only performed the engagements which the necessities of his father's family constrained him to take upon himself. The Son of God had no necessity laid upon Him by anything but His own and His father's infinite love to become surety for such worthless creatures as we are. Judah might entertain a reasonable hope, either that the governor of Egypt would feel the force of his generosity too much to make him suffer by it, or that he might by other means soon recover his liberty. Jesus knew that when He took our debt upon Him He must pay it all. May we all know the love of Christ that passeth knowledge, and feel its constraining power upon our hearts, that we may do justly, and love mercy, and walk humbly with our God!

LECTURE 20

Joseph makes himself known to his brethren, and soothes the anguish of their troubled spirits.

xlv 1–5

VER. 1. *Then Joseph could not refrain himself before all them that stood by him; and he cried, Cause every man to go out from me. And there stood no man with him, while Joseph made himself known unto his brethren.*

JOSEPH had now heard enough, and more than enough, to satisfy him that his brethren sincerely loved Benjamin and their father; that they would not, on any consideration, have done now what they once did against himself; and that it was now time to discover himself to his brethren, and to give full scope to all the fervour of his brotherly love. Every word of Judah's speech pierced his heart. He recognised in his brother a heart congenial with his own. He fondly hoped that all his brethren would now show themselves worthy of their venerable father, for he saw that they were all tenderly interested in his peace and comfort. He blushed to hear Judah frequently repeat these words, "Thy servant our father." He deeply felt the distress of his own mother's son standing silent before him, under a load of unmerited accusations, supported by proofs which appeared indubitable. He could no longer endure the sight of one so dear to him trembling in anxious suspense about the sentence that should determine his own fate and that of his beloved father. Joseph's heart was strongly agitated by the tenderest and most powerful passions, filial and fraternal love, compassion, joy, and grief. He could contain himself no longer. Scarcely could he articulate the orders that he gave to all his servants to leave the presence-chamber, for none of them were allowed to stand with him whilst he made himself known unto his brethren.

If his servants had been present, they must soon have learned what treatment Joseph had once received from his brethren ; and it was not to be expected that they would so easily forgive the injuries done to their lord as their lord himself could do. Time could not fail to bring to light some part of their bad conduct, but Joseph took all the measures that were in his power to save their reputation. " Charity covers a multitude of sins." Where is our love to our brethren if we entertain no regard to their character and to their feelings ? If we love them as ourselves, let our love be discovered in its proper effects. Surely we will not divulge those things that will lessen our own reputation, if we can conceal them without sin and without danger.

Joseph could not have given all the scope he wished to those warm affections which he felt in his heart, whilst his ordinary attendants were present. We delight to exchange our thoughts with those whom we love, without witnesses. "There stood no man with him, whilst Joseph made himself known to his brethren."

VER. 2. *And he wept aloud : and the Egyptians and the house of Pharaoh heard.*

The strong passions that wrought in the heart of Joseph found a vent in the tears which streamed from his eyes. Tears are not dishonourable to the best or bravest men on earth. Jesus Himself wept in the days of His flesh. Many were the tears of sorrow which Joseph had shed in the days of his affliction. Even the joys that followed in his exaltation brought tears from his eyes. He had not tasted such pleasure since the time when he had left his father's house as at this moment, when he found his brethren so well disposed towards Benjamin and towards their father, and when he could indulge in the pleasing hope of soon again enjoying the society of his father, and of all his father's house; yet he wept aloud. His tears were mingled with such expressions of his vehement affection, that the house of Pharaoh heard, and were amazed. They could not comprehend what these transports of passion meant, or in what they originated. Surely some strange thing had happened to their lord, who seemed to have lost his usual self-command. The speech which they had heard was so moving that, very probably, many of Joseph's attendants wept at the hearing of it. Perhaps their tears were not dried up when they left his presence. But what was the cause of these strong emotions which now seemed to overpower his constancy they could not understand, till they heard that the men were Joseph's brethren.

The joys of the next world will set us above all the pains which are often mingled with the most delicious pleasures of the present. The Lord God will wipe away all tears from the eyes of the righteous in their state of perfection.

VER. 3. *And Joseph said unto his brethren, I am Joseph; doth my father yet live? and his brethren could not answer him; for they were troubled at his presence.*

Strong passions obstruct the voice, or render it inarticulate. Joseph's flood of tears, for a time, made him silent, and astonished his brethren. At last he found power to utter a few words, "I am Joseph; doth my father yet live?" It seems probable, from these words, that his brethren hitherto knew him not by the name of Joseph, but of Zaphnath-paaneah, or some title of office. He thought his first name *Joseph* sufficient to awaken their recollection of their long-lost brother. For a long time he had made himself strange to them. They never formed the least suspicion that he stood in any nearer relation to themselves than to other strangers that came into the country to buy corn. They had, indeed, been unable to account for some parts of his behaviour, and many conjectures might come into their minds; but the true reason of his behaviour could not have been guessed by the wisest man upon earth. The name of *Joseph* half explained the mystery. The sound of it recalled his countenance to their minds. Could they have looked to him with composure, they would have seen the once well-known features of his beautiful countenance, though considerably altered by the vicissitudes of more than twenty years of an eventful life. But in the present state of their minds they knew not what to think. Was it possible that this man could be their brother, or was he some other man of the same name? If he was Joseph their brother, whence the flood of tears that had gushed from his eyes, or why did he ask them if his father was yet alive? Apparent impossibility vanishes before the testimony of one's own senses. It was surely their brother Joseph that now spoke to them, and inquired concerning his father's welfare. Things may be true which are not only very improbable, but in appearance impossible. Nothing is impossible with God. He can raise the poor out of the dust, and the prisoner from his dungeon, and set him with princes.

"Doth my father yet live?" Had not Joseph already heard that his father still lived? If he could not believe the words of his brethren, he might have seen the truth of them in Judah's solicitude to preserve his father from being swallowed up by over-much grief. But men wish to have pleasant pieces of intelligence repeated and confirmed again and again, when they have no reason to doubt of them. This is the reason why believers in Jesus take pleasure to hear those truths often sounded in their ears which they already know and believe. That Jesus died and rose again, according to the Scriptures, are truths which we learned when we were children; and there are too many who would rather hear discourses on any other subject in religion, than on those which they think they already know as well as any preacher in the country. But God forbid that we should cease to glory in the cross and in the life of our Redeemer, or that the preachers of Christ should determine to know anything amongst their hearers save Jesus Christ, even Him who was crucified, and who lives for us!

"And his brethren could not answer him, for they were troubled at his presence."

Shame and terror took possession of their hearts. They were covered with confusion, when they found themselves in the presence of the man whom they had hated without a cause, whom they had stripped of his coat of divers colours, whom they had thrown into the pit, whom they had intended to assassinate, whom they had actually sold into Egypt, and whom they had represented to himself as one who was unfortunately lost in the days of his youth, and whom their father believed to have been torn in pieces by wild beasts. Every circumstance of their malevolent conduct rushed into their minds. They wished that the wings of a dove had been given them, to flee far away from the face of their deeply injured brother. They were ashamed and confounded, because they felt the reproach of their youth.

Fear, too, co-operated with shame to distress them. They had no reason to think that Joseph meant to do them any hurt. They had every reason to think that his heart overflowed with kindness to them. But we have already seen how their hearts were disposed to meditate terror on every occasion. The consciousness of guilt roused fear in their hearts, when there was little or no cause of fear, and even when there was cause to rejoice. Joseph now had them in his power. Although they were his brethren, they had been his enemies, and their enmity had been more inexcusable than if they had been sons of Esau. What if their brother, now so highly exalted above them, should make them feel the power of his arm in the infliction of vengeance? If a man find his enemy, will he let him go well away? If Joseph did not take advantage of his greatness to destroy or enslave them, was it to be expected that he would conceal their crimes from the people and the king of Egypt? Would they not be rendered so hateful to Pharaoh and to his people, that it would be difficult for them to make their escape out of that land into which they had sold their brother? There was a prophecy in their family, that the seed of Abraham would be sore afflicted by strangers for a very long space of time. Now the time might be come for the verification of this prediction, and their misery would be greatly embittered by the reflections of their own consciences, for they could not but acknowledge that their own hands had made these cords with which they were bound.

s

Such tormenting thoughts as these would crowd into their minds. They had sinned, and now their iniquity had found them out. When they were thrown into prison, their own consciences condemned them before God; but now, to the testimony of their consciences was added the presence of him whom they had so greatly wronged. He was not only present as an unexceptionable witness, but he was raised so high above them, that he could have pronounced and executed, if he had pleased, such a sentence as their crime deserved.

When your consciences arraign you for any part of your criminal conduct, consider that "God is greater than your hearts, and knoweth all things." Consider that although the remorse of your consciences is exceeding painful, that remorse is but a small part of the punishment that shall come upon you. What would you think of having those persons against whom you have sinned brought into your presence to publish their wrongs? What if they should one day be exalted, like Joseph, to a throne of judgment, to pass sentence upon you? This is no fanciful supposition. It will actually be the case if your sins continue marked in the book of God against you. "Your children, that have cast out devils, shall be your judges," said our Lord to those Pharisees who blasphemed His gracious works. May we not say, that those persons whom you have wronged, though perhaps greatly your inferiors, shall be your judges, under the universal Judge? They will rise up against you at the last day. He who executes righteousness and judgment for the oppressed will grant them the sight of their desire upon their enemies, and of much worse evils than they now desire, if charity dwells in them. If they are to be ranked amongst the just, hear what Paul says, and tremble : "Do ye not know that the saints shall judge the world?" The proud, and all that do wickedly, shall be ashes under the feet of the righteous, in the day that the Lord shall do this. Have you sinned against Christ, by rejecting His salvation and breaking His laws? "Behold, he cometh with clouds, and every eye shall see him; and they also that pierced him, and all kindreds of the earth shall wail because of him. Even so, amen." In that day it will be found that many pierced our blessed Lord who never beheld Him with their bodily eyes till they saw Him in the clouds of heaven.

Joseph's brethren were struck with confusion and alarm, yet they were safe, and they were soon happy; for Joseph, who might have been their judge and their avenger, was their brother and their friend. Consider whether you wish to have Christ at the last day for your friend and Saviour, or your destroyer. "He shall come without sin unto salvation" to all who take refuge under the shadow of His meditation. But He will come in flaming fire, "taking vengeance upon all them that know not God, and that obey not the gospel of our Lord Jesus Christ."

Ver. 4. *And Joseph said unto his brethren, Come near to me, I pray you. And they came near. And he said, I am Joseph your brother, whom ye sold into Egypt.*

It was pleasant to Joseph to speak words of kindness unto his penitent brethren. But he wished, likewise, to have them in his arms, that he might seal his kindness by the kisses of his mouth. The kisses of an enemy are deceitful; but the kisses of a faithful friend, long absent, or after long alienation, are delightful testimonies of mutual affection. Before his brethren could receive his embraces with pleasure, it was necessary to give them fuller assurance that he had cordially forgiven his wrongs.

"And he said unto them, I am Joseph your brother, whom ye sold into Egypt."

He assures them that he was their brother still, although they had sold him into Egypt. The relation between them was not dissolved, the duties and charities of it were not cancelled. An angry man remembers those things that fired his passion. A generous man, when he is injured, calls to mind what will soften it. When we are provoked, let us endeavour to keep the command of our thoughts, and to call up those considerations to view which will most effectually subdue or soften our resentment. We have been wronged or insulted; but the man who did us the wrong is entitled to our charity. He is made of the same blood with ourselves.   He is perhaps a child of God, a brother in Christ, a member of that body to which we belong. If we ought not to hide ourselves from our own flesh, we ought much less to hate those who are our brethren, both in the flesh and in the Lord.

But if Joseph remembered that he was their brother, why does he call up to view their hateful conduct?   Was he one of those hypocrites in charity who will forgive, but will not forget offences?   Very far from it; but he saw in their faces the impressions of shame and fear produced by the bitter remembrance of their guilt, and he wished to restore them to friendship with themselves, that they might be restored to friendship with him.   "He said, I am Joseph your brother, whom ye sold into Egypt."

VER. 5. *Now therefore be not grieved, nor angry with your-selves, that ye sold me hither : for God did send me before you to preserve life.*

Had they not good reason to grieve and be angry with them-selves?   Did not Joseph wish them that repentance which is so absolutely necessary for salvation?   Undoubtedly.   He had used some severe methods to inspire them with grief and hatred of their sin, and he was far from wishing that their goodness should be as the morning cloud, or as the early dew, that passeth away.   If we truly repent of our sins, our sorrow and shame for offending God will not be expelled by the assurance of pardon, either from God or man.

But when men are mourning even for sin, they may carry their grief to a dangerous excess.   Paul did not desire the great offender at Corinth who had disgraced the church to be overwhelmed with excess of sorrow.   Although he had treated that poor man with greater severity than Joseph did his brethren, for he had commanded him to be delivered to Satan for the destruction of his flesh, yet he would not suffer him to remain without comfort when grief had overwhelmed him, lest Satan should find an opportunity to do him mischief, which Paul did not intend.   "Sufficient to such a man is this punish-ment which was inflicted of many : Ye ought rather to forgive him, and comfort him, lest perhaps such an one should be swallowed up with over-much sorrow : Lest Satan should get an advantage over us ; for we are not ignorant of his devices."

When sinners justify or excuse themselves, they ought to be awakened by sharp reproof. When Joseph had no reason to think that his brethren were sufficiently sensible of the atrocity of their guilt, he treated them with a severity which brought their sin to remembrance in all its horrors. When he saw them deeply humbled, and overwhelmed with confusion, he administered healing consolation. "Be not grieved, nor angry with yourselves, that ye sold me hither." By the grief and self-reflections against which he exhorted them is not to be understood that grief and self-abhorrence which are essential to repentance, but that kind of grief which was now wringing their hearts, and preventing them from accepting his fond embraces. They were not to consider their fault as a crime too great to be forgiven, either by that God or that brother whom they had offended. They were not to mourn as if there was no hope left of a cordial reconciliation with himself. Whilst they were angry at their corrupt tempers, which had prompted them to sell their brother into Egypt, they were not to imagine that Divine Providence was unable to prevent the mischievous consequences which their sin might have produced ; nor were they to indulge anger against one another for the part which some of them might take in prompting the rest to the commission of an action which now appeared so hateful to them all.

"Blessed are they that mourn," says our Lord, "for they shall be comforted." We ought by all means to mourn for sin. But the promise to the mourners is in effect a prohibition of that sorrow which does not admit of comfort. If comfort is the portion of the mourners, they must not mourn as if there were no remedy for the evils which they have brought upon themselves.

"Be not grieved nor angry with yourselves, that you sold me hither : for God did send me before you to preserve life." Here a doctrine is taught which is full of mystery, but no less full of comfort. When Jacob's envious sons sold their brother into Egypt, God sent him thither. The holy God made use of the wickedness of his brethren to accomplish His own gracious purposes. Marvel not that God is said to do those things which are done by the hands of wicked and ungodly men. We find that ascribed to God in one place of Scripture which is in another place ascribed to the great enemy of God. The Lord was displeased with Israel, and moved David against them to say, "Go number Israel and Judah." Satan stood up against Israel, and provoked David to number Israel. Surely the wrath of men, and the malice of Satan, shall praise God. They can do nothing without His permission. They can do nothing without His providence overruling all their malicious contrivances, and directing them in a subserviency to His own purposes, 2 Sam. xxiv. 1 ; 1 Chron. xxi. 1.

You know that the righteous God hates all sin with a perfect and irreconcilable hatred. He cannot tempt any man to evil. He is of purer eyes than to look upon sin ; yet no sin can be committed without His knowledge, or in opposition to His holy counsels. Sinners are as really the ministers of His providence as saints, and He glorifies Himself by the wickedness which He hates and punishes as well as by that holiness which He loves and rewards. When Joseph was sold into Egypt by the envy of his brethren, that he might never attain that pre-eminence which seemed to be portended by his dreams, God sent him into Egypt, that he might both attain the promised grandeur, and might be the happy instrument of saving many lives. "God did send me before you to preserve life."

There is a season for everything, and a time for every purpose, under the sun. The time of everything was determined by God in His eternal counsels, and His wisdom appears glorious in His arrangement of the events of providence. When Jacob's family was to come into Egypt, Joseph was sent before his father and his brethren, that they might not all perish with hunger. Who knows what is good for a man all the days of his vain life, which he spendeth as a shadow ? When Jacob lost his dear Rachael, she left behind her two sons ; one of them was an amiable boy at the time of her death. Jacob thought that she would not be wholly dead to him whilst these two children, her representatives, lived. They would live under his eye, and cheer him with their growing virtues. His beloved wife seemed to die to him a second time when Joseph was torn from him, and he seemed to lose her a third time when Benjamin was carried to a strange land, from whence he might never return. All these things, he thought, were against him. Yet God, by depriving him of Joseph, sent a man before him by whom he and his house should be fed. It was necessary that Benjamin should be sent likewise, that he might have comfort in all his sons, by the proof which they gave of their reformation. But Joseph was to be sent long before, both that he might acquire that high station which enabled him to afford subsistence and protection to the whole family, and that he might prepare the means of life in famine.

" God sent me before you to preserve life "—to preserve not only the life of his father's family, but the lives of the whole nation of Egypt, and of multitudes in the neighbouring countries. God is pleased often to afflict the sons of men by His sore judgments, and famine is one of the heaviest of them. Yet He remembers mercy in the midst of wrath, even to the unthankful and to the evil. Those arrangements of providence by which life is preserved in famine are often very surprising to the most thoughtless of mortals. God opens His hands liberally, and supplies the wants of every living thing. His liberality is wonderful in the worst of times, especially to His own people. God had a special regard to Jacob's family when He sent Joseph into Egypt to preserve life. Jacob, in his last days, could not forget the bounty of that God which had fed him all his lifelong. And we ought never to forget that goodness which has fed all the past generations of men, and has provided rich supplies in days of famine to them that fear Him.

The greatest part of men, in thinking of their misfortunes or their blessings, think little of the great Author of their being, and manager of their concerns. They feel irritation of spirit against those men whose bad conduct has caused their miseries, and are grateful to the persons to whom they reckon themselves indebted for favourable circumstances in their condition; but they do not raise their minds to Him who has said, "I form light, and create darkness; I make peace and create evil; I the Lord do all these things." Joseph was taught by God to acknowledge and revere His providence in all that befell him. He saw the hand of God in his afflictions, and saw goodness and mercy in them, and could cheerfully forgive those who were God's instruments in bringing him low. He saw the hand of God in his exaltation, and kept in view the end for which he was raised on high. He was not immoderately dejected by adversity, for he knew that his God would do him no hurt that would not be overruled for his good. His soul was not lifted up within him by prosperity, for he knew that, not for his own benefit chiefly, but for the benefit of others also, he was advanced to the government of Egypt, and blessed with the knowledge of things to come.

"Now therefore be not grieved, nor angry with yourselves, that ye sold me hither: for God did send me before you to preserve life." Joseph, in these words, endeavours to revive the dejected spirits of his brethren, by turning their attention to the gracious operations of Divine Providence, bringing much good to themselves, and to many others, out of their own bad conduct. What we have done, we cannot undo; and we cannot prevent the natural tendency of sin to produce the most miserable effects to ourselves, and perhaps to others. Joseph's brothers had sold him into Egypt. He might there have died under the effects of bad usage, or of the despondency of his own spirits. He might have been corrupted by the infectious example of idolators. His father might have pined to death in his grief for the misfortunes of his favourite son. His brethren might have been plagued in this world, or punished with eternal burnings in the next, for their wickedness. Such consequences might have been expected as the natural or penal effects of their guilt. Such consequences have been felt from less aggravated iniquities by thousands and millions of transgressors. "The wages of sin is death."

But Joseph was still alive, and uncorrupted in his principles or practice. Jacob was enabled patiently to bear his heavy calamity, and there was joy before. him more than sufficient to compensate all that he had suffered. His sons were so far from being punished as their iniquities deserved, that their lives, and the lives of their little ones, were to be preserved by the man whom they had sold into Egypt. His grievous afflictions were steps to that grandeur and power which enabled him to do such eminent and needful services to his father's family. "The archers had sorely grieved him, and shot at him; but his bow abode in strength, and the arms of his hands were made strong by the hands of the mighty God of Jacob, that he might be the shepherd and stone of Israel."

When we consider what our sins deserve, and what have been the miserable effects of the sins of multitudes of our fellow-men, we will find abundant cause of thanksgiving to that Providence which has, in innumerable instances, counteracted the natural tendency of our iniquities; and has preserved us from the pain of seeing misery diffused around us as the fruit of our doings. Blessed be God, who has restrained us from doing half the evil to which we are prompted by our perverse dispositions, and who hath prevented a great part of those evils which might otherwise have followed our evil works. We have still greater reason to be thankful when we see good brought out of our evil, either to ourselves or to other men. Joseph's brethren sold him into Egypt, and God made use of their sin to perform His purposes of mercy to their father's house.

Yet we must not think that the nature of sin is altered by the use that God makes of it. Poison does not cease to be poison because it may enter into the composition of healing medicines. " If our unrighteousness commend the righteousness of God, what shall we say? Is God unrighteous who taketh vengeance? God forbid; for then, how shall God judge the world?"

LECTURE 21

Joseph comforts his brethren, and sends a kind message by them to his father.

xlv 6–13

VER. 6. *For these two years hath the famine been in the land : and yet there are five years, in the which there shall neither be earing nor harvest.*

WE are too ready in word and in tongue to forgive those who have offended us, whilst in deed and in truth we retain a bitter resentment of our wrongs ; and if we do not inflict or wish some visible judgment to come on them, we wish that they may feel in their own hearts a painful remembrance of what they have done. But Joseph so entirely forgave his sinning brethren, that he wished for them the same peace and pleasure that he wished for himself. To restore tranquillity to their troubled minds, he directs their attention to that gracious Providence which overruled their iniquity to his own advantage and theirs. "Be not grieved, nor angry with yourselves, that ye sold me hither : for God did send me before you to preserve life." These words needed explication. Two years of famine had reduced the family of Jacob to distress. They had been under the necessity of fetching corn from Egypt. But must they all have died unless they had received supplies from Egypt? Possibly they might have found some other shift for the preservation of their lives during these two years. But these two years were but the beginning of the sorrows of famine. They were to be followed with other five years, in which there was to be neither ploughing nor sowing through the greater part of the fertile country of Egypt. Every succeeding year would be more grievous than the former. Many were likely to lose their lives. God could find out a way to preserve the family He had chosen; and the way that He was pleased to take for this end was by sending Joseph into Egypt before his father and his brethren. Let us not distrust the providence of God in the worst of times. In the mount the Lord will be seen. Let days and years of hardships follow one another in long succession, God knows them all before they come, and knows what provision to make of all needful supplies and relief. " Man does not live by bread alone, but by every word which proceedeth out of the mouth of God."

" There are five years in which there shall neither be earing nor harvest." Let not the ploughman complain of the cold and dreary days in which he must follow the plough. Let not the reaper complain of the toils of harvest. What if days should come in which there were neither earing nor harvest? You must encounter some bitter blasts. You must toil and sweat in your labours; but he that plougheth plougheth in hope, and he that reapeth reapeth in hope, that he shall eat the labour of his hands. Those are evil times in which there is no hire for man or beast, for him that goeth out or for him that cometh in.

"There shall be neither earing nor harvest." For what reason? Because the people knew that there would be no crop, they would not cultivate the ground, or cast that seed into the earth which would produce no increase. Hope is necessary to every business that is transacted. Who will labour without hope of advantage? And it is no less necessary in the affairs of religion than in the affairs of life. Those who say, " What profit shall we have if we pray unto God?" are the men who restrain prayer before Him. " He that cometh unto God must believe that he is, and that he is the rewarder of them that diligently seek him." It is the will of God that he who plougheth should plough in hope, and that he who thresheth in hope should be partaker of his hope.

Ver. 7. *And God sent me before you to preserve you a posterity in the earth, and to save your lives by a great deliverance.*

Joseph here repeats what he had already said, that it might make the deeper impression on the minds of his brethren, to dispel their fears, and inspire them with confidence in himself, and with gratitude to the God whose mercy so wonderfully prevented them.

"God did send me before you to preserve life"—not only to preserve the lives of those who already existed, but to preserve a posterity in the earth for Abraham and Jacob. These patriarchs and their children looked forward with pleasure to the time when their seed should be numerous as the stars of heaven, and when that blessed seed should come into the world, in whom all the families of the earth were to be blessed. But that these promises might be accomplished, it was necessary that the present race should be preserved, that they might become the progenitors of successive generations to praise the Lord. If Isaac had perished on Mount Moriah, what would have become of the promise to Abraham? If Jacob's sons had died with hunger, what would have become of the promise to Jacob, that in his seed all the nations of the earth should be blessed? If we rejoice in these good tidings, that to us was born in the city of David a Saviour, let us give thanks to that Providence, which by sending Joseph to Egypt, preserved to Jacob a posterity in the earth, from which the Saviour was to take His flesh. It was impossible that the family could perish which was to give a Saviour to the nations.

We see from this observation of Joseph one great reason why we ought to bless God for those mercies to our fathers by which they were preserved from destruction. They were preserved for our sakes as well as their own. None are suffered to die till they have brought into existence those who were to proceed from their loins. "Thus saith the Lord, As the new wine is found in the cluster, and one saith, Destroy it not, for a blessing is in it; so will I do for my servants' sake, that I may not destroy them all." When wrath came upon the Jews to the uttermost, they were not all destroyed. For the elect's sake the days of destruction were shortened ; and not only for the elect's sake who lived at that time, but for the sake of those elect persons that might spring from them at the distance of thousands of years.

" And to save your lives by a great deliverance." The daily preservation of our lives is a great mercy. Every interposition of Providence to save us from danger is a wonderful mercy. But some deliverances are singularly great on account of the greatness of the danger from which they preserve us, or the singular circumstances attending them. Such deliverances ought to be carefully remarked, that we may praise God according to the greatness of His mercy. Such was the deliverance of Lot from Sodom ; such was the preservation of the house of Jacob from the horrors of the general famine in the days of Jacob ; such was their deliverance from the land of Egypt. All our deliverances will be admired by us if the spirit of adoption dwell in us. All deliverances will be lost upon us if the principle of selfishness reign within us.

Grandeur has its attendant troubles, and snares, from which we may infer the vanity of what is most admired among the sons of men. Yet when greatness meets with a generous and holy temper of mind, it is a great blessing to the possessor, because it enables him to do much good which cannot be done by ordinary men. We have no reason to envy the great, for it is very probable that if we were in their places, we would be less happy and less holy than we are. Yet great men who are fitted by God to do the duties of their places have great reason to be thankful. And that their stations may be a blessing to themselves and others, they ought to consider who it is that hath exalted them, and for what ends that they may fulfil the gracious designs of Providence. Joseph did not think that God had first humbled and then exalted him that he might eat royal dainties, and enjoy the acclamations of the multitude, and see them bowing their knees before him. He knew that God had sent him into Egypt, and exalted him to power, that he might save many lives, and he diligently employed himself in those noble services to Egypt and to his

father's house which he was exalted to perform. Thus David
saw that God had exalted his kingdom for the sake of His people
Israel, and devoted all his days to their service. If we are
negligent of the duties of our places, whatever they are, or if
we neglect those special duties for which God furnishes us with
singular advantages, what account will we render to our Judge
for those talents with which we are intrusted?

VER. 8. *So now it was not you that sent me hither, but God:
and he hath made me a father to Pharaoh, and lord of all his
house, and a ruler throughout all the land of Egypt.*

Joseph's brethren certainly sold him into Egypt. They had
indeed no views to one place more than another when they sold
him. But they knew that the Ishmaelitish merchants who
bought him were travelling into Egypt, and would probably
dispose of him in that country. Joseph himself had already
said to them, " I am Joseph your brother, whom ye sold into
Egypt." How, then, does he say, " It was not you that sent me
hither, but God?" God undoubtedly sent him into Egypt, but
was it not by their hands that he sent him?

Words have not always the same meaning from different
mouths. Had such words as these been spoken by Joseph's
brethren, we would have justly thought they were speaking
a lie, and almost a blasphemous lie, by endeavouring to transfer
their criminal behaviour to God. Adam said nothing but what
was strictly true when he said, "The woman whom thou gavest
to be with me, she gave me of the fruit, and I did eat;" yet
in these words we discover the corrupt disposition of the
speaker. He wished to transfer his own guilt to his wife, and
almost charged Divine Providence with it. He said in effect,
that if God had not cursed him with a wicked wife, he might
still have been innocent and happy. Thus, if Joseph's brethren
had said, " It was not we that sent you hither, but God," we
might have justly said that they charged God foolishly, and
wished to exculpate themselves by attributing that conduct
for which they deserved so much blame to that Providence
which can do nothing wrong.

But when Joseph is the speaker of these words, the plain

meaning is, that he entertained no harsh sentiments concerning their conduct, but considered it, and all the effects of it, as a step of Divine Providence for his good. Their intention was too manifest. They meant evil against him. But his thoughts were so much occupied by God's kind intentions, that he forgot theirs. When God says, "I will have mercy, and not sacrifice," the meaning is, not that God will not have sacrifice, but that He will have mercy in preference to it. Thus, when it is said, " It was not you, but God, that sent me hither," the meaning is, my coming to Egypt is more God's work than yours. God was the first cause, they were but instruments overruled by Him for the accomplishment of His own purposes. It was the will of God both that Joseph should be brought to Egypt, and that the malevolence of his brethren should be the means used for bringing him to it. The Lord of hosts permits much evil in the world. We are amazed that the God who hates all sin should permit so much sin to find place in a world which He governs with an absolute sway. But here we find that He not only permits it, but makes use of it. No sinner can do any evil that He has not intended to use for the advancement of His own glory. It is only in some cases that we can see what God can bring out of so much evil; but from these cases we may learn what He does in other cases of a like nature. Joseph was sold into Egypt by the envy of his brethren, but it was not they only, but God that sent him into Egypt. Their envy remained with themselves. Its effects on Joseph did him no hurt, but much good. If any hurt was done to him, it was good in the event. But God's design took its full effect in His own glory, and in saving many people alive. Thus our Lord Jesus Christ was sent into Egypt by God, when He fled from the wrath of Herod. He suffered many things in the course of His life ; He endured a painful and ignominious death, but we know that He was made perfect through sufferings, and that they were all appointed for Him by a Providence which could not err, that He might be an all-accomplished Saviour to us —" For it became him, for whom are all things, and through whom are all things, in bringing many sons unto glory, to make the Captain of their salvation perfect through sufferings."

" And he hath made me a father to Pharaoh." It it said, chap. xli. 43, that " Pharaoh made Joseph to ride in the second chariot which he had, and they cried before him, Bow the knee." Some commentators tell us that the word which we render *Bow the knee* is not to be understood as a Hebrew, but as an Egyptian word, which signifies the father of the king. This opinion derives some probability from what Joseph here says to his brethren. It is not likely that he would have taken to himself this high title of father to the king without the king's own authority. Pharaoh had said to him, " In the throne will I be greater than thou ; " yet he gave him the management of all the affairs of his house and kingdom ; expected his own subsistence from him, and treated him with all the respect which a son shows to his father.

" God hath made me a father to Pharaoh." He was greatly indebted to the king of Egypt, but he was infinitely more indebted to the God of heaven. It was God that brought him to the knowledge of Pharaoh, and gave him favour in his sight. It was God that exalted him by the ministry of Pharaoh, and furnished him with knowledge, wisdom, and authority to be an eminent benefactor to Pharaoh and to his kingdom. He looked beyond his brethren to God when he thought upon his affliction, and beyond Pharaoh to God when he thought of his exaltation. Thus he bears his afflictions with meekness, and his elevation with humility.

" God sent me into Egypt, and made me father to Pharaoh and lord of all his house, and ruler throughout all the land of Egypt." Better is the end of a thing than the beginning thereof. When he first came to Egypt, he became a servant to one of Pharaoh's servants. Now he becomes a father to Pharaoh, and a lord over the whole kingdom, the greatest at that time in the world. We ought not to fix our views upon detached circumstances in our condition, without taking into account those other circumstances which are connected with them. Had Joseph fixed his attention only on the sorrows which he had endured in consequence of his brethren's envy, his soul would have been disquieted and ruffled. His brethren might have appeared to him the authors of all his misery, and he would have found it difficult or impossible to forgive their trespass from his heart, and to love them as brethren; but he considered his miseries as the occasions and means of his happiness.

He saw "that God had brought him through fire and water, and caused men to ride over his head, that he might be brought to a wealthy place." He told his brethren that they had done him no real hurt, but had been the instruments employed by Divine Providence to bring him to glory and honour. He was so far from harbouring bitter resentment against them, that he ascribed to them, under God, the dignity which he enjoyed, and the happy opportunity put into his hand of diffusing plenty through all the land of Egypt, and of preserving all his father's house from the miseries of famine. "All things work together for good to them that love God;" and those who love God should observe how He brings good out of evil to them, that they may learn how to forgive their enemies. We are not exasperated against those whom we esteem our benefactors. Injuries are benefactions when they promote our best interests, and it is our own fault if they do not. We cannot expect such results to our afflictions as those of which Joseph speaks to his brethren. But what are all the glories of this world compared with a participation of God's holiness, which is the consequence of all sanctified affliction! If we cannot follow Joseph's example, we may speak as cheerfully as Joseph himself did of our afflictions, and of the advantages which they bring. Bear every injury with the meekness and gentleness of Christ. Consider what you suffer as the allotment of gracious Providence for your benefit, and you will certainly be able to say, that you have learned by your afflictions to keep God's statutes. And this is more than if you could say that you were advanced to the highest honours among men. The highest honours among men endure but a moment. "But our light afflictions, which are but for a moment, work for us a far more exceeding and eternal weight of glory."

T

VER. 9. *Haste ye, and go up to my father, and say unto him,*
Thus saith thy son Joseph, God hath made me lord of all Egypt:
come down unto me, tarry not.

We are not surprised that Joseph was now impatient to
communicate to his father the happy tidings of his life, and his
glory in Egypt. We rather wonder that he did not hasten his
brethren's return with the happy news when they came down
for the first time; or that he did not send intelligence by other
means of conveyance long before he saw their faces. Certainly
he expected no greater pleasure in this world than again to
behold the loved countenance of Israel his father, and to hear
the words of his mouth, which were always full of kindness or
of instruction to him in his earliest years. But all Joseph's
steps were guided by wisdom, and by divine direction. Now
everything was removed out of the way which might render it
unadvisable to inform his father of his condition, and Providence had so ordered matters, that he could entertain a reasonable hope of prevailing on his father to come down to Egypt.
He requests, therefore, his brethren to hasten to Canaan, and
tell their common father how great a man he was become, and
how desirous he was to employ all his power and wealth for his
benefit, if he would come and dwell with him. We too often
render our pleasures tasteless or vexatious by too much haste to
enjoy them. By patience and prudence we are prepared to
enjoy them without danger of losing them, or turning them into
bitterness.

"Thus saith thy son Joseph." He was not forgetful that he
was Jacob's son, although he was become a father to Pharaoh.
If a man were advanced from a shepherd's cottage to a throne,
he would be unworthy of that life which he enjoys if he could
forget the father that begat him, and the mother that bare
him.

"Thus saith thy son Joseph, God hath made me lord of all
Egypt." This part of the message would give Jacob the pleasure
of knowing that Joseph had not forgotten the language of Canaan
in the midst of a people of strange language. He remembered
not only his father, but his father's God, and the lesson which

his father had often taught him, to ascribe all the happy events of his life to the providence of God.

" Come down unto me, tarry not." He could not arise and go to his father, otherwise he would have been happy to revisit his native land, that he might again behold his revered countenance, and ask his blessing. But the lord of Egypt was called to employments that rendered his presence necessary in that country. His father had no necessity laid upon him to abide in Hebron. On the contrary, he was called by the providence of God to leave a country in which bread was not now to be found.

VER. 10. *And thou shalt dwell in the land of Goshen, and thou shalt be near unto me, thou, and thy children, and thy children's children, and thy flocks, and thy herds, and all that thou hast.*

Joseph speaks as if he had all power in the land of Egypt, and would take it upon him to assign one of the best and most convenient districts in that land to his father as his habitation. From this it appears that Pharaoh had not promised more than he performed to Joseph, when he was advanced to his high office. He had now been at least nine years in office, and his power was still so great, and appeared to be so well established, that he could promise a quiet habitation and plenteous accommodations to his father for many years to come. His mountain stood strong by God's favour, and he could promise what he knew he was raised up by God to perform.

"And thou shalt be near unto me." Joseph knew that these words would be sweeter than music to his affectionate father. From the words of Judah, he had learned what bitter griefs his father had endured by his own separation from him. He rejoiced greatly that God had put it into his power to compensate to his father all those floods of tears which the sorrows of parental tenderness had for so many long years drawn from his eyes. What happiness might such a son and such a father hope to give and receive, if Providence allowed them to live together for the remainder of their joint lives, after such a long and mournful separation ! Jacob could not certainly wish for a greater felicity than to be with Joseph till the time should come when angels would carry him to Abraham's bosom, which was far better.

Joseph could not leave his government to go to his father. Jacob could not leave his large family to come to Joseph, but he could bring them all with him to enjoy the protection and bounty of his beloved son : " Thou shalt be near unto me, thou, and thy children, and thy children's children, and thy flocks, and thy herds, and all that thou hast." Parents, especially in old age, wish to be near to as many as possible of their children. And dutiful children wish to be near their parents, to show them that respect, and administer to them those comforts, which they are entitled to expect. Relations, who are taught by nature to love one another, ought to be thankful to God when He allows them the pleasure and benefit of one another's society ; and they ought to behave so as that their mutual society may be a benefit and pleasure.

VER. 11. *And there will I nourish thee ; for yet there are five years of famine ; lest thou, and thy household, and all that thou hast, come to poverty.*

Joseph knew that his father Jacob was once rich in flocks and herds, in gold and silver, in man-servants and maid-servants ; but he knew likewise, that riches are not for ever, and that in bad times poverty will often come upon the rich like an armed man. Often have those who once lived in the greatest affluence been reduced to dependence on the liberality of other men.

In the prospect of the long continuance of famine, Joseph was solicitous to preserve his father's family from feeling its bad effects. Almost all fathers interest themselves deeply in the prosperity and welfare of their children. Why should not children interest themselves as warmly in the comfort and welfare of their parents when they are old? If a man will not part with what he has to his father and mother when they need his assistance, he is not a true son of Jacob. He hath denied the faith, and is worse than an infidel. A dutiful son will have no greater pleasure in the use of what he has acquired than in supplying, or, if possible, preventing, the wants of those who gave him birth. Joseph did not wait till his father became poor, but importuned him to come to Egypt, with all that he had, and to partake of his own wealth, that he might not come to poverty.

VER. 12. *And, behold, your eyes see, and the eyes of my brother Benjamin, that it is my mouth that speaketh unto you.*

What the brethren of Joseph now saw and heard was so passing strange, that it was a difficulty with them to believe their own eyes and ears. Joseph therefore calls them to observe that he was now speaking to them without an interpreter. They might all have recollected the features of his face and the sound of his voice. Even Benjamin, who was but a child when Joseph left Canaan, could not but know that it was Joseph who was speaking to them.

But the real state of the matter was, that the backwardness of Joseph's brethren to receive his embraces was the effect of shame rather than uncertainty. They could not doubt that it was the mouth of Joseph that spoke to them. They could scarcely doubt of his kindness.

They yet found it very difficult, or impossible, to believe that he retained no resentment at all of their cruel usage of him. They were conscious that they deserved severe rebuke and punishment; and they also probably felt that they could not have from their heart forgiven one who had treated them as they had treated Joseph. It has been frequently observed that it is much easier to forgive the injuries which are done to us, than to believe that the injuries which we have done are forgiven.

Under the influence of shame, and of some remaining fear, they still stood at some distance from Joseph. To engage their confidence, he desires them to observe that it was their own affectionate brother that spoke to them, and that Divine Providence had turned all the grounds of complaint which he seemed to have against them into causes of joy and thanksgiving.

VER. 13. *And ye shall tell my father of all my glory in Egypt, and of all that ye have seen; and ye shall haste and bring down my father hither.*

It is unpleasant to hear a man talking again and again of his own wealth and grandeur. It is not good for a man to eat much honey; so for a man to speak of his own glory is not glory, but shame. How, then, does Joseph speak so much of his own grandeur? Are we to suppose that he was puffed up by a fleshly mind? Far from it. His treatment of his brethren and of the Egyptians affords us sufficient evidence that he walked humbly with his God when he was lord of Egypt as well as when he was Potiphar's servant.

But he wished greatly to turn away the thoughts of his brethren from that wretched state to which they had reduced him, unto that happy state to which they had advanced him. Whilst they considered how they had sold him, they found it almost impossible to believe that he could retain for them the kindness of a brother; but if they could have fixed their thoughts on the happy changes of his condition, they might have been persuaded that the sense of their wrongs was buried in the joy of his exaltation. His afflictions appeared to be blessings in disguise. And bitter resentment against the instruments of his affliction would have been ingratitude to that God who brought so much grandeur out of them. Remember, that the God who commands you to forgive injuries is wonderful in counsel and excellent in working. He can turn them to your advantage; He will turn them to your advantage if you obey Him; you may know by your obedience to the command of forgiving your enemies that He has turned them to your benefit; and if you believe that He is faithful to His promise of making all things work together for your good, the precept of forgiveness will not be grievous.

Joseph likewise spoke of his glory in Egypt, and desired his father to be informed of it, because he knew that it would give much pleasure to his father, and enlarge his heart, and open his mouth to praise that God who had been so gracious to him in the person of his beloved son. An affectionate son takes great pleasure in giving pleasure to his father. A lover of God takes pleasure in telling what God has done for him, that his friends may magnify the Lord with him. "He hath delivered us from so great a death," says Paul to the Corinthian believers, "and doth deliver, in whom we trust that He will yet deliver us; ye also helping together by prayer for us, that for the gift bestowed upon us by the means of many persons, thanks may be given by many on our behalf," 2 Cor. i. 10, 11. He sent Tychicus to the Ephesian believers to tell them all his state, that they might assist him by their prayers and thanksgivings.

Joseph had perhaps another end in view when he desired his brethren to tell his father of his glory. This part of the message might give them the hope of finding forgiveness with their father. When he learned what they had done against their brother, he must have been shocked at their unnatural barbarity; but by hearing of Joseph's glory, he could perceive that God had sent him into Egypt by their hands to accomplish his prophetical dreams. The grace of God, in giving such a favourable issue to Joseph's afflictions, would reconcile Jacob to the men who had brought those afflictions upon him. Joseph himself felt the force of this consideration on his own spirit. Very probably the same consideration had a happy influence on the Church of Christ when many of those men who had been partners in the guilt of crucifying Him were converted to the faith. Those who first trusted in Christ must have thought with horror of the atrocious guilt of the men who embrued their hands in His blood. Yet they did not hesitate to receive these murderers into their holy society, nor retain any resentment against them for their outrages against their Lord, whom they so dearly loved. God had, by hands cruel and unjust, inflicted that death upon Christ which was their own life; and they rejoiced to share the blessings purchased by His death with those who killed Him.

" Ye shall tell my father of all my glory in Egypt." Joseph knew that his father, who loved him so dearly, would rejoice greatly to hear of his glory in Egypt. And if we love our Lord Jesus Christ, will we not greatly rejoice to hear of that glory in heaven to which He was exalted, after suffering those afflictions upon earth, to which Joseph's afflictions could bear no comparison? and after suffering for our sins, that we might be preserved from the awful consequences of our guilt, and might be advanced to a seat with Him on His throne? It was but a little time that Jacob could share in the prosperity of his son. He had reason, from the word of God to Abraham (Gen. xv.), to fear that the advantages to be expected from going down to his son in Egypt would be followed with a deplorable servitude to his seed; but we know that when Christ comes to receive us to Himself, the days of our mourning will be ended, and the day of everlasting joy commence.

"And ye shall haste and bring down my father hither." When you forgive those that trespass against you, it will give them pleasure to oblige you, if they are truly penitent; and by putting it in their power to do you a favour, you will lighten them of a part of that load that lies upon their hearts. Joseph now saw that his brethren could not forgive themselves for what they had done against him; but he lets them know that they had it in their power, in some degree, to compensate his former miseries by using their influence along with his to hasten down their father to Egypt. One of his griefs had been, that in Egypt he could not see his father's face; but for the pleasure of again beholding him, he would account himself indebted to his brethren if they could prevail on him to make no tarrying in doing what he would find at last to be absolutely necessary. Unless Jacob's sons had lingered before they came the second time, they might have been in Egypt many days sooner. If they suffered themselves to be detained in Canaan for but a few weeks after their return, the time would appear very long to Joseph, whose heart was now eagerly set on a reunion with his father. When he saw but a distant probability of meeting with his father, he patiently bore what could not be remedied. But now hope kindled his desires; and when hope is deferred, it maketh the heart sick.

LECTURE 22
Joseph's interview with Benjamin.
xlv 14

VER. 14. *And he fell upon his brother Benjamin's neck, and wept ; and Benjamin wept upon his neck.*

JOSEPH'S bowels had yearned over his brother Benjamin at the time when he stood at his own bar arraigned as a thief, and so confounded with the unworthy charge, that he could not answer a word for himself. Now, when there was no further occasion for concealing what was in Joseph's heart, his affection broke forth in all its force. Words were insufficient to express half the tenderness of his soul. He sprung into Benjamin's embraces, and held him fast, and was relieved from an oppression of joy by a flood of tears.

Benjamin was little less transported than Joseph. The transition from passions of the most gloomy kind to the sweetest joys that mortality can taste, was almost too hard for him to bear. But tears came, likewise, to his relief. He wept upon Joseph's neck.

Benjamin could remember how pleasant his brother Joseph had been to him before the time that he was supposed to have been torn in pieces by the beasts of prey. Benjamin was not then too young to feel the loss of such a brother. He joined his tears with the tears of his father, and this probably was one of the many endearments by which the heart of Jacob was knit to Benjamin. He knew that his other sons were displeased with his own partiality to him, and did not think their sorrow for his loss was so sincere or strong as Benjamin's.

Benjamin had often listened to his father speaking of the virtues and of the unhappy fate of Joseph. He no more expected to see him in the land of the living than to see his fathers Abraham and Isaac raised up again from their graves in the cave of Machpelah. What overwhelming joy poured into his heart when that crafty tyrant who wished to make him a thief and a slave was found to have no existence, and his own much-lamented brother appeared in his place, as if the lions which devoured him had rendered up their prey, and bone again come to its bone! We have heard of many whose life was unable to sustain the impetuous tide of joy which rushed into their souls when those friends were found to be alive who had been supposed dead. We should not have wondered if Benjamin had died with joy, or fainted in Joseph's presence. But the tears which he wept on Joseph's neck unloaded his heart of its excess of pleasure.

Benjamin's loved image had been deeply engraven on Joseph's heart. In Benjamin he saw his long-lost mother. Yet his fondness was not confined to this brother. Reuben, and Simeon, and Judah, and all the other sons of Jacob were his brethren, the sons of the same venerable father.

VER. 15. *Moreover he kissed all his brethren, and wept upon them : and after that his brethren talked with him.*

They were all dear to him, and he greatly desired a place in their hearts. His kisses and his tears were genuine expressions of his kindness, and sure tokens that all their offences were to him as if they had never been committed.

His brethren were now assured of his love, and could talk with him. One great reason why those who have committed injuries are with difficulty reconciled to the persons whom they have wronged is, that if the persons injured really forgive, they are often deficient in their expressions of forgiveness. Joseph not only forgave his brethren, but gave them such assurances of his forgiveness, and such endearing testimonies of his love, as made them ashamed of their doubts. Long after this time they grieved the heart of their brother by the discovery they made of suspicions concerning him still lurking in their hearts. But at this time their suspicions were driven from them by Joseph's affectionate behaviour; and friendly converse succeeded to that tempest of passion which had nearly overwhelmed them.

This converse was now very different from that which they held at the governor's table. When they were eating and drinking with him as the lord of Egypt, he avoided a discourse which might have betrayed an intimate acquaintance with the history of their family; and they were guarded in their answers to his questions, that they might betray none of those family secrets that were little to their credit. Now Joseph asked a thousand plain questions about his father, about the wives and children of each of his brethren, about his sister Dinah, about his grandfather Isaac, who was now gone to the bosom of Abraham, and had expected to find Joseph there before him, but was not disappointed when he understood that his beloved grandson was still on earth, adding to that treasure of good works which was to follow him. The answer that Joseph received to his questions sometimes excited sadness and sometimes joy; but, on the whole, he saw that still God's paths were mercy and truth to the seed of Abraham. Happy will it be for us if we can make such a good improvement of that part of the history of the patriarchs which God has given us, as Joseph did of what he heard from his brethren.

VER. 16. *And the fame thereof was heard in Pharaoh's house, saying, Joseph's brethren are come: and it pleased Pharaoh well, and his servants.*

Joseph, when "he revealed himself to his brethren, wept aloud, and the house of Pharaoh heard." They could not understand what it was that wrought such a mighty commotion in the heart of a man so eminent for wisdom. Their curiosity was soon gratified. Joseph had carefully concealed from the Egyptians those parts of his own history which were disgraceful to his brethren, but he now wished it to be known that they were come to Egypt. The fame of their arrival soon spread, and reached the ears of Pharaoh and of all his servants.

Joseph was such a wonderful man, that Pharaoh justly supposed his family were in possession of secrets of wisdom hid from the generality of mankind, and thought that if they were settled in his country, they might be a blessing to his kingdom. He was sensible that it had derived already greater benefits from Joseph than he could repay, and was glad that his brethren were come to partake of the fruits of their brother's wisdom. He resolved that the whole family should partake of his gratitude and bounty.

It is too common with great men to forget the favours done to them by mean men, or to think that they are only duties performed which are entitled to little recompense. But this king of Egypt had such a sense of his obligations to Joseph, that he did not think all the honours conferred upon the man whom he had exalted almost to a throne from a prison were a sufficient recompense for his merits. He was a man of a very different temper from that king of Egypt in the following age, who remembered not Joseph. We are, indeed, to ascribe the gratitude of this prince not so much to the goodness of his dispositions as to God's providence. Joseph had already suffered what measure of affliction seemed to the Divine wisdom expedient for him, and now, according to the days wherein he hath been afflicted, it was the will of God "to make him glad." Pharaoh's heart was therefore inclined to favour him with a warm and steady friendship. But we ought not to deny Pharaoh the just praise of his gratitude to Joseph because it was the fruit of God's kindness to His faithful servant. Who is the man that can say there is any good thing in him which he has not received? In our flesh there dwelleth no good thing; if we were as holy as Paul, or if we do anything that is good, it is not we, but the grace of God with us that does it. Moral virtues come from His good providence; Christian virtues from His special grace.

"And it pleased Pharaoh well, and his servants." It is perhaps more wonderful that Pharaoh's servants continued so long to favour Joseph, than that the king himself was so firmly attached to him. The servants of princes, if we may believe the records of history and the memoirs of courts, are too often disposed to view with an unfavourable eye those who are raised above themselves, however deservedly, if they were once their inferiors, especially if they were aliens. Joseph's merits, indeed, with all the Egyptians, were such, that Pharaoh's servants could not but perceive and acknowledge them. Yet the spirit which is in man lusteth so strongly to envy, that the respect in which Joseph was for a long space of time held by the court of Pharaoh may well be considered as a singular testimony of the favour of that God in whose hands are all the hearts of the children of men. Joseph's goodness, wisdom, and affability were means by which his reputation was preserved and the hearts of the people conciliated. Yet in his early days he had such experience of the unreasonableness of envy, that he must have been duly sensible of the good hand of God towards him in maintaining his lot, and in securing to him the goodwill of all around.

VER. 17, 18. *And Pharaoh said unto Joseph, Say unto thy brethren, This do ye; lade your beasts, and go, get you unto the land of Canaan; and take your father and your households, and come unto me: and I will give you the good of the land of Egypt, and ye shall eat the fat of the land.*

We cannot but applaud the generosity of this prince, which is extended not only to Joseph's father, but to all his father's house: "Lade your beasts, and go up to the land of Canaan, and take your father and your households, and come unto me." Pharaoh will not only afford sufficient means of subsistence to old and young amongst them, but they shall eat of the fat of the land. This generous gratitude to Joseph was well merited. All that had been done for Joseph's own family, or might yet be done, was little to what Joseph had done for Pharaoh's kingdom. All his subjects were indebted to Joseph for the means of preserving life, and therefore he was glad to find an opportunity for extending his goodness to all the kindred of this public benefactor. May we not learn from the example of Pharaoh what we owe to our Maker and Redeemer? Our goodness cannot extend to God. But there are some on earth whom He honours with the titles of friends. Our goodness can extend to the saints, to the excellent ones of the earth. Of these our gracious Lord says, " Whosoever shall do the will of my Father in heaven, the same is my mother, and sister, and brother."

VER. 19. *Now thou art commanded, this do ye ; take you wagons out of the land of Egypt for your little ones, and for your wives, and bring your father, and come.*

" Now thou art commanded." Some commands are expressions of kindness. Pharaoh not only permits, but enjoins Joseph to furnish every conveniency for the accommodation of his father's family, that they might not find any embarrassment to retard their journey to Egypt. Joseph's modesty might have hindered him from availing himself of the full extent of the king's favour, if he had not been required by the royal authority to spare no expense in a business so pleasing to his master. Thus God shows His grace to us no less in His commandments than in His promises. We are enjoined by the authority of Heaven to make large demands on that treasury which can never be exhausted. If we are not rich in spiritual blessings, we not only distrust the goodness, but disobey the precept of the Lord God Almighty : " This is the work of God, that we believe on Him whom He hath sent." Christ enjoins us to ask and receive, that our joy might be full; and He is displeased when we ask little or nothing in His name.

" Now you are commanded, this do ye ; take you wagons out of the land of Egypt for your little ones, and for your wives, and bring your father, and come." When Jacob fled from Laban, he had no carriages for his wives and his little ones, and therefore he was under a necessity of travelling slowly. It does not appear that he ever thought of providing those conveniences for his family which are found in so great plenty amongst us. He was a plain man, and trained up his family to bear fatigue, and to want many things which other men might think necessary to their happiness. Pharaoh kindly considered all that might be needful for such a long journey to women and children. He would not have Jacob detained in the land of Canaan till he could provide carriages for his family, nor would he have the women and children exposed to excess of fatigue by a journey of such length.   There are wagons in plenty in the king's offices, and Joseph is not only allowed, but commanded, to send as many of them to wait upon his father as would be of any use.   " The liberal man deviseth kind and liberal things."

VER. 20. *Also regard not your stuff ; for the good of all the land of Egypt is yours.*

Frugality is certainly a virtue which none but fools will despise.   Christ himself taught His disciples to practise it : " Gather up the fragments, that nothing be lost."   Yet there are times and cases in which the ordinary rules of frugality ought to be set aside.   Pharaoh did not wish Jacob's sons to encumber themselves with all that stuff which might have been useful to them had they remained in Canaan.   He desired them to leave behind them such pieces of furniture as were of little value, or difficult conveyance, and assures them that they should be no losers although they left everything, whether greater or lesser, of value in their tents behind them : " Also regard not your stuff, for the good of all the land of Egypt is before you."   Joseph had already made the king rich, and was every day increasing his riches, and it would be no sensible diminution of his accumulating wealth to enrich the whole family of Joseph's father to the full extent of their needs and desires.

If the good of all the land of Egypt was before these men, they had no temptations to encumber themselves with the furniture of their tents, or to be vexed on account of anything that might be left behind them, or damaged in their journey. Rich men are fools if they suffer themselves to be disquieted with trifling losses.   And why should those who have all the riches of the better country before them give themselves any disquiet about the perishing things that belong to the earthly house of this tabernacle ?   The heirs of heaven are rich in the midst of poverty ; although they have nothing, they possess all things.   Never let them give less credit to the promises of their Heavenly Father than Jacob's sons gave to the king of Egypt. "Let God be true, and every man a liar."

VER. 21. *And the children of Israel did so : and Joseph gave them wagons, according to the commandment of Pharaoh, and gave them provisions for the way.*

Beware of pride. Joseph's brethren could not bear the thoughts of his exaltation above them, and therefore they sold him into Egypt, that they might never more see his face. Yet see how they are reduced to the necessity of acknowledging his power and accepting of his bounty. If their haughtiness had not been humbled, they would have scorned his favours. But hard necessity on the one side compelled them, and his generosity on the other side sweetly constrained them, to agree to his kind proposals. They did as Pharaoh commanded, and as Joseph requested them to do. They accepted of the greatest favours from the man to whom their pride had made them deadly enemies. We know not to whom we may be under a necessity of owing very important obligations before we leave this changeable world. Let us behave justly and discreetly to all men, that we may not have our faces covered with blushes, if Providence should exalt those above us who are now below us. What unexpected changes take place in the course of a single life !

"Joseph gave them wagons, according to the commandment of Pharaoh, and provisions for the way." It is very probable that the commandments of Pharaoh were the suggestions of Joseph himself, for Pharaoh commanded him to do for his brethren what he expressed his intention of doing before Pharaoh knew that his brethren were come. It was Pharaoh's wisdom to follow the counsels and to comply with the wishes of Joseph; and it was an instance of Joseph's integrity, that without Pharaoh's commandment he would not make use of the royal treasures for the benefit of his father's family. He was well entitled to the means of doing all that he did for them; but a servant must not take from his master, without leave, what he may consider as the due reward of his services.

Ver. 22. *To all of them he gave each man changes of raiment ; but to Benjamin he gave three hundred pieces of silver, and five changes of raiment.*

It is still a common custom in the East with rich men to testify their love to their friends, or their esteem for strangers, by presents of garments. Some of them have their wardrobes furnished with great variety of raiment for this purpose. The fashion of clothes never changes with them as with us, and therefore they do not become useless, if proper care is taken of them.

Joseph doubtless gives to all his people changes of raiment suited to his high condition, but he gave to his brother Benjamin five changes of raiment; and thus he published to his brethren the superior regard which he entertained for him as the son of his mother as well as of his father. It is not always a token of partiality to love one son or one brother more than another, and it is not always unwise to show the superior regard we entertain towards those who are connected with us by the same ties of blood. One may deserve more kindness, and more public testimonies of kindness, than another. Virtues form a more endearing connection than blood. And good offices, from relatives as well as from other persons, call for grateful returns. When Joseph gave to Benjamin five changes of raiment, he was so far from showing any disrespect to his other brethren, that he paid them a compliment which, I believe, was very grateful to them. He showed his confidence in their good dispositions towards Benjamin. They had discovered their envy against himself on account of the coat of divers colours by which his father distinguished him from his brethren. If Joseph had not firmly believed that there was now a complete revolution in their temper, he would not have honoured Benjamin with such open testimonies of his partial fondness. He certainly did not design that Benjamin should be stripped of his fine robes like himself; but he knew that his brethren would never, on any consideration, bring again upon themselves the guilt of those sins whereof they were now ashamed.

U

Ver. 23. *And to his father he sent after this manner; ten asses laden with the good things of Egypt, and ten she-asses laden with corn and bread and meat for his father by the way.*

He wished his father to partake of the best things of Egypt before he set his foot in the country. True love is never slow in producing its fruits. Those children who honour and love their parents as they ought will joyfully seize opportunities to testify their regard and add to their happiness. It was a pleasure to Isaac to eat of the venison which his eldest son procured for him by hunting. It would afford far more pleasure to Jacob to partake of the fruits of the attention and kindness of his long-lost Joseph. Yet he derived far more pleasure from Joseph's goodness to his brethren than from the presents sent unto himself. He had no reason to doubt of Joseph's warm affection to himself, but it would fill him with joy unspeakable to find his son exhibiting the highest pattern of meekness and of the forgiveness of injuries that the world had ever yet beheld. The greatest pleasure of an aged saint is to see his children walking in the truth, and causing "their light so to shine before men, that others, seeing their good works, may glorify their Father who is in heaven."

Joseph gave to his brethren provision for the way to Canaan, and to his father he sent sufficient provisions for the way to Egypt. He did not send a superfluity of provisions even for his beloved father, to enable him to continue longer in the land of Canaan, for he hoped soon to have him with himself. You will not say that Joseph discovered too little love to his father when he did not put it in his power to linger in Canaan; because he loved his father, he wished to see him in Egypt. Do you, then, think that God does not love His poor people in this world because He does not give them more than they need to use in this land of their pilgrimage? Does He not rather show His love by giving them only so much of the good things of life as will satisfy all their reasonable desires, without laying them under too strong temptations to forget that better country which ought to be ever in their view?

When Joseph came to Egypt, his brethren had stripped him of his coat of many colours, and received money for him from the Ishmaelitish merchants. When he sent his brethren from Egypt, he gave them change of raiment, and loaded them with presents to themselves, and to their father, and to their little ones. The good things of Egypt sent by him to Jacob were not all designed for his own personal use, but for his large family. Joseph teaches us by his example how to observe the apostolical precept of overcoming evil with good. He had no opportunity of reading these solemn maxims : " If thine enemy hunger, feed him ; if he thirst, give him water to drink ; " or that command of our Lord and Saviour : " Love your enemies ; do good to them that hate you." But he was taught by the grace of God to exercise fervent charity to offending brethren. And if we do not follow the example of Joseph, and the more affecting example of Him who was constantly doing good in the course of His life to a thankless generation, and who gave His life for His enemies, can we hope to stand in the assembly of the just at the great day with those men who never enjoyed our advantages, and yet obeyed that law which is now so much more powerfully enforced, that the old commandment of love may be called a new commandment, because the darkness is past, and the true light now shineth ?

Beware of deceiving yourselves with hypocritical pretences to the forgiveness of injuries which still rankle in your breasts. Can you not give pleasant words to your offending brethren ? Or, although your words be good, are your deeds not correspondent to them ? Joseph's tongue was the law of kindness. His words were like the honey-comb, sweet to the taste, and pleasant to the troubled spirits of his brethren. He did everything that was in the power of man to regain the affections of his brethren, and to preserve them from feeling the bitter effects of their own cruel behaviour.

A certain man differing with his brother (one of the ancient Greek philosophers), threatened never to be reconciled to him. His reply was, " But I will force you to love me ; " and he made his words good. It was wonderful that any man was ever an enemy of Joseph. It would have been still more wonderful if those who were his enemies had not become his friends. May the Spirit that dwelt in all the ancient believers, the Spirit that was given without measure to Christ, and is given to all that obey Him, work in our hearts that love which beareth all things, and which covereth a multitude of sins!

LECTURE 23

Joseph's brethren return to their father,
and inform him of Joseph's glory in Egypt,
and of his ardent desire to have his
father with him. Jacob is almost
overpowered with the tidings.

xlv 24–28

VER. 24. *So he sent his brethren away, and they departed:
and he said unto them, See that ye fall not out by the way.*

JOSEPH had enjoyed some hours of exquisite felicity in the
presence of Benjamin and of all his brethren, yet he sends
them away. He deprived himself for a time of the joy
of their society that he might see them again with greater
pleasure when they returned to abide with him all the days of
their life, and brought with them their father and their little
ones. He did not so much as keep young Benjamin with himself. He knew that his father would often look out with
wishful eyes for his sons, and if he did not see Benjamin in
their company, terror might seize upon his spirit before he
could be informed why he did not make his appearance with his
brethren. Joseph was willing to deny himself comfort to give
comfort to his father.

Before his brethren departed, he gave them a friendly advice,
which in the present circumstances was seasonable and necessary :
" See that ye fall not out by the way;" or, as the Seventy render
it, " Be not angry by the way." The original word may signify
any strong commotion of mind, under the influence either of
fear, or grief, or anger.

Joseph had seen the violent agitation of their minds, both when they were put in prison and when he made himself known to them. He had heard Reuben speak words which were daggers to the hearts of his brethren, by which he wished to impress their guilt upon their consciences. And Joseph was afraid lest they should either feel more uneasiness than he wished them to do in their own minds, or exasperate one another by reflections on their former conduct. Simeon had already suffered much from Joseph himself, and Joseph would have been sorry if Reuben, or Judah, or any of the brethren, in the course of the journey, had added to his grief, or perhaps ruffled his spirits, by putting him in remembrance of that fierce rage which he too often displayed in the days of his youth.

Joseph was now a happy man, and he desired to make all his brethren happy, and to preserve them from everything that might have made them unhappy, and particularly from quarrels amongst them.

He certainly wished them to bring forth the fruits of repentance, but for this end it was proper to warn them against any expression that might exasperate the minds of one another. True penitents are not disposed to load other men with the guilt of their own sins, even when their neighbours have drawn them into the snares by which they have fallen. They know that they were drawn away of their own lusts, and enticed, when they complied with the temptation either of Satan or of their fellow-men. They know, too, with respect to the latter, that although a part of the guilt belongs to them, yet their own share is what they are chiefly concerned with, and that the causes of reflection do not lie wholly on the one side. Simeon had greatly sinned against his brethren when, by the fury of his vindictive spirit, he had been hurried into that cruel behaviour on several occasions in which he had drawn his brethren into a participation with himself. If he had not set them the example, and inflamed them by his passionate words, they would perhaps never have thought without horror of those crimes whereof they were now ashamed. But, on the other side, ought they not to have checked Simeon, or any of the brethren that concurred with him? By their consent to participate they tempted him to hold fast, and to accomplish his purpose. He might have been convinced of his folly had they remonstrated against his proposal. Had they refused to concur with him, he could not have carried it into effect. Let us not judge one another, for God is the Judge of all, and often He sees that we have a share in that guilt which we condemn in our fellow-sinners. If we confess our sins, and take the guilt of them to ourselves, "God is faithful and just to forgive us our sins." If we lay the guilt of them upon other men, we must abide the judgment of God. Adam our father had little reason to reflect on Eve for giving him the forbidden fruit. She tempted him to sin, but he tempted her to impenitence in sin. Adam called his wife's name Eve, because she was the mother of all living. He gave her this name after the promise of the seed who was to destroy the works of the devil. But if this promise had not been given, he might have called her by a name which signified the very reverse, and have taken the blame of it to himself; for whatever her own fate might have been, she would not have communicated death to posterity if he had not taken and eaten of the fruit.

"See that ye fall not out by the way." Joseph knew that, in the course of their long journey, their discourse would naturally turn to the memorable events that must have made so strong an impression on their minds, and that whilst they thought with shame upon their behaviour to so kind a brother, they might be ready to say something that would tend to mutual irritation, or to conceive a displeasure against one another for observations that were not intended to exasperate. Without a strong guard both on their tongues and their hearts, they were in danger of conceiving mutual resentments, hurtful to their comforts and to their souls. Joseph not only forgave them, but exhorted them to forgive and forbear one another. And if Joseph forgave them all as far as any of them had wronged him, it was highly reasonable that they should forgive one another. He was a peacemaker by his example as well as by his exhortation. All the children of God ought not only to be peaceable, but peacemakers, as far as their power and opportunities extend. The blessing of the peacemaker came upon the head of Joseph, and upon the crown of the head of him who was separated from his brethren. "The fruit of righteousness is sown in peace of all them that make peace."

VER. 25. *And they went up out of Egypt, and came into the land of Canaan unto Jacob their father.*

We have no account of their communication by the way, but we cannot be mistaken in supposing that they employed a great proportion of their thoughts and discourse on the wonderful turn that Providence had given to their affairs; on the terror that seized their hearts when they were examined concerning the cup; on the surprising discovery of their generous brother; on the strange vicissitudes in his condition; on the necessity they were laid under to accept of his bounty, and the bounty of his royal master; on the unexampled goodness of the man whom they had sold into slavery; on the impression that the tidings they carried would make on the heart of their father. It was almost impossible that they should at this time think or speak of any other subject, and they must have been more hardened than we have any reason to think they were, if such thoughts and discourse did not leave a happy impression on their minds. They had not only been witnesses of some of the most astonishing works of Divine Providence, but had been deeply interested in them. If their consciences were awakened by their imprisonment, it is reasonable to think that their hearts were deeply affected with the Divine mercy which preserved them, and which so wonderfully provided for the supply of their wants. They could not think without shame on their own conduct to Joseph, when they considered his kindness to themselves. Did not their hearts burn within them when they talked to one another by the way of his kind words, of his affectionate embraces, of the care that he took to dispel every uneasy thought from their mind?

"They came unto Jacob their father." The good man was happy when he saw them. Simeon and Benjamin were not left behind. His soul was filled with the praises of that goodness which had preserved them in the way which they went, and restored them safe to his arms. But he soon was made to understand that he was furnished with materials for thanksgiving beyond what he had ever imagined.

VER. 26. *And told him, saying, Joseph is yet alive, and he is governor over all the land of Egypt. And Jacob's heart fainted, for he believed them not.*

When we are to inform our friends of events likely to throw them into excèssive transports of grief or joy, we endeavour to prepare them for the tidings by awakening such a degree of hope or fear as we suppose them able to bear, that their minds may not be shocked by an abrupt discovery of what they are soon to know. It is very possible that Jacob's sons might endeavour to prepare their father's mind for hearing of Joseph's life and glory in Egypt. We are not to suppose that everything that passed between the father and the sons is recorded; but whatever mode they used to make known the joyful news, it could not be expected that Jacob could hear them without strong transports of passion.

"Joseph is yet alive." If they had told him that Abraham or Isaac had returned from the dead, he could scarcely have been more surprised. How was it possible that Joseph should not have been heard of for more than twenty years if he had been still alive?

"He is governor over all the land of Egypt." This, if possible, was still less likely to be true. Would the high-minded Egyptians suffer a man to rule over them who was a stranger, and who, if he was still alive, must have appeared to them a poor exile? Was it to be supposed that a nation of idolaters could submit to the government of a servant of the God of the Hebrews? Or if Joseph had been alive, and had by some strange vicissitude obtained a station of such eminence, was it credible that he should never yet have sent information to a father whom he so tenderly loved of his life and prosperity?

We are ready to believe what we wish to be true; and yet a consciousness of this disposition may lead us to suspend or refuse our belief to those facts which above all others we desire to find true. When the disciples of Jesus heard of His resurrection, they believed not for joy. The news were too good to be believed without surer evidence than is required for ordinary events. Jacob could not believe that, after so long and so heavy mourning for his favourite son, he should at last find that he was still alive.

It is well for us that God, who knows our frame, ordinarily suits both the sorrows and the joys of life to our capacity for bearing them. Immoderate joy is too hard for us, as well as immoderate grief. Historians tell us of many to whom it has been fatal.

"Jacob's heart fainted within him when he heard of the life of his son, for he believed them not." The report agitated his mind to such a degree that his frame could not sustain the shock. There seemed to be certain proofs both that Joseph was dead and that he was not dead. One moment he believed that Joseph must be alive. His own brethren, who well knew him, and who had seen him in Egypt, were the reporters of it; and was it to be supposed that they would all agree in telling to their father a manifest falsehood? What end could they propose to themselves by renewing that grief in their father's heart which they had formerly seen with such tender sympathy? On the other hand, it was incredible that the long-lamented son of Jacob should be still alive, or that the man who had treated Jacob's sons with so much injustice should be their brother Joseph, who was so kind and generous, and who loved his father so well when he lived in his father's house.

There was an inexplicable mystery in the affair. The extremes of joy and grief alternately seized on the old man. But grief predominated. His soul was enfeebled in his weak body by the conflicting passions. When his mind was settled in the persuasion that the good news could not be true, the anguish of his soul was doubled by the short interval of pleasure which he had enjoyed.

It is but little that we can bear whilst we are in our mortal bodies. And this is one advantage of an intolerable load of anguish, that it destroys the capacity of suffering pain. Thus the miserable escape from the bitterest moments of distress, or perhaps from all the miseries of this life. But, after all, it is but a lamentable escape that is made from the miseries of this life, unless we are secured against all the miseries of another life. If Jacob had died through the alternation of grief and joy in their extremes when he heard the happy but doubtful tidings, he would have found himself in the bosom of Abraham ; but when grief destroys the sinner, he finds himself in a condition to bear, without end or interruption, these unutterable woes, one moment of which would make an utter end of the present life.

VER: 27. *And they told him all the words of Joseph, which he had said unto them : and when he saw the wagons which Joseph had sent to carry him, the spirit of Jacob their father revived.*

Men are said in scripture language to faint when they are sore oppressed, and nearly overwhelmed by strong passions, although they should not be wholly deprived of sensation. If Jacob fainted to such a degree as to lose for a time the possession of his faculties, he did not remain long in that state, but was soon able to attend to the account which his sons gave him of their journey, and of the happy discovery which they had made. His body was very feeble, and his fond attachment to Joseph raised a violent tempest of passion in his mind when he was told of his life, and of his glory in Egypt. But that habitual exercise of resignation to the will of God, by which Jacob had hitherto been enabled to bear the weight of his afflictions, prepared him for enduring new trials of his patience better than could have been expected ; and God upheld him with His powerful arm, that he might not sink into the grave. He could not yet die, for he was yet to perform very important services to God, and to see much of the goodness of the Lord in the land of the living. His sons told him all the words of Joseph ; and in telling him these words, they could not avoid telling him in effect that they had been the authors of all the misery which the good man had sustained in the imagined loss of his favourite son. It is reasonable to think that they would endeavour to tell the eventful story in the way that they thought least likely to awaken their father's resentment against themselves, and best fitted to convince him that they deeply repented of what they had done; and they could not have found out better arguments for softening their father's displeasure, or a more forcible method of expressing them, than by using the words of Joseph himself. Jacob would be charmed to hear that his dear son referred all that had befallen him to the providence of a gracious God, and retained such a cordial attachment to brethren who had done him such a cruel injury. If Joseph forgave them, Jacob must forgive them also. When Joseph trusted Benjamin in their hands, after loading him with singular marks of his affection, it was plain that he believed their repentance to be genuine, and their envy to be extinguished; and why should not Jacob rejoice that his sons were much better men than they once had been? When they told him all that Joseph had said, they told him what impression his words had made upon their minds. He saw good reason to think that their sorrow had wrought repentance that would not be repented of. We ought to mourn bitterly when our friends bring guilt upon themselves, but we ought not on that account to withdraw from them our charity. We ought to rejoice greatly when they are humbled for their offences, and bring forth fruits meet for repentance. The incestuous person at Corinth had brought great dishonour on the Church, and exposed it to great danger, by his abominable wickedness. Yet Paul tells the Corinthians that when he appeared to be overwhelmed with grief, they ought to forgive and to comfort him. The crime and the repentance of Jacob's sons were matters as interesting to their father as the life and glory of Joseph. But at this moment the concerns of Joseph occupied his mind to such a degree that he could think of nothing else. When he saw the wagons which Joseph had sent to carry him, he believed the truth of the report. Surely his sons had not collected so many wagons to impose an incredible lie upon him, and a lie so dishonourable to themselves. The wagons which he saw were better constructed than any to be found in the land of Canaan. The proof was complete. Jacob's appre-

hensions were now completely banished. Joy took full possession of his soul. His spirit was revived.

VER. 28. *And Israel said, It is enough ; Joseph my son is
yet alive : I will go and see him before I die.*

"Israel said, it is enough." "I have full evidence that
Joseph is alive. I could not be better assured of this fact if I
saw him with mine own eyes ; and my joy is full. All the
happiness that the world can give is mine. Were all the
kingdoms and glories of this world to be given me, they could
not afford me satisfaction. But, blessed be God, my son Joseph
liveth, I will go and see him before I die, and then I will die
with gladness, when it pleases God to call me out of the world."

Consider what these things are which can afford you most
pleasure in this world. Bless God if you possess them, or have
recovered them when they seemed to be lost, and fret not
because you are not allowed to enjoy everything that you
wish. The life of your children is more valuable in your
estimation than gold or silver, houses or lands. Then be
thankful to God as long as your children are spared, although
God should think fit to deny you those other things which He
is pleased to bestow upon some of your neighbours. If God
has taken from you those things which you formerly possessed,
and left you the beloved fruit of your bodies, remember the
words of your Lord : " Is not the life more than meat, and the
body than raiment ?" Job lost both his children and his substance in one day, and yet he blessed the name of the Lord,
who had taken only what He gave.

But perhaps you have lost the most beloved of your children.
You saw them die. You carried them to the grave. No hope
is left you that you shall ever again see them in this world.
Whilst you read these words, " Joseph my son is yet alive,"
you cannot prevent the uneasy comparison between Jacob's
condition and yours : " My son or my daughter, in whom I
placed my chief earthly joy, is torn from me for ever."

Yet Jacob thought it was enough that Joseph was yet alive,
although his beloved Rachel was still in her grave. He was
not so unreasonable as to dream that the dead must be raised

from their graves for him before the general resurrection.
When you mourn for the dead, think on those who are alive.
None of your beloved friends have been in a literal sense
restored to life, yet perhaps some of them have been delivered
from great deaths.   Their restoration to health was almost as
surprising to you as it was to Jacob to hear that his son Joseph
was yet alive.

" My son Joseph is yet alive."   What transports of joy did
Jacob feel when he spake these words !   They put us in mind
of what was said by the father of the prodigal son when he
returned to his father's house.   " This my son was lost, and is
found ; he was dead, and is now alive."   When a sinner is
brought back from all his wanderings to God, he is alive from
the worst kind of death.   His Heavenly Father rejoiceth over
him with joy and singing.   The day of his conversion is the day
of the gladness of Christ's heart.   It furnishes angels with
songs of gladness, because an addition is made to their blessed
society.

Are any of our children living in sin, alienated from the life
of God through the blindness of their minds ?   Seek to turn
them from the error of their ways.   Your success, if God smiles
upon your labours, will give you joy like that which the good
old patriarch tasted.   If your joy be less transporting, it will
be more durable.   Jacob knew that Joseph, though yet alive,
was not to live always.   But he that liveth and believeth in
Christ shall never die.

From the transports which Jacob felt at the report that
Joseph was still alive, we may form a faint conception of the
joys of the just at the general resurrection.   When Jesus said
to Martha, " Thy brother shall rise again," she said, " I know
that he shall rise again in the resurrection at the last day."
And we all know that if Jesus died and rose again, then them
also that sleep in Jesus will God bring with Him.   What
pleasure would it give you to be assured that all those beloved
friends whose loss you have deplored shall rise again to live with
you in the present evil world !   Should such a favour be granted
to you, it would make the earth too pleasant.   It is a much

greater and sweeter ground of comfort to us, if our faith is vigorous, to have the sure hope of meeting with our friends in a better world, where there is no more death, nor sorrow, nor crying.

Our friends who have died in the Lord are yet alive. They live with God in heaven. We cannot go and see them before we die. But as soon as we die, we shall go and see them, and to see Christ, which is far better, and to dwell with them and with Him for ever and ever.

" It is enough." Not that the patriarch thought it enough to hear that Joseph was living. Although he was assured of the truth of the report, yet his happiness was still in hope.

" I will go and see my son." The sight of Benjamin would have an hour before this time appeared to him sufficient happiness for this world. But now he cannot be happy unless he see Joseph likewise. The beloved Rachel will be again alive to him when he is blessed with a sight of his lost and best-beloved son. Much trial must be undergone, and some dangers may be encountered, by a body worn out with age and grief, before he can set his eyes upon Joseph. But what will not Jacob do, or suffer, or risk to obtain another sight of that son whom his soul loved? Love is a mighty affection of the heart. It is as strong as death. It wrought so powerfully in the martyrs that they would have encountered a thousand deaths that they might see the Beloved of their souls as He is. They were persuaded that a day, an hour, a moment of His presence in heaven was incomparably more than sufficient to counterbalance all the infernal tortures which their enemies could inflict.

" I will go and see my son before I die." Long had Jacob been thinking of death. When Joseph was lost, he said, " I will go down to the grave mourning for my son." But he will not now go down to the grave mourning, for his son who was lost is found. He will go to see his son, and die with joy.

Jacob well knew that he had nothing to fear after death. If he had not been well assured that he should die in peace with God, he could not have looked forward with such composure to his latter end. A subject of infinitely higher importance than the sight of Joseph ought to have engrossed his thoughts. But when our calling and election is made sure, it is desirable, before we die, to see all our children, to give them our last advices, and to recommend them to the protection of that God who had fed us all our lifelong, of that Angel who hath redeemed us from all our troubles.

When parents must die at a great distance from some of their children, they have this comfort, that the throne of grace is accessible to them, and that God, whom they have served, gives them good encouragement to commit the beloved fruit of their bodies to His care. He is a God afar off as well as near, and can answer our prayers, however distant from us the subject of them may be. If Joseph had never seen the face of Jacob after he went to Egypt, the blessing of Jacob would have come down upon his head. The prosperity of Joseph was an answer to the prayers of Israel, for many prayers had the holy patriarch presented to God on his behalf before he went to Egypt. Jacob could not pray for him by name when he supposed him to be dead, yet, even then, the prayers of Jacob for his family included Joseph, and were heard in his behalf.

LECTURE 24
Jacob, at Beersheba, is encouraged by God to go down to Egypt.
xlvi 1–4

VER. 1. *And Israel took his journey with all that he had, and came to Beer-sheba, and offered sacrifices unto the God of his father Isaac.*

BEERSHEBA was made famous by the journeyings of Abraham and Isaac. Abraham planted a grove in Beersheba, and there called on the name of the Lord, the everlasting God. "And he sojourned in the land of the Philistines many days." In the same land, too, Isaac sojourned many years, and at Beersheba obtained remarkable testimonies of the favour and protection of the God of his father. To this place Jacob came and consulted the God of Abraham and Isaac about his journey to Egypt. He had indeed said that he would go to Egypt before he came to Beersheba, but he never undertook any important journey till he acknowledged God, who directed all his steps.

We all ought, when we propose to go into such a city, and continue there, to say, "If we live, and the Lord will," we shall do it. But Jacob had peculiar reasons for inquiring the mind of God concerning his journey to Egypt. He was a stranger and sojourner in the land of Canaan by Divine appointment, as were his fathers Abraham and Isaac. He lived in the faith of the promise, that this good land should be given to his seed. If he had left it without Divine direction on account of the

x

famine, it might have been thought that he was weary of waiting upon the Lord, or that he did not think the promised land sufficiently good to recompense his waiting so long for it under such discouragements.

Greatly did Jacob long to see Joseph. But his most ardent passions were under the government of religion. He would rather have died without seeing Joseph in this world, than go to see him without a warrant from that God whom he loved more than all his sons, and more than his life. When his father Isaac once thought of fleeing to Egypt from a famine, he was prohibited by God.

Jacob now went to Beersheba, and sacrificed to the God of his father Isaac. Isaac had been forbidden by God, in a time of famine, to go down to Egypt ; and if the God of his father had prohibited him also from going to Egypt, he was disposed cheerfully to give up the hope of seeing his son. Joseph was very dear to him, but a good conscience towards God was dearer.

" He offered sacrifices to the God of his father Isaac." It is said, chap. xxxi., that he " sware by the Fear of his father Isaac." Jacob knew that He was the God of Abraham as well as Isaac ; but it ought to be remembered that, although we are better acquainted with Abraham than with Isaac, Jacob was better acquainted with Isaac. He could remember to have seen Abraham, and to have heard of those golden sayings that used to come from his lips. Often he had heard Isaac speak of Abraham's faith and love to God, and of the mercy and truth which God showed to Abraham. But he was probably more deeply impressed with what he had seen in Isaac than with what he had heard of Abraham. Possibly he might think himself so much Abraham's inferior in the noblest qualifications, that he might derive more comfort to himself from God's goodness to Isaac than from the instances of His kindness to Abraham. From that goodness and mercy which followed Isaac all his life long, it appeared that the mercy shown to Abraham extended to his seed, though not equal to himself in those graces and virtues by which God is glorified, and in which He takes pleasure.

Beersheba was the place in which the King of Gerar and the

captain of his host confessed that Isaac was the blessed of the Lord, and that it would be dangerous to be found enemies to a man whom God so visibly favoured. The experience of Isaac wrought hope in Jacob. He knew and believed that his father's God was his own God also, and would grant him all that protection and help which had been granted in his own time to his father, and before his time to his grandfather Abraham.

"He offered sacrifices." From the time of Adam's fall, sacrifices were offered by the believing patriarchs. They expressed, by offering them, their sense of the demerit of their offences, and their hope of pardon and acceptance through that better Sacrifice which was to be offered when the fulness of the times should come. Good men in every age were convinced that they were sinners before God, that they were undone unless they were pardoned, and that they must be indebted to the counsels of Divine wisdom for pardon in a way consistent with the glory of Divine righteousness.

All Jacob's family came with him to Beersheba, not only because he did not intend to return to Hebron, but because he would have them all to attend on the solemn services he was to perform to God. The religion of Jacob was different from the religion generally professed in Canaan. He showed that he was not ashamed nor afraid to be singular in his religion, when he offered sacrifices to the God of his father Isaac; and he endeavoured to train up all his children and his grandchildren in his own religion, that they might set their hope in his God, and in the God of his fathers Abraham and Isaac, and that they might not learn the way of the heathen around them, or of those heathens into whose land they were going. We must not do our good works to be seen of men. Yet we must make our light to shine before men, and chiefly before our families. Happy are those fathers who need not be ashamed to say to their children, "These things which ye have seen and heard in me do, and the God of peace shall be with you."

VER. 2. *And God spake unto Israel in the visions of the night, and said, Jacob, Jacob. And he said, Here am I.*

The historian, in this and in the foregoing verse, and in

several other places, calls Jacob by the name Israel. He received this glorious name from God when he wrestled with the Angel and prevailed. This name, so graciously given him by God, was a great encouragement to him to seek the Lord in every time of distress. "O Thou that hearest prayer, all flesh shall come unto Thee;" those persons especially whom Thou hast blessed with testimonies of Thy grace in hearing their prayer.

From the history before us, it appears that Jacob was still the same man as when he met God at Peniel, and that the Lord was still the same gracious God to His aged servant as in the days of youth. He will not leave His petitioners when they are old and gray-headed. And the remembrance of God's kindness to them in the days of their youth will embolden their approaches to Him when old age overtakes them with all its infirmities.

"God spake unto Israel in the visions of the night." It was not now the first time that God spake to Israel in the visions of the night. He was not now in such distress as when God first spake to him at Bethel in visions of the night, when he was lying on the cold ground with a stone for his pillow. God can speak to men at what time and in what manner He pleases. David's reins often instructed him in the night-season.

"And said, Jacob, Jacob." The Lord called him by his first and ordinary name *Jacob*, perhaps to put him in mind of what he was in himself. He was now, by Divine mercy, honoured with a very glorious name, but he must not forget that he was only Jacob when God met with him in his early days. He might have been exalted above measure with the revelations made to him if he had forgotten what he once was. That we may be duly sensible of the value of Divine favours, and that we may not abuse them as a gratification to pride, let us not forget what we formerly were, and what we must still have been if the Lord had not blessed us with undeserved favours.

"Jacob, Jacob." God speaks once, yea twice, that He might waken Jacob's ear to hear His voice. Thus, when the Lord came the third time to Samuel, He stood, and called, as at other times, Samuel, Samuel. Something of importance was to be spoken to these holy men, when God addressed them in language expressive of such kindness and such earnest desire to be heard.

Both Jacob's ears were open to the voice of God. Here am I, cried the good man. He was prepared to hear, to consider, and to obey what God should be pleased to speak. "Speak, Lord, for Thy servant heareth."

In whatever manner God speaks, we ought to say, Here we are, O Lord! ready to receive Thy commandments. We are all here before God, said Cornelius, ready to hear whatever shall be commanded thee of God. If God had forbidden Jacob to go to Joseph, he could have mortified his desire of seeing his son, as readily as Abraham, at the command of God, offered up Isaac his son upon the altar. No instance of self-denial can be so unpleasant to a man who loves God as disobedience to the will of God.

VER. 3. *And he said, I am God, the God of thy father: fear not to go down into Egypt; for I will there make of thee a great nation.*

That we may hear the Word of God with due reverence, and obey His voice, let us never forget what God is. What comparison is there between God and the greatest of the children of men? Can God lie? Can He promise what He is either unable or unwilling to perform? Can He enjoin any service which He has not a good right to require?

Let us not forget the relation in which we stand to God as His creatures, or the more endearing relation into which He is pleased to take us by His grace. "I am the God of thy father." Jacob well knew that Isaac had ever found God faithful to all His gracious engagements. It is true that all the patriarchs died not having received the promises, yet they all died in the faith; and they all, in the course of their lives, enjoyed rich experiences of the faithfulness of the promises. "As for the Lord, His word is tried; He is a buckler to all them that trust in Him." Abraham and Isaac trusted in the word of the Lord, and were never ashamed of their confidence. And Jacob, who had now lived the best part of his mortal life, found that there was no change in that God who had been the shield and the exceeding great reward of Isaac as well as Abraham. We ought not to forsake our father's friend, far less ought we to forsake or to distrust our father's God. "He is our father's God, and we will exalt Him" by our faith and gratitude, by our praises and services, Exod. xiii. 2.

God showed wonderful kindness to the three famous patriarchs, by taking from them a name and a memorial by which He would be known to all the generations of their posterity. He accounts it His honour to be trusted. He honours those who honour Him with their confidence, and publishes His kindness and fidelity to them as an encouragement to others to hope in His word. Our Lord Himself, in His lowest abasement, thought on the faithfulness of God to the ancient believers as an encouragement to His own faith : "But thou art holy, O thou that inhabitest the praises of Israel. Our fathers trusted in thee : they trusted, and thou didst deliver them. They cried unto thee, and were delivered : they trusted in thee, and were not confounded," Ps. xxii. 3-5.

"I am the God of thy fathers ; fear not to go down into Egypt." It is not the will of God that His servants should lead uncomfortable lives. He appeared unto Abraham in the plains of Mamre, and said to him, "Fear not, Abraham." He said to Isaac, in Beersheba, "Fear not, for I am with thee." To Jacob, in the same place, He said, "Fear not to go down to Egypt." We often find Him addressing like comfortable words to the seed of Jacob : "Fear thou not, for I am with thee ; be not dismayed, for I am thy God. Fear not, thou worm Jacob, and ye men of Israel ; I will help thee, saith the Lord, and thy Redeemer, the Holy One of Israel. Fear not, O Jacob, my servant, and thou Jeshurun, whom I have chosen," Isa. xli. 10, 13 ; xliv. 3.

The seasons when God administers His comforts to His people are generally the seasons when they stand in the greatest need of them. At this time Jacob needed support to his heart in the view of going to Egypt. He perhaps saw little difficulty in his way when he first thought of it. His joy at hearing of

Joseph's life and glory was so rapturous that nothing seemed difficult. But when he deliberated coolly on the subject many new thoughts about it sprung up in his mind. Was it lawful for him to go to Egypt? Was his body able to bear the fatigues of it? Was it safe for his family to go to a land of idolaters, governed by a great king, who required allegiance from all who dwelt within the bounds of his country? In Canaan he was an independent prince, who could go from one country to another at his pleasure. But in Egypt, he must be in some measure under the government of the King of Egypt; and it was not to be expected that Joseph or his seed should always be lords of it.

The word of God, "Fear not to go down into Egypt," was sufficient to answer all objections against the journey. If God commands us to banish all fears, we certainly have nothing to fear, for there is everlasting faithfulness in His precepts as well as in His promises. Fear not to do anything that God requires. Hath not He commanded you? Is it possible that we can err by doing His will?

But God graciously fortifies Jacob against fear, not only by His command, but by irresistible reasons drawn from His own power, from His covenant, and from His promises. "I am God (or the strong God), the God of thy father Isaac," and consequently thy God, for the covenant was established with Jacob as well as Isaac. "Fear not to go down into Egypt, for I, the mighty God, the God of thy father Isaac, will there make of thee a great nation. I will go down with thee into Egypt, and I will also surely bring thee up again; and Joseph shall put his hand upon thine eyes."

"I am God, the God of Isaac, and I will make of thee in Egypt a great nation." The mighty God increases or diminishes nations at His pleasure. The God of Abraham, and Isaac, and Jacob had already promised to multiply their seed as the stars of heaven. Those patriarchs probably till this time believed that the land of Canaan was to be the country in which their seed should grow into a great nation. Abraham was informed that His seed should be afflicted in a strange land; but Jacob was now told that they were to grow into a nation in Egypt. The patriarchs looked forward with joy to the completion of this promise of a numerous seed. They saw in the light of it that they were to be the fathers of the most highly favoured nation in the world, of that nation that was destined to enjoy the previous privileges of the covenant; that nation out of which the seed was to come in which all the families of the earth should be blessed. The patriarchs desired a better country than the land of Canaan, even a heavenly. And the pleasure of the hope of heaven received no small addition from the charming prospect that every succeeding age would bring a new race, sprung from themselves, to share in their felicities.

We who dwell in Britain, under the government of a race of princes whose dominion extends over the whole island, and many other countries, cannot easily understand how the seed of Jacob became a great nation in Egypt. But the words *great* and *little* have no determinate meaning. We call ourselves a great nation, and other nations small ones that cannot be compared with ours for extent of country or number of people. Thus Jacob's seed became a great nation in Egypt compared with those nations with which Jacob had any acquaintance (unless we may except the nation of Egypt, of which he had only heard, for neither he nor his father had ever sojourned in that land). In the land of Canaan Joshua conquered one and thirty kingdoms, and yet the whole extent of Canaan was not equal to that of Scotland.

It might seem strange to Jacob that he should grow into a great nation in that country where his seed was to endure great tribulation; but he believed the word of God, and Moses attests the accomplishment of it. The more the children of Israel were oppressed, the more they multiplied and grew. When they came out of Egypt, their numbers amounted to six hundred thousand footmen, from twenty years of age and upward, all that were able to go forth to war, besides the whole tribe of Levi, and all the women, and old men, and children, of all the tribes of Israel.

VER. 4. *I will go down with thee into Egypt; and I will also surely bring thee up again: and Joseph shall put his hand upon thine eyes.*

The chief pleasure of Jacob in the land of Canaan was, that God was with him in all his sojournings. Rachel was taken from him by death; Joseph was taken from him, being torn, as he supposed, by wild beasts; but the Lord was always with him to direct all his steps, and to refresh his soul with the assurances of his loving-kindness. But the presence of God was not confined to the land of promise. God had been with him in Mesopotamia. God promised to be with him in the way in which he was now going, and in the country to which he was going. No enemies would be able to destroy him; no accident to deprive him of the possession of his soul; no death to terrify him, if God was with him. We may walk, not only with safety, but with joy, through the valley of the shadow of death if God be with us. Though our heart and our flesh fail us, God will be the strength of our hearts, and our portion for ever.

How blessed was Jacob, having such a promise as this to sweeten all his trials! But have not all Christians the same promise to cheer their spirits under every trial? The intention of the Gospel is to give us the knowledge of salvation, that our fellowship may be with the Father and His Son Jesus Christ, that our joy may be full. "Fear not," says the Lord, "for I am with thee." Think upon the precious comforts of these words whenever you are dejected by solitude, by affliction, by temptation, by fear. If we could believe and apply them, light would spring up out of darkness.

But must Jacob bid a perpetual farewell to the holy land, where his fathers served God for more than two hundred years, the land in which they hoped their seed would dwell for ever, under the protection of God Almighty? No. Jacob must leave this land at present, because it was polluted by the sins of its inhabitants, and punished by the sore judgment of famine, from which the family of Jacob was not exempted. A necessity is laid upon him to go to Egypt, that his family might not die with hunger; but I will surely, said God, bring thee up again. The Lord did not say that He would bring him up again as soon as the remaining five years of famine were ended. It might be inferred from the words of the promise that he was not to be brought up again as long as he lived, for there he was to become a great nation ; and he neither expected nor wished to live till he became a great nation. But the views of the holy patriarchs were not confined to the time of their earthly life. Neither Abraham, nor Isaac, nor Jacob ever dreamed that they were to have their lives prolonged till their seed should become as numerous as the stars of heaven. Had God told them that they would be kept on earth till their seed was so greatly multiplied, they would have thought the declaration a threatening, and not a promise.

Jacob no doubt felt the same sentiments in his mind at this time which David expressed when the Lord told him that He would establish the throne of Israel in his family : "Who am I, O Lord God ? and what is my father's house, that thou hast brought me hitherto ? And this was yet a small thing in thy sight, O Lord God! but thou hast spoken concerning thy servant's house for a great while to come ; and is this the manner of men, O Lord God ?"

"I will also surely bring thee up again." The promise was expressed in strong language, that every doubt might be banished from the patriarch's mind. It could not be accomplished without a very wonderful display of Divine power. But Jacob was a true son of Abraham ; he was persuaded that what God had spoken He was able also to perform.

Jacob's body was brought up again from Egypt when he died. But this was a small thing. It was only a pledge of the fulfilment of the promise in its true meaning. We need not be greatly moved with anything that befalls us in life or death if God be with us to deliver us. If we are driven to the uttermost parts of the earth, there shall God be with us, and His right hand shall hold us. If we go to the nether parts of the earth, God is there also. Dying believers sleep in Jesus, and them that sleep in Jesus God will bring with Him. All Christ's sheep are in His own and His Father's hand ; and none shall pluck them out of these Divine Persons' hands. No enemy shall be able to prevent their complete possession of all those felicities which they hope to enjoy in the better country. It was only in the person of his seed that God brought up Jacob from Egypt to possess the earthly inheritance; but he was received in his own person into the inheritance of the saints in light. And to that inheritance shall all the true sons of Jacob be brought when they die. It is of small importance to us where we die, if we are blessed with the living hope of " that inheritance which is incorruptible, and undefiled, and which fadeth not away."

" And Joseph shall put his hand upon thine eyes." The time was to come when Israel was to die, but God vouchsafes to comfort him with the sure hope that he should die in peace and comfort, and that his favourite son should close his eyes in death. He was to die amongst strangers, yet in the bosom of his own family. His dear son was to do the last offices for him, and in these last offices he was to taste the goodness and faithfulness of God.

It is wonderful how solicitous old men sometimes are about those circumstances of their death and burial which seem to be of no great consequence. When death comes, it is so speedily over, that we need not give ourselves much trouble in thinking about the circumstances which may attend it. But the promise to Jacob, that Joseph should close his eyes, was an assurance to him, not only that God, in love to him, would order the circumstances of his latter end to his own satisfaction, but that he should not again leave Joseph. Long had Joseph been lost to him, though still alive, but he need no more give place to any uneasiness about a life so precious to him. Joseph was to survive his father, and his father was to enjoy his society till death. No parent amongst us knows that any of his dearest friends will live to close his eyes. We have often known parents lament that they had lived so long in a valley of tears to bemoan the loss of those whose youth and vigour promised a long continuance of life. Jacob has been almost the only father who could certainly say that he would not live to mourn over the best-beloved of his children. David knew that Solomon would outlive him, but he saw the miserable end of a son not less dear to his heart.

Perhaps it may appear strange to some that God should now comfort Jacob with a promise concerning the life of Joseph, when he had given him no information, for more than twenty years that Joseph still lived, but left him under all that sorrow for an imaginary loss which other parents feel for the real loss of their children. We must not pretend to penetrate the depth of Divine counsels. God withholds at one time that consolation from His people of which they stood in great need, and at other times gives them an extraordinary measure of consolation. But it would be a great error to suppose that the ways of God are unequal. He has always good reasons for what He does, although He is never bound to tell us what they are, and does not always, in this world, think fit to inform us. This we know, that God's people are not always equally fit for receiving comfort, they do not always equally need in the day of tribulation, and they are not always equally entitled to it, according to the gracious rules of God's procedure towards those whom He loves. God meeteth those who rejoice and work righteousness, those who remember Him in His ways. His own people provoke Him to deny His comforts when they are negligent or cold in their endeavours to please Him by a cheerful obedience and submission to His will.

When Jacob saw his son's coat red with blood, he too hastily concluded that he was torn to pieces, and did not give unto God the glory due to His name, by duly resigning himself to the providence of God, and seeking from Him those consolations which He allows to His afflicted people. He resigned himself to his grief, and said, "I will go down to the grave mourning for my son." When the consolations of God are so small with us, that we think them insufficient to relieve our sorrows, God may withhold them in righteous judgment. Can we reasonably expect those favours which we despise, as if they were not worthy to be sought? God does not value His consolations at so low a rate as they are too often valued even by His own people, and by withholding or diffusing them, will give them juster notions of their necessity and worth.

But when Jacob heard that his son was alive, he consulted God about going to Egypt, and the Lord blessed him with new discoveries of His grace, and cheering prospects for the time to come. His heart was now set at rest, and he would look forward to his long journey, and to all the remaining part of his mortal life, with joy and hope. "The Lord is good unto him that waiteth for Him, to the soul that seeketh for Him."

LECTURE 25

Jacob goes down to Egypt with all his family and all his substance.

xlvi 5–27

VER. 5. *And Jacob rose up from Beer-sheba: and the sons of Israel carried Jacob their father, and their little ones, and their wives, in the wagons which Pharaoh had sent to carry him.*

BESIDES the continual pilgrimages of Jacob in the land of promise, he was more than once under the necessity of making long journeys to distant countries. He fled to Mesopotamia from his father's tents, when he was unconnected with a family which he could call his own. He returned from Mesopotamia to Canaan at the end of twenty years. He then thought that his distant journeyings were at an end. He would now have nothing more to do but dwell in tents, going from place to place in the land of promise, till the time should come when he was to be received to everlasting habitations. But none of us can tell what is before us in this changeable world, or where we may be called to lay our bones. Our comfort is, that the earth is the Lord's, and the fulness thereof; and that the angels of God can conduct our souls, when we die, as easily from one place as from another. If we are Christians, whether we live or whether we die, we live and die unto the Lord. Whether, therefore, we live or die, we are the Lord's, and shall be with Him for ever.

When Jacob was fleeing to Padan-aram, he saw a delightful vision at Luz in the land of Canaan, and received pleasant promises from God. Having obtained such mercy from God, it is said that he lifted up his feet, and came into the land of the people of the East. He was animated by the dicoveries which God gave him of His love, and went on his way rejoicing. The promises given him at Beersheba had the same effect. They gave him new spirit and vigour. His bodily strength was now almost exhausted; but he was strengthened with strength in his soul, and the cheerfulness of his heart, like a medicine, did good to his bones.

He could not travel on foot to a distant country, as he had done in the days of his youth. It was necessary for him to travel in a wagon. Let none of us expect to enjoy the vigour of youth in old age. From the day when sin came into the world death wrought in the bodies of Adam and of his children. And from the time that there were old men in the world, it has been always found that human strength gradually decayed after it came to its perfection, till the time that man went to his long home. Why should men glory in that strength which may be weakened in the middle of the way, and shall certainly be weakened in the end of it?

Divine Providence was ever kind to Jacob, and provided seasonable supplies for his wants. When he was not able to travel on foot, wagons were at hand to carry him to Egypt, and his sons were careful to perform every office to him that could make his journey pleasant.

Dutiful children can do much to soften the uneasiness of old age to their parents. Job was feet to the lame, and eyes to the blind, and caused the widow's heart to sing for joy. How much more ought young men to supply the place of hands, and feet, and eyes to their parents, when these members of their bodies are rendered unfit by infirmity to perform their offices! Let parents endeavour to retain the affections of their children when they are in a state of dependence, and, unless the children have lost all sense of duty and gratitude, they will requite their parents under the infirmities of declining years.

Jacob well deserved the grateful respect of his sons. They were little children during the course of the last long journey which he was obliged to undertake, and he prayed and wrestled with God for them when they were in danger, and used all possible means to appease their enraged uncle, that he might not smite the mother and the children with himself, and moved slowly along the road as the women and children were able to bear the journey.   Now Jacob himself was a child in strength, and his children enjoyed the vigour of youth, and recompensed their father's tender cares by their care of him on their present journey.   " The sons of Israel carried Jacob their father, and the little ones, and their wives, in the wagons."

It is the custom among rude nations for men to take all possible ease to themelves, and to devolve every drudgery on their wives.   We often read with pain of the hardships imposed on their women, who must, in their journeyings, carry their little ones on their backs, whilst their lordly husbands move along at their ease, without feeling any concern for the misery which they impose on their female companions.   Civilisation is a precious blessing to mankind, and the female sex have special reason to bless God for its benefits.   They have still more reason to bless God for the light of revelation, which best teaches men and women what they owe to one another.   What treatment women received from the Canaanites we learn only from the treatment which they receive in other countries in the same stage of society.   But the family of Jacob had learned from God to give honour to the wife as the weaker vessel.   The men burdened themselves with the most laborious part of the work necessary to be done, and placed their wives in the wagons along with the children.   It will always be found that when the true religion is best understood, women will be treated with most respect.   Politeness, in refined nations, will procure them the exteriors of respect, but will not secure them against snares and injuries, which are often more pernicious than the rudest treatment of the Indian savage.

Ver. 6. *And they took their cattle, and their goods, which they had gotten in the land of Canaan, and came into Egypt, Jacob, and all his seed with him.*

Jacob left Mesopotamia with much cattle and substance,

which, by the blessing of God, was increased in the land of Canaan. We are not told how he was able to keep his cattle alive in the time of the famine. But seldom have famines been so terrible as not to leave some small portion of sustenance for the beasts. A part of the cattle might perish, and in that which remained the dismal effects of the famine appeared. Joseph was tenderly solicitous for his father, that he might not come to want, and put it in his power to retain the property of his flocks and herds when the Egyptians sold all that they had to Pharaoh.

Jacob's sons brought not only their cattle, but their goods with them, which they had gotten in the land of Canaan. Pharaoh had desired Jacob not to regard his stuff, because the good of all the land of Egypt was before him ; but he wished not to take advantage of Pharaoh's goodness, or to owe greater obligations to him than he found necessary. He inherited the spirit of Abraham, who would not give occasion to have it said that the King of Sodom made him rich. We must not haughtily refuse obligations from those who are willing to confer them when we need their kindness ; but we ought to be diligent in business, and careful in using what we have gained by it, that we may be as little burdensome as possible to our friends. A Christian ought not to be mean-spirited, or to snatch like a dog at everything that is offered him ; and a provident care of what is our own may preserve us from temptations to such contemptible behaviour. Christ Himself taught His disciples frugality in the use of those things which He could have easily multiplied by a word from His mouth, Matt. xiv.

VER. 7. *His sons, and his sons' sons with him, his daughters, and his sons' daughters, and all his seed, brought he with him into Egypt.*

Jacob's trials were more numerous than those of his father or his grandfather ; but he had some comforts, too, above others, for God, who distributes to His people all their trials and comforts, uses to balance the one with the other. When Abraham was old, whilst he was yet alive, he thought it necessary to send away all his sons from him except Isaac. When Isaac

Y

was old, Esau found it necessary to depart from him to the land of Mount Seir. Jacob, till the day of his death, had all his sons with him except Joseph, who was sent away by Providence to provide food for his household; and with him, too, he dwelt during the last seventeen years of his life. Some of his children gave him no satisfaction by their behaviour. Yet it was a great comfort to him, and it may be presumed that it was a great blessing to them, that they were near to him, that he might give them all the instructions and admonitions which they needed. They dwelt with Jacob when they had families, and doubtless he was very useful to their little ones in training them up in the way in which they should go. His blessing prevailed above the blessings of his progenitors, for all his descendants made a part of the seed promised to Abraham by Isaac. And he used all diligence to inspire them with just views of the value of the promises, and of the excellency of the true worship of God. Thus he spent his old age in the last services which he could perform to God and to his family, and died in the cheering hope that the pure religion, which he so dearly loved, would be kept up amongst all his seed.

He did not leave any one of his sons, or of his grandsons, behind him in the land of Canaan. And it does not appear that any of them were unwilling to accompany him. They paid him a becoming deference as their common father. We have been already told that his sons carried him in the wagons which they had brought from Egypt. We are here told that Jacob brought all his sons, and his sons' sons, with him into Egypt. His sons took all the trouble of the journey upon themselves. Their father kept all the authority in his own hands, and none of his sons grudged it to their venerable father. They were all happy to be under his direction, and considered him as the bond of their union. Families are happy when the heads of them are qualified to govern in the fear of the Lord, and all the younger members are disposed to obey. If there are disputes and strifes among them, the authority of the head is necessary, and may prove useful in removing them.

" His daughters, and his sons' daughters, and all his seed,

brought he with him into Egypt." When we read of daughters, we are not to infer that there were more than one, for the plural is sometimes used for the singular. Thus, ver. 23, we read of the sons of Dan, when we have an account of no more than one son. Jacob is said to have brought his daughters with him, by whom we may understand, not only Dinah, but his sons' wives, whom he considered as his daughters, and treated with all the affection and care due to such a relation. But we read only of one daughter of his sons—Sarah, the daughter of Asher. All those Jacob brought along with him; and if there had been more of them, he would not have left them behind. Daughters were dear to him as well as sons. Their outward comfort, as well as their precious souls, were the objects of his tender concern. And why should any parent behave partially to the offspring of his own body, as if he thought that his daughters were more distantly related to him than his sons? They may probably leave the house, and become the property of a man whom they love more than father or mother. But is it not as probable that the sons will leave their father and mother, and cleave to women whom they take into a nearer relation than that of children to their parents?

VER. 8-14. *And these are the names of the children of Israel, which came into Egypt, Jacob and his sons, &c.*

As some of Jacob's great-grandchildren are mentioned in this list, we may reasonably presume, both that the seven years of plenty did not commence immediately upon Joseph's advancement, and that Jacob's children were married, and had distinct families early in life. Hezron and Hamul, the grandchildren of Judah, were grandsons, likewise, of the wife of one of his sons, and therefore Judah must have been at that time pretty well advanced in life; and yet, from the youth of Benjamin, we may infer that none of the sons of Jacob could be beyond middle age. A long time after the promise of a numerous seed to Abraham, he had no child. Isaac was sixty years of age, and Abraham a hundred and sixty, before any more children of the promise were born. Jacob was advanced in life before the birth of any of his children. Thus was the faith of the patriarchs tried by long delays in the accomplishment of the promise. But now the promised seed began to increase speedily in number. Early in life, each of Jacob's sons had sons born to them, and some of them were grandfathers when they had arrived at the middle period of life. God will hasten His word in His own time, and not sooner.

Reuben brought with him four sons; Simeon, six; Levi, three; Judah, three sons and two grandsons; Issachar, four sons; Zebulun, three. They, no doubt, were all covetous, like their father and mother, of many children; and God bestowed this gift upon them in different measures, according to His own will. None of them had so large families as many persons whom we have known in our time, although their father had the promise given him of great fruitfulness. Even after God was visibly proceeding to the accomplishment of the promise, room was left for the patience of faith. One of Simeon's sons, in distinction from the rest, is said to have been by a Canaanitish woman. This circumstance would not have been observed if it had not been an uncommon thing in the family to marry the daughters of Canaan. We cannot have forgotten how solicitous Abraham was that his son should not marry a Canaanitess, and what grief of heart Isaac and Rebekah endured for Esau's marriage with women of Canaan. Besides the ungodliness that generally prevailed in the country, there was another reason why it was unsafe for sons of Abraham to marry the daughters of their neighbours. It might have formed a too close and very dangerous connection with the nations that were to be destroyed for their wickedness, to make room for the children of Israel. If a man will not be satisfied without a wife trained up in evil practices, he may prevent a part of the mischief to be expected from the unhappy connection by removing to a distance from all her ungodly friends. A man ought to remember that by marriage he not only finds a wife, but gains a new set of relations, who are likely to be either a blessing or a curse to him. It is a question whether Simeon, by leaving Canaan, prevented the mischievous consequences to be dreaded from his family connection with the Canaanites.

His son Shaul was removed from the influence of his mother's friends; yet we find long after, that this tribe was distinguished by judgments procured by flagrant iniquities. It was one of the princes of Simeon that perished by the hand of Phinehas, as the great ringleader in the abominable business of Peor. This tribe was not half so numerous when it entered into the land of Canaan as when it entered into the wilderness, so memorable for the rebellions and punishments of Israel.

In the list of Judah's family we have an account of two young persons who left their carcasses in Canaan—Er and Onan, it is said, died in the land of Canaan; but why, then, do we hear of them in this place, which promises to give us an account of those who went down with Jacob to Egypt, and not of what happened in Canaan? We must not suppose that there are any useless repetitions in the Bible. The story of Er and Onan is called back to our mind that we may not forget how dangerous it is to provoke the Lord. They were very young persons when they perished in their iniquity. Let not the young take liberty to sin, in the presumptuous hope that they will repent and find mercy when they are old. What if God should root them out of the world before the time come that they have set for repentance, and make them a warning to other young persons, that their time is not in their own hands!

"The sons of Judah : Er, and Onan, and Shelah, and Pharez, and Zarah; but Er and Onan died in the land of Canaan. And the sons of Pharez were Hezron and Hamul."

Er and Onan were lawfully begotten sons of Judah, by whom he hoped that his family would be built up. Pharez and Zarah were illegitimate, yet Er and Onan perished childless in the wrath of God; Pharez and Zarah built up the house of Judah. One of them became a father in early youth. Many great kings, and the Great King, who is Christ the Lord, descended from him. Let no man boast of the honours of his birth if he lives under the power of that corrupt nature with which we are all born. Let not children born of fornication think that God has utterly cast them off from His people. The dishonour of their birth is, in God's eye, their parents', and not their own.

Christ sprung from Pharez. The mother of Pharez, as well as his brother Zarah, is mentioned in the list of his ancestors by Matthew.

Ver. 15. *These be the sons of Leah, which she bare unto Jacob in Padan-aram, with his daughter Dinah : all the souls of his sons and his daughters were thirty and three ; [or, all the souls, his sons and his daughters, were thirty-three ; i.e., all the souls already mentioned, consisting chiefly of his sons and daughters, but including likewise Jacob himself.]*

These heads of families in Israel were born by Leah in Padan-aram. The children of these patriarchs might, in some sense, be said to be born by Leah, as she was their mother ; but they were not born in Padan-aram. Yet perhaps, in the language of the Hebrews, she might be truly said to have born them all in Padan-aram, because she bore them in the persons of their fathers, none of whom were born in the land of Canaan. Thus, Levi, in some sense, paid tithes in the loins of his father Abraham.

The sons of Jacob were, in more senses than one, strangers in the land of promise. They were neither born, nor did they die in it; and whilst they lived in it, they ordinarily went about from place to place, dwelling in tents.

Leah was very thankful to Divine Providence for making her the mother of several children ; and we find that this greatly desired blessing of children was multiplied to her. Almost the half of Jacob's seed that came into Egypt were her offspring, although she did not live to see them all, for before this time she was buried with the father and grandfather of her husband.

All Leah's sons were heads of families and fathers of tribes in Israel. But poor Dinah was only an aunt in Israel. She had taken a false step in youth, which clouded all her future days. Unhappily, she was too fond of amusement, and when she went to see the daughters of the land, met with a seducer or ravisher. From that time she appears to have lived desolate in her father's house. We know no more of her but what is here said. She could not be very young when some of her brothers brought grandchildren with them into Egypt. To what misery do young persons often subject themselves through the whole course of their lives by one imprudent piece of conduct, which too frequently leads to others still worse! Let young women keep themselves pure, if they wish to enjoy peace and pleasure in old age.

If our translation of the last part of this verse is just, it seems probable that the transcribers of the ancient copies made a slight blunder, by placing the third for the second letter of the alphabet, and thus making the number of Leah's descendants thirty-three instead of thirty-two. But it is probable that Jacob himself was intended to be included in this part of the list.

VER. 16-18. *And the sons of Gad, &c.*

" Cast out the bond-woman and her seed," said Sarah to Abraham, " for the son of the bond-woman shall not be heir with my son, even with Isaac." But here we find the sons of the bond-women, Zilpah and Bilhah, ranked with the sons of the free-women, Leah and Rachel. Let us adore the sovereignty of God, who chooses whom He pleases, either to be members of His Church on earth, or heirs of the everlasting kingdom. He confirmed the word of Sarah by commanding Abraham to turn Ishmael out of his house, although the thing seemed grievous to him when it was required by his wife, from the love which he bore to his son. But he granted the wishes of Jacob, to have all his descendants made partakers of the same privileges. On his death-bed he said, under the influence of the Divine Spirit, "Dan shall judge his people, as one of the tribes of Israel." Sovereignty appears, not only in choosing or rejecting whom God pleases, but in the favours which He is pleased to bestow on His chosen. Abraham was as well beloved as Jacob, and yet a great part of his descendants were left in the same state with the other nations, who soon lost the true knowledge of the true God. But all Jacob's sons, by the concubines as well as by their mistresses, were patriarchs in Israel.

VER. 19-22. *The sons of Rachel, &c.*

" The Lord maketh the barren woman to keep house, and

to be a joyful mother of children." Rachel was indeed a joyful mother only to her first child. When he was born, she expressed her hope that God would add to her another son. This son was added, but he was the son of her sorrow. By these two sons she became the mother of fourteen grandchildren, and of three tribes in Israel.

We have in this place an account of Joseph's family; for although he was in the land of Egypt, he trained up his sons as grandsons of Jacob. It is said of the good Emperor Theodosius that he accounted it a greater honour to be a member of the Church of Christ than to be lord of the Roman Empire. Joseph was like Moses, who chose rather to take his portion with the Hebrew strangers than be called the grandson of the King of Egypt.

Benjamin went down to Egypt with no less than ten children, although he was still his father's darling, as the son of his old age. If parents and children are wise, the pleasure of the parents in the children will not be diminished, but increased, by years. The qualities of ripened age in well-behaving persons are not less amiable, but attractive of a stronger affection than those which are discovered in childhood, when the character is not so fully developed or so well ascertained as in more advanced years.

Ver. 23-25. *And the sons of Dan : Hushim, &c.*

Although Dan had only one son, his children are spoken of in the plural number, because the mention of this one son is a full enumeration of his family. The same way of speaking is used in the account which Moses gives of his family, Num. xxvi. In which passage, as well as in the account given (Num. ii.) of the number of the tribe, we find that it was the largest in Israel, except the tribe of Judah. The beginning of these two tribes was small. Only one of Judah's lawfully begotten sons survived the judgments of God upon his family. Dan had only one son, Benjamin had ten ; and yet the tribe of Benjamin was the least of all the tribes. Those of Judah and Dan were the greatest. Who can tell any man how few or how many his descendants will be at the distance of a thousand or a hundred years? If we know not how few they may be, let us not indulge too fond expectations of pleasure when we see our children like olive-plants round about our table. If we cannot tell how many they may be, let us spare no pains to induce our children, and our household after us, to keep the way of the Lord. We cannot estimate the quantity of good which may be done by our endeavours to transmit our religion to our children's children.

VER. 26, 27. *All the souls that came with Jacob into Egypt, &c.*

Thirty-two descendants of Leah, sixteen of Zilpah, fourteen of Rachel, seven of Bilhah, together with Jacob, make in all seventy persons, sixty-six of whom, besides Jacob himself, came down at this time into Egypt, where Joseph with his two sons already were. Jacob said to God, when he was travelling from Padan-aram, "With my staff I passed over this Jordan, and now I am become two bands." What would he now say when he descended to Egypt with eleven bands, expecting to find another in the land to which he travelled? Doubtless his heart would expand with thankfulness to God, who had graciously given him so many children, and had preserved so many of his descendants alive (for two of them only had died), and kept them all under his own eye, that he might train them up for God, and use all the means in his power to prevent the covenant and the wonderful works of God from being forgotten when he should go to sleep with his fathers.

Jacob had the pleasure, which few enjoy, of seeing all his children's children, and of living with them till they were all capable of receiving all the instruction that he thought it necessary to give them. It seems probable, from Num. xxvi., that all his children's children were born before he went down to Egypt, where he lived seventeen years. From this circumstance, as well as from several others, it seems highly probable that Joseph was more than thirty-nine years of age when Jacob went down to Egypt, and consequently that the seven years of plenty did not commence in the year when Joseph was exalted to his high station.

It is remarkable that of all Jacob's seed that went down to

Egypt, two only were of the female sex—Dinah, the daughter of Jacob, and Sarah, the daughter of Asher. Many have justly remarked that the almost equal distributions of men and women through the world is a decisive proof that there is a God who governs the world. There have been not a few who lived to see nearly as many descendants as Jacob; but perhaps never any man saw half the number of sons, and so few daughters among them. It is observed of all the antediluvian patriarchs that they begat sons and daughters. None of Jacob's sons appears to have begotten a single daughter, except Asher; although all of them, except Dan, were fathers of more than one son. We cannot pretend to account for this singularity in Jacob's family, yet may take the liberty to observe one good purpose served by it. It obliged Jacob's grandsons to go out of their own families to seek wives. Judah married a Canaanitess, his only wife, for aught we know. We know, at least, that all his lawful children sprung from one wife. It is not an improbable conjecture that his deep sense of his guilt in the matter of Tamar turned his thoughts ever after from the female sex. Simeon seems to have had only one of his sons by a Canaanitish woman. The other wives in Jacob's family were in all probability descendants of Abraham, by the sons of the concubines, or by Esau. And thus Abraham's prayers for his other sons besides Isaac did not utterly fall to the ground. A part of Ishmael's posterity by his daughters made a part of the posterity of Isaac, in whom Abraham's seed was called. There is no reason to think that Jacob would advise his children to take wives of their neighbours amongst whom they dwelt, when himself went to the country of Syria for a wife, and for a wife of that country kept sheep.

In these seventy persons that went down to Egypt Jacob saw the progenitors of a race like the stars of heaven for multitude. He believed God's promise; and not much more than two hundred years after this time, there came out of Egypt no less than six hundred and three thousand and five hundred and fifty men of his descendants able to go forth to battle, besides a whole tribe devoted to the services of religion.

The Lord can soon make a little one to become a thousand; and a small one a strong nation. The spiritual seed of Jacob became still more numerous, when the twelve apostles, the patriarchs of the spiritual Israel, begat thousands and ten thousands of children to Jesus Christ through the Gospel. " Who hath heard such a thing? who hath seen such things? Shall the earth be made to bring forth in one day? shall a nation be born at once? for as soon as Zion travailed, she brought forth her children."

LECTURE 26
The meeting of Jacob and Joseph.
xlvi 28–30

VER. 28. *And he sent Judah before him unto Joseph, to direct his face unto Goshen; and they came into the land of Goshen.*

JACOB met with no such difficulties and dangers in the course of this last journey as in former journeys from or to the land of Canaan. When he went from his father's house to Mesopotamia he was fleeing from his brother Esau, without a companion, and found it necessary to lodge in the open fields. When he fled from Mesopotamia to Canaan Laban pursued him, and he was credibly informed that Esau was coming against him with four hundred men. We do not find that any of the Arabs or of the Philistines came to attack him on his way to Egypt. God stays His rough winds in the day of His east wind. Jacob had suffered much of late from the absence of his two favourite sons, and his body was become unfit to bear what he endured in former times. The strength of God's people will be according to their days, or their days according to their strength.

When Jacob was approaching towards Egypt, or to the royal city, he sent Judah before him to Joseph to direct his face to Goshen. He could not travel with such speed as he desired, to see the son so dear to his heart, but doubted not that his son, when he heard of his approach, would come forth to meet him. Thus they would both gain some hours of happiness. Besides, it seemed proper that Joseph and the house of Pharaoh should have warning of the approach of such a large company before they made their appearance. A good man will guide his affairs with discretion.

"And they came unto the land of Goshen." Thus far God fulfilled His word to Jacob, "I will go down to Egypt with thee;" and doubtless the good man firmly believed that the other promises would be no less exactly accomplished, when the time appointed was come. All the promises were never intended to be fulfilled at once; but experience worketh hope, for the mercy of the Lord endureth for ever, and His truth is to all generations.

VER. 29. *And Joseph made ready his chariot, and went up to meet Israel his father, to Goshen, and presented himself unto him; and he fell on his neck, and wept on his neck a good while.*

As soon as Joseph heard that his father was approaching, he made ready his chariot to go down and meet him. He was impatient to see a father who loved him so dearly, and whom he so dearly loved. Love laments the absence of the beloved object, and seizes the first opportunity that offers to enjoy what it so greatly longed to possess. How strange is it if any man shall call himself a lover of Christ, who feels no ardent desires to see His beauty and to enjoy the pleasure of His presence! If a man discovers no wishes to enjoy the company of his father or mother, you will think that he scarcely believes himself to be their offspring. Is Christ truly beloved by us if we feel not as strong an attachment to Him as children discover to their parents, from whom they have long been separated? Or does love to Christ produce the same effects which disaffection produces when our fellow-creatures are its objects? Do not men willingly deceive themselves when they pretend to love a person to whom they say in effect, Depart from us, we desire to have no fellowship with thee?

Joseph sent wagons only for his father, and his father's house, but made ready a chariot for himself, to come and meet with his father. Did he wish to show himself a greater man than his father? Certainly this was not his intention. He would cheerfully have exchanged his carriage for his father's if it would have contributed to his father's satisfaction; but he well knew that Jacob never chose to travel in a chariot. He was a plain man, living in tents from his early days, and never desired the conveniences enjoyed by princes. When we desire to show our regard to our friends, let us consider their taste and habits of life. What would be a grateful present to one would give no pleasure to another. Solomon, with all his wisdom, did not always attend to this obvious rule of conduct.

A wagon was better fitted for Jacob coming to Egypt at the head of his numerous family, many of whom were little ones, than one of the King of Egypt's chariots would have been. But it was proper that Joseph should appear with an equipage suited to the station to which the king had advanced him. The swift horses of his chariot would soon bring him to the much-desired presence of his father.

"He went up to meet Israel his father, to Goshen, and presented himself to him; and he fell on his neck, and wept a good while." It would be a vain and needless attempt to describe the joy that Joseph felt and gave when he saw that father whose distance from him he had mourned for more than twenty years. How much are those men to be pitied who love only their own persons, and scarcely ever felt the charities of father, son, or brother, or the joys of friendship! They may congratulate themselves on their exemption from the pains which often attend the social affections; but a man who has lost his appetite for his daily food may with as good reason congratulate himself because he does not feel, like other men, the cravings of hunger. When men are entirely swallowed up by the concerns of their own dear persons, they may taste the pleasures of a beast, but they cannot relish nor understand the pleasures of a human creature.

Joseph expressed his fervent affection to his father by weeping upon his neck; and this he continued to do for a considerable time before he could give vent to his joy in articulate words. Those tears were more delicious than any of the joys which men express by smiles upon their countenances, or by the sound of trumpet. His joy was too great for utterance.

He was now richly recompensed for all the bitter tears which the envy of his brethren or the rage of his mistress had extorted from his eyes. Pleasant were the moments when he wept on the neck of Benjamin. His pleasure seems to have been still greater when he wept on Jacob's neck ; it is said that he " wept on it a good while."

The tears of love are sweeter than the laughter of joy, arising from a happy change in one's own circumstances. Paul could not forget the tears of his son Timothy, shed when they parted from one another. These tears were the tears of grief, and yet the remembrance of them was pleasant to Paul, because they expressed the tender affection of a son whom he so dearly loved. How joyful must they both have been when Providence suffered them again to meet !

Ver. 30. *And Israel said unto Joseph, Now let me die, since I have seen thy face, because thou art yet alive.*

Never did a parent taste greater pleasure in seeing his son alive who had been really dead than Jacob now felt in seeing Joseph alive. We may justly except the Virgin Mary. She knew that her blessed Son would certainly rise the third day. Her faith was not shaken by her Son's death to such a degree as that of the disciples—or rather, perhaps, it was not shaken in any degree. Yet undoubtedly her joy at seeing her Son and Saviour raised from the grave far exceeded the pleasure that the fondest of other parents could enjoy, were the dearest of their departed children to be raised up from their graves. But neither the widow of Zarephath, nor the woman of Shunem, nor Jairus with his wife, were more fully persuaded of the death of their children, whom they received again raised to life, than Jacob of the death of his son Joseph ; nor did any of these parents love their children so dearly as Joseph was beloved by Jacob.

Love was the spring of all this joy, which Jacob found himself unable to express. Observe one of the excellencies of love, for which it will be valued by all who wish to enjoy true happiness. It is a spring of pleasure which selfish men cannot enjoy. It makes the happiness of our friends our own. Love will be a great part of the happiness of the heavenly state. The felicity of all the angels and all the redeemed saints in heaven is the happiness of every one of them. We may speak a much bolder word. The happiness of their Father and their Redeemer is their own. The blessedness bestowed on themselves gives them joy unspeakable, but not so much as the boundless felicity of him whom they loved better than themselves. Christ told His disciples that if they loved Him as they ought to have done, they would have rejoiced at the thought of His going to the Father, although themselves were to be left behind. What joy, then, must it have given them to be received up to the place to which He went, there to behold His glory, and to be ever with Him!

It must be confessed that upon earth love is often the cause of pain as well as of pleasure, although, even in this valley of tears, the pleasures of love, regulated by religion, incomparably exceed the pains; and the pains which attend it are often preparatory to, and mingled with pleasure. Jacob could not have so greatly rejoiced to see Joseph at this time if he had not long mourned for his loss. His sorrows were now richly repaid. He would have given his life with pleasure for this happy sight of Joseph living, after he had been so long numbered by his father with the dead. "Now let me die, seeing I have seen thy face." Life was now more pleasant to Jacob than it had been for many past years. Yet pleasant as it was become, he would have parted with it without sorrow, because the pleasure he enjoyed would not suffer the approaches of sorrow. As a man that has found a precious treasure which he did not expect would not feel much pain in losing a small sum of money, because his gain exceeds his loss; so Jacob, had he died at this time, would have thought the loss of his own life a small matter, when he had gained a more precious life than his own.

A certain Greek, at the Olympic games, had the pleasure of seeing three of his sons victorious in different combats. His pleasure was more than doubled by the affection of his sons, who came and placed on his head those crowns which they had obtained as the reward of their victories. The spectators, transported at this instance of parental felicity, cried out,

" Die " (naming him), " die at this time, you can never die in a happier time." The father himself was transported to such a height of joy that he expired on the spot. If Jacob had died when he met with Joseph he would have felt no pain. The excess of his pleasures would have swallowed up the sorrows of death. Love is stronger than death, and can overcome all its terrors. We read of martyrs who endured the most cruel deaths which malignity could devise, and yet professed that they felt no pain. Their fortitude cannot be accounted for on the ordinary principles of human nature. They no doubt were strengthened with might by the Spirit in the inner man, yet love to Christ was the powerful means by which He invigorated their souls in the awful moment. They died for him whom their souls loved. He was with them, and they hoped soon to be with him.

" Now let me die in peace, since I have seen thy face." He knew that he was not long to enjoy Joseph's company on earth. The days were now drawing nigh when Israel thought he must die. Happy as this meeting was, the joy of it was soon to be terminated by death. How happy will that meeting of friends long lost to one another be which death will not terminate ! When we meet in heaven with those whom we loved on earth, the crown of our felicity will be the certainty that we shall part no more.

Jacob little thought at this time that he had yet seventeen years of life before him in this world. Yet those seventeen years soon passed away, and death was not terrible to him. It was a great alleviation of the sorrows of death that Joseph was at hand to close his eyes, and brought himself under a solemn promise to carry up his body to the sepulchre of his fathers. But his chief pleasure in seeing Joseph at this time, and in Joseph's filial behaviour at his death, was, that he saw the truth and kindness of God to him, both in meeting with Joseph and in Joseph's behaviour. God had promised to conduct him to Egypt, and to spare the life of Joseph to close his eyes in death. Perhaps the remembrance of this promise brought his death into his mind when he saw his beloved son.

z

"'Now let me die, since I have seen thy face, because thou art yet alive." Jacob said nothing of Joseph's greatness, although he certainly rejoiced in his son's prosperity, but he accounted life more valuable than grandeur. Although he had found his dear son in a poor condition, he would have praised the God of his mercies. What reason have we to confess our ingratitude to God when we are unthankful either for our own life or for the life of our children, because God has not been pleased to give to us, or to them, those great things which we greedily desired to satisfy our lust, or because He has taken some things away which were given only for a time!

If Jacob rejoiced in the mortal life of Joseph, what thanks do we owe to God if He has given to ourselves and to our children, who were dead in trespasses and sins, that new and better life which shall never end!

Perhaps some may think that the good old man need not have been transported with such joy to find his son alive who was thought to be dead. When he was daily looking for death to himself he must have expected soon to see him in a world where there was no death. The separation between them was likely to be much longer by finding Joseph in a world which himself was soon to leave, than it would have been if the sight of this darling son had been deferred for a few years longer. This is true. When seventeen years more had passed, Jacob was parted from Joseph for all the remaining time that Joseph was to live on earth, and he was then but in the midst of his days. Yet Jacob justly esteemed it a great mercy to himself to find Joseph again in the land of the living. It was on earth that the good man needed this consolation. In heaven he was assured that whatever pleasure he found in the society of Joseph, yet his absence would make no void in his felicity. No earthly person was so dear to him as Joseph. In heaven he was to be in the bosom of Abraham. He was to dwell with all the spirits of the just who were now made perfect, and with an innumerable company of angels. Yet their society was to constitute but a small part of his happiness. God Himself was Jacob's portion on earth as well as in heaven, but the full and immediate enjoyment of God was not to be expected in this world. Whilst he was at home in the body he was absent from the Lord. He tasted and saw that the Lord was good; and if all his family had been laid in the dust, it is hoped that he would still have thought himself happy, although for a time he would have been in great heaviness through this sore temptation. But, eminent as Jacob was in faith and fervency of spirit, he had not attained such a measure of patience as Job. When Joseph seemed to be lost, he spoke of nothing but the other world, and seemed to despair of ever seeing any more good in this world. When Joseph was recovered, he lost not his views of the other world. Joy made him now as willing as grief had formerly made him desirous to die. Yet he had now seen the goodness of God in such a way as he had never expected to see it in the land of the living, and he hoped that he would be able to spend the small remainder of his life, not only with greater comfort, but more thankfully to God, and more usefully to men.

It is pleasant to give scope to our thoughts on this happy moment of the much-afflicted patriarch's life. We should have been happy to have been informed more fully of the sweet converse that happened between the happy father and the happy son, and of the pious reflections that arose in the mind of Jacob, when the transports of his joy had so far subsided as to leave him at liberty to think and to speak with composure.

There was one kind complaint that Jacob would surely make to his son, Why did you not take the first opportunity to inform your mourning father that you were alive? What answer Joseph made we cannot say. There were circumstances known at the time, perhaps, when this history was written, which cannot now be known, that accounted for this apparent neglect. Jacob was certainly satisfied with Joseph's account of the matter. When a man of acknowledged goodness neglects something that seems to be his duty, he may, for what we know, be very blameable, for no man is absolutely perfect in this life. Yet we ought not to pronounce him in the wrong till we know his reasons, if there is a possibility that he might have been in the right. If he is not present to give his reasons, or if we have no right to require an account of them, or if he is dead, let him enjoy all the credit that his known behaviour in other parts of his life demands, and let him not be judged for what he probably had good reasons to do, or not to do, although we know not what these reasons were.

Some of Jacob's thoughts on this occasion may be suggested to us by his known character. We can scarcely doubt of his pious reflections upon that kind Providence which had ordered all his affairs in perfect wisdom, contrary to his own wishes and fears. He must have now condemned himself for what he had once, or perhaps often said, "All these things are against me." He was now ready to weep for those tears which he had formerly shed when he was dissatisfied with that Providence which he now found to be so wonderfully gracious.

We may run into mistakes when we infer men's behaviour from their character. Neither good men nor bad men are always themselves. Yet we cannot think ourselves in an error when we suppose that Jacob's exercises of heart at this time were such as might be expected from so holy a man, on an occasion so wonderful. It will, however, be more profitable for us to consider what instruction in righteousness we may derive from what is plainly recorded in the history ; for we are not to suppose that it can be of little use to us to consider with attention those wonderful facts recorded in the Bible, to which there is nothing like in the course of our own lives.

"Let me now die, because I have seen thy face, and thou yet livest." In the time of the sweetest joy that earth could afford him, he speaks of dying; and the Apostle Paul advises us, when we rejoice, to call to remembrance our mortality, that our joys may be moderated in a suitableness to our condition : "This I say, brethren, the time is short; it remaineth that both they that have wives, be as though they had none ; and they that weep, as though they wept not ; and they that rejoice, as though they rejoiced not ; for the fashion of this world passeth away."

Although our days are few and full of trouble, we ought to be thankful that comforts are intermingled with our troubles. Old age is the time of life when men say that they have no pleasure in it. But we are sullen and discontented creatures if we do not thankfully receive those favours of Providence by which God is pleased often to sweeten the bitterness of the last days of life. If we have few remaining days of life left us, pray that they may be gladdened with testimonies of the Divine favour, Ps. lxxxix. 46, 47. Yet let us not forget that we are in the evening of life, that the sun, and the moon, and the light, and the stars will be darkened more and more, and that we must go to our long home, where, if we have not attained a meetness for better enjoyments, everlasting darkness must be our portion.

The prospect of dying and leaving Joseph did not discompose the patriarch ; for all his days (from the time that he knew the Lord, and believed His promise) he had been seeking a better country, where all his treasure was laid up.

We may in some measure learn from Jacob's words how we may be fitted for dying. He was so full of joy that the pains and cords of death at this time could not have brought him that trouble and sorrow which are ordinarily felt in the last moments of mortals. But is it possible that we can attain such joys in this world of miseries as will swallow up all the bitterness of death ? From the things or persons of this world we cannot expect such transports of pleasure. Jacob himself, when he was settled in Goshen, would find other considerations than the life of Joseph necessary to sustain his heart in the view of leaving the world. He knew, as well as Job, that he had a living Redeemer, and that though, after his skin, worms destroyed his body, yet in his flesh he should see God.

Old Simeon, who waited for the consolation of Israel, found all the horrors of death annihilated by a sight of what he had long wished and hoped to see. A firm faith, and a lasting hope in Christ, would enable us to die, not only without terror, but with joy and gladness. It was Jacob's hope of the salvation of

Christ that cheered his soul when he saw death actually making its approaches, Gen. xlix. 18.

The joys of God's salvation can alone swallow up the sorrows of death. And who would not be ready to die a thousand times, if he was fully persuaded that the living Redeemer stands ready to receive his departing soul?

LECTURE 27

Joseph gives his brethren directions what
account of themselves they should
give unto Pharaoh, and procures a royal
mandate for settling them in the land of Goshen.
xlvi 31–34; xlvii 1–6

VER. 31. *And Joseph said unto his brethren, and unto his
father's house, I will go up, and shew Pharaoh, and say unto him,
My brethren, and my father's house, which were in the land of
Canaan, are come unto me.*

JOSEPH, no doubt, continued for some time in sweet converse with his father, but did not overlook his brethren.
They were all welcome, and he behaved in such a manner
as to make them sensible that they were welcome to Egypt, to
partake in his prosperity. · They were shepherds compelled to
leave their own country. Joseph was the lord of Egypt, yet
he was not ashamed to acknowledge his relation to them, either
before the people or before the king: "I will go up and shew
Pharaoh, and say unto him, My brethren, and my father's house,
which were in the land of Canaan, are come unto me." The
heart of Joseph was not exalted above his brethren by the
superiority of his station, nor alienated from them by their
malicious conduct to himself. He was persuaded that they had
repented, and his resentments, if they ever existed, were now
obliterated. He was far superior to them in station, but it was
his highest honour to be a son of Abraham and of Israel. Those
who from a high station to which Providence has raised them

look down with coldness or contempt upon their poor kindred, forget the absolute uncertainty and constant mutability of all earthly things. They do not consider that pride debases the highest below the meanest of mankind ; that the devil himself was made what he is by pride; and that He who is fairer and greater than the children of men is not ashamed, in His exaltation, to call the poorest believer upon earth a brother, saying, " I will declare thy name unto my brethren."

It was a proper instance of respect to the king, as well as to his brethren, to inform Pharaoh that they were come to his country from the land of Canaan at his desire. Pharaoh told Joseph that in the throne himself only was to be greater, and Joseph did not forget the respect due to so kind a prince—" I will say, My father and my father's house are come."

VER. 32. *And the men are shepherds, for their trade hath been to feed cattle ; and they have brought their flocks, and their herds, and all that they have.*

Joseph well knew how greatly shepherds were detested by the Egyptians, and yet he would not conceal from the king that he was sprung from a race of shepherds. His credit was too well established to be overturned by the knowledge of this connection, and it was necessary that his brethren's occupation should be known to the king, that he might assign them a dwelling convenient for their flocks and herds.

We need not be ashamed of any lawful profession ; sin only brings shame. The want of a lawful occupation would be shameful to the great bulk of mankind; none of us came into the world to eat up the fruits of other men's industry, without doing something (if God has given us ability) to compensate, on our own part, for the labours that others must take for our good.

Pharaoh had desired Joseph's father not to put himself to any trouble with his stuff, because the good of all the land of Egypt was at his service. But he would be pleased to hear that the good man did not wish to abuse his kindness. All that Jacob desired from him for himself and his family was the supply of those provisions which bad seasons had denied to the land of Canaan. Those are best entitled to our bounty who wish to be no further troublesome than imperious necessity compels them. Improvident persons, who trust to the bounty of others, deserve to feel want, that necessity may teach them frugality and diligence.

VER. 33. *And it shall come to pass, when Pharaoh shall call you, and shall say, What is your occupation?*

It was to be expected that Pharaoh would call for Joseph's brethren, and converse with them. His long friendship for Joseph would make him desirous of seeing his brethren, and perhaps of honouring them with employment in his service. It was right that Joseph's brethren should consider beforehand how they should behave if they were called into Pharaoh's presence. First impressions concerning them on the king's mind might be very useful or very hurtful to their interests. A wise man will consider how he ought to converse even with his equals or inferiors, and still more, how he ought to converse with great men, if he is honoured with their attention. Æsop, it is said, gave this advice to Solon at the court of the rich King of Lydia : " Either converse not with kings, or let your discourse be such as will please them." Solon's answer was better than Æsop's advice : " We ought either never to converse with kings, or to say things that may be useful to them."

Joseph well knew Pharaoh's way of thinking, and could guess what would be one of Pharaoh's first questions to his brethren—What is your occupation? The king would not ask whether they had any occupation. He would take it for granted they had not been through life eating the bread of idleness. There are some who think that idleness is the basis of happiness. They imagine that those are the only happy persons who have nothing to do but to gratify the impulse of the moment. But nothing can be plainer from experience than that idleness is a source of constant misery, and the nurse of those vices that are most prejudicial to both soul and body. Is it not far better to have something in view as the object of daily prosecution than to be put every morning to the trouble of discussing in our own minds what we shall do through the day? If we desire to have nothing at all to do, instead of thanking God for making us living and rational creatures, we will be disposed to envy the dust below our feet, or the stones of the field.

"What is your occupation?" If you have none, the devil will find you employment. If you have a lawful occupation, be diligent in doing the duties of it. No occupation will be an honour or advantage to the man who is careless about the duties which it requires. No occupation dishonours a man who walks with God in it, and serves his generation according to the will of God, whose providence assigns us our stations. Paul, even when he was intrusted with the most glorious of all offices, was not ashamed to provide bread for himself and for his companions by labouring with his hands in his original profession of making tents. The same apostle declared it to be an important part of the mind of Christ, that "if any man did not work, neither should he eat."

VER. 34. *That ye shall say, Thy servants' trade hath been about cattle from our youth even until now, both we, and also our fathers: that ye may dwell in the land of Goshen; for every shepherd is an abomination unto the Egyptians.*

Why was every shepherd an abomination unto the Egyptians? As we have no authentic history of the Egyptians in this early period except what we find in the Bible, we cannot certainly say whether this abhorrence of shepherds was occasioned by cruel depredations, which are said to have been made in Egypt by an army of Phœnician shepherds; or whether the principles of that senseless idolatry which the Egyptians practised in latter ages had already begun to infect the hearts of that people with hatred to all that were not as blind as themselves. We know that many ages after the time of Joseph, Bagoas, a favourite eunuch of Artaxerxes Ochus, King of Persia, was filled with such infernal rancour against his master for killing a bull, whom the Egyptians considered as a god, that he not only murdered that prince, but substituted another body instead of his own to receive the funeral honours intended for it; gave the real body of the king to cats to be devoured, and turned some of his bones into hilts for swords, because he thought that death was too gentle a punishment for the murderer of a god. It is not, however, probable that in the time when Joseph was regarded as an oracle in Egypt, the people would entertain such wild notions as afterwards disgraced that country. Pharaoh exalted Joseph to his high station to teach wisdom to his senators. He undoubtedly made no secret of his abhorrence of all idolatry, and yet was in favour both with the king and the people. Yet that mystery of iniquity might be working at that time which afterwards gained such prodigious accessions of foolishness and madness. Such is the corruption of the human mind, that the powerful efforts made by eminent champions for truth in different nations, when men began to multiply after the flood, were not attended with any permanent effects. In the days of Moses, the great-grandson of Levi, it appears that the worship of cattle was not only begun, but was become so popular that it would have been dangerous for the Israelites to have sacrificed to the Lord in Egypt such beasts as He required for His altar.

Whatever was the reason of the abhorrence entertained by the Egyptians against shepherds, it was unjust; and yet it was not peculiar to the men of that blinded nation, to conceive an aversion to a profession in itself lawful. We find publicans joined with harlots, in the common language of the Jews in our Lord's time. The publicans too generally deserved the ill name under which they lay; but one reason why they deserved it so well was, that it was so commonly given them. Take away men's good character from them, and you remove a necessary fence against temptation, and one powerful excitement to virtuous and praiseworthy conduct.

Amongst ourselves there are often prejudices found in men of one profession against another, for which no plausible reason can be given. There are certainly businesses attended with strong temptations that are too often fatal to the virtues of those that undertake them. It will be our wisdom to shun such professions; but if they are necessary for society, those who are placed in them by Divine Providence, and who continue

virtuous, are not to be blamed for the sake of their employment, but to be respected for their firm resistance to those
temptations by which others are seduced. Why should we
ascribe to men faults that are not their own? or why should we
attach dishonour to employments necessary for the welfare of
mankind?

Joseph by no means advised his brethren to conceal their
occupation from the King of Egypt, although it was dishonourable in the sight of the Egyptians; but, for this very reason,
advised them to make it publicly known, that he might assign
them a habitation by themselves, where they would not be
mingled with the people of the land. He foresaw that it would
be dangerous for the house of Jacob to be mingled with the
Egyptians; and when the king knew that they followed a profession hated by his own people, he would see the propriety of
settling them on the borders of the country, where there would
not be an intermixture, that might give occasion to variance
and strife. All wise kings will promote peace amongst their
subjects, and endeavour to prevent every occasion of contention.

Some may perhaps think that Joseph was not sufficiently
attentive to the aggrandisement of his kindred. He had
obtained a high place in the government, which made him a
very great man; might he not have procured places of high
respectability for Judah, who was a man of talents, and for any
other of them that was qualified to occupy them with honour?
He was so far from recommending them to the king as persons
fit to be employed in the government of the country, that he
rather wished to keep them at a distance from public employment. He desired them to give such an account of themselves
to the king as would effectually exclude them from posts of
honour, unless it could have been considered as an honourable
office to be made ruler over the king's cattle.

Joseph was far from grudging to his brethren a share in his
honour any more than in his wealth. He did not reckon his
honours enviable. He found them attended with a load of care,
and with no small danger. By the grace of God the load had
been made easy to him, and he was preserved from the snares

to which he was exposed. But he had a special and a clear call to his high office. He was raised up to be the preserver of Egypt and of his father's family. His brethren had not the same call with himself to an eminent station, and he thought it would be safest and best for them to continue employed in that occupation which had employed their time from their youth. It was evident that it was owing neither to a mean opinion of his brethren's talents, nor to an indifference about their welfare, that he wished them to continue shepherds. He did not wish his own sons to be mingled with the Egyptians, or to occupy such places of trust as would separate them, like himself, from their brethren of the house of Jacob. He was far better pleased with his father's adoption of them than he would have been with a royal decree assigning them the highest station in the kingdom as their hereditary right.

All wise men will consider that situation as best for their children and friends that will be esteemed best on a death-bed, or in another world. If you are more solicitous about the outward than about the spiritual prosperity of your children and friends, can you rank yourselves amongst those of whom the apostle speaks when he says, "We look not at the things which are seen, but at the things which are not seen; for the things which are seen are temporal, but the things which are not seen are eternal?"

Let no Christian despise persons of mean occupations. The time has been when those occupations that are now esteemed the meanest were accounted honourable. Abraham, and Isaac, and Jacob, and David were shepherds. Joseph certainly would not have desired to be a greater man than his father, for any other reason than the superior advantages which it afforded him for usefulness.

"Thy servants' trade hath been about cattle from our youth, both we and our fathers." The Egyptians abhorred shepherds, and therefore would not desire to have the house of Jacob incorporated with them; yet it was to be hoped that they would not conceive a bad opinion of them for professing the same occupation with their fathers. The Egyptians made it a rule, that the children of persons of any particular profession should follow the same profession. They might think that the Hebrews were unfortunate, but could scarcely reckon them blamable for walking in the steps of their fathers.

"That ye may dwell in the land of Goshen." This was the land in which Joseph wished them to dwell, both for its fertility, and because it was nearer to the land of Canaan than any other part of Egypt. He might, by his own authority, have placed them in it, but he wisely desired that the king himself might allot to them their habitation. Servants ought not to be forward in using that power with which they are intrusted either for their own personal benefit, or for the advantage of their relations. Many ministers of state have contracted much hatred by partial kindness to relations. Many have obtained much praise by their disinterested distribution of honours. We may practise much selfishness or much self-denial in the affairs of our friends as well as our own. Our friends are, in some sense, parts of ourselves. It was an evidence of the holiness of Moses that when he was king in Jeshurun he paid no regard to kindred in the choice of the men who were to be intrusted with the most honourable offices, or in the rules that he gave for the distribution of estates. He had particular directions from God for all his regulations, but he discovered a cheerful acquiescence in the will of Heaven when other families were raised above his own. He earnestly desired to see the goodly land, but he never requested the Lord to appoint a peculiar portion in it to his own sons. He had an offer of the whole land to his family if he would have let God alone to destroy the rest of the people for their sins; but if Israel must perish, it was his desire that he and his father's house might perish with the rest of the people, rather than live to mourn over their unhappy fate.

CHAP. xlvii. 1. *Then Joseph came and told Pharaoh, and said, My father and my brethren, and their flocks, and their herds, and all that they have, are come out of the land of Canaan; and, behold, they are in the land of Goshen.*

Joseph, in the height of his prosperity, did not forget that he had a superior. Dearly as he loved his father and his brethren, he did not settle them in the possessions which he intended for them till he obtained Pharaoh's consent. Those are likeliest to retain their power, and enjoy it with the least envy, who use it with modesty and moderation.

There are too many who say and do not. They will readily make promises either to God or man, but either forget to perform them, or take their own time for it. But Joseph immediately performs what he promised to his father and brethren. He had said to them, " I will go and show Pharaoh that my father and my brethren are come," and he delayed not to accomplish his word. Happy as he was in the company of his father and brethren, he did not indulge himself in the pleasure of talking or eating and drinking with them when they continued without a settlement, but immediately took the proper steps to procure for them such a place of abode in Egypt as he thought most convenient for the pasture of their flocks and herds. He did not indeed present a formal petition to Pharaoh ; this he knew to be needless ; he could obtain what he desired in an easier and more honourable way, for he knew the king's readiness to oblige him, without putting him to the necessity of solicitation for gifts.

VER. 2. *And he took some of his brethren, even five men, and presented them unto Pharaoh.*

He did not single out such of his brethren as made the finest appearance, or were best qualified to shine in the presence of the king, but took five of those that most readily occurred to him without selection. So the expression in the original seems to imply. He was an honest man, and wished Pharaoh to form no other opinion concerning his brethren than what they would be able to support.

He did not at this time take all his brethren with him to court. It was probably necessary that some of them should continue to take care of their father, and of their little ones, and their substance. Matters of ceremony must be managed so as not to interfere with the care of necessary business.

This was perhaps the first time that any of Joseph's brethren appeared in the presence of a great king. None of the princes of Canaan could be compared for power or grandeur with the King of Egypt. These men would doubtless feel no little solicitude when they were to appear before an august personage as petitioners for his favour. But it was their comfort that they were introduced into the royal presence by a brother who loved them, and who was loved and esteemed by the king; and may we not be emboldened to come into the presence of the everlasting King, by the consideration that our blessed Mediator is not ashamed to call us brethren, and that His interest in the court of heaven is sufficient to procure us everything we need? His merits more than counterbalance our unworthiness, and His intercession will procure for us the audience of all our prayers.

Ver. 3. *And Pharaoh said unto his brethren, What is your occupation? And they said unto Pharaoh, Thy servants are shepherds, both we, and also our fathers.*

Pharaoh did not ask whether they had an occupation—this he took for granted; but he asked them what their occupation was. He wished to afford them some employment for which they were qualified by their former habits of life. A wise man will not rashly relinquish that occupation in which his employment has long been, nor will he rashly take another man out of that employment to which he has long been accustomed. As we are to make the first choice of our occupation by considering the talents which God has given us, if we find ourselves called upon to choose a new employment, it will be our wisdom to choose (if we are at liberty to choose) some business for which we are in some measure fitted by our former employments. God has often called men to professions very different from their former ones; but He can give what new powers He pleases to any of His creatures. It is easy with Him to make shepherds fit to rule over men, or to qualify fishers of the inhabitants of the waters to be fishers of men. God could give Joseph wisdom sufficient for the government of a great kingdom; but Pharaoh could not qualify men whose trade had been in cattle from their youth to manage his affairs of state.

" And they said unto Pharaoh, Thy servants are shepherds, both we and also our fathers." "I dwell amongst mine own people," said the woman of Shunem to Elisha, when he would have procured to herself, or to her husband, a place at court, or in the army. Joseph's brethren appear to have been of the same mind, when the king asked them concerning their occupation ; they returned him an answer which left them no room to hope for a higher place than to be rulers over his cattle. Their brother Joseph was in a very high station, but they did not envy him, or wish to share in his grandeur, but readily complied with his advice, by telling the king that they had been shepherds, and that they had been trained up by their father to the pastoral life.

VER. 4. *They said moreover unto Pharaoh, For to sojourn in the land are we come ; for thy servants have no pasture for their flocks ; for the famine is sore in the land of Canaan : now therefore, we pray thee, let thy servants dwell in the land of Goshen.*

Joseph's brethren did not come to take up their perpetual residence in the land of Egypt. Their necessities drew them to it for a time, but their hearts were in the Land of Promise. They told Pharaoh that they wished only to be accounted strangers and sojourners in his country. Pharaoh might have been better pleased with them if they had proposed to place themselves entirely and for ever under his government, but they honestly told him their wishes. Never give any man reason to think that you intend to do what you are not resolved to perform. What mischiefs and contentions might men escape if they would always speak truth in their hearts !

" For thy servants have no pasture for their flocks in the land of Canaan." It seems the famine was still more severe in the land of Canaan than in the land of Egypt. This was a great trial to the faith of Jacob and his sons, but from what they said to Pharaoh, it appeared that the land of Canaan, after all they had suffered in it, was still considered by them as their own country. They had left it for a time ; they could not

2 A

dwell in it without losing all their cattle, for which they could with difficulty find subsistence for the two former years. In five years more a great part of the cattle of Canaan was likely to perish; yet they would not renounce their interest in that land with all its inconveniences for a portion, either in the land of Egypt, where they were now sojourners, or in the land of Chaldea, from whence their fathers had come. They believed the promise to be not only true, but good. The Land of Promise could not secure its inhabitants against famine. It might be more grievously afflicted than other lands, but it was the land that the God of their fathers had spied out for them, and given to them for an everlasting inheritance.

Their request to the King of Egypt was a modest one, and extorted by hard necessity. " Since the famine hath forced us for the time to leave the land of Canaan, we pray thee to let thy servants dwell in the land of Goshen." They do not ask him to supply them with all they needed, but only that they might be suffered to dwell in the land of Goshen under his protection; nor did they specify any particular district in this land. For any part of it in which they could find pasture they would thank him. Be modest in your requests to men; desire liberal things in your requests to God, who cannot be impoverished by giving.

VER. 5. *And Pharaoh spake unto Joseph, saying, Thy father and thy brethren are come unto thee.*

The men had now presented to Pharaoh their humble petition. They were but shepherds, and the offspring of shepherds, a set of men whom Pharaoh was taught by his education to abhor. But they were Joseph's brethren, who was not ashamed to acknowledge his relation to them. Pharaoh could not despise men so nearly related to the saviour of his country. He will not therefore suffer the principles in which he had been trained up to obstruct his bounty to those men. Joseph had well deserved, not only the highest honours to himself, but the royal liberality to all his father's house.

VER. 6. *The land of Egypt is before thee; in the best of the land make thy father and brethren to dwell; in the*

*land of Goshen let them dwell: and if thou knowest any
men of activity among them, then make them rulers over my
cattle.*

Those who seek least will obtain most from a man of a
generous spirit. All that Joseph's brethren sought was a liberty
to sojourn in the land of Goshen. The king ordered Joseph to
assign them a place for dwelling in the best part of that province.
If one district in the land of Egypt was better than another,
there let the house of Joseph's father be placed. A truly
grateful man will take pleasure to oblige, not only those
who have done him eminent services, but also those that
are related to them by blood, or connected with them by
friendship.

"And if thou knowest any men of activity among them,
make them rulers over my cattle." Although Pharaoh was
disposed to employ under him the brethren of Joseph, yet their
relation to him must not be held for a sufficient recommendation,
even to very indifferent posts, either in the court or household.
A very wise man may be the brother or the father of a very
foolish man. Other things being equal, the favour due to such
a man as Joseph may procure honourable or lucrative stations
to his relations, but personal merit must always be the chief
recommendation.

Ability and diligence are necessary to all those that stand
before kings; how much more in those who are called to
minister in holy things to the King of Zion! Pharaoh would
not entrust the care of his cattle to a man destitute of the
requisite qualifications, although he had been his favourite's
brother. Would it not, then, be exceedingly unreasonable and
wicked to choose ministers of the Gospel, or any kind of office-
bearers in the Church, from regard to their connections according
to the flesh? Let nothing be done by partiality. If a man is
not furnished with spiritual gifts, he cannot be called to feed
Christ's sheep, although he were the son or brother of the best
man that ever lived. When deacons were to be chosen under
the direction of the apostles, the rule given to the electors was,
not that they should choose men nearly related to Peter or

John, not that they should choose men nearly related according to the flesh to Christ Himself, but that they should choose men full of the Holy Ghost, to be appointed over that business. Pharaoh's maxims of government are a reproof to all who, from partial consideration, give honour unto fools—"As every one has received the gift, so let him minister the same, as a good steward of the grace given him by God."

LECTURE 28

Joseph introduces his father to Pharaoh,
assigns to his father and brethren
the place of their residence, and supplies
them with food convenient for them.

xlvii 7–12

Ver. 7. *And Joseph brought in Jacob his father, and set him before Pharaoh : and Jacob blessed Pharaoh.*

JOSEPH was not ashamed of his brethren, or of their occupations, still less was he ashamed to call himself the son of Jacob. To be the son of this man he accounted a greater honour than to be next to Pharaoh on the throne of Egypt, and wished his children to have part with the sons of Israel, rather than with the posterity of Poti-pherah, priest of On, although the greatest, or one of the greatest, families in Egypt, after that of the king.

He would have presented his father to the king along with his brethren, but the old man needed some repose after the fatigues of his journey before he could make his appearance in the palace. Men of the most hardy constitutions must yield to the decays of nature when they live to be old. The best men feel the infirmities of age when they are permitted to live long in this world of changes. Let it satisfy them that immortal vigour is the portion of the children of the resurrection.

When Jacob was refreshed after his fatigues, Joseph, with great pleasure, introduced his venerable father to the king, who longed to see the father of one to whom he was so greatly indebted. Jacob never courted the friendship of the great, but he could not do less than wait upon his son's benefactor, especially at a time when he stood in need of favours from him to himself, and to all the other branches of his family.

"And Jacob blessed Pharaoh." The word which we render *blessed* is sometimes used to denote an ordinary salutation. The salutations used amongst the pious Hebrews were real prayers addressed to God for the welfare of the person saluted. When one said to another, Peace be to thee, or, The Lord be with thee, he expressed his desire, in a short prayer to God, for the best blessings to his friend or neighbour. Perhaps it would not be desirable to have this form of salutation restored, unless persons were more generally disposed to lift up their souls in holy ejaculations to God when they meet with their friends. The form, without the spirit of prayer, would be an expression of profaneness rather than piety.

But Jacob had accustomed himself to think of God, and to lift up his heart to Him upon every occasion; and without doubt, on the present occasion, he blessed Pharaoh with a very devout temper of spirit. There was none now living upon earth to whom he reckoned himself so much indebted as to the prince who had raised his beloved son from a dungeon almost to a throne. He saw the kind providence of God to himself in what Pharaoh had done for Joseph, and most earnestly prayed that blessings might come down in rich abundance on the head of the man who was the instrument of Providence in conferring so much happiness on himself, and on the men who were dearest to him of any in the world.

"Bless them that curse you," says the apostle. "Bless, and curse not." If we ought to bless even them that curse us, how fervently ought we to pray for them who do good to us, to those whom we love, that the Lord may render their benefits into their own bosoms sevenfold!

Ver. 8. *And Pharaoh said unto Jacob, How old art thou?*

It is probable that Pharaoh's curiosity to know how old Jacob was proceeded from observing the marks of extreme old age in his countenance. There were probably at this time older men in the world than Jacob, but few, if any, that appeared to be older. Much had he suffered in the course of his life; much had he suffered of late from grief and anxiety. Many more years of life spent in ease and prosperity would have made less impression upon his body, than a few years of such sorrows as had kept hold of Jacob's mind since Joseph was torn from him; and the griefs that he had felt more than twenty years before were redoubled when Benjamin, the only remaining son of her that bare him, seemed to be in danger of coming, like his brother, to an untimely end. Some think that the appearance of Jesus Himself, in the days of His flesh, suffered such alterations from His continual griefs, that He was thought to be a great deal older than He really was. He was few years more than thirty when it was said to Him, "Thou art not yet fifty years old." In this world you cannot avoid suffering grief, but make no needless griefs to yourselves, and suffer not passion to usurp the place of reason, if you desire to preserve the vigour of your constitution till it is weakened in the course of nature. Old age is attended with more infirmities than you wish; you need not prepare sorrows for it beyond those which it is impossible to avoid.

When we see the marks of old age, we are desirous to know the number of the years that one has lived. This is an innocent curiosity, and it may not be altogether useless. There are duties owing to the aged; and the older a man is, we should be the more careful to perform them. He is nearer to that period of existence when he must be removed beyond our reach. If we are deficient in our duties to the young, we and they may live to supply what has been wanting, and correct what has been wrong. This indeed is but an uncertain hope. But we are almost sure, that if we are not careful at present to perform our duties to our aged friends and neighbours, their death will soon render the wrong for ever irreparable. "Whatsoever thy hand findeth to do, do it with thy might," especially those things that never can be done unless they are done quickly.

But it is to be regretted that a bad use is too often made of our knowledge of the great age of some of our neighbours. We think that we may live as long as they have lived, or may yet live, and thus are encouraged to defer our preparation for our latter end to a period of age which we may never reach; or if we should reach, will find ourselves less qualified than at present to attend to the things that belong to our eternal peace.

It is of small importance to us to know how old our neighbours are; but it may be of great use to know and consider how old we ourselves are. The days that are past may be lost, and worse than lost, to us, but they are marked down in a book which shall one day be opened. What good have we left undone that ought to have been done? What good things have been so negligently performed, that they might as well have been left undone? That amiable prince, Titus Vespasian, lamented one evening that he had lost a day, because of that day he could remember no good action. Have not we lost many of our days? what if they are all lost days? what if all that has been hitherto done by us should be produced against us in the day of trial to our condemnation? What need have we to redeem our time! Although we are yet young, we know not how few days may be left for what has hitherto been neglected; if we are old, we know that our days will not be many.

VER. 9. *And Jacob said unto Pharaoh, The days of the years of my pilgrimage are an hundred and thirty years: few and evil have the days of the years of my life been, and have not attained unto the days of the years of the life of my fathers in the days of their pilgrimage.*

Jacob's life had been very unsettled. He fled to Mesopotamia from Canaan, and back to Canaan from Mesopotamia. In Canaan he went from place to place, and now he was in his old age compelled to leave it for all that remained of his days. But when he speaks of the days of the years of his pilgrimage, he used the language he had learned from his fathers. He speaks of their pilgrimage as well as his own; and the sense in which they all spoke of their pilgrimage is given us by Paul when he says, " That they confessed themselves to be strangers and pilgrims on the earth," and "thereby declared plainly that they sought a country." They were sensible that they neither had nor would have in this world a continuing city, "but they sought one to come, whose builder and maker is God." In this sense we all ought to consider ourselves as pilgrims; we are all on our journey to another world, and all true Christians are travelling towards a better country. Whilst David sat on a throne, he considered himself as a pilgrim: "We are strangers with thee, and sojourners, as all our fathers were." In a land where we are strangers and pilgrims we cannot expect that ease and tranquillity which are expected by men flourishing in palaces, or in settled habitations of any kind. We must endeavour to bring and to keep our mind to our condition, for it is certain that we cannot bring our condition to our mind. Let us remember, that when a few years are past, our pilgrimage will be at an end, and we shall enjoy an everlasting rest in our Father's house.

Few in our time of the world have such a long and weary pilgrimage as Jacob. "The days of the years of my pilgrimage are an hundred and thirty years." Threescore and ten years have summed up the lives of the greatest part of men for more than three thousand years. Jacob's days were now almost double of that sum. He might at least hope to complete the double of it; and we have some reason to think that some in his time had attained to a greater number of years before they left the world. He was the shortest lived of any of his line from the days of Adam, although we read of none of his descendants that attained to his years in the days of their earthly pilgrimage; yet Job appears to have lived after him, and lived many more years. He must have approached near two hundred years of age before he died, for he lived a hundred and forty years after the destruction of his first family.

"Few have been the days of the years of my pilgrimage." *Few* and *many* are relative terms: a hundred and thirty years make a life of extraordinary length in our days. Long before our time, it was said of Anna the prophetess, that she was of a great age, when she was probably not many years above a hundred, Luke ii. And in the time of David,

Barzillai, at the age of fourscore, is called a very aged man. In the days of Job an aged man was one that had lived a century or more than a century, and yet Bildad says our days on earth are as a shadow. Jacob and Bildad counted their days few, because they came far short in number of the days that man used to live in the generations that lived before them. "Ask now of the times that are past, and prepare thyself for the search of their fathers, for we are but of yesterday, and know nothing, and our days on earth are as a shadow."

When Jacob was yet a child in his father's house, a hundred and thirty years would appear to him a very long space of time. They would appear a very long time to his son Joseph, or to Pharaoh, if he was not himself an old man; but they appeared but a few days to Jacob, after they were gone from him. Those years that appear many in prospect, appear but a few days when we look back to them. Say not, therefore, that you have yet many days of life before you, you will eat, and drink, and be merry; you know not when your souls are to be required from you: but although you should live a hundred years twice told, and rejoice in them all, what will they appear when they are at an end, but as yesterday when it is past! "A perpetuity of bliss is bliss!" A hundred years of bliss is nothing to a creature that must be supremely blessed or wretched through endless ages.

"Few and evil have the days of the years of my life been." It is certain that many of the few days of Jacob's life were spent in grief. Besides the years of bitterness that he spent in lamenting Joseph's unhappy fate, and the other deaths in his family, that drew many tears from his eyes, the sins of his children were the cause, not of days, but of years of sorrow. They were so heinous that the bitter remembrance of them must have kept possession of his mind till his dying day. But to what purpose did he speak of the calamities of his life in this short intercourse with Pharaoh? Not to bespeak the pity of that prince, for he was already assured that Pharaoh would do for him everything that he wished. Far less did Jacob intend to express any dissatisfaction at that kind Providence which had tempered the bitterness of his cup with many rich mercies. Perhaps the good man's griefs had given such a direction to his thoughts that complaints of the vanity and vexation of human life were become habitual to him, and he might think it his duty to take every opportunity to impress his juniors with a sense of that painful but important truth, that happiness is not to be expected in a life where the clouds are ever returning after the rain. He had seen it expedient often to speak to his sons of the evil days that he had seen, and might very justly suppose that a hint on this subject would be useful to the King of Egypt. There are none who stand in greater need of admonition concerning the evils to which men are exposed in this world than those who have more of the good things of this life than their heart could wish; and none are so fit to give an impressive force to such admonitions as old men, who have passed through many changes.

"Few and evil have the days of the years of my life been." One would almost think that Job had heard the story of Jacob's interview with Pharaoh. "Man that is born of a woman," says he, "is of few days, and full of trouble." Yet the thought is so obvious to a man who knows anything of human life, and especially to one who has shared largely in the evils of life, that it might as readily present itself to the mind of that patient sufferer as to the mind of old Jacob. Indeed, we must be great strangers both to the world and to ourselves if we have not yet learned a lesson for which we have far more than ten thousand instructions. We must be very unacquainted with the Bible if we do not believe that doctrine on which the wise preacher so largely insists, that all things on earth are vanity.

Since there is so much evil mingled with human life, we ought rather to rejoice than to mourn that our days are few. Indeed, if nothing were to be expected beyond the grave, we would rather wish to endure all the evils of life a great while longer, than to lose our present existence. But if an eternity of joy in the presence of Christ awaits us, why should we regret the brevity of our life of sorrows? The night is soon spent, for it is not long, and the day will soon come. Paul speaks in stronger language than Jacob of the brevity of life, but in softer language of the evils of it, when he compares the present suffering state of Christians with the prospects set before them in the Gospel. " Our light afflictions, which are for a moment, work for us a far more exceeding and eternal weight of glory; whilst we look not at the things which are seen, but at the things which are not seen; for the things that are seen are temporal, but the things which are not seen are eternal."

" And have not attained to the days of the years of the life of my fathers in their pilgrimage." The fathers whom he had in his view were Abraham and Isaac. If he had been comparing his own years of life with those of his more ancient progenitors, the difference would have been still greater. Nahor only, the grandfather of Abraham, lived but a year longer than Jacob.

The length of human life decreased rapidly after the Flood, till it came to its present standard. We need not greatly regret the change that has taken place in the duration of men's abode upon earth. Unless men were better than a great part of our race are, they live long enough; and it is probable they would be a great deal worse if a longer term of life were allowed them. As for ourselves, if we are true followers of Jesus, we need not mourn that we are kept no longer at a distance from Him whom our souls love. If we are not followers of Jesus during the short space of our life, it is likely that we would become worse if we were to live a hundred or two hundred years. Julius Cæsar, when he was fifty-six years old, said that he had lived long enough for nature and glory. We have lived long enough for God and for ourselves, if we are found in Christ, and have done all that service for God which He intended us to do in this world.

Jacob did not envy his fathers for the length of their lives, nor was he dissatisfied that God had not allowed him a length of days equal to theirs. Perhaps he mentioned the long lives of his progenitors to Pharaoh, either because he saw that prince expressing signs of wonder at the length of his own life, or perhaps he designed by this remark to express his deep sense of the shortness of human life which was allotted to the generation then living on the earth. When men saw human life shortened from generation to generation, they were loudly called to consider how few their days were, and how necessary it was to do with their might what their hands found to do. When men in general had lived little more than half the time that their great-grandfathers had lived, they were more likely to be impressed with the shortness of their time on earth than we, who live as long as men used to do three thousand years ago, although our lives consist of fewer days in reality. He who dies at the age of a hundred years will be thought to have died in childhood, when the Lord makes the days of His people as the days of a tree.

VER. 10. *And Jacob blessed Pharaoh, and went out from before Pharaoh.*

Jacob blessed Pharaoh when he came into his presence, and again blessed him when he went out of it. It is a good thing to do good to good men. They will return in prayers and blessings, if they cannot otherwise return, what is done to them in their persons and families. The prayer of such a wrestler with God as Jacob availeth much.

Jacob went out at this time from Pharaoh's presence. From what we know of the disposition of this prince, and of his attachment to Joseph, we have reason to think that this was not the last time Jacob saw him. Pharaoh put a high value on a man in whom the Spirit of God was, Gen. xli. And he must have seen that Joseph's father, as well as Joseph himself, was a man in whom was the Spirit of God. His wisdom made his face to shine. But how far the King of Egypt profited by his conversation with Jacob or Joseph we are not informed. It is evident that he learned much wisdom for government from Joseph, but it is not so plain that he learned from either of these patriarchs the best kind of wisdom. He appears to have continued too warmly attached to those priests, whose doctrines were very different from theirs. But let us not intrude into those things which we cannot know.

VER. 11. *And Joseph placed his father and his brethren, and gave them a possession in the land of Egypt, in the best of the land, in the land of Rameses, as Pharaoh had commanded.*

If Joseph had given them a possession in the best part of the land, without express orders from Pharaoh, it would have opened the mouths of the Egyptians, not only against himself, but against the house of his father. But when Pharaoh commanded him to place them in the best part of the conntry, he not only had a right, but counted it his duty, to give this testimony of his affection to his father. We ought not, on pretence of impartiality, to deal worse with our friends than with other men. To be partial in their favour would be unjust; to turn our partiality against them would be unnatural.

If Jacob had not been placed in one of the most fertile districts of the land of Egypt, Joseph would have affronted the king by disobeying his command, and counteracting his generous intentions. Thus, when we refuse to receive the precious blessings which God gives us in the Gospel, we are chargeable, not only with an unnatural contempt of our own mercies, but with the guilt of disobedience to the Divine commands, and contempt of the Divine goodness. Let us never say to a generous prince, and least of all to the Prince of the kings of the earth, Thy gifts be to thyself.

How richly was Joseph repaid for all his sufferings when he was made a father, not only to Pharaoh and to the Egyptians, but to all his father's house! The greatest pleasure of such a man as Joseph consists in doing good; and he took pleasure most of all in doing so much good to his father's house, and to the servants of the God of his father, and in giving so much pleasure to his father's heart in the last period of his life.

Joseph was none of those children whose affections are warm and active under the influence of some occasional impulse, but cold and selfish when that impulse has spent its force. His kindness to his father's family was unwearied.

VER. 12. *And Joseph nourished his father, and his brethren, and all his father's household, with bread, according to their families.*

It is needless to inquire at whose expense Joseph afforded

such large supplies to his father's family. He was first just, and then generous. He was entitled to a large revenue, which would enable him to practise liberality to a great extent. It is plain, from what we have already seen, that he used no more freedom than he was expressly warranted to do with the king's property under his management.

Do good to them that hate you, and to those friends that have wronged you. If the envy of Joseph's brethren had been gratified to its full extent, he would have either been cut off without leaving a posterity behind him, or he and his posterity would have lived in an indigent and abject condition. But he took care that none of all the members of the families of his brethren should want a liberal supply of all that they needed, or could wish to enjoy. The Lord made him the "shepherd and the stone of Israel," "and he fed them in a good pasture, according to the integrity of his heart, and the skilfulness of his hands."

Some young persons are called by Providence to support their infirm parents, or to be fathers to their brethren and sisters. Others, perhaps, will pity them, because they are under a necessity to take upon themselves the burden of a family before their time. But if they are possessed of natural affection to any considerable degree, they will rejoice in opportunities to requite their parents, either in their own persons, or in the persons of their children. They may be compelled to labour, while other young persons find leisure for diversion. They must expend some part of the fruits of their labours on their fathers' families, whilst others are enriched by the fruit of their parents' industry. Will they think themselves less happy on these accounts than other persons of their time of life? If they do, they neither regard the commands nor the providence of God. Good works, if the Bible is true, are far more profitable, and in the end more pleasant, than riches, or than all the delights of sense. "It is a good thing that a man bear the yoke in his youth." It is your honour and advantage to honour your parents, whether dead or alive.

LECTURE 29

Joseph gains for the king all the money of Egypt, with the cattle and land, which he returns to the people upon easy conditions.

xlvii 13–26

VER. 13. *And there was no bread in all the land; for the famine was very sore, so that the land of Egypt and all the land of Canaan fainted by reason of the famine.*

"GIVE us this day our daily bread." This is a petition which Christ teaches Christians, whether poor or rich, to offer up to God. Rich men may perhaps say that they have no need to ask daily bread. They have land or money which will procure them bread, and everything else that they need, as long as they live. But how do you know that your riches will not take wings and flee away from you? or what if your land should refuse to yield its ordinary increase? Your grounds are not more fruitful than the land of Egypt or Palestine, and yet in these lands no bread was to be had for several years but from the King of Egypt's granaries, "and all the land of Egypt and Canaan fainted by reason of the famine."

The inhabitants of the land were sunk into despondency. Bread is the staff of life. The want of it would speedily prove fatal? and scarcity of bread not only weakens the body, but dispirits the soul. What reason have we to bless God that we have seldom or never known by experience the horrors of famine, or even the anxiety of fear about the necessaries of life! Let the affluent express their gratitude to God, by their readiness to distribute their bread to the hungry.

VER. 14. *And Joseph gathered up all the money that was found in the land of Egypt, and in the land of Canaan, for the corn which they bought: and Joseph brought the money into Pharaoh's house.*

The price of corn must have been high beyond what had ever been known, and we cannot blame Joseph for taking a large price, especially when we consider that he was only a servant. If a man sends his servant with corn to a market, he must require the current price for it, although it should be double or triple what it had formerly been. We can do what we will with our own, but not with that which is another man's.

The people in Egypt and Canaan were willing to give all their money for corn, and were glad that they had money to give in exchange for what was so very necessary to their comfort, and even to their existence. Do you grudge to pay for what you cannot want? Of what use is money, but to procure the things that we need? and we ought to thank God in times of scarcity when corn can be had for money, and money can be had to purchase corn. No doubt many were reduced to great distress at this time, before the money of the land was exhausted. The rich would have a part of their money left when the poor were ready to die for want of necessaries. How the poor were preserved from perishing at this time we are not informed; but we know that Joseph was both a wise and a merciful man, and had sufficient influence with his master to procure seasonable relief for their necessities. The very end of Joseph's advancement was to prevent the dreadful effects of the famine; but it is not to be expected that the sacred historian would give us a particular account of every part of Joseph's administration. From the instances of it left on record, we have no reason to doubt that the blessing of him that was ready to perish came upon Joseph, and that he caused the widow's heart to sing for joy. Joseph's behaviour to his brethren and their families would be an instruction to Pharaoh in the care of his people.

When it is said that all the money of the country was re-

2 B

ceived by Joseph, the meaning probably is, that the greater part was brought to him for corn. None was left in the hands of the common people, and little in the hands of the most affluent. But Joseph did not enrich himself with that money which came so abundantly into his hands. He brought it into Pharaoh's house, reserving nothing for himself but the lawful and known reward of his labour. He certainly had good opportunities to heap up riches without end to himself. He could not have been easily detected if he had secreted a part to his own use; and if his mind had been tainted with covetousness it might have found out many pretences to excuse him to himself; but he knew that an all-seeing eye was upon him, and abhorred the thought of sinning against God. What would thousands of gold and silver have availed him if he had brought that curse upon himself which is the portion of the unrighteous!

VER. 15. *And when money failed in the land of Egypt, and in the land of Canaan, all the Egyptians came unto Joseph, and said, Give us bread: for why should we die in thy presence? for the money faileth.*

How pitiable was the condition of the people of Canaan at this time! There was no Joseph among them to buy up stores of food against the time of famine: what means they used to obtain supply, or what methods a gracious Providence used to preserve them from utter destruction, we are not informed. This we know, that the iniquity of the Amorites was not yet full, and the time was not yet come for their destruction. The great Preserver of man and beast punished them for their iniquities, and perhaps suffered some of them to perish with hunger. Yet the nations of Canaan had a much longer space for repentance allowed them, which they did not improve, and therefore, about two hundred and fifteen years afterwards, were almost exterminated by the sword of the Lord, and the sword of Israel.

The Egyptians felt the famine very severely, but were not reduced to the same pitiable distress with the Canaanites. They deserved to feel the effects of famine, because they had not been careful to lay up provision for themselves, when they ought to have known that the famine was coming. When the plague of hail was predicted by Moses, those of the Egyptians who feared the Lord secured their servants and cattle against it, and those who feared not the Lord lost their servants and cattle. It is very probable that some of the Egyptians, in Joseph's days, would lay up corn for themselves. Joseph would not have hindered them, but rather praised them, for doing well for themselves. The far greater part, however, either disregarded the word of the Lord, or trusted to Joseph to provide supply for their necessities. It was therefore highly reasonable that they should comply with the equitable terms which he proposed for their relief; and they had reason to rejoice that when they would not put themselves to the trouble of laying up provisions for their own use, there was a man who had done it effectually. Let not the poor, in time of famine, envy the rich, but let them give thanks to God that what they want others have, who are bound by the law of God, and inclined by principles of human nature, to preserve their poorer neighbours from perishing by hunger. You say, perhaps, that you are less indebted to Providence than many of your neighbours ; and perhaps you say what is true. But before you complain of the hardships to which you are doomed, consider what claims you have upon God. Is He your debtor? If He has received anything from you, He will recompense it ; if He has received nothing, let Him dispose of His own property according to His own pleasure ; and give Him thanks for those merciful appointments of His law and providence, by which the members of human societies are made instrumental in averting calamity from one another, and in conferring mutual benefits.

The famished people of Egypt knew that there was bread, and to spare, in the king's granaries, and that he had committed to Joseph the disposal of it ; to him therefore they came, and said, " Give us bread : for why should we die in thy presence?" There was certainly no reason why they should be suffered to die, although their money was spent. The corn collected in the granaries would have been useless without eaters, and the king would have been a king no longer if all his subjects had died ; yet it was highly reasonable that he should receive a price for his commodities, from men that had houses and lands in their possession.

Ver. 16. *And Joseph said, Give your cattle; and I will give you for your cattle, if money fail.*

Was not Joseph taking advantage of their poverty when he furnished bread to them on such hard conditions? Was it not enough for them to part with all their money, without being compelled to dispose of their horses and asses, their kine and their sheep? To this question the answer is easy. We are well assured that Joseph was not an extortioner. How could that man be an extortioner who would rather expose himself to the imminent danger of an ignominious death, than sin against God by indulging the lust of the flesh? How could that man be an oppressor of the Egyptians whom the people acknowledged to be the preserver of their lives? It was not to be expected that the inspired historian would tell us all that passed between the Egyptians and Joseph, and therefore justice requires that we should judge of his behaviour from his character, when nothing is found in his behaviour that may not be accounted for in a perfect consistency with justice and generosity.

If you happen, in a time of scarcity, to be entrusted with the disposal of another man's corn, will you give it away gratuitously to those who come and tell you that all their money is spent? Will you not rather ask them if they have no cattle, or anything else as good as money? or if they should have nothing at all to give in exchange for the necessities of life, are you on that account bound to give them what is not your own? You must remember that the corn was not Joseph's, but Pharaoh's ; and it is required in stewards that a man be found faithful.

But why did not Joseph use his influence with Pharaoh to give his corn to his poor subjects without money, and without price! There is no doubt that he used his influence to procure such favours for Pharaoh's subjects as seemed to him best calculated to promote the mutual interests of king and subjects.

Nor have we any reason to think that the good man was mistaken in his opinions on this subject. Who can presume to say that, all things considered, it would have been better to give the people corn without price, than to require their cattle as the price of it? No man can pretend to say what circumstances, known or unknown to us, came under consideration in determining this point. Joseph knew them all, and was as well qualified as he was entitled to give his opinion in the king's council; for although he was the prime minister, we have no reason to think that he would venture upon measures of great importance without taking the opinion of other counsellors of the king. He was too wise a man to restrain wisdom to himself, or to expose himself to envy and reproach, by taking upon himself the whole burden of all the most delicate measures of government. He was the oracle of the kingdom, by the deference that was paid to him, rather than claimed by him ; and he certainly had the good sense to manage affairs in such a manner as to cut off occasion from those that would seek occasion to speak reproachfully.

We must not think that Joseph did not consider the case of the poor ; there is every reason to believe that he considered it so wisely, that none of them seem to have perished by the famine, which will appear very wonderful when it is considered that the rich were reduced to great poverty. Unless very wise and very merciful precautions had been taken the poor must have lost their lives, before the rich had expended for bread, not only their money, but everything they had.

It was not less just to take their cattle than their money. It might indeed have been deemed ungenerous or inhuman to have deprived the people for ever of the use of their cattle. But there was little reason to be afraid that the king would keep all this property in his own hands. It would not have been consistent with his own interest, nor with the character of his government under Joseph's administration. But it might conduce to the general benefit, to take out of the people's hands for the present that part of their property which was now become the king's, that they might be the better disposed to submit to those regulations for the general benefit which Joseph had in view.

Ver. 18. *When that year was ended, they came unto him the second year, and said unto him, We will not hide it from my lord, how that our money is spent; my lord also hath our herds of cattle; there is not ought left in the sight of my lord, but our bodies, and our lands.*

Those who have lived in the habit of receiving alms are often too loud and frequent in their complaints of poverty. They think (but they are mistaken in their thought) that they will receive the larger bounties when they are clamorous in their lamentations. But it is only extreme necessity that will extort confessions of poverty from those who have all their days lived in affluence. To this hard necessity were the Egyptians reduced, when all their money was spent, all their cattle sold, and nothing left them but their bodies and lands.

But when men are very poor, it is a great comfort to know that there are rich persons who will be ready, on reasonable terms, to administer relief. The Egyptians knew that Joseph had laid up provisions against the time of famine, and would not suffer them to be famished. They would not conceal their distress from one who was so able and so ready to give them that relief which they needed. With how much greater confidence may we have recourse to Jesus in all our distresses! "He will deliver the needy when he crieth, the poor also, and him that hath no helper: He will spare the poor and needy, and will save the souls of the needy."

Ver. 19. *Wherefore shall we die before thine eyes, both we and our land? buy us and our land for bread, and we and our land will be servants unto Pharaoh: and give us seed, that we may live and not die, that the land be not desolate.*

A brave man, it has been often said, will prefer his liberty to his life; and there are certainly cases in which it would be shameful cowardice not to venture life for our liberty, and for the liberty of our country. When it is our duty to maintain the public liberty against oppression, we ought not to count our lives dear to us, that we may serve our generation according to the will of God. But when the providence of God gives to men a just right over our liberties, or when we cannot, without sin, expose our life for our liberties, greatness of mind appears in a cheerful compliance with the will of God. " Art thou called in the Lord, being a servant? Care not for it, but if thou mayest be free, use it rather; for he that is called in the Lord, being a servant, is the Lord's free man."

The Egyptians had nothing to give for corn but their bodies and their lands. And these they were willing to sell, but it was to a good master, for that bread which they could not want. How precious are the fruits of the earth! We know not the value of them, because we have seldom or never known want. A man will give not only all that he has, but himself also, for the staff of life. Such bargains, indeed, are not known amongst us; we have the happiness to live in a land of liberty. But bargains of this kind were not uncommon in certain periods of society, even in Britain; nor were they without examples amongst the Israelites in their own fruitful country. But God, by His merciful law, provided for the comfort, and for the eventual liberty of His people, when they should find a state of servitude necessary for their present subsistence.

If men pinched with poverty were so willing to part, not only with their land, but with their liberty, for that meat which perisheth, what value should we set on that meat which endureth unto everlasting life! With what cheerfulness ought we to devote ourselves to the service of Him who hath given His own flesh to be the food of our souls!

VER. 20. *And Joseph bought all the land of Egypt for Pharaoh; for the Egyptians sold every man his field, because the famine prevailed over them: so the land became Pharaoh's.*

No injury, it has been often said, can be done to a man without his own consent. This maxim needs limitations. There are certainly many cases in which great injuries may be done to men without their own consent. If the Egyptians had offered themselves as slaves to Pharaoh when there was no valid and necessary reason for it, Joseph could not have righteously accepted of the surrender of their liberties. But it was surely better for them to sell themselves and their land to Pharaoh, than to want bread. Possibly Joseph might have been better pleased with them if they had only sold their lands, and made no mention of their bodies; but when they voluntarily offered their bodies as well as their land, it is a question whether he would have acted wisely and justly towards his master, had he refused to accept of what seemed so cheerfully offered. And we will afterwards find that Joseph wisely took measures to prevent any bad consequences to the people from their seeming forwardness to rush into slavery. It is probable that the king's yoke was heavier to the people after their bargain than before it. But there is reason to believe that they would bear it with greater cheerfulness.

VER. 21. *And as for the people, he removed them to cities from one end of the borders of Egypt even to the other end thereof.*

When the Egyptians sold their land, they were so well pleased with their bargain, that they thought little of what they had given in exchange. Thousands of gold and silver are not so precious to a man at other times as a plain piece of bread in a time of extreme famine. But when their present hunger was satisfied, and provision laid up for many days to come, they might have found it difficult to reconcile their minds to the change of their condition, if they had lived in the constant view of those possessions which were once their own. Joseph wished to accustom them to the consideration of their land as Pharaoh's property, by removing them to cities at a distance from their former dwellings. When a rich man becomes suddenly poor, he can scarcely believe that his condition is so different from what it once was as he finds it to be. He is ready to call those things still his own which now belong to another man. It will be useful for him to have them removed from his sight, that his mind may accommodate itself to its present circumstances, and thus a less space of time will be necessary to heal the wounds of his spirit.

Perhaps, too, Joseph might wish, by this removal of the people from their former possessions, to place them in a condition favourable for the improvement of manufactures. He knew the value of labour properly employed, and how much the assembling of multitudes into cities contributes to the advancement of those arts by which a nation is enriched. We find Egypt famous in after-times for its manufactures and arts of various kinds, Isa. xix. A man so wise as Joseph at the head of the administration would no doubt do what lay in his power to introduce or encourage those arts by which human life is improved, and a nation is made to prosper.

One thing may be inferred from the removal of the people to fenced cities, that Joseph was under no apprehension of seditions or rebellions among them. Nothing has more frequently roused nations to sedition than the want of bread, especially when there was any reason, or shadow of reason, to think that the measures of government tended to raise the price of it. Joseph appears to have been confident that his measures were such as not only would bear the strictest scrutiny, but could not excite discontent amongst the multitude. The historians of later times tell us that no nations were more prone to raise tumults against the government than the Egyptians. But Joseph was so far from oppressing the people, or doing anything that tended to alienate their minds from himself, that he cared not how many of them were assembled in one place. When they met together from different parts of the country, their ordinary subject of discourse, from time to time, would be the distress which had compelled them to sell their lands, the miseries of the famine, and the methods taken by government to relieve them; and Joseph had no apprehensions that the tendency of such discourse would be prejudicial either to himself or to the king. Let us all endeavour so to act on every occasion that we may have no reason to stand in fear of the scourge of the tongue. We cannot hinder men from speaking of us what they please. But if our conduct is worthy of commendation, we may hope either that the voice of reproach will not be heard, or that it will soon be put to silence.

VER. 22. *Only the land of the priests bought he not ; for the priests had a portion assigned them of Pharaoh, and did eat their portion which Pharaoh gave them: wherefore they sold not their lands.*

Here let it be observed that the inspired historian speaks not of Joseph, but of Pharaoh. Joseph was not the man who assigned to the priests their revenue. We cannot blame him for giving them that portion which Pharaoh allotted them. He could not have justly detained it. The reason why the generosity of Pharaoh to the priests is here mentioned is to account for Joseph's not buying their lands when he bought the lands of the other Egyptians.

Pharaoh testified his respect to the gods of the country, and to its sacred rites, when he was so liberal to the priests; and from this circumstance it appears too probable that, although he admired the wisdom of Joseph, he did not learn from him the best of all kinds of wisdom. Such is the blindness of the human mind, that we will more readily receive any kind of knowledge than that in which eternal life consists, and hold faster than any other errors those which of all others are most pernicious. But how far Joseph might reform the errors of the priests themselves we cannot know. It is too well known that in after-times no nation in the world was given to more senseless idolatries than the Egyptians.

If the Egyptian priests had been faithful servants to the true God, as Pharaoh no doubt supposed them to be, he would have deserved praise for the respect which he showed them. " He that despiseth you, " says Christ to His ministers, " despiseth me ; and he that receiveth you, receiveth me ; and he that receiveth me, receiveth him that sent me." What can be more reasonable than to minister to those in carnal things who minister to us in spiritual things? It is shameful to those who are taught the best of religions, and the only true religion, to be less willing to give a decent support to those servants of the living God, who show them the way of salvation, than heathens were to show their liberality to the teachers of error.

It is of high importance to form right notions of religion, that we may not misspend our zeal and liberality in our endeavours to promote its interests. Hence many thousands of gold and silver have been expended on the worship of false gods.

Through man's blindness in ancient times, they generally expended those treasures on error that might have been employed to great advantage in the cause of truth. It was promised, and has been in some measure fulfilled, that in the days of the Gospel kings should be nursing-fathers to the Church, and that the people of distant regions should bring gold and incense to Zion, and show forth the praises of the Lord, Isa. xlix. and lx.

VER. 23. *Then Joseph said unto the people, Behold, I have. bought you this day and your land for Pharaoh: lo, here is seed for you, and ye shall sow the land.*

These words of Joseph would have a pleasant sound in the ears of the Egyptians. There were seven years in which it was needless to sow. The husbandmen languished in idleness and dejection; the land languished when there was no agricultural work to do; but now they are told that the labours of husbandry were to be resumed. Seed was given them to sow the fields that were once their own, and were still to be their own, for all the purposes of a comfortable subsistence. Let us thank God for the assurance given us, that whilst the earth continues seed-time and harvest shall not cease. The temporary interruptions of the returns of seed-time and harvest in particular places do not render the promise of God of none effect.

The people of Egypt had been long sustained without the ordinary labours of the seed-time and harvest. Perhaps many of them had learned a habit of idleness from the discontinuance of their labours. But they must now again labour or perish. When men are able to work, and have opportunities for profitable labour, they ought to starve if their hands refuse to labour. Joseph laid up corn only for the years of famine. The manna which God gave to the children of Israel in the land that was not sown ceased when they came to Canaan. It was not the will of God that the necessity of labour should be superseded amongst them. We have great reason to be thankful when God allows us to eat the labour of our hands, although we are not fed, like the fowls of heaven, with the meat for which we have not laboured.

VER. 24. *And it shall come to pass in the increase, that ye shall give the fifth part unto Pharaoh, and four parts shall be your own, for seed of the field, and for your food, and for them of your households, and for food for your little ones.*

"Better is the end of a thing than the beginning of it." We must always wait for the end of God's works, and often for the end of men's works, before we can pass a judgment upon them. If Joseph had not been a man of unimpeachable integrity and goodness, we might have supposed that he dealt hardly with the Egyptians when he accepted of their lands and their bodies as a price for the corn. But now we see clearly what his intentions were. It was highly reasonable and just that Pharaoh's revenue should be improved by that royal economy which was the salvation of Egypt; and it was worthy of the royal bounty to make a rich present to the impoverished people, that they might live with comfort, and yield a cheerful obedience to the benign government under which they lived.

We must not suppose that Joseph returned to the people their lands under such easy conditions without consulting the king, and obtaining his consent. A faithful steward will always endeavour to do justice between his master and the man with whom he transacts business on his master's behalf. But he will exercise generosity no farther than he knows himself to have his master's concurrence. He may very warrantably advise his master to perform acts of generosity, when he sees a good reason for it. But he must not perform them at his own discretion, if he does not wish to forfeit the character of an honest man. The Lord, it is said, commended the unjust steward, who allowed his master's servants to reduce the sums standing against them in the books of account. But beware of misunderstanding the words of Christ. The commendation of the wisdom of the unjust steward was not a commendation of his unjustice.

The best charity is not always that which freely gives to the poor what they need. It may be better charity in many cases to give them what they need for a price which they are able to give, or on conditions which they are able to perform. Thus, whilst their indigence is relieved, no encouragement will be given to idleness, or to covetousness. It is highly probable that Joseph, by his bargain with the Egyptian landholders had it in his power to do a much greater service to the country than he could have done by making them a present of the corn they needed. The poorer sort of the people, who are the most numerous in every country, must have spent everything they could turn into money before the richer part of them. A present of corn at that time would have benefited only the rich; for to those who had neither money nor land, he must certainly have extended his bounty, although we are not informed of the particular instances of it. It is evident that they were not suffered to perish. But by taking from the rich their cattle and lands, he would have it in his power to restore to many of the former proprietors what had been bought by their wealthier neighbours, before the famine had reduced them likewise to poverty.

If this observation should be esteemed only a conjecture, yet it is certain that in one of the most delicate conjunctures which could happen to a nation, he acted with such justice, generosity, and wisdom, as to gain the high approbation of the people; and we need not doubt that he had the approbation of the king likewise, without whose consent he transacted no business of importance.

VER. 25. *And they said, Thou hast saved our lives: let us find grace in the sight of my lord, and we will be Pharaoh's servants.*

It is difficult in a time of famine to please the poor by all the benefactions which it is in the power of the affluent to confer. As the property of the rich tends, through the corruption of human nature, to make them insolent and high-minded, want too often makes the poor discontented and unthankful. It was the honour of the Egyptians, as well as of Joseph, that they entertained a grateful sense of his services to the nation.

Gratitude to public benefactors is not too common in the world. The Egyptians themselves, in process of time, forgot what Joseph had done for them, but not till that generation was laid in the dust.

" Thou hast saved our lives : let us find grace in the eyes of my Lord." These words were delightful to the ears of Joseph. A man of a disposition abounding in benevolence must have felt a pleasure that passes description in the consciousness that he deserved the acknowledgment of a whole people for saving their lives. Do good, and you shall have the pleasure and the praise of it. If you meet not with gratitude for your benefactions from men, remember God's promise, that what good things any man doth, the same shall he receive of the Lord.

We have it not in our power to be such public benefactors as Joseph. But, as we have opportunity, let us do good to the bodies or to the souls of men. The saving of one soul from eternal death is a greater work than the saving of a whole nation from that death which can only be deferred for a few years. " Brethren, if any of you do err from the truth, and one convert him, know, that he who converteth a sinner from the error of his ways shall save a soul from death."

The blessings of a whole nation, and doubtless of many in other nations, came upon Joseph. The blessings of all the nations of the saints, and of all their generations, shall come upon Jesus Christ, who hath saved us from eternal death, by giving us the true bread from heaven. Let us all say unto him, " Thou hast saved our lives, Thou hast redeemed us with Thy blood ; let us find grace in Thy sight, and we will serve God with our bodies, and with our spirits, which are His."

VER. 26. *And Joseph made it a law over the land of Egypt unto this day, that Pharaoh should have the fifth part ; except the land of the priests only, which became not Pharaoh's.*

Pharaoh, directed by the counsels of Joseph, made a perpetual edict, securing at the same time his own royal prerogatives, and the rights which his bounty conferred on the people. The greater part of the nations of the eastern and southern regions of the world have the will of the prince for their law. And perhaps the kings of Egypt, as well as other countries, too often exercised a despotic power; but by the law here mentioned the king renounced all right to invade the property reserved for his subjects. If this law had not been made, tyrants in after-times might have claimed to themselves the right of property on every man's estate, except those of the priests. They might have alleged that, by the bargain made with Joseph, the kings of Egypt were not only the rulers, but the proprietors of all the lands, and perhaps of the cattle too, belonging to their lay subjects. But all such vexatious pleas were obviated by that constitution which assigned the fifth of all the product of the lands, and nothing more, to the king.

The king gained much, and the people lost almost nothing of what had once been theirs. Before the famine they probably paid a tenth of the products of their land to the king; and when he needed extraordinary supplies the subjects would either find it necessary to raise them in the form of taxes, or, what was worse, would be exposed to partial and oppressive exactions, to supply the royal exchequer. At present the Grand Signior is not understood to have a right to impose new taxes on his subjects when his necessities require new supplies. But what is the consequence? What his ministers do not claim as a right they must procure by extortion. The rich revenue from this time possessed by the kings of Egypt might be expected to supply, not only their ordinary, but their extraordinary wants, and to enable them to carry on every useful enterprise for the benefit of the kingdom, without laying any new burden upon their subjects. Thus it was to be hoped that the people would as cheerfully pay the king's proportion of the increase of their fields as tenants amongst us with good leases pay their rent to their landlords. Their rent for ground, though very low, was all the burden laid on them for every purpose of government. When we consider the extraordinary fertility of the land of Egypt, we will see no reason to doubt of the people's ability to pay the king's proportion of the increase of their lands, without depriving themselves of any of those comforts which any reasonable man would desire.

"Joseph made it a law." The law was no doubt made by the king with the advice of his counsellors. But the honour of it is given to Joseph, because he was the chief and the first adviser. Men of great influence have it in their power to do much good by other hands than their own. And the good they do by others, as well as by themselves, if it is done from proper motives, will turn to their praise, and honour, and glory, at the time of Christ's appearance.

"The lands of the priests became not Pharaoh's." The priests of false gods have for the most part obtained better rewards from men than the ministers of the true religion ; yet these have no reason to complain. They expect their reward from God. If they look every one to his gain from his quarter, they are not the servants of Christ. However the faithful servants of Jesus may be despised or overlooked by those to whom they minister the Gospel of Christ, they are authorised to expect better rewards than any of the princes of the world could bestow. Their converts shall be a glory and joy to them in the day of the Lord. "When the chief Shepherd shall appear, they shall receive a crown of glory, which fadeth not away."

LECTURE 30

Jacob obtains from Joseph a solemn promise to bury him in the land of Canaan.

xlvii 27–31

VER. 27. *And Israel dwelt in the land of Egypt, in the country of Goshen; and they had possessions therein, and grew, and multiplied exceedingly.*

IT is not of great importance to determine whether by the name Israel in this place we are to understand Jacob himself, or his family, now beginning to multiply into a nation, for many ages afterwards known by the glorious name of this progenitor. It is, however, most natural to understand the name in this place of the whole family, as the plural number is used concerning Israel in the last part of the verse. It was the happiness of this venerable patriarch that he lived, through the last part of his life, in the presence of all his descendants. Abraham had the pleasure to spend his last years (and Isaac spent his whole life) in the Land of Promise. Jacob found it necessary to spend his last years, and to die, in a strange land. But he had this great advantage above his father and grandfather, that his sons did not leave him, and that he found no necessity of sending them away to other countries. This would be counted a precious advantage by such a man as Jacob, and the more so that some of his children stood in great need of his admonitions. He was the teacher and dispenser of divine ordinances among them; and we hope that, through his ardent

2 c

prayers, and the supply of the Spirit of God, the labours of his old age were not in vain. What his children had seen, and feared, and suffered would probably be of great use to them, when they had so experienced a saint for their instructor.

"Jacob dwelt in the land of Egypt, in the country of Goshen." Although Jacob found it necessary to settle in the land of Egypt for the remaining part of his life, it was a comfort to him that his family had a separate settlement, and was not scattered among the worshippers of strange gods. No doubt he trembled at the thought of the influence that the bad example of the Egyptians might have upon his seed when he should be taken from their head. But in the multitude of his thoughts within him, the comforts of God would delight his soul. He was conscious that he was called, both by the providence and the word of God, to bring down his family to Egypt, and he knew that he would be brought again out of Egypt. The Lord had promised both to himself and to Abraham that their seed should not be left in that country, but be brought in safety to that land which God had spied out for them; that land which was to be made, by the Divine favour, the glory of all lands. What though we should be strangers and foreigners in a land where we are exposed to dangers and difficulties, if we are assured by God Himself that He will in the end conduct us to a better country!

Jacob's seed could not yet possess the land promised to their father. When they came into Egypt they were only threescore and ten men; but the good man not only knew by the promise that their number would increase till they became a great nation, but his eyes saw the promise going on to its accomplishment. They grew and multiplied exceedingly before as well as after his death. Abraham and Isaac saw but few sons of the promise, and yet they did not stagger in the faith of it. Jacob too had formerly believed it whilst he had no seed, and now he had the pleasure of seeing with his eyes that the expectation of believers shall not always be forgotten. The fulfilment of God's precious promise in the numbers of his descendants was more pleasant to him than the joy of seeing a numerous family around him. He saw the glory of the mercy and truth of God which had hitherto followed him all the days of his life, and he believed that they would shower down blessings on his seed through all generations.

VER. 28. *And Jacob lived in the land of Egypt seventeen years: so the whole age of Jacob was an hundred forty and seven years.*

Jacob told Pharaoh that the days of the years of his pilgrimage had been few, and had not attained to the days of the years of his fathers in their pilgrimage. It appears from these words that he thought himself near to the end of his life when he came to Egypt, yet seventeen years of life were before him. Many have lived longer in the world than they expected; but many more have died sooner. Job said, "Mine eye shall no more see good," and yet lived a hundred and forty years longer, and spent them all in prosperity. The man in the parable, who said he had stored up goods for many years, lived not to enjoy them a day longer.

Jacob did not weary of his life during the seventeen years of his abode in Egypt. He patiently and cheerfully waited all the days of his appointed time, although he was willing to leave the world whenever God should be pleased to call him out of it. Perhaps his coming to Egypt was the means of his living so much longer than he seems to have expected. He was worn out with grief in Canaan, because it seemed in many things to go evil with his house. But in Egypt he saw Joseph, and what was still better, he saw the loving-kindness of the Lord in the life, and prosperity, and family, and piety of Joseph. A cheerful heart does good like a medicine. Perhaps he never spent any years with more pleasure than the last seventeen years of his life. Although he was not exempted from the weakness and pains which are almost the inseparable attendants of great age, yet he enjoyed a quiet life under the protection of his great and good son, the glory and the comfort of his declining years. He appears to have enjoyed as good health as an old man could expect, till the days drew near when Israel must die. He was not now encumbered with the cares and vexations of the world. Doubtless he spent his days in the service of God, and brought forth such fruits in his old age as might be expected from a patriarch within a near view of the end of his pilgrimage. He was a true son of Abraham, who commanded his children and household after him to keep the way of the Lord, and enjoyed happy opportunities, which Abraham wanted in the last period of his life, for training up all his seed in the way wherein they should go.

In all, Jacob lived a hundred and forty-seven years; Isaac lived to the age of a hundred and eighty; Abraham to the age of a hundred and seventy-five. Jacob's life was shorter than theirs, but he lived as long as he wished in the land of his pilgrimage. He was happy with his son Joseph. The vicinity of that beloved son was a support to his declining years, which for a long time he had no expectation of enjoying; and unexpected mercies have a peculiar sweetness. Yet it would give him little pain to leave Joseph, that he might go to Abraham and Isaac, and, what was far better, to God Himself, the fountain of felicity.

Few of us will live half so long as Jacob, and why should we wish to live longer than our fathers have done? If our days are few, let them be well improved. John Baptist lived not many more than thirty years, and was followed to the other world by a greater number of good works than the greater part of those who have lived whole centuries. Josiah did not live forty years, yet he too left a precious name behind him, and had reason to rejoice that he was taken away from the evil to come. Pursue the great end of life whilst you live, and you will not die too soon. "Precious in the sight of the Lord is the death of his saints."

Ver. 29. *And the time drew nigh that Israel must die: and he called his son Joseph, and said unto him, If now I have found grace in thy sight, put, I pray thee, thy hand under my thigh, and deal kindly and truly with me; bury me not, I pray thee, in Egypt.*

"Israel must die." The man who had power over the angel and prevailed must die. He did not wish to live always in this world, and he must not expect to go out of the world in the manner in which Enoch had left it. Abraham was dead, Isaac was dead, and he was not better than his fathers. We possess consolations in the view of dying which these patriarchs wanted. They died without receiving the promise; Jesus had not then died to destroy the sting and the power of death. Yet, confiding in the promise of God, they could look without terror through the doors of the shadow of death. Israel was not like too many of us, who put away the thoughts of death when the infirmities of our bodies warn us of our approaching end. When the days were drawing near that he must die, he sent for his son Joseph, to inform him of his wishes concerning the disposal of that body which was to be left behind him on earth.

Our death is every day making a nearer approach to us. To-day we are twenty-four hours nearer to our latter end than yesterday, and three hundred and sixty-five days nearer to it than we were a year ago. At all times we are inexcusable if we endeavour not to be found ready; but those are more than doubly inexcusable who are warned by the decay of their strength that death is approaching, if they banish it from their thoughts, when they ought to be hastening their preparations to meet it with firmness.

"He called his son Joseph." Joseph was ever ready at Jacob's call. The lord of Egypt did not forget that he had a father, whom he was still bound to honour and obey. That greatness makes a man little which exalts him above any of the duties that he owes to his relatives, whatever be the difference of their condition. Joseph's time was almost engrossed by the weighty affairs of the nation; but he could manage his affairs with such discretion as to redeem time for domestic and for all relative duties and comforts.

"He called Joseph, and said unto him, If now I have found grace in thy sight." Was this the language of a father to his son? As the children should not lay up for the parents, but the parents for the children, so children should rather entreat the favours of their parents, than parents of their children. Yet parents, on some occasions, may find it proper rather to entreat than to command their children. Children should obey and honour their parents as long as they live. But parents are not to expect the same degree of obedience from them in every part of life; because, in the progress of reason, and of human affairs, children are entitled to new privileges, and laid under obligations to new duties. They have a right, when they come to the years of maturity, to judge for themselves concerning matters in which they were formerly bound to acquiesce in the judgment of their parents. They enter into new connexions, the duties of which are not less sacred than those which they owed to their parents. Joseph was in high office under Pharaoh, and he was a husband and a father. Jacob had no right to demand anything from him that he could not perform consistently with the duties of these relations.

Even when parents have a right to command, it will be no diminution of their dignity in many cases to entreat. Paul was the spiritual father of Philemon, and when he might have commanded him to comply with his desires in favour of Onesimus, yet, for love's sake, he rather besought him. Christ Himself condescends to entreat us by His ministers to accept of His blessings: "We pray you, in Christ's stead, be ye reconciled to God."

"If now I have found grace in thy sight, put thy hand under my thigh, and deal kindly and truly with me; bury me not, I pray thee, in Egypt." Jacob was certainly a man that feared an oath. The man who does not fear an oath, is not only a bad man, but one of the worst of sinners, Eccles. ix. Yet you see that the good man did not think it unlawful to give or to require an oath when there was a good reason for it. He requested Joseph to put his hand under his thigh, and swear to him that he would not bury him in Egypt, but in Canaan. Be not righteous overmuch. Never take the name of God rashly and presumptuously into your lips; but God graciously allows His name to be used in matters of importance for the good of society. He is glorified when His name is used in oaths on proper occasions with due reverence, as well as by other acts of worship, Ps. lxxiii. 9.

The mode of swearing used by Abraham and Jacob is different from that which we now use; but they were both prophets, and had the mind of God. Whether the putting the hand under the thigh was a known symbol of subjection, or whether it had a reference to the Christ, who was to come out of the loins of the patriarchs, certain it is, that the practice of these venerable patriarchs gives no just pretence for any of the superstitious modes of swearing now used in the Christian world.

"Put thy hand under my thigh, and deal kindly and truly with me; bury me not, I pray thee, in Egypt." If other men are entitled to kindness and fidelity from us, much more the parents of our flesh. Nor are we to forget what we owe them when their breath leaves their bodies. Jacob desires Joseph to give him his solemn promise that he would bury him where he desired to have his body laid, when it was become a lifeless carcass. And if respect is due to the breathless dust, it is still more due to the living representatives of our fathers.

"Bury me not, I pray thee, in Egypt." Jacob certainly never dreamed of any virtue in the relics of deceased saints. He left the bodies of his venerable progenitors behind him in the land of Canaan, and ordered his own body to be carried away from Egypt, whilst his seed were to remain in that land of exile. He knew that they were to suffer grievous afflictions in Egypt before they left it, but did not apprehend that his dead body, or any member of it, would give them any comfort or help in the evil day. "Bury me not, I pray thee, in Egypt." Why was the good patriarch so averse to a sepulchre in Egypt? Did he foresee that the mode of burial in Egypt would give rise to the senseless fables concerning the invisible world, which made a considerable part of the religious belief of the heathens? The reason why he wished to be buried elsewhere we learn from his own words—

VER. 30. *But I will lie with my fathers, and thou shalt carry me out of Egypt, and bury me in their burying-place. And he said, I will do as thou hast said.*

Why did the good man wish to lie in death with his fathers? He certainly knew that dead bodies cannot enjoy the pleasure of fellowship with the bodies of those whom they once most dearly loved. He knew that the way to heaven at the resurrection was equally near from Egypt as from Canaan; nor is it likely that he thought of Canaan as the common rendezvous of the just at the time when their happiness was to be completed.

But Jacob had all the sensibilities of a man, as well as the piety of a most eminent saint. It is natural for men to wish to be joined in burial with their friends that were dear to them. That much-lamented hero, Lord Nelson, is said to have expressed a wish in his latter will to be buried by the side of his father, unless the king should order otherwise. It was one of God's threatenings against the King of Babylon, whose reign was to terminate the glory of that proud city, that he should not be joined in burial with his predecessors, but cast forth as an abominable branch, because he had destroyed his land, and slain his people. Although we know that we can have no converse with our friends in the house of silence, and that we can enjoy no pleasurable feelings from their presence; yet it gives us some pleasure, while we yet live, to think that our dust shall mingle with the dust of those whom we love.

But thoughts of this kind were surely not Jacob's chief inducement to wish that he might be buried at Hebron. Had he been buried in Egypt he might have hoped to mingle his dust with that of persons no less beloved by him than his father, and no less worthy of his love. But the apostle tells us that "by faith Jacob gave commandment concerning his bones." He believed the promise, that the land of Canaan should be given to him in the persons of his seed. By sending his dead body to that land, he published to his seed and to the world that he believed and embraced the promise; that he was well satisfied, both with the country and with the security given him for the possession of it, although he was but a stranger and sojourner in it during his own life, and was laid under a necessity of leaving it before the end of his life.

" All these," it is said, "died in faith." Their faith continued firm under every trial of it to the end of their lives, and when they found themselves dying, they publicly professed their faith, for the benefit of survivors. Jacob published his faith, not only to his children and his children's children, now living in Egypt, by the orders given about his funeral, but to all the following generations of his descendants. He hoped that when they heard of his care to have his body carried to Canaan, they would all be excited to consider that land as their country, and to set a high value on that promise which secured it to them as their perpetual heritage.

He did not think that he would find an easier passage to heaven from Canaan than from Egypt, but he looked upon the promised land of Canaan as a figure of that better country which all the patriarchs sought.

When God promised to Jacob that he would surely bring him up again from Egypt, the good man did not think that the promise was of none effect, because he never again with his own eyes beheld that country which he so dearly loved. He probably understood it to signify that he was to be brought up again in the persons of his seed, for it was joined with another promise, that was to receive its accomplishment by his dying in Egypt—Joseph was to put his hands upon his eyes. He waited all his days for the promised blessings, and when he died without them, he wished it to appear to the world that he was not disappointed. He would go when he was dead to Canaan, if he could not go whilst he was yet living, and thus in a double sense the promise would be accomplished; and the accomplishment of it in the first sense would be a sign for the establishment of the faith of his seed concerning its more important accomplishment.

"And he said, I will do as thou hast said." Children ought not only to obey their parents in the Lord, but to give them all reasonable satisfaction of their intentions to obey them in things on which their hearts are set. Though Joseph had done what his father had said, yet if like the son in the parable, who repented of his refusal, he had said, I will not, Jacob must have died without the pleasure of hoping that he should sleep in the same burying-place with his fathers. The son who said, "I will not go," and yet went, was much to be preferred to him who said, "I go, sir," but went not; yet if there had been another son, who both said, I go, sir, and went, he would have deserved more praise than either.

Ver. 31. *And he said, Swear unto me. And he swear unto him. And Israel bowed himself upon the bed's head.*

Why did Jacob require an oath from Joseph? We have heard with pleasure a story of a certain philosopher (Xenocrates), who being called before a court to bear testimony in a certain cause, the court refused to take his oath, because they thought the word of such a man was as good as his oath. Did not Jacob think his son's word as good as any oath that could be sworn? Certainly Jacob's desire of an oath was not for the confirmation of his own belief of Joseph's word, but rather to give Joseph a powerful argument with Pharaoh, to obtain leave for burying his father in Canaan. Heathens, if they are not sunk into the grossest immoralities, reverence an oath. It might have been hoped that Pharaoh would not have refused any favour to Joseph that he might think proper to ask; and yet the fear of losing so excellent a servant, if he should be seized with a desire of ending his days where he had spent the sweetest time of his life, might have induced Pharaoh to hesitate in granting him leave to revisit the scenes of his early years.

"Joseph sware unto him." Was not Joseph afraid to swear the oath? Abraham's servant would not swear an oath proposed by his master without an explanation: "What if the friends of the woman will not suffer her to come to this land, must I carry back thy son to the land of his nativity?" Might not a man of such a tender conscience as Joseph have likewise said, "What if Pharaoh should not give me leave to carry thee up to Canaan? In this case I must be free from the obligation of the oath."

Joseph certainly feared an oath as much as Abraham's servant, but there is a great difference between a tender and a scrupulous conscience. He had no reason to think that Pharaoh would refuse him leave to perform his father's dying requests. If he had scrupled the oath, as it was proposed by Jacob, he would have betrayed an unworthy distrust of a generous master. His swearing it without conditions, was a strong plea for procuring Pharaoh's consent. And Joseph wished to give his father all the satisfaction he desired, or could desire, about a matter in which he appeared so deeply interested.

"And Jacob worshipped, leaning upon the top of his staff." So we are authorised by Paul to understand the last words of the verse. The dying patriarch was revived by the dutiful behaviour of his dear son, by the prospect of lying in the same burial-place with his fathers, and especially by the prospect of having his faith in God's promise publicly declared, by the circumstances of his funeral, to the glory of God, and to the advantage of his seed. He was filled with gratitude to his dear son, and especially to that God whose mercy he saw sweetening the last days of his life.

When we cannot praise God and serve Him as we wish to do, let us do it as we can. Jacob was now too feeble to perform his devotions in the manner to which he had been accustomed. He could not now go to an altar built for sacrifices of praise; but he exerted all the vigour left him, and with the help of his staff, on which he leaned, he performed his devotions in such a posture as showed his reverence and joy.

By faith he worshipped, leaning upon the top of his staff. His faith excited his joy, and gratitude, and confidence. His faith prompted him to publish to all who were present his lively sense of the loving-kindness of the Lord.

In the faith of the promise he worshipped God, and gave glory to him for giving him the promise, for the many assurances he had received of the truth of the promise, for all the joy and comfort derived from it in the course of his pilgrimage, and for the happy prospects before him in the light of the promise. He blessed God that the land of Canaan was to be the everlasting possession of his seed; that himself, with his fathers, had been enabled through life to give them a good pattern of faith in the promise; and that he was now to be joined with his blessed fathers, not merely in burial, but in possession of the better country.

Were our faith like Jacob's, we would be ready to bless the Lord at all times. Our praises would be in waiting for Him, when we meet with any new discoveries of His kindness. Living and dying, we would abound in the fruits of righteousness, which are by Jesus Christ to the glory of God.

LECTURE 31
Joseph visits his dying father with his two sons.
xlviii 1–7

VER. 1. *And it came to pass after these things, that one told Joseph, Behold, thy father is sick: and he took with him his two sons, Manasseh and Ephraim.*

WE have already heard that Jacob felt the approach of death in the decay of his strength. Here we are told that he was seized with sickness before he died. There are many things that come alike to all. "Lord, he whom thou lovest is sick," said the messenger of Martha and Mary to Jesus. Jesus could command away both sickness and death; yet the man whom he loved was sick unto death, and died of his sickness. Let us be prepared for all those evils that in all probability will sooner or later overtake us. If we were such men as Jacob or Lazarus, sickness would not be terrible to us. If the great Physician is our friend, we shall be either well or sick as He sees good for us.

Joseph was informed that his father was sick. He would not enjoy his father's presence so much as he wished, or so much as his other sons did (grandeur has always its incumbrances), but he was careful to be always seasonably informed of everything that happened to the good old man, and when he heard of his sickness, delayed not to visit him. At all times children ought to honour their parents; but sickness, or the approaches of death, call upon them to give more than ordinary testimonies of their affection and sympathy to persons who ought to be so dear to their hearts.

Although Joseph's love to his father was sufficient to draw him to his father's house, yet he might at this time have in view likewise his own advantage. A visit to a good man on his death-bed brings its own reward with it, when he acts like himself, or when he enjoys those comforts in sickness which God frequently bestows on those that love Him. Joseph knew that from his father's mouth he would hear words full of grace, and fit to make impressions on his heart that would last as long as he lived. He brought his two sons along with him to share in the benefit. He knew that it would give his father great pleasure to see the two young men, and hoped that the words of their blessed grandfather would make an indelible impression upon their hearts, as well as his own.

"Manasseh and Ephraim." These young persons were probably now grown up to men. Yet they were the only children of their father. Joseph was to be a fruitful bough, "even a fruitful bough by a well:" yet for a long time his family was small. The beginning is often small when God intends greatly to increase the latter end, for He shows His power by making a little one a thousand.

The very names of the young men would awaken the gratitude of the dying patriarch to the God who had dealt so kindly with his beloved son, when he was torn away from his father's protection. They proclaimed God's goodness to Joseph, and the sense that Joseph had of God's goodness in causing him to forget his affliction; and in making him fruitful in the land of his exile.

VER. 2. *And one told Jacob, and said, Behold, thy son Joseph cometh unto thee: and Israel strengthened himself, and sat upon the bed.*

When Jacob heard of the coming of Joseph, this instance of filial affection called to Jacob's remembrance the long train of kindness heaped on himself and on his family by his favourite son. It gave him still more pleasure by calling to his mind the faithfulness of God, who said to him, "Joseph shall put his hand upon thine eyes." Death had no bitterness for the man who so fervently waited for God's salvation, and obtained such testimonies of His loving-kindness and truth.

It is well known to us all that the mind has a powerful influence on the body, and that strong passions sometimes communicate to it an extraordinary degree of strength. Jacob felt his strength return to him when he heard Joseph's name, and exerted all his vigour to receive him with proper marks of his gratitude and love, and to speak to him of those things that might leave the sweetest and best impression on his mind.

Ver. 3. *And Jacob said unto Joseph, God Almighty appeared unto me at Luz in the land of Canaan, and blessed me.*

God strengthened Jacob on the bed of languishing, and Jacob employed that strength which God gave him in speaking of the mercy and faithfulness of God. Doubtless he had often presented to God such requests as those which one of the best of his sons offered up in his old age : " O Lord, thou hast taught me from my youth, and hitherto have I declared thy wondrous works. Now also, when I am old and gray-headed, O God, forsake me not, until I have shewed thy strength unto this generation, and thy power to every one that is to come." The wishes of Jacob were gratified. He spent his best days in publishing the wonders of the providence of God, and his faithful promises to Joseph and to his other children. We have only a specimen, but it is a delightful specimen of his last words and dying speeches.

We need not trouble ourselves in inquiring what particular reason Jacob had for speaking, on this occasion, of a variety of subjects to Joseph his beloved son. His wishes concerning his burial were already known, and Jacob gave himself little more trouble about them, for he knew that Joseph would do all that he had formerly said. His great view in all that he now said was to establish the faith of Joseph in God's word, and to guard him against the temptations of Egypt, and of grandeur. Although no man had ever showed a firmer attachment to his religion than Joseph, yet, like all other men, he needed help from God to keep him from falling, and he needed those means of establishment which God is wont to bless. The instructions,

and admonitions, and dying advices of parents are of great use
at all times, but they were peculiarly useful in the patriarchal
ages, when the means of knowledge and grace were far from
being so abundant as those which we enjoy.

Jacob begins his short discourse to Joseph with an account
of the first remarkable manifestation of God's special favour
which he enjoyed. Some think that the Almighty's appearance to Jacob at Luz was the means of his conversion. But
Jacob's unworthy behaviour to his father Isaac when he
obtained his blessing by fraud, is no proof that Jacob was then
unconverted. It is, however, probable, or rather evident, that
the vision of God at Luz was a blessed means of great increase
of grace and spiritual improvement. From the time that he
enjoyed it he might be in some sense a new man, although
formerly he had been a very different man from his brother
Esau. He saw the glory of the Lord. His heart was raised
far above the joys and sorrows of life. The Lord made him to
forget his father's house, in the same sense as Joseph afterwards
did, and prepared him for encountering all those hard trials
which were before him. He could not till his last day ot life
forget what he had seen at Luz. Doubtless he had spoken of
it to Joseph long before this time ; but his pleasure in speaking
of it was great, and he wished Joseph never to forget it. If
even Paul was in danger of being lifted up above measure
with the abundance of revelations made to him, Joseph might
need preservatives against the bad use he might be tempted to
make of the favours of Providence. He was exalted to great
honour and power in Egypt. What if the devil might find
auxiliaries, even in Joseph's family, to draw away his heart
from Canaan to Egypt ! He had it in his power to procure
the most elevated stations for his sons. Asenath, the daughter
of one of the noblest families in Egypt, might think it a hard
matter to have her children placed in the same manner with
the abhorred shepherds of Palestine. What if Manasseh and
Ephraim should be tempted to think that it was better to enjoy
the dignities of Egypt than to suffer the reproach of the God
of Abraham ! The vision of Bethel was a powerful preserva-

tive from all such temptations. Joseph was in high favour with an earthly king, but what was the favour of Pharaoh to the grace of God! It was great to be the Lord of Egypt; but it was incomparably greater to be a favoured servant of the Most High, and to be assured of those blessings which proceed from the special love of the Lord God Almighty.

" God Almighty appeared unto me at Luz." The name of that place where God appeared unto Jacob when he fled from the face of his brother Esau, was Luz at the first. And Luz was the name by which it was still generally known, although Bethel became afterwards its common name. God's people will never forget those places where they have been blessed with remarkable manifestations of His favour, especially when their circumstances were such as to render these manifestations highly necessary and seasonable. Jacob was in great distress at the time when God appeared to him at Luz; and the remembrance of his distress inflamed his love to the God who knew his soul in adversity. When God called him to go again to that delightful place where he had enjoyed such remarkable fellowship with God, " Let us arise," said the good man to his family, " and go up to Bethel, and I will make there an altar unto God, who saved me in the day of my distress, and was with me in the way which I went."

" At Luz, in the land of Canaan." Goshen, in the land of Egypt, was the place where Jacob had obtained a comfortable settlement in the days of famine. But Luz, in the land of Canaan, was the place where Jacob had, for the first time, an uncommon instance of divine mercy in the visions of God. Egypt was the country in which Joseph had been aggrandised by an earthly prince; but Canaan was the land where God ordinarily appeared to Joseph's progenitors, and assured them that it should be the inheritance of their seed.

No man hath seen God at any time, and yet God had been seen by Jacob both at Luz and at Peniel. There is a sense in which God may be still seen by men upon earth. His power and His glory have been often seen in the sanctuary. Although we do not expect such sensible communion with God as the

2 D

ancient patriarchs, yet such communion with Him, as is no less real and beneficial, is attainable by all who love Him. " He that keepeth my commandments," says Jesus, " he it is that loveth me, and my father will love him ; and I will manifest myself to him." No wonder that we do not enjoy those distinguished favours which we seldom seek with earnestness of desire. But blessed are all that seek God with their whole hearts ; they shall find Him, and their hearts shall rejoice, and their joy death itself shall not take from them. The remembrance of the Divine visits to Jacob at Bethel would be sweeter, perhaps, to him at this time than they had ever been before. He was now about to enter into the immediate presence of God. His views of God had excited ardent longings for clearer manifestations of His glory, and these longings were now to be fully satisfied. He had seen God darkly, as through a glass, but now he was going to see Him face to face, and to know even as he was known.

" God Almighty appeared to me at Luz." The Lord was known to the patriarchs by the name of God Almighty. Jacob was well informed of all the pleasant discoveries that God had made of himself to Abraham. He had been informed by Isaac, or perhaps by Abraham himself, that in the year before Isaac was born, the Lord had appeared unto Abraham, and said to him, " I am the Almighty God ; walk before me, and be thou perfect, and I will establish my covenant with thee, and I will multiply thee exceedingly." God had, besides, revealed Himself by this name to Jacob at Luz, in the second vision of God which he saw at that happy place. There God said unto him, " I am God Almighty ; be fruitful and multiply ; a nation and a company of nations shall be of thee." At the time of the vision Jacob was in greater perplexity than at the time when he fled from the face of his brother. He had been trembling for the life of his family, exposed to the rage of the Canaanites by the murder of the men of Shechem. But this name of God, the Almighty, gave him strong consolation. If all the nations of Canaan had combined against him he was safe. They could not have destroyed that seed to which the Almighty had promised to give the land for their possession. He was persuaded that what God had promised He was able also to perform. And now he reminds Joseph of that great name which had so mightily supported the faith of his progenitors. It was better to trust in the Lord than to put confidence in princes. It was better to trust in the Almighty than to put confidence in Pharaoh. The strength of Pharaoh would be his shame if his trust was placed on it, and confidence in the shadow of Egypt would be his confusion. But the arm of the Lord could never be shortened, and none who trusted in His word could be disappointed.

"God Almighty appeared unto me at Luz, in the land of Canaan, and blessed me." There Jacob was blessed with precious promises, pleasant to his heart, because they contained not only assurances of the love of God to himself, but assurances likewise of rich blessings to his seed for a great while to come. Joseph and all his brethren were deeply interested in this appearance of God, and in the blessing which their father received : "He blessed me."

VER. 4. *And said unto me, Behold, I will make thee fruitful, and multiply thee, and I will make of thee a multitude of people ; and will give this land to thy seed after thee for an everlasting possession.*

Did not Jacob promise to himself more than God had promised him? We find in the account of what God said unto him at Luz, both when he fled from his father's house, and when he returned to it (Gen. xxviii. 35), that a promise was given him of a very numerous seed, and the land of Canaan for their inheritance ; but we do not find in any of these accounts any mention of the perpetuity of this inheritance. Yet we have no reason to think that Jacob added any unwarrantable comments of his own to the faithful and true sayings of God. He knew how to compare spiritual things with spiritual. By the words which the Almighty spoke to him at Luz, he was assured that the blessing of Abraham was to come upon himself, and upon his posterity ; and he knew that by the covenant made with Abraham, the land of Canaan was secured for ever to his seed. The term *for ever* is, however, to be understood sometimes in a limited sense. The good land was secured by the promise to the seed of Abraham and Jacob, till the time came when God should create, as it were, a new world, by introducing a new dispensation of grace among men. Jacob was assured by the promise that, for a long series of generations, if not through all ages, his seed should possess the land under Divine protection. Other nations might dwell for many ages, or for ever, in their own country, but they did not dwell in the Lord's land. Their possessions were not secured to them by a Divine covenant. They enjoyed no special proof of the love of God in the place of their residence, or in the privileges annexed to it. The land of Israel was dear to the lovers of God, because they saw the Divine mercy and faithfulness to Israel in their possession, and in all those distinguishing privileges which they enjoyed.

The Lord is abundant in goodness and truth. He will not disappoint the hopes excited by His word in the hearts of His people. If Abraham and Jacob understood the promise of an everlasting inheritance in Canaan to signify that they should dwell in it as long as the earth endures, we have reason to believe that God will accomplish this after a long interval. The Jews have now lived in exile for seventeen hundred years, but the day is yet coming when the Lord will be the God of all the families of Israel, and they shall be His people. Then it is highly probable they will again return to their own land, and glorify God, because His truth endures to all generations.

The whole land of Canaan could not at this time be inhabited by the seed of Jacob. If all the ancient inhabitants of the country had been driven out to make room for them the land would have been a desolate wilderness, and the wild beasts of the field would have multiplied beyond measure. But that God who designed the land for His people promised to multiply them, that they might fill the land. Jacob was to become, not only a nation, but a multitude of nations. They were to increase in number till they were like the stars of heaven, or the sand of the sea. Then they would be literally equal in number to many of such nations as were in the time of the patriarchs scattered over the face of the earth.

But when this great multiplication of seed was promised to Jacob as Abraham's heir, the Apostle Paul teaches us to take a still more extensive view of its meaning. "Abraham," he says, "having been justified by faith while he was uncircumcised, received the sign of circumcision, that he might be the father of all them that believe, though they be not circumcised." "Therefore," adds the apostle, "it is of faith, that it might be by grace, to the end that the promise might be to all the seed, not to that only which is of the law, but to that also which is of the faith of Abraham, who is the father of us all; as it is written, I have made thee the father of many nations, before him whom he believed, even God, who quickeneth the dead, and calls those things which be not as though they were."

The mention of this promise concerning the seed of Jacob was more than sufficient to establish the soul of Joseph against all temptations to separate himself from his brethren, any farther than his present condition compelled him to do. And are not the words of Paul more than sufficient to persuade us to seek justification by the faith of Christ? All who believe unto righteousness are the true seed of Abraham and Israel. What though they have not their dwelling in the earthly Canaan! They shall sit down with Abraham, Isaac, and Jacob in the kingdom of God.

VER. 5. *And now thy two sons, Ephraim and Manasseh, which were born unto thee in the land of Egypt before I came unto thee into Egypt, are mine; as Reuben and Simeon, they shall be mine.*

Reuben was the first-born of Jacob, "but forasmuch as he had defiled his father's bed, his birthright was given to the sons of Joseph, the son of Israel," 1 Chron. v. 1. It seems that, according to the law or custom of the primogeniture, when Reuben lost his birthright, it fell to the first-born, not of the concubines, but of Rachel, who was a free woman, as well as Leah, the mother of Reuben. Yet this honour done to Joseph may perhaps, with more propriety, be ascribed to his father's love under the direction of God; for the sons of the concubines were admitted to all the privileges of the other sons of Jacob, and their first-born sons were older than Joseph. That Providence which gave the birth-right to Jacob instead of Esau gave the birthright to Joseph rather than to Asher or Dan. These sons of Jacob were sufficiently happy that they were not sent out of their father's house, like the sons of Abraham's concubines. Reuben had reason, indeed, to lament his degradation; but he had himself only to blame, and had great cause to bless God that a single portion in the heritage of Jacob was reserved for him, notwithstanding of what he had done to provoke his father and the God of his father to anger. It might have seemed hard to him, if his repentance for his sin had not been sincere, that although he had been Joseph's only friend in his distress, his birthright was to be transferred to Joseph. Yet he had just reason to be pleased with the manner of expression by which his father assigned the double portion to Joseph—"Thy two sons, Manasseh and Ephraim, shall be mine; as Reuben and Simeon, they shall be mine." Reuben and Simeon had been offenders; but still they have a portion in Israel, and shall be fed with the heritage of Jacob.

We need not give ourselves much trouble about the ill-will of men, if God is on our side. Joseph's brethren did all that lay in their power to exclude him from a part in the heritage of Jacob. He was sold into a strange country; and had not the Lord been with him in a very remarkable manner, he would never have again seen the good land, far less would he have transmitted a title to possessions in that land to his seed after him. But through the favour of God, he was now assured of a double share.

Let us observe the great mercy of God to Jacob. It was not without Divine direction that he adopted the two sons of Joseph. He had long given up his son for lost, and now he finds in him two sons. Each of Joseph's sons is a son, and not merely a grandson, to the good old man. It was a high gratification to the dying patriarch to find himself authorised to give such a testimony of his favour to that son whom he loved more than his life.

It may be further observed that the kindness showed, not so much by Jacob as by the God of Jacob, to the two young men would be a powerful attractive to their hearts, and a means of persuading them that it was more for their interest to cast in their lot with the people of the God of their father, than with the family of Poti-pherah, the priest of On. They might have hoped to make a distinguished figure in Egypt if they had been willing to conform their practice to the manners of that country. But they were taught by their father, and by God, that a part in the heritage of the seed of Abraham was incomparably to be preferred to a kingdom in any other part of the world. If they associated themselves with the people of God, they could not reasonably hope to escape the reproach and afflictions of that people; but they had a rich portion of their blessings secured to them, which might be an abundant compensation for all that they might lose, or for all that they might be called to endure.

VER. 6. *And thy issue, which thou begettest after them, shall be thine, and shall be called after the name of their brethren in their inheritance.*

It does not appear that Joseph ever begot any more sons, but Jacob was careful to settle his affairs with sufficient precaution, and to cut off as much as possible all occasions of dispute from his children, when himself should be laid in the dust. Many fatal contentions might have been completely obviated, if parents had always been equally careful to provide against every danger of contention amongst their offspring.

Jacob spoke under the direction of the Spirit of God, but the Spirit was given him only by measure. It was not given him to know whether Joseph should have any more sons of his own body than Manasseh and Ephraim; but it was made known to him that Joseph should have a very numerous seed by these two sons. This sufficed him; and he left directions, that if Joseph should have any more immediate sons, they should take their stations in Israel under the banners of Manasseh and Ephraim.

VER. 7. *And as for me, when I came from Padan, Rachel died by me in the land of Canaan in the way, when yet there was but a little way to come unto Ephrath: and I buried her there in the way of Ephrath; the same is Beth-lehem.*

What train of thought led Jacob at this time to speak of Rachel and her burial! It is often not easy for us to explain the train of our own thoughts or discourse. Yet we may form a conjecture of the circumstances that brought Rachel at this time into Jacob's mind, and of the reason why he spoke of her burial in the ears of her son, and her two grandsons, who were adopted sons. The sight of these dear children of Rachel brought their beloved mother into Jacob's mind, and he knew that Joseph and his two sons would be deeply affected by the mention of their mother, and might have good impressions made upon their hearts by the mention of her early death and burial in the Land of Promise.

She was not suffered to remain with Jacob many years; but it was to be hoped that she had lived long enough with him to know the value of his religion, and of those promises which were given him as the ground of his faith. She lived to accompany him into the land of Canaan, and to find a grave in it, though at some distance from the place where Jacob wished his body to rest.

It was not to be supposed that Jacob could carry on a long discourse at this time. But what he said of Rachel was sufficient to call up several other things to the minds of Joseph and of his two sons. Joseph already knew the reason why she was not carried to the cave of Machpelah, and he might be excited by the thought of her burial in the way of Ephrath to desire that his own body might be carried for burial to the land of Canaan. This would be a noble testimony of Joseph's faith and of his high regard to the promise.

The land of Canaan might be endeared to Joseph's seed by hearing that their mother Rachel, as well as their father, was buried in it. We find that the King of Persia heartily sympathised with Nehemiah's affliction when he heard that the place of his father's sepulchres lay waste.

We have not Jacob's reasons for wishing to be buried in any particular spot. It will not be of great importance to us to be buried with our fathers; but the consideration of their death and burial may have a happy tendency to hasten our preparations for our latter end. Soon will the time come when the grave will be ready for us, and we shall say to the worms, Ye are our mother and our sisters. But blessed are the dead that sleep in Jesus, in whatever spot of the earth their bones are laid. If we believe that Jesus died and rose again, we believe also that them who sleep in Jesus will God bring with Him.

LECTURE 32
Jacob blesses the two sons of Joseph.
xlviii 8–16

VER. 8. *And Israel beheld Joseph's sons, and said, Who are these?*

"REMEMBER thy Creator in the days of thy youth, before the evil days come, when thou shalt say, I have no pleasure in them;" when the sun, and the light, and the moon, and the stars are darkened; and when those that look out at their windows cannot any longer enjoy the light of heaven. Isaac and Jacob were so dim-sighted when they were old that they could not distinguish the well-known faces of their own children. But it was their happiness that when they could not discern visible objects, they beheld the things which were not seen.

VER. 9. *And Joseph said unto his father, They are my sons, whom God hath given me in this place. And he said, Bring them, I pray thee, unto me, and I will bless them.*

Joseph considered his sons as a gift bestowed upon him by God. Thus Jacob, when he was asked by Esau, Who are these with thee? answered, The children which God hath graciously given thy servant. We think that rich men are bound to thank God for their wealth. Do we not esteem our children a part, the principal part, of our earthly treasure? Surely we would not part with them for silver and gold. The loss of them would afflict us more than the loss of all our money. Ought we not to bless God, then, on their account, especially when we find comfort in their good behaviour? There are some children, indeed, who tempt their parents to lament the day in which they were born. But we must not think that we have a right to withhold our gratitude from the God of our mercies because our children give us too good evidence that they are not exempt from that corruption which is common to our race. When we are dissatisfied with their behaviour, have we not great reason to be thankful that their space of repentance is lengthened out? But when their conduct is as good as we have any reason to expect in the present state of human nature, let us thank God, both for giving them to us and for preserving them from so many of the evils that are in the world.

" Bring them near to me," said Jacob, " that I may bless them." He had already adopted them, and he wished to give them the blessing, not only of a father, but of a patriarch. We cannot bestow such blessings on our children as Isaac and Jacob gave to theirs. But nature disposes us to love them, and grace teaches us to show our love in earnest prayer for their welfare. Let young children endeavour to behave in such a manner as to entitle them to the blessings of their parents. There is a promise of long life and prosperity to the children that honour their parents. This promise encourages parents to plead for the Divine favour to dutiful children.

Ver. 10. *Now the eyes of Israel were dim for age, so that he could not see. And he brought them near unto him; and he kissed them, and embraced them.*

We have already seen a proof that the eyes of Israel were become dim. But we shall soon see a proof that he saw what none else could see. He saw future things in the light of God. The eyes of his mind were enlightened to behold the gracious works of his God, in fulfilling His promises to himself and to his father. This is a consolation, under the loss of sight, granted to few. There is not now a prophet, or any that can penetrate into the dark abyss of future events, by a light of revelation immediately granted to himself. Yet this is the happiness of all that believe on God, that they can behold those future things in which they are most deeply interested, in the light of those revelations which were given to the holy patriarchs, and prophets, and apostles, to be communicated to the Church, for the instruction of every generation of mankind.

Israel did not so soon lose the use of his eyes as his father Isaac had done. God knows what His people need, and what they can bear. Isaac had no long journeys to perform in his old age. Jacob had the use of his eyes when he most needed them. No doubt he now felt the privation of his sight. He would have taken much pleasure in beholding the face of his new sons, Ephraim and Manasseh, as well as the countenance of his much beloved Joseph. But this was a small matter; he saw the face of God with joy, and knew that he would soon be satisfied with His likeness. Neither the loss of money, nor the loss of sight, nor the loss of the present life, can make that man miserable whose hope is in the Lord his God.

When Isaac was dim-sighted, his wife and his son Jacob conspired to impose upon him. But Jacob was not treated by his sons in old age as he had treated his own father. Joseph was ready to perform every soothing act of kindness, and probably the other sons of Jacob now did what they could to sweeten the distresses inseparable from the decay of nature.

Joseph brought near his two sons with great pleasure to Jacob. It is likely, when he brought them with him, he intended to ask a blessing for them, and now he brings them forward to receive a richer blessing than he expected.

Jacob kissed them, and embraced them, as a testimony of his love, and a seal of their adoption into his family as immediate sons and heirs.

How happy were these two young men! They might have been Egyptian princes: but they accounted it a far greater happiness to be sons of Jacob, and children of the covenant made with Abraham. The embraces and kisses of the good old patriarch were far superior in value to all the honours which the King of Egypt could confer. Happy was the dying patriarch. He was not only assured of heaven to himself, but assured likewise that Joseph, and that Joseph's seed, would be blessed on the earth. If his former days had been few and evil, his last days were good. God can make those days which are commonly accounted the evil days of life, the best of all our days.

VER. 11. *And Israel said unto Joseph, I had not thought to see thy face: and, lo, God hath shewed me also thy seed.*

"Rejoice, O sinner! in the days of thy youth; walk in the way of thine heart, and in the sight of thine eyes. But know, that for all these things God will bring thee to judgment." What will you think of your licentious pleasures when the hand of death is upon you, and eternity full in your view? Why should you plant beforehand thorns for your dying pillow? "Mark the perfect, and behold the upright man." You thought his life was joyless, because he could not indulge himself in those pleasures which his conscience reprobated; but he was preparing joys for those hours, in which those who have their portion in this life must bid an eternal adieu to all those pleasures for which they have any relish. Jacob was now dim-sighted, and could not see his own children. He saw himself approaching to the end of life, and yet his heart is full of joy, and his mouth is filled with the praises of God. He tasted the loving-kindness of the Lord in the kisses and embraces of his two sons, and said to Joseph, "I had not thought to see thy face, but lo! God hath shewed me thy two sons." All that happiness which he now enjoyed he considered as a testimony of God's favour. The mercy of his Heavenly Father, in his outward enjoyments, gives him incomparably greater pleasure than the same enjoyments could give to a man governed merely by the feelings of nature. Parental love is, in itself, the source of rich pleasures, when children are dutiful and virtuous; but religion greatly sweetens, whilst it sanctifies, the common enjoyments of life. The sisters of Lazarus were happy to see their brother raised from the dead, because they dearly loved him; but their joy in that happy event was derived chiefly from the love of Jesus and the glory of God, which they saw in the miraculous work performed for their comfort and joy of faith, John xi.

When we see Jacob embracing and kissing his sons, and hear him blessing God for showing him such tokens of His favour before he left the world, we are reminded of a similar, but more interesting instance of happiness, in a dying saint. Old Simeon saw Jesus before he left the world, and took Him up in his arms, and blessed Him, and thanked God, saying, "Lord, now lettest thou thy servant depart in peace, for mine eyes have seen thy salvation." Jacob was a happy man, but far less so than Simeon. He was only waiting for God's salvation, and died in faith, not having received the promise. Yet his eyes, too, saw the salvation of God in the light of the promise, and in the pledges given to establish his faith in the promise. When he had two of his beloved children in his arms, he remembered the promise of an innumerable progeny, in which was included the Saviour whom Simeon received into his arms. Jacob probably did not yet know from which of his sons the Messiah was to come. When the birthright was given to Joseph, it was a natural conclusion that he might, in all likelihood, be the father of Messiah. But he knew, with certainty, that from whomsoever Christ should derive his birth, he was to be the Saviour of every believer of his race.

The pleasures and the bitterness of life in their succession greatly enhance one another. Sorrow succeeding joy is doubled, and so are joys succeeding sorrows. When Jacob was blessed with the embraces of the sons of Joseph, he thought of the time when Joseph himself was not—"I had not thought to see thy face : and, lo ! God hath shewed me thy sons." What would he not have given to see the face of Joseph, without any sons to perpetuate his name? And now God had given him a sight, not only of his son, but of his son's sons. Joseph was now doubled to him in those children that were to be the fathers of a numerous race. Jacob's soul blessed the Lord, who had brought happiness to him out of despair, and multiplied that blessing of which he thought himself for ever bereaved. The time may come when we will think with joy of our present sorrows. The remembrance of them will double our pleasures, and inflame our hearts with gratitude to God, when He gives us the "oil of joy for mourning, and the garment of praise for the spirit of heaviness."

" God hath caused me to see thy seed." The good man almost forgot that he had lost his sight. He spoke as if he had been able, not only to embrace his sons, but to feast his eyes with their blooming countenances. It is foolish to lose the sense of our pleasures in griefs. It is happy to lose the remembrance of our griefs in our joys. Fools know how to make themselves miserable amidst the best means of happiness. Thankful Christians know how to make themselves happy in the midst of many evils.

VER. 12. *And Joseph brought them out from between his knees, and he bowed himself with his face to the earth.*

He brought them out from between his father's knees, for the old man was unable long to support the efforts of his weak arms, and the transports of his soul. Joseph therefore removed his sons, to place them in a posture proper for the solemn occasion; and expressed his reverence to his father and his gratitude to God, by bowing himself to the earth.

Although Joseph was a very great man in the eyes of the people of the land, his heart was not haughty, nor his eyes lofty. There are many who can bear adversity much better than prosperity. Joseph was tried and approved in both. And he deserves as much praise, at least for the modesty and humbleness of mind which he discovered in his grandeur, as for the firmness and patience with which he bore the tempests of calamity.

When the Egyptians knew Jacob only as the father of Joseph, Joseph himself considered it as his highest honour to be the son of Jacob, and one of the heirs of the blessings promised to Abraham. He revered his father; and instead of thinking that he had done anything extraordinary in feeding all his father's family, he felt the liveliest gratitude for the affection which his father showed him in the persons of his two sons.

VER. 13. *And Joseph took them both, Ephraim in his right hand toward Israel's left hand, and Manasseh in his left hand toward Israel's right hand, and brought them near unto him.*

Joseph observed the ordinary rules of ceremony, when he presented his eldest son to Jacob's right hand. The sons of Jacob sat by him according to their birthright, when they ate with him. It was natural to think that his own eldest son should stand at Jacob's right hand to receive the blessing. He knew that his father had obtained the blessing and the birthright, although he did not come into the world so soon as Esau; but Esau was not one of the seed in which the covenant with Abraham was to be established. He knew that the birthright was transferred from Reuben to himself, but Manasseh had done nothing to forfeit the primogeniture. Joseph therefore behaved with propriety when he placed him at Jacob's right hand. God might give the chief blessing to whom he pleased. Joseph pays a proper regard to the rights of nature, till he is assured that they were set aside by God.

VER. 14. *And Israel stretched out his right hand, and laid it upon Ephraim's head, who was the younger, and his left hand upon Manasseh's head, guiding his hands wittingly; for Manasseh was the first-born.*

The imposition of hands was designed for different purposes, on different occasions. When Jacob laid his hands upon the heads of Joseph's sons, he marked them out as the persons whom he solemnly blessed in the name of the Lord. He signified by this action that the blessing was to come upon the head of Joseph, and upon the crown of the head of him that was separated from his brethren. "Blessings," says Solomon, "are upon the head of the just." The imposition of Jacob's hands, when he blessed the sons of Joseph, taught them that the God who spake by the significant actions, as well as by the mouth, of their venerable father, would crown them with loving-kindnesses and tender mercies, with these gifts which are from above, and come down from the Father of lights.

Jacob in crossing his hands made it evident that although his eyes were dim, he could clearly see those future events which he predicted. If he had not acted by the direction of the Divine Spirit, he would have complied with the wishes of Joseph, by giving the preference to his first-born. Jacob probably loved Manasseh as dearly as Ephraim. But he moved his hands, and spake with his tongue, as he was moved by the Holy Ghost. As a man and a father, he would have

been of the same mind with Joseph ; but as a prophet, he gave
the richest blessing to him who was to partake most richly of
the blessings of heaven. What ! was he to withstand God ?
His father Isaac had given the blessing to a son to whom he
did not intend to give it, but found it impossible to counteract
the councils of Heaven. He trembled very exceedingly when
he found how God had frustrated his intentions. Jacob was
too wise to follow the example.

Neither Joseph nor Manasseh had any reason to be dissatisfied. God may bestow His blessings according to His own will.
We ought to have our hearts filled with the praises of God if
He gives us an inheritance among His chosen, although He give
to others a larger share in that inheritance. The nine disciples
of our Lord, who were not taken to the mount of transfiguration,
had no reason to be dissatisfied because they were left in the
plain, but great reason to be thankful that they were numbered
with the twelve. It would ill become preachers of the grace of
God to repine at the glory of its sovereignty. The Lord will
have mercy on whom He will have mercy, and will show them
His mercy in the manner and measure that seem good to Himself. If the first are made last, and the last first, what have
we to say ? " Even so, Father, for so it seemed good in thy
sight."

VER. 15, 16. *And he blessed Joseph, and said, God, before
whom my fathers Abraham and Isaac did walk, the God which
fed me all my life long unto this day, the angel which redeemed
me from all evil, bless the lads.*

He blessed Joseph in blessing his sons. Those are unnatural
fathers who do not wish all happiness to their sons and
daughters. Those are not religious parents who are not as
truly thankful to God for blessings bestowed on their children
as for their personal blessing. King David was not displeased,
but gratified, when his friends prayed that " God might be
with Solomon, and make his throne greater than the throne of
their lord King David."

" Bring near the lads to me, and I will bless them." How
did he bless them ? In the form of a prayer to God, for the

2 E

best blessing to come down upon their heads. Yet this prayer is likewise a prophecy. He prayed not only in the exercise of that faith which is required in all our prayers, but in the faith of particular revelations made to him concerning the future fate of Ephraim and Manasseh. The Spirit of God directed him to express his mind in the form of a prayer and his expressions were attended with correspondent affections. He most ardently desired from God those blessings which he requested, and was well assured that they would not be denied.

"The God before whom my fathers Abraham and Isaac walked." These holy patriarchs lived all their days in all holy obedience before God, from the time He made Himself known to them as their own God. They endeavoured to approve themselves to Him, and depended on Him as their shield and salvation. We are not children of these holy men if we walk according to the course of this world. Those who walk in the steps of the faith of our father Abraham will justify their faith by their works.

The holy conversation of Abraham and Isaac did not procure the blessing to their posterity, for the promise to Abraham and his seed, that he should be the heir of the world, was not made through him, but through the righteousness of faith. Yet that faith, which is always attended with holiness, was necessary for receiving the promise. Those children of Jacob that came out of Egypt had a promise given them of entering into God's rest, and yet came short of it through unbelief. God, on the contrary, says of Abraham, "I know that he will command his children and his household after him to keep the way of the Lord, to do judgment and justice, that I may bring upon Abraham that which I have spoken of him." And to Israel the Lord said, "I will multiply thy seed as the stars of heaven, and will give unto thy seed all these countries, and in thy seed shall all the nations of the earth be blessed : because that Abraham obeyed my voice, and kept my charge, my commandments, my statutes, and my laws."

Abraham and Isaac walked before God in the faith of His promise; and it would have been unworthy of the Divine faithfulness and goodness to have failed in the performance of what He promised to their seed. Jacob's sons had no reason to say in their hearts, " We have Abraham and Isaac to our fathers, and therefore we must inherit the blessing, whatever our conduct be." The fate of Er and Onan was an awful proof that God had not brought Himself under any obligation to suffer sin in the children of Isaac, in whom Abraham's seed was called. The words of Jacob under consideration contain indeed an encouragement to his children to look for the performance of the promise made to Abraham ; but they contain at the same time an implicit admonition to follow the example of those holy patriarchs, if they desired to be blessed with faithful Abraham.

Jacob might have added his own name to the names of Abraham and Isaac. Perhaps his modesty kept him from mentioning it, or perhaps it did not seem necessary. His own behaviour was well known to Joseph and his sons. It is likely that although Jacob was conscious of his constant endeavours to walk before God unto all pleasing, he did not think his name worthy to be mentioned with the names of his pious progenitors. Paul did not think himself meet to be called an apostle, because he had persecuted the Church of God. Jacob might, on account of his miscarriages, think himself unmeet to be ranked with those patriarchs whose names were to be held in everlasting remembrance. But if such was his thought, he stood single in the opinion. No man ever thought him inferior to Isaac, or greatly inferior to Abraham.

" The God which fed me all my life long unto this day." When Jacob was going to Padan-aram he vowed a vow, saying, " If God will be with me, and will keep me in the way that I go, and will give me bread to eat, and raiment to put on, so that I come again to my father's house in peace, then shall the Lord be my God." He desired not great things for himself, but to be preserved from evil, and fed with food convenient for him. The Lord gave him what he sought, and he praised the name of his generous benefactor. When he says that God fed him all his lifelong, his meaning is, that the Lord had been his shepherd, and had kept and led him, as well as supplied all his wants. And he observes with thankfulness that God had fed him all his lifelong unto that day. The Lord fed him when he was in his father's house. The Lord fed him when he procured his food by toil at Laban's house. The Lord fed him when his beloved son supplied all his wants. In whatever way we obtain the necessaries and conveniences of life, God is the giver of them. And we ought at all times to be penetrated with a sense of that goodness which follows us all the days of our life. A son gratefully acknowledges the goodness of his mother who suckled him at her breast, and supplied all the wants of his early years. He will not forget what his father did to enable him to live comfortably in the world. How much more ought we gratefully to remember that Divine kindness which has preserved us from so many evils, and loaded us with benefits from the time that we came into the world unto this hour.

Although Jacob did not choose to speak of his own good conversation, yet he did not overlook the goodness of God to him. He hoped that his sons would be impressed with lively gratitude to that God who had been so kind to their father, and would see it their interest, as well as their duty, to place their confidence in Him, who never forsakes any that trust in Him. "I will not leave thee," said God, "till I have done that which I have spoken to thee of." Jacob on his death-bed gives his attestation from experience to the truth of this promise—"The God who fed me all my life long unto this day—"

VER. 16. *The Angel which redeemed me from all evil, bless the lads; and let my name be named on them, and the name of my fathers Abraham and Isaac: and let them grow into a multitude in the midst of the earth.*

"Few and evil have the days of the years of my life been," said Jacob. Good men are not exempted from the common fate of the sinful sons of Adam. In the course of their short life upon the earth they sometimes see many evil days. But they have this great advantage, that they know where to find refuge from the tempest. They have a Redeemer who is mighty to save; the Lord of hosts is His name!

The angel which redeemed Jacob from all evil was not a created angel. He did not pray to his fathers Abraham and Isaac, who were now equal to angels, but to that God who had fed him all his lifelong, and to the Angel who redeemed him; and it is evident that the Angel who redeemed him was not a different object of worship from the God who had fed him. Distinct persons are meant, but the divine essence must be the same in both. The God who had fed him, and the Angel who redeemed him, are but one undivided object of his prayers, when he seeks the best blessings to the young men whom he so dearly loved.

" The Angel that redeemed me from all evil." His afflictions were many, but the Son of God, the messenger of the covenant, delivered him from them all ; he delivered him from the wrath of Esau, from the impositions of Laban, from the revenge of the Canaanites, who were sore displeased with him for the wicked-ness of his.sons, which he could not prevent. By this Angel Jacob was redeemed from evils far worse than men ever had it in their power to inflict. He was redeemed from all his iniquities, and from their penal consequences. Jesus has in every age been the Redeemer of His people. Never since the world began was there a sinner saved but by the merit, and blood, and power of Christ. What praises are sufficient for Him who redeems our lives from destruction, who delivers us from death, who preserves us from everlasting misery ! " Bless the Lord, O our souls, and all that is within us ! " Bless Him who saves us from our sins, and from those evils that we have brought upon ourselves by our sins.

Joseph could not be ignorant who this Angel was to whom Jacob addresses his prayer. He had doubtless often heard him speak of that glorious night when he wrestled with the Angel, and prevailed, and obtained a blessing for himself and for his seed. With great propriety, Jacob, blessing his children, spoke not only of the God who had fed him, but of the Angel who gave him his blessing at Bethel and Peniel. That Angel gave a gracious answer to those petitions which he offered up for his seed with himself, never forsook him through his life, and continued his kindness to his seed through every succeeding generation. " In all their afflictions the Lord was afflicted, and the Angel of his presence saved him. In his love and in his pity he redeemed them, and he bare them and carried them all the days of old."

How pleasantly did Jacob speak of his God and Redeemer in the view of death! He looked back with joy on the many signal mercies of his life, and he looked forward with joy to the innumerable mercies which he expected from his God, and the God of his fathers, to their seed and his own seed. Let the people of God walk before Him with all circumspection through life. It may be that, when they are dying, they will taste the joys of sweet reflection on God's past mercies, and the pleasures of hope, not only concerning their own eternal welfare, but concerning their remnant.

" The God that fed me all my life long unto this day, the Angel that redeemed me from all evil, bless the lads." This prayer was not much different in meaning from Paul's prayer for all the churches, " That grace might be unto them, and peace from God our Father, and the Lord Jesus Christ." Jacob was not more sincere or more fervent in praying for grace and mercy to his sons than Paul in his prayer for all the churches. The members of them all were his children or his brethren.

" And let my name be named on them." His name was already named on them, and he wished it might always be named on them. He desired that they would not take the name of their mother's family, although to the Egyptians it appeared a far greater name than Abraham's or Jacob's. If their names should have been inscribed in the registers of the royal family, Jacob would by no means have consented to their exchanging their interests in his own family for such splendid honours. Although he did not glory in the flesh, he justly esteemed his God, and the covenant of his God, the glory of his family ; a glory which it would have been impious in the highest degree to exchange for anything in earth or heaven.

" Let my name be named on them." Let them be called my children, and let them stand in the same relation to Abraham and Isaac with my other children. Such honour was bestowed on Manasseh and Ephraim, and such honour have all the saints. They are not all Israel that are of Israel, but believing Gentiles are a part of the Israel of God. The name of Christ Himself is named upon them. Blessed are the overcomers; Jesus will write upon them the name of His God, and the name of the city of His God, the new Jerusalem that comes down out of heaven from God; and He will write upon them His own new name. Let us all endeavour to be an honour and a praise to that worthy name by which we are called. "Lord, visit us with thy salvation, that we may see the good of thy chosen, and rejoice in their joy, and partake of the gladness of thy nation."

LECTURE 33
The same subject continued.
xlviii 17–22

VER. 17. *And when Joseph saw that his father laid his right hand upon the head of Ephraim, it displeased him : and he held up his father's hand, to remove it from Ephraim's head unto Manasseh's head.*

THE ways of God are often so strange that His own people may be displeased with them. When the Lord smote Uzza, it is said that David was displeased because the Lord had made a breach upon him. We must not, however, ascribe the fault to any of them, without sufficient evidence that they deserve the charge. Joseph was displeased because his father laid his right hand, not upon the head of Manasseh, but on the head of Ephraim. But if he had thought that his father guided his hands wittingly by Divine direction, when he gave Ephraim the preference, Joseph undoubtedly would have found no fault with it, but adored that sovereignty that gave the preference to the youngest, while it conferred rich blessings on both.

From Joseph's behaviour we cannot certainly infer that, like Isaac, he loved the first-born better than the youngest. But he was sorry that an honour was not given to the eldest which he would naturally expect, and bestowed on the youngest, who did not expect it, and who would not have been hurt by the want of it. A man of landed property may love all his sons with an equal affection, or he may love his youngest better than his first-born, and yet be very unwilling that the youngest should obtain that estate which the eldest had a right from the common rule of inheritance to expect.

Parents are not to be blamed, but approved, for interesting themselves in the honour as well as the prosperity of their children, if their tenderness is subjected to the rules of reason and piety. Isaac sinned in his solicitude to give the blessing to Esau. Joseph is not to be blamed for wishing to rectify a supposed mistake of his father Jacob.

He did not know that his father's hands, as well as his tongue, were guided by the Holy Spirit; and if he mistook the elder for the younger, Joseph ascribed it to accident, or to a blameless infirmity. Joseph had no intention to find fault, but to set him right. His displeasure was not a sullen, rude expression of dissatisfaction at his father's conduct. Joseph was incapable of such unnatural conduct to such a father. His displeasure was an evidence of his profound reverence. He placed such a high value upon a single testimony of his father's regard, that he wished it not to be transferred from that son who seemed best entitled to it, though to another equally beloved. There is a kind as well as an ill-natured displeasure. Because Jacob was dear to Joseph, Joseph was displeased that Jacob gave that honour to one which the other might more reasonably expect. "He held up his father's hand to remove it from Ephraim's head unto Manasseh's."

VER. 18. *And Joseph said unto his father, Not so, my father : for this is the first-born ; put thy right hand upon his head.*

Fathers ought not to be above advice from their sons when they need it, nor ought they to take it amiss when their sons take the liberty to offer objections to their opinions and conduct, when there is an appearance of reason for it, provided these objections are made with that deference which is due to the judgment and authority of parents. Joseph, in the present case, was mistaken, but the mistake was very excusable ; and the objection which he made to his father's conduct was only to what appeared to him an unintentional deviation from the ordinary rules which decency prescribes.

Jacob did by no means take it amiss that Joseph pretended to set him right.

VER. 19. *And his father refused, and said, I know it, my son, I know it: he also shall become a people, and he also shall be great: but truly his younger brother shall be greater than he, and his seed shall become a multitude of nations.*

Joseph was displeased with Jacob, and Jacob refused to comply with Joseph's wishes. Yet there was no interruption of reverence on the one side, nor paternal love on the other. We may refuse requests to those whom we love, and we may grant requests to those whom we hate. We may grant what some ask because we do not love them, and we may refuse what others ask because we love them. Yet when we refuse to comply with the requests of our children and friends, we ought to do it in a friendly manner. Jacob did not hurt the feelings of Joseph by refusing to remove his hand from the head of Ephraim to Manasseh. "I know it, my son, I know it. The position of my hands is not accidental and unmeaning, but intentional and significant. You have no reason to be jealous for the honour of your first-born. He is dear to me; he is a favourite of Heaven; he shall be great: his younger brother shall indeed be greater; but the greatness of Manasseh will not be lessened in reality, or in the estimation of the wise, by the superior greatness of Ephraim."

If the king should be pleased to make my youngest son a marquis, and his eldest brother an earl, would the eldest complain of partiality in the sovereign? Would he not rather be astonished at the unexpected and unmerited bounty, not only to himself, but to one whom he loved, or ought to love, as a son of the same father. And is there any one of our race that deserves more from God than my sons deserve from their prince? "Who hath first given unto God, and it shall be recompensed unto him again?"

God, in the course of His providence, from the earliest ages of the world, has often preferred the younger to the elder branch of a family, and in innumerable instances has made it evident that He does not follow the rules which men would prescribe to

Him in the distribution of His favours. One reason for it is, that we may learn not to glory in the flesh, but in the Lord. Were he to dispense His bounties according to such rules as might appear reasonable to us, our high thoughts of human worth would be cherished. We might lose all impressions of the right that He has to do what He will with His own ; and when we receive His singular favours, would be tempted to sacrifice to our own net, and burn incense to our own drag.

"He also shall become a people, and he also shall be great." The Scripture too truly informs us of that spirit of envy which so generally abounds in the world, and poisons the enjoyments of human life. The half of men's grievances would be at an end if they would cheerfully enjoy the bounties of Divine Providence, without mixing comparisons of their own condition with the conditions of other men, whom they cannot think better than themselves. Perhaps men whom you count less respectable, or worse than yourself, feed on the finest of the wheat, and the fat of fed beasts, when you must live on barley-bread and fishes. But they are not so much inferior in any respect as Herod and Pilate were inferior in dignity to Jesus, who fed on barley-loaves and fishes, when the Roman governor and the tetrarch of Galilee fed on royal dainties. If God be pleased to shower down blessings on a bad man, He gives him only what He has a right to give, without asking your advice ; and His bounty to him lays Him under no obligation to deal as bounteously with you. You have all that you can claim, and a great deal more. Consider the bread you eat, the raiment you put on, all the various gifts of Providence which you enjoy. It is probable that you enjoy many comforts and honours which others want who are better than you. Ephraim was greater than Manasseh. Had Manasseh any reason to be disquieted? He too was great, though not so great as his brother. Jacob taught him to consider what was promised to himself that he might not envy his brother, but thank that God who dealt wondrously with them both.

"But truly his younger brother shall be greater than he." "How shall I curse whom God hath not cursed?" said Balaam.

He was so far from being able to curse, that he was compelled to bless the people whom God had blessed. Isaac desired his son Esau's venison, that he might be refreshed by eating of it, and bless his son before he died. But God gave Jacob the blessing intended by him for Esau. Joseph wished to have the precedency in the blessing for his first-born; " but verily," says Jacob, " his younger brother shall be greater than he." Devise, labour, toil, from morning till night, for yourselves or for your families, you and they shall enjoy what God has appointed for them, and nothing less or more; for " of God, and through him, and to Him, are all things, to whom be glory for ever." One part of the glory which we ought to ascribe to the Giver of all good is thankfulness for that share of good things (whatever it be) which is allowed to us, and for that share of them which we may be enabled to leave to our children after us. We will labour in the fire for very vanity if we attempt to alter the decrees of God, or to prevent their execution.

"And his seed shall become a multitude of nations." We must take the word *nation* in the sense in which it was understood in the days of Jacob or Moses, that we may know how this prediction was accomplished. At what time Moses wrote this book we know not. If he wrote it about the time when the children of Israel came up out of Egypt, which it is probable he did, if not before that event, the children of Ephraim exceeded those of Manasseh by more than eight thousand. Before Moses died the children of Manasseh were much more numerous than the children of Ephraim. But Moses faithfully records the words of Jacob, in the full assurance that, if they were not accomplished in his own time, they would be accomplished in God's time. In later times we find that Ephraim was the chief of the ten tribes that separated themselves from the children of Judah. We have no account of the comparative numbers of the tribes; but we know that Ephraim was frequently the royal tribe, and that it gave a name to the whole kingdom.

Perhaps it may be thought that it would be no great comfort for Joseph to know that his race should be so numerous, unless he had likewise been told that his children would be worthy of their progenitors. But this was what neither Abraham nor Isaac could know. They had even the pain of seeing some of their children, whilst they were yet in the world, walking in the ways of sin. They knew that their posterity were to enjoy advantages above all the other nations in the world, for the knowledge and service of God. They had sufficient reason to hope that many, but not all, of their descendants would partake of the saving grace of the Most High, and that of their seed a Saviour was to be born, who was to be the light of the Gentiles, and the glory of His people Israel.

We must not pretend to search into the secrets of the Divine counsels. God will have mercy on whom He will have mercy. He never will bind Himself to extend His saving mercy from generation to generation, to all the offspring of the most approved saints. But when Manasseh and Ephraim were assured that their seed would be very numerous, they could not but see of what great advantage it would be to keep their place among the sons of Jacob. What pleasure could they have enjoyed in the prospect of thousands and millions of Egyptian idolators deriving from them their origin! But it must have given them great satisfaction to leave an inheritance among God's chosen to a multitude of nations.

VER. 19. *And he blessed them that day, saying, In thee shall Israel bless, saying, God make thee as Ephraim and as Manasseh: and he set Ephraim before Manasseh.*

Jacob not only told Joseph that he should be the father of two tribes in Israel, but assured him likewise that neither of them should be smaller than the other tribes. They were to make such a figure in Israel, that when one man blessed another, he would desire no better a model of blessedness than Ephraim and Manasseh. We have a specimen of such a form of blessing in the book of Ruth, iv. 11. 12—" The Lord make the woman that is come to thy house like Rachel and like Leah, which two did build the house of Jacob ; and let thy house be like the house of Pharez, which Tamar bare unto Judah, of the seed which the Lord shall give thee of this woman."

Manasseh had no reason to repine, but much reason to

rejoice, in the prospect of a seed which should make his name famous in Israel, as a pattern of benediction. Yet Jacob again intimates that Ephraim was to be greater than Manasseh. As Jacob laid his right hand upon the head of the younger, contrary to Joseph's declared intention, so he names Ephraim before Manasseh. But why does the venerable patriarch give so many indications of the superior glory of the younger son? Was he not afraid of awakening the jealousy of the elder? Did he not remember what he had suffered for giving such a manifest superiority in his affection to Joseph? All that we can say is, that it seemed good to God, not only to give the superiority in His providence to Ephraim, but to signify His purpose beforehand to the heads of these tribes; and we may learn, from the frequent repetition of this instance of Divine sovereignty, that it is the will of God to have His sovereignty known and acknowledged by His people. The sons of Jacob had already brought heavy punishment upon themselves by their unwillingness to allow Joseph that superiority which was intended for him. Joseph was qualified to teach his sons a cheerful acquiescence in the will of God. And we have no reason to think that Manasseh was unwilling to learn this lesson. He made no attempt to disunite himself from the congregation of Israel that he might enjoy a share in the grandeur of his mother's family. Nor did Joseph reply against God, when he was informed that his eldest son was not to enjoy precedency to his brother.

There might probably be another reason why Ephraim was so repeatedly assured beforehand of the grandeur of his family in Israel. He was to meet with heavier trials in his family before he left the world than any other of Jacob's sons. Several of them were to perish by an untimely death. Their father Ephraim mourned for them many days, and called a son afterwards born to him Beriah, because it went evil with his house.

In the midst of his griefs he would no doubt remember the words of his father Jacob. The hope of their accomplishment would mitigate his sorrow. He was assured that, although his beginning was small, his latter end should greatly increase. There were no sorrows like unto his sorrows among his brethren, but he was afterwards to enjoy the pre-eminence amongst the greatest part of the tribes of Israel. Great is the advantage which those who live by faith have over those who walk by sight. They can at all times see light in the midst of darkness. When the night comes, they know that the morning also will come, and that the Lord their God will make their darkness light.

VER. 21. *And Israel said unto Joseph, Behold, I die: but God shall be with you, and bring you again unto the land of your fathers.*

"I die." The good patriarch had suffered many sore calamities in the course of his life. He had been tossed with many tempests, but was now comforted by the sight of a peaceful haven. He could speak of his death without fear or sorrow. The joys of death far overbalance its sorrows, to those who, like the ancient patriarchs, are seeking the better country.

Jacob, by speaking of his death, prepares Joseph for meeting with that stroke of affliction which he had reason to expect. We have heard of the transports of Joseph when his father came down to live with him at Egypt. Seventeen years had now passed away greatly to his satisfaction in the vicinity of his father. But now the day approaches when Israel must no more be seen by his affectionate son. It was needless to conceal from him what he would soon see with his own eyes; but his father teaches him how to endure the shock with patience.

"I die; but God shall be with you." Joseph's heavenly father could not die. "The Lord liveth, and blessed be our Rock." His earthly father was about to leave him; but the God of his father, who was his own God, would never leave him nor forsake him. If the Lord be with us, He will abundantly compensate the want of all earthly friends. If we see the light of day, we can want the torches or candles that give us light in the night.

Joseph felt for his brethren no less than for himself. He saw that they would lose in Jacob, not only a father, but a ruler, a guide, an instructor, an intercessor with God on their behalf. "But God shall be with you," said Jacob. "He will be with thee and with thy brethren. He will preserve and bless you in this strange land, and in his time he will bring you again into the land of your fathers."

We have no account of the reason why Jacob did not prepare to return to the land of his fathers after the days of famine were at an end. Perhaps he thought that it might appear an ungrateful return to Pharaoh for all his favours to speak of returning to the land of Canaan as soon as the famine was at an end; or the distresses of Canaan, after plenty was restored to Egypt, might render it inconvenient for Jacob's family to take up their dwellings in it; or the remembrance of the odium raised against him for the slaughter of the Shechemites, or other circumstances unknown to us, might render it more eligible to continue in the land of Egypt than to return to the land of his fathers. The last verse of the chapter gives us reason to conclude that Jacob met with troubles in the land of Canaan of which we were not informed in the course of his history.

But whatever enemies Jacob had in the land of Canaan, or whatever the reason was of his continuance in Egypt, he still retained his attachment to that good land which God had promised. He knew that his seed were to be afflicted and oppressed in a foreign land. And perhaps the prediction concerning their pilgrimage and their afflictions set his mind at rest about his continuance till death in that country whither Providence had sent him. He probably knew that it was determined by God for his seed to live a long time in Egypt, and to be there brought low by affliction, before they obtained their settlement in Canaan. God had expressed His purpose; and good was the word of the Lord concerning him and his seed. Although they were to be afflicted, yet the Lord was to be their Protector. Although it now appeared that, till the end of four hundred and thirty years from the calling of Abraham, they would not be suffered to leave Egypt, at the end of these years they were to be brought out with great substance.

"God shall bring you to the land of your fathers." Canaan was in present possession the land of the seed of Ham; it was by promise the land of Abraham and Isaac. Although they were strangers and pilgrims in it, they called it their own. God had spoken in His holiness, and they rejoiced. Kirjath-arba was theirs, Kirjath-sepher was theirs, Salem was theirs, Shechem was to be the possession of their seed. The whole land, from Mount Lebanon to the river of Egypt, and from the river to the hindermost sea, was already theirs by the promise of God.

"Behold, I die : but God shall be with you, and bring you to the land of your fathers." "All flesh is grass, and all the goodliness of it is like the flower of the field ; but the word of the Lord shall stand for ever." Let this living word be our consolation when our friends die. Joseph could not tell, and Jacob could not inform him, how the word of promise was to be accomplished. They knew no more about their deliverance than Abraham was enabled to inform them, that God would judge the land where they were oppressed, and bring them out with great substance. Their business at this time was to believe and embrace the promise, to account themselves strangers when they were at a distance from the Land of Promise, and leave the manner of its accomplishment to God. "Hath he said, and shall he not make it good ? "

VER. 22. *Moreover I have given to thee one portion above thy brethren, which I took out of the hand of the Amorite with my sword, and with my bow.*

Was Jacob a man of war ? Or if he made a conquest from the Amorites, was the conquered territory left vacant for the sons of Joseph, till the people of Israel should go to take possession of the land of Canaan ?

Agesilaus, when he was forced to return to Greece from the dominions of the King of Persia, said that he had been drawn out of the country by thirty thousand archers, meaning, by thirty thousand pieces of money, stamped with the figure of an archer. With that money the Athenians had been bribed by the ministers of the King of Persia, to make war upon the Lacedemonians, that Agesilaus might be compelled to return to the defence of his country. Some think that Jacob's sword and bow are to be understood in this place in a like sense ; and that the piece of ground which he left as a heritage to Joseph was that piece of ground which he had bought with a hundred

2 F

lambs (as it stands in the original), or with a hundred pieces of silver, as it is with propriety rendered in our translation.

Others think that by Jacob's conquest is understood the conquest that he was to make in the persons of his posterity. He no doubt might speak of this conquest in the prophetical style, as if it had been already effected, to express his full persuasion that the land would be subdued by his posterity. Yet this, as well as the foregoing sense, seems to depart too far from the obvious meaning of the words.

This portion of ground seems to be that portion of land which he bought from the men of Shechem. When he left that place it is probable that the Amorites had taken possession of it; and that Jacob, by Divine direction, had driven out the invaders of his land with an armed force of children and servants, and perhaps, too, of allies. We know from Abraham's campaign that a holy patriarch may be a soldier and a hero. Jacob, as a prince, had power with God, and with man too he prevailed.

It is certain that Jacob would not have engaged in either an unjust or needless war. But he might have reasons unknown to us for girding on his sword, and showing to the inhabitants of Canaan that, although he was a lover of peace, he was not afraid to fight in the defence of his just rights. The warmest lovers of peace may sometimes find that war is the best or the only means for enjoying peace.

According to the Greek translation of the LXX., Shechem was the place which Jacob gave to Joseph. It is certain that the place was at least near to Shechem, for we read (John iv. 5) that when Jesus was passing through Samaria He came to a city called Sychar, near to that parcel of ground which Jacob gave to his son Joseph. It is not to be supposed that Jacob thought of retaining this place for his son Joseph, as his purchase, or his conquest. It was certain that it would be occupied by the people of Canaan, who would reckon themselves entitled to keep possession of it as long as they were able. It was to be reconquered, as well as other parts of the country, before the children of Joseph could obtain possession of the legacy. Nor could it be valuable, for its extent, to a man who was lord of Egypt.

Yet on another account it would be of high value in Joseph's eyes. It was the gift of his father, a gift of special love; a gift by which he testified that he loved Joseph more than any of his brethren; a gift bestowed by him on his death-bed, at the time when he wished to leave the last proof of his affection to his favourite. It was, besides, given to him by Divine warrant, and God thereby gave testimony of His acceptance of Joseph's eminent services to the family which He had chosen to distinguish by His favours.

The tribes of Israel were to have their portions assigned to them by lot; but Joseph was to have this portion without a lot, as a testimony of his father's grateful love. In this view the children, or supposed children, of Joseph set a high value on this portion of land, as long as the commonwealth of Israel subsisted. "Art thou greater" (said the woman of Samaria to Jesus) "than our father Jacob, who gave us this well, and drank thereof himself, and his children, and his cattle?"

More than two hundred years passed before the children of Israel obtained possession of this portion of ground which Jacob left them. Yet at last they obtained it, and were happy in it, as a testimony of their father Joseph's virtues. They had more reason to value this heritage than Naboth to set a high value upon the possession which the lot had assigned to his ancestors. Endeavour to walk so as to please God, and to leave a blessing to your children, or to your children's children. If God does not presently accomplish His promises to the children of His servants, there is no reason to think that they are forgotten. God has not yet forgotten His promises to Joseph. In the latter days God will be the God of all the families of Israel, and they shall be His people. He will yet be a father to Israel, and Ephraim shall be His first-born. It may indeed seem incredible to us that God should now be able to accomplish any promise to the remnant of His people, in such a visible manner as to enable us to observe and acknowledge His faithfulness to particular tribes. But if it be marvellous in our eyes, should it be marvellous also in the eyes of the Lord? When God shall be pleased to make Judah and Ephraim one stick in his hand, the truth of the promises to Joseph may with propriety be acknowledged, in the mercies bestowed on that part of the seed of Jacob which was separated from Judah. All the tribes that shook off the government of the family of David were associated under the standard of Ephraim, and by intermarriages, the descendants of the different tribes would be mingled with one another. Although it is certain that our Lord came out of Judah, yet it is not unlikely that He derived His birth likewise from Ephraim, and other sons of Jacob, in the same sense when He descended from Lot, and even from Ham, Matt. i. Certain it is, however, that the Lord knows from what progenitors all men on earth descended, and that His eyes are still upon the natural seed of Jacob, to perform in due time the promises made unto their fathers, perhaps more gloriously than He has ever yet done, except in the single instance of His raising up Jesus out of the seed of David. He hath already performed the great promise in raising up a horn of salvation to His people in the house of His servant David. The fulfilment of this promise is a sure pledge of the performance of all that was ever promised to the nation, in its utmost extent of meaning. As concerning the Gospel, the Jews were enemies in the time of the apostles for our sake, and they still continue enemies; but as touching the election, they are beloved for the Father's sake. They have now continued many days, and they may yet continue many more days, without a king, or priest, or image, or ephod, or teraphim; but afterwards they shall return and seek the Lord their God, and David their king, and shall fear the Lord and His goodness in the latter days.

LECTURE 34
The burial of Jacob.
l 1–14

VER. 1. *And Joseph fell upon his father's face, and wept upon him, and kissed him.*

"JOSEPH," said God to Jacob at Beersheba, "shall put his hands upon thine eyes." This no doubt Joseph had done, although we are not expressly informed of it ; and now, when he saw that his father was a lifeless carcass, he gave way to the excess of his grief, and fell upon it, and wept and kissed it. The soul had fled to the regions of blessedness, but Joseph kissed and watered with his tears what remained to him of his best friend.

"All things are vanity and vexation of spirit." What can riches and power do for men in the time when they stand in the greatest need of comfort? All the treasures and all the power of Joseph or of Pharaoh could not have detained Jacob one day or one hour longer in this world. No man hath power over the spirit to restrain it within its earthly habitation; neither is their any discharge of this warfare. It is our joy that God alone is .the Lord of life ; yet we cannot but grieve when His stroke removes from us those whom above all others on earth we loved, and a great ransom cannot deliver them. We can scarcely conceive the transports of joy which Joseph felt when he first saw his father in Egypt. For seventeen years his father's vicinity was one of the chief pleasures of

his life.   What, then, must he have felt when his father, his
guide, his best friend on earth, left him for ever?   No more
was he to behold the venerable countenance of the man who
was his spiritual father, as well as the father of his flesh!   No
more was he to hear those words of truth and wisdom from
Jacob's mouth, which he had often heard not only with joy,
but with unspeakable advantage to his soul.   In losing his
father, he had lost anew his grandfather Isaac, and his great-
grandfather Abraham, whom Joseph had never seen in person;
but his father was not less venerable in his eyes, and used to
communicate to him all the holy instruction which that patriarch
transmitted to his posterity.   The doctrines which holy men in
those times learned from their pious ancestors, and taught
their children and their households after them, were the same in
effect that we now learn from the Bible.   The instructions we
receive from our teachers ought to be heard with earnest
attention.   We will not always behold their faces, or hear
them with our ears.   But if we lay up their words in our
hearts, they will continue to speak to us when they are dead.
Joseph doubtless enjoyed this comfort when he wept over his
father's body.   The precious truths which he had often heard
from his father's mouth were indelibly written on his heart.

When your fathers die, you must mourn.   Your hearts
must be hard as rocks if you do not : but beware, whilst
they are yet alive, of laying up for yourselves materials of
grief that will not admit of comfort.   Joseph could never have
forgiven himself if he had been conscious of embittering his
father's days, by despising his counsels whilst he was yet alive.
We are not told what Reuben, or Simeon, or Levi felt on the
present occasion.   Their sensibilities were not so strong as
those of Joseph, but their self-reflections must have been bitter.
Joseph's tears were attended with secret consolation.   Their
griefs were tinctured with the most painful and tormenting
passions.   Yet it may be hoped that their hearts were made
better, for they must have felt that the pleasures of their sins,
which lasted but for a moment, were not to be compared to the
lasting pain which was the natural consequence.   There is joy

in grief for the loss of the dearest friends, if stinging remorse is not mingled with it.

VER. 2. *And Joseph commanded his servants the physicians to embalm his father : and the physicians embalmed Israel.*

The physicians did what they could for Israel while he was yet alive, but they could not turn old age into youth, nor avert death.

Joseph commanded them now to embalm the dead body of his father. None in the world were so expert in performing this office for the dead as the Egyptian physicians. There are dead bodies in Egypt, and dead bodies brought from it to other countries, which still preserve in part their form, although they have been now several thousands of years in the state of death. The bodies of Jacob and Joseph might still have been preserved as objects of curiosity, if they had been kept in some of the Egyptian repositories of the dead.

Joseph could not preserve his father alive, or redeem him from death, but he will spare no trouble or expense in doing what he could for him. His dead body was preserved from corruption, as far as human power or art could go. Natural affection will prompt all dutiful children to perform the ordinary funeral honours to their parents. But it can be no honour to their memory for private persons to affect extraordinary magnificence on such occasions. Joseph abounded in wealth, and a very honourable burial was due to Jacob, on account of his own rank, and the rank of his son. Yet more respect was showed to his dead body than Jacob himself desired ; he wished much to be with his fathers at Machpelah, but of the embalming of his body he said nothing.

VER. 3. *And forty days were fulfilled for him ; for so are fulfilled the days of those which are embalmed : and the Egyptians mourned for him threescore and ten days.*

In embalming dead bodies, it was necessary to give the drugs time to operate, that they might produce their designed effect upon the body, to prevent it from corruption. Was so much time, and pains, and expense employed on a dead body to preserve it from the common consequence of death? What excuse is left to us if we cannot bestow as much time and care as to be secured against the terrible consequences of death to both soul and body? Are there not some who act as if they thought less time was necessary to prepare for heaven than the Egyptian physicians thought necessary for seasoning the dead body of a man, to preserve it from putrefaction. Who will pity such persons when they eat of the fruit of their own ways!

"And the Egyptians mourned for him threescore and ten days." Thirty days of mourning were thought a sufficient mourning for the illustrious dead among the Jews. So long did the children of Israel mourn for Aaron, and again for Moses. The seventy days here mentioned are thirty days allotted to mourning, added to forty days for embalming, which are likewise days of mourning; for it is to be supposed that the mourning began at the time when the good man died. If it had discontinued at the end of the forty days for embalming, there would have been no time at all set apart for the peculiar ceremonies of mourning.

This long mourning for the death of Jacob was a great honour done to the venerable patriarch, chiefly for the sake of his son. All the Egyptians saw how dear Jacob was to their lord, and thought they could not pay a more agreeable instance of respect to him than by mourning for his father. We afterwards find good kings in Israel greatly lamented when they died. The singing men, and the singing women, and all Judah, and most of all the prophet Jeremiah, lamented for Josiah when he died.

It is decent in subjects who can afford the expense to wear mourning apparel for their deceased princes, and for those deceased relations of their princes who may be supposed to have been dear to them. But the wearing of black is only a public profession of sorrow. When good and great men die the heart ought to feel the stroke of Providence. Those who were pillars of society are then removed, and we ought earnestly to deprecate the evils that must follow if Providence is not pleased to repair the loss.

When we wear mourning apparel our clothes will rise up in judgment against us if we do not call to mind our own mortal condition, and think seriously of our own dissolution. Our bodies are not made of brass, any more than the bodies of those whom we pretend to deplore. A loud voice comes from their graves, proclaiming that to-morrow, or when a few years are gone, we must be with them.

VER. 4. *And when the days of his mourning were past, Joseph spake unto the house of Pharaoh, saying, If now I have found grace in your eyes, speak, I pray you, in the ears of Pharaoh saying.*

Joseph was lord of all the land of Egypt, and yet he was Pharaoh's servant : he did not forget his condition amidst all his grandeur. We must always remember what we owe to our superiors, as well as what our inferiors owe to us.

He certainly had sufficient credit with Pharaoh to procure his permission to bury his father in Canaan without solicitation from other favourites. Yet he disdains not to use the interest of other servants of Pharaoh in his favour. He did not, like some favourites of princes, claim all the power of the kingdom for himself, nor endeavour to engross the king's ear. Those who use their power and favour with princes most moderately are most likely to enjoy it without envy or danger.

It is likely that Joseph had a reason at this time for employing friends as his agents with the king. Princes in the East have often discovered an irreconcilable aversion to anything that wears a gloomy appearance, or that puts them in mind of death. Mordecai would not have been permitted to sit in the gate of the King of Persia whilst he wore mourning apparel. The Father of Mercies looks with a compassionate eye on mourners when they come into His presence. But a wise man will be cautious of obtruding his sorrows on his fellow-men without knowing their dispositions. The house of feasting is, by a great part of men, preferred to the house of mourning, although that is the end of all men, and the living ought to lay it to their hearts.

VER. 5. *My father made me swear, saying, Lo, I die: in my*

grave which I have digged for me in the land of Canaan, there shalt thou bury me. Now therefore let me go up, I pray thee, and bury my father, and I will come again.

The Egyptians were very jealous of the honour of their country, which they esteemed "the glory of all lands." They might have thought that Joseph, who had received such honours in their land, did not discover a grateful sense of their favours if he had carried his father's body to be buried in another land without giving a good reason for it. The old man had been treated with great generosity by Pharaoh. Did his son grudge his body to that land which had supplied his numerous family with food when he could find none in the land of Canaan? Joseph wished to obviate any such reflections, and therefore produced reasons for his requests, which he knew would fully satisfy the king's mind, and the minds of his people. Jacob had digged a grave for himself in the land of Canaan, and in that place of it where his father and a part of his own family were buried. He had not only expressed a strong desire to be buried in that grave, but he had brought his son Joseph under the sacred engagement of an oath to do what he desired. "Now therefore," says Joseph, "let me go up, I pray thee, and bury my father, and I will come again." He was sure the reasons he gave him would not only procure the king's consent to his proposal, but banish every suspicion of disrespect in making it. He would not be accounted deficient in his affection to his king and benefactor because he was a dutiful son, who paid a regard to his father's dying wishes. He would not be esteemed a disloyal subject because he desired leave to perform a solemn oath. On the contrary, he would have lost all credit with the Egyptians themselves if he had acted otherwise than he did. Nor would his father be thought ungrateful to a king and nation from whom he had received such favours when he wished to lie in death with his forefathers, in the grave which he digged for himself.

It may seem strange that Jacob should have been in such haste to dig a grave for himself more than seventeen years before he died. But it is likely that he did not expect to live so long as he did. His heart almost died within him when he was made to believe that Joseph was torn in pieces by some wild beasts; and although he had not met with so many evils in the course of his life, he might have dug a grave for himself without the imputation of folly or melancholy. The most healthy and prosperous ought to remember that they will one day need a grave; nor will we impair our cheerfulness by thinking of our latter end if we entertain the well-grounded hope of happiness beyond the grave.

VER. 6. *And Pharaoh said, Go up, and bury thy father, according as he made thee swear.*

Pharaoh was at all times ready to gratify the wishes of his prime minister, and yet it is probable that he would have felt some reluctance to gratify his wishes at this time if his father had not taken an oath from him. The king had been so long accustomed to repose in Joseph as his counsellor, and the manager of his affairs, that the burden of government might appear too heavy for him in Joseph's absence. But when Joseph had given not only his word, but his oath to his father, there was no room left for choice. A solemn oath must be observed. The name of God must not be taken in vain. Those Christians who disregard the obligation of oaths are worse than a great part of the heathens. We read of a famous Lacedemonian, who said that children are to be caught with baubles, and men with oaths; but his impiety was execrated by his fellow-heathens. The foundations of human society are subverted when oaths are treated with contempt.

VER. 7. *And Joseph went up to bury his father: and with him went up all the servants of Pharaoh, the elders of his house, and all the elders of the land of Egypt.*

All Egypt did Jacob honour at his death. All (or a great part of) the ministers of Pharaoh, and of the governors of the provinces, attended the funeral. None absented themselves but such as were not able to attend, or those who were under a necessity of continuing at home, to carry on the necessary business of the king and of the nation.

This honour was procured to Jacob by his son's favour with

the king, which he still retained after he had been more than twenty years in office. It was a mournful saying of the famous Wolsey, that "if he had served his God as well as he had served his king, He would not have forsaken him in his old age." Joseph was a faithful servant to his king, but he was a faithful servant also to his God, in whose hand are the hearts of kings, and of all their people. The wisdom, the justice, the moderation, and gentleness of Joseph were the means by which he retained the favour of both prince and people; but they were only the means. It was his God that first gave him favour, and afterwards maintained what he wrought for him.

The great cavalcade which attended Jacob to his long home, through a part of two different countries, would spread the fame of the good man, and revive the remembrance of him in the land of Canaan. And it was much for the interest of religion that his name should be known. In his life he had showed forth the lovely virtues by which religion is recommended. Let us always be careful to behave so that those who remember our names when we are in the dust may find no pretence to speak evil of us, or of the ways of God on our account.

VER. 8. *And all the house of Joseph, and his brethren, and his father's house: only their little ones, and their flocks, and their herds, they left in the land of Goshen.*

Joseph's brethren, no doubt, cheerfully concurred with him in doing honour to their father, and in observing his last injunction. They had been fully persuaded that he did them no injustice in valuing and loving Joseph so much more than themselves. They were penetrated with grief for the loss of their best friend. Whilst they attended the funeral they must have bitterly reflected on themselves for the griefs which they brought upon his grey hairs; and it is to be hoped that the country through which they travelled brought to their remembrance many things which they had seen in their progenitors, or heard from their mouths. Attendance on funeral solemnities would be of great use to us if our minds were disposed to make a due improvement of them. We ought to remember those who have gone before us to heaven, and to follow their faith, "considering the end of their conversation."

They left their little ones, and their flocks and herds, in the land of Egypt;—whether because the king would not have been willing to lose so many useful subjects, or whether they thought it safer to dwell in Egypt than in Canaan, where they had certainly made themselves obnoxious to the fierce resentments of many of its inhabitants. God, for the sake of Jacob, had preserved them from the revenge of their neighbours the Shechemites. When he was taken from their head they might reckon themselves safer under the protection of the King of Egypt than in that land which was promised to their seed at the distance of about two hundred years. It is probable, too, that they might be directed by a Divine oracle to continue in Egypt.

VER. 9. *And there went up with him both chariots and horsemen: and it was a very great company.*

Jacob never affected splendour in his life; he was willing to be a servant in the country of Syria, and for a wife he kept sheep. Yet he is honoured with a funeral as splendid as if he had been a king. Such honours done to a man after his death can be of no value to him. It was the happiness of Jacob that his dead body was under the protection of his God, and was to rise again in glory and incorruption at the last day, Luke xx. 37. Yet the affectionate heart of Joseph was agreeably soothed by the sight of so large a company of the first men of Egypt. His grief was mitigated by the respect paid to his father's memory, and to himself; and may it not be hoped that the discourse of some of the company was turned by the occasion to the character of Jacob, and to those marvellous events which procured him so much consideration from the King of Egypt? The history of Jacob and Joseph contained a series of proofs that their religion was from the living God, the Maker of heaven and earth. The cause of true religion was therefore likely to be promoted by the ceremonies attendant on the funeral.

VER. 10. *And they came to the threshing-floor of Atad, which is beyond Jordan, and there they mourned with a great and very sore lamentation: and he made a mourning for his father seven days.*

It is not certain whether Atad is the name of a man, or whether the place received its name from the thorns abounding at that time in the country. But it seems strange that Joseph should choose this place as a scene of solemn mourning for his father. Had not the Egyptians mourned sufficiently in their own country? or if they must spend some days in mourning in the land of Canaan, why was not the field of Ephron chosen for the place of it?

Perhaps Joseph went to excess in his solemn mourning for his father. But he may be excused. He loved his father dearly in the days of his youth, and his love was greatly increased by his long separation from him. Seldom has the love of a son to his father equalled Joseph's love to Jacob. His grief was proportioned to his love, and he found relief in seeing others sharing in his grief, and in hearing the mournful voice of those that were skilful in lamentation. Men of the best dispositions ought to keep a strict watch over their spirits when their dearest friends die. There was indeed much cause for grief when the best man on earth was carried out of it; but there was much cause too for joy, for he had left blessings behind him to his house, and had arrived at the end of his painful pilgrimage. Joseph certainly knew that he was now in possession of that salvation for which he had so long waited, and that he would not have exchanged his present situation for all the joys and glories of the world.

The threshing-floor of Atad might be a more proper place than the field of Ephron for this solemn mourning in the land of Canaan. What if the inhabitants of the country where a part of Jacob's property lay had looked with an evil eye on such a large company of men continuing seven days amongst them? They would have had a better pretence for supposing that some bad design was in agitation, than Joseph had to impute bad designs to his brethren when they came to Egypt to buy corn. In every part of his conduct Joseph dealt wisely. Whilst his heart was pierced with sorrow he did not forget those rules by which at other times he acted, to prevent occasions of mischief.

VER. 11. *And when the inhabitants of the land, the Canaanites, saw the mourning in the floor of Atad, they said, This is a grievous mourning to the Egyptians; wherefore the name of it was called Abel-mizraim, which is beyond Jordan [or on the side of Jordan].*

The Canaanites would be astonished to see the Egyptians expressing their sorrow by all the ordinary signs of it for seven days together, and no doubt mourning women would be employed to excite sorrow, or the outward tokens of it, amongst the multitude. Surely, thought the Canaanites, this man must have been greatly admired or greatly beloved in Egypt. Never were such cries of grief heard, never were so many tears shed for a single man, amongst the people of another nation. Thus Joseph procured honour to his father's memory in Canaan as well as in Egypt.

Remember, when you mourn to an uncommon degree for the death of your beloved friends, your behaviour will be observed. Consider whether you are honouring your profession or not by your tears and sighs.

The place was from henceforth called Abel-mizraim, the mourning of the Egyptians. There were several other places in Canaan that had Abel for the beginning of their name; for in a world where there is so much sin, sorrow is to be expected. The name of this place would keep in the memories of the people of Israel an event worthy to be remembered. It would call up to their minds the edifying history of Jacob their father, and of his son Joseph, and that gracious working of Divine Providence by which Joseph was exalted to honour, and was "made the shepherd and stone of Israel." It will be very useful to us also to keep their histories in everlasting remembrance, as we find it recorded in the book of God.

VER. 12. *And his sons did unto him according as he commanded them.*

Not only Joseph, but all his sons, did as he commanded

them; they were all equally forward to do him honour at his death, and to execute his dying charge. The greatest part of men entertain a warm regard for their dead parents, although there are too many who embitter their days whilst they are yet alive. If your parents are yet spared to you, behave towards them as you will wish to have behaved when you lay their heads in the dust.

Men are to be commended for their care to execute the will of deceased parents, and yet their own conduct in this instance may in too many cases be applied to reprove and condemn another part of their behaviour. Is more regard due to a dying father of our flesh than to a dying Redeemer, whose blood was shed for our salvation?

VER. 13. *For his sons carried him into the land of Canaan, and buried him in the cave of the field of Machpelah, which Abraham bought with the field for a possession of a burying-place of Ephron the Hittite, before Mamre.*

How precious was the dust of those saints that were buried in the cave of Machpelah! yet we never find that this dust was worshipped by the sons of Jacob, or that any place of sacred worship was erected over their dead bodies.

Jacob, by the care of his sons, was buried in his own grave, dug by himself, and purchased by Abraham along with the rest of the field. It was fit that these men should have a possession of a burying-place. Although in life they were but strangers and sojourners, yet the grave was to be their long home. Jesus did not in death receive those honours which were done to Jacob. Few attended His funeral; many of His warmest friends dared not to do Him honour on that occasion. His enemies set a guard before His grave, which was not His own property, although he was Lord of all. But the grave was not to be His long home. He needed the use of a friend's sepulchre only for a few days. He was buried, but He rose again the third day, according to the Scriptures.

Kings and counsellors of the earth have often built magnificent tombs for themselves. They pleased themselves with the prospect of being interred in state, and of lying under a splendid dome. But, like other men, they must say to corruption, "Thou art our father, and to the worm, Thou art our mother, and our sister." "Blessed are the dead who die in the Lord." "They sleep in Jesus." Their dust is as much under His care as the dust of the ancient patriarchs. God is still their God; and as He hath raised up Jesus, He will raise them up also by Jesus.

LECTURE 35

Joseph's brethren obtain from him new assurances of his forgiveness and protection.

l 14–21

VER. 14. *And Joseph returned into Egypt, he, and his brethren, and all that went up with him to bury his father, after he had buried his father.*

THE time was not yet come to put the children of Israel in possession of the promised land. They must therefore return to Egypt, to the place of their former dwelling, till the time of that promise come ; and they certainly knew that it would be vain to strive against God. Their head was taken from them. Their loss would be their gain if they were disposed, like David, to say, "Though my father and mother should both leave me, the Lord will take me up."

All that went with Joseph returned after Jacob was buried. They could do no more for the good man whose death they so greatly lamented. We may attend the funerals of our deceased friends, and let the world see how much we loved them when they were with us, but we cannot preserve their bodies from consuming in the grave ; far less can we stretch forth our hands to their departed spirits. If we can do anything for their souls, let it be done whilst they yet live with us. "Whatsoever thine hand findeth to do, do it with thy might, for there is no work nor device in the grave ; " and no work can be done for those who dwell in that place of corruption.

Ver. 15. *And when Joseph's brethren saw that their father was dead, they said, Joseph will peradventure hate us, and will certainly requite us all the evil which we did unto him.*

Their father was dead, but they had a second father still alive. If they had known the heart of Joseph, they would still have thought that they had a father on earth as well as in heaven. But their consciences turned what should have been their pleasure into pain. They were stung with remorse for their own former conduct, and tormented with the apprehensions that the time for Joseph's revenge was now come. His veneration for his father had restrained his hands till this time, but now it would be seen that their sin was too great to be forgiven.

Their thoughts of Joseph were formed from what they saw in the greater part of men; and it is to be feared that what they felt in themselves might infuse those unreasonable suspicions into their minds. For a far less injury than they had done to Joseph some of them had destroyed a whole city.

"The days of mourning for my father are at hand," said Esau, "and then I will kill my brother Jacob." Joseph's brethren knew this piece of history; but they knew also that Esau relented before his father's death. Why did they suppose Joseph to be a second Esau, or worse than Esau? Surely his former behaviour might have banished all such thoughts from their minds, and had actually banished them. But their present dejection of spirit at their father's death disposed them to entertain dismal thoughts, which would not have been admitted at another time. Their affliction and fear brought their sin again to remembrance, and renewed their apprehensions of vengeance. We have reason to think that they had sincerely repented; and no true penitents will be condemned by God, but they may be condemned and, in some degree, punished by themselves.

"He will certainly requite us all the evil which we did unto him." The light of conscience tells us that we deserve to be requited according to our works; and it is so common for men to requite their own enemies according to their works, as soon as it is in their power, that it is difficult for us to believe that any will act otherwise, when he can do it without damage to himself. But have we not many instances on record in the Bible and other histories, of men who have loved their enemies, and blessed those who cursed them? Whatever men may do who live under a worldly and selfish spirit, men who are led by the Spirit of Christ will observe His laws, and walk in His steps. You do great injustice to a true Christian if you think that he is no better than other men. There is indeed flesh as well as spirit in him. He may feel too strong resentment against those who have wronged him. He may, like David, in a fit of passion, threaten to destroy his enemy, but his hands will be stayed, and the corrupt workings of his heart will be powerfully checked when he considers the mercy of God to himself, and the strict charges he has received to render no man evil for evil.

Ver. 16. *And they sent a messenger unto Joseph, saying, Thy father did command before he died, saying.*

Who were those messengers whom they employed to solicit pardon from their brother? Benjamin was probably one of them; with him they might send such of their servants as they could best trust.

They were ashamed or afraid to venture into the presence of Joseph, that they might solicit pardon for themselves; but they found others whom they could trust on a business that seemed to them so necessary and important. Men were born to be useful to one another; and none are so high as not to need benefits from their fellow-men. Joseph himself employed intercessors on an important business with the king; yet his brethren might have saved themselves the trouble of sending an agent for the present business.

They sent messengers unto Joseph, saying, Thy father did command before he died, saying, Ver. 17. *So shall ye say unto Joseph, Forgive, I pray thee now, the trespass of thy brethren, and their sin; for they did unto thee evil: and now, we pray thee, forgive the trespass of the servants of the God of thy father. And Joseph wept when they spake unto him.*

Did Jacob really leave orders to carry this message to Joseph ? There is great reason to think that he did not ; he knew Joseph too well to think that such a message was necessary ; or if he had thought it necessary to solicit Joseph's kindness in behalf of his offending brethren, Jacob would rather have solicited in person than left his name to his brethren to be employed for that end. If he had supposed that Joseph retained any secret resentments, he would have endeavoured to extinguish them, or to guard against their consequences, in one of his last interviews with him. He spake twice to him, and once to all the brethren, about his burial in the land of Canaan. The conciliation of their minds to one another would have been a more important subject for his last charge if any mutual alienation had been suspected. The words of the request are therefore to be considered as the words of Joseph's brethren, and not of his father. They took an unwarrantable liberty with their father's name ; but a guilty conscience has often urged sinners to use still more unjustifiable artifices.

"Forgive, I pray thee, the trespass of thy brethren, and their sin ; for they did unto thee evil." They make an ingenuous confession of their offence. They could not do less if they expected to be forgiven, for it was too well known to be concealed. Yet how common is it for men to hide or varnish over their offences, when they are well enough known, not to themselves only, but to those whom they have offended. Wo justly complain that so few are disposed from the heart to forgive offences. But we have reason likewise to lament that so few who have given offence show a ready disposition to take the proper steps for obtaining forgiveness. When you labour to hide or extenuate what cannot be hidden or extenuated, you but hold it up to the light, and turn the eyes of your neighbours to observe it.

Although the words of the petition were not the words of Jacob, yet Joseph knew that they expressed what would have been his father's mind in the case which his brethren supposed. And doubtless Joseph's regard for his father was such that he would have forgiven his brethren for his sake, although nobler motives had been wanting. But his forgiveness would not have been circumscribed within the limits of his father's life. His father's will, as we have already seen, was sacred to him when the old man was not alive to thank him. Those who love a father will be ready to forgive his children their offences.

"Forgive, I pray thee, the trespass of thy brethren." There is a strong motive for pardon in this expression. Brethren, for the sake of their common parents, ought to forbear and to forgive one another. But there is a much more powerful motive in the request which they presented in their own names: "And now, we pray thee, forgive the trespass of the servants of the God of thy father." Joseph reckoned himself bound to do much for his father, but incomparably more for his father's God.

His brethren made a good profession in these words. They called themselves the servants of their father's God. They had in some instances been very undutiful to God, but they served a God who pardons iniquity, transgressions, and sin. Although we are conscious of many provocations, let us not leave the service of this glorious Master, or despair of finding acceptance through a Mediator, in our endeavours to please him. We hope that the practice of the sons of Jacob was now suitable to their profession; if this was the case, we will find some of them at the last day as illustrious monuments of the grace of God as almost any of those pardoned transgressors of whom the Scriptures give us an account—"There is forgiveness with God, that he may be feared."

"Forgive the trespass of the servants of the God of thy father." All His servants are dear to Him, and He will be greatly displeased if we harbour cruel resentment against those whom He loves. If God forgave Simeon and Levi their offences against Himself, if He forgave all of them their wickedness in selling Joseph, it certainly was to be expected that Joseph would forgive them also. The injury done to him was not to be compared with the offence committed against God in selling him.

Joseph himself was a servant of God, and was bound to forgive his fellow-servants. What comparison could be made between the forgiveness which he received and daily expected from God, and that forgiveness which was asked from him? Although Joseph was an eminently holy man, yet the debt for which he needed and received forgiveness from God, was, to that debt which his brethren owed to him, as ten thousand talents to two hundred pence.

Joseph could not but rejoice to see God served and worshipped by his fellow-men. He wished to be the companion of them that feared God, and to give them all possible encouragement to hold on in the course of righteousness. If he had resented the conduct of his brethren to such a degree as they feared, he would have done much hurt to religion. He would have put it out of their power to do that service to God which they wished. At a time when the servants of God were so few in number, the damage would have been incalculable. At all times the lovers of God may be expected to encourage the hearts, and strengthen the hands, of their fellow-servants. If we, to gratify our pride, or revenge, or any selfish disposition, disable the servants of God from doing their work, or discourage their hearts, or weaken their hands, we oppose the end of our creation. Instead of glorifying God, we will not suffer Him to be glorified by those that would. Woe to the world because of offences. They must come, but woe to the man by whom they come; and they come by those who refuse to forgive their offending brethren, especially when the offenders repent of what they have done. The Christians at Corinth thought they were giving a proof of their zeal for holiness when they would not forgive that penitent criminal whom they had spared too long in their society. But Paul warned them by all means to forgive him, and to confirm their love towards him, that Satan might gain no advantage against them, for they were not ignorant of his devices.

"And Joseph wept as they spake unto him" by their messengers. If Joseph had been of a haughty spirit, he would have been angry with his brethren. He had already from his heart forgiven them, and had given them very abundant proofs that their conduct was erased from his memory. Did they imagine that he was for seventeen years playing the part of a hypocrite, with words of kindness in his mouth, and gifts in his hand, and malignity in his heart? For a recompense of his kindness, he had expected the esteem and cordial affection of his brethren. Were vile suspicions of his sincerity all the return they made him? But Joseph imputed their message not to ingratitude, or to any habitual disbelief of his sincerity, but to the grief and fear occasioned by the new situation in which the death of their father had placed them whilst they were in a strange land, where the power of government was lodged with himself. If Joseph had ever ascribed their fears to habitual distrust of himself, his heart would not have been inflamed with indignation, but melted with compassion and grief. The soft passions operated powerfully on Joseph's heart. The fierce passions never found with him a cordial reception.

VER. 17, 18. *Joseph wept when they spake unto him.—And his brethren also went and fell down before his face; and they said, Behold, we be thy servants.*

Where now were their mouths with which they said to Joseph, Shalt thou indeed reign over us? or shalt thou have dominion over us? They were not the same men; affliction and fear had humbled them to the dust. They had seen the hand of God stretched out to baffle their devices, and to exalt their brother. They had been long habituated to a dependence on him, and would now have been glad to sell him their liberty for their lives, which seemed to be at his mercy.

Be not proud. It is pride that makes us scorn the thought of being placed below those who are now our equals. Be still, and know that the Lord is God, and that He brings down the high and exalts the low, according to His own pleasure. The day may come when you will be glad to be indebted to the favour of those whom you now despise; and if your prosperity make you proud, it will be good for you to meet with those adversities which are needful to abase you. It is better to be of a lowly spirit with the humble than to divide the spoil with the great. Joseph's brethren are not to be greatly praised for humbling themselves at his feet. They would have behaved in a manner more respectful and grateful to him if they had placed all that confidence in him to which his generosity entitled him; yet we are pleased to find so great an alteration in their present from their former conduct. They act like men who accepted the punishment of their iniquity, and humbled themselves under the mighty hand of God.

VER. 19. *And Joseph said unto them, Fear not: for am I in the place of God?*

None but tyrants delight to see their neighbours depressed in spirit and tormented with fear any farther than their abasement may be necessary for themselves. It was the earnest wish of Joseph to banish every gloomy and disquieting thought from the minds of his brethren. All the sorrow which he wished them to feel was that godly sorrow which worketh repentance unto salvation not to be repented of.

"Fear not: for am I in the place of God?" These words seem to signify that God is the great avenger of sin, and that Joseph was not so presumptuous as to place himself in the room of Him to whom vengeance belongeth. He was indeed a magistrate to whom the sword was given by God to execute vengeance upon evil-doers. Yet he could not execute vengeance as a magistrate upon his brethren. for the offence committed against himself long before he was ordained to his high station. The invitation which he gave them to come and dwell with him was an implied promise that he would not use his authority against them, but treat them as if they had never offended him. Joseph lived long before the time when God said, by Moses, "Vengeance is mine; I will recompense it, saith the Lord." Yet we may warrantably suppose that he knew the truth taught in these important words. What can be more presumptuous than for a man to usurp the prerogatives of the Judge of all the earth! Yet this prerogative is usurped by every man who gives indulgence to an unforgiving spirit. If the fear of God possess our hearts we will endeavour to walk in the steps of our blessed Redeemer; who, when He was reviled, reviled not again; and when He was threatened, insulted, and crucified, committed Himself to Him that judgeth righteously, and even made intercession for those transgressors that crucified Him.

Although the words, in this view of their meaning, convey an awful admonition to men of a revengeful spirit, yet our translators here seem to have mistaken their meaning. It is not consistent with the well-known character of Joseph to suppose that he meant to refer their punishment to God, rather than take it into his own hand; or that he so much as wished to alarm them with the apprehensions of a more dreadful punishment than any which he could conflict. His heart was melted with compassion, and he wished to heal the painful wounds of their broken spirits.

Am I under God? This translation is not less agreeable to the original than our ordinary translation, and gives us a sense entirely comfortable to Joseph's views, and to the sentiments expressed in the following part of his words, Am I or am I not under God? Am I not as much His subject as you are? It is plain that His providence has sent me by your agency to Egypt, not to destroy you, but to save your lives. If I should make use of the advantages which He has given me to execute a mean vengeance for injuries done to myself, I would incur the dreadful guilt of fighting against God, and of abusing His great goodness to the service of sin.

When you are strongly solicited to avenge yourselves, consider whether you are, or whether you are not, under God. Are you His servants, and not the servants of your own corrupt lusts? Then, fulfil not the lusts of your mind, but the command of Him who hath said, "Avenge not yourselves." Are you governed by His providence? Think not that any situation in which He places you will authorise you to break His law. However highly you may be exalted, you are as much below God as you were in your lowest condition; and your power is given you, not to rebel against your Benefactor, but to give you new opportunities for serving and honouring Him. Happy will it be for us if we can always keep in our minds this truth, that we are under God. When we presumptuously violate His law, by executing that vengeance which He prohibits, do we not say that we are above Him? Who is the Lord that we should obey Him? We know not that He is our superior, and therefore we will take vengeance on our enemies with our own hands, and at our own pleasure.

VER. 20. *But as for you, ye thought evil against me; but God meant it unto good, to bring to pass, as it is this day, to save much people alive.*

"O Lord, I will praise thee; for thou wast angry with me, but thine anger is turned away," Isa. xii. 1. Our translators give a version less literal, but more just, of the original word of this passage—"O Lord, I will praise thee; for though thou wast angry with me, thine anger is turned away." They might have, with equal propriety, rendered the words before us, "Though ye meant evil against me, God meant it unto good." Joseph by no means intended to upbraid his brethren with what they had thought against him. His mention of their intentions was designed only as a contrast to the gracious intention of God. It may, however, be observed, that in what Joseph said to them on the same subject when he made himself known to them, he made no mention at all of the wickedness of their thoughts. At that time they were less able to bear it. But before their father's death they had time to know that he could mean nothing that was unkind. After so many proofs that he still loved them, notwithstanding of all that they had done and intended, they might bear the hint that he now gave them. All that he could intend by it was to acknowledge what was too plain to be denied, or to suggest the necessity of repentance towards God. But in the very sentence in which he confessed that their views were bad, he gives them a very convincing evidence that, whilst his principles of action continued to be what they had ever been, he would not remember his wrongs to their prejudice—"God meant it unto good, to bring to pass, as it is this day, to save much people alive." He saw that God's views were thoughts of mercy and kindness, both to himself and to his brethren; and under the impression of this intention of Providence, how could he be guilty of so great a wickedness as to destroy or hurt those very persons whom God had exalted him to protect? He might then have been compared to a servant who is hired to give their portion of food to his fellow-servants, and kills them with hunger, that he may spend it on his own lusts.

When you meet with injuries, consider what may be the intention of Providence in suffering you to meet with bad treatment. Your enemies intend ill, but surely God intends no ill to any of those who trust in Him.

In everything He permits to be done, however bad, He must intend good to them that love Him. And will you not bless God for those thoughts toward you, which are thoughts of peace, and not of evil? But if you bless God, do not curse men whom He overrules by His providence as the instruments of His kindness; they have thought evil against you, but that evil will not light upon you. It may recoil upon themselves. They deserve your pity. The displeasure of God will be sufficiently heavy for them without your displeasure. God knows how to turn their evil into your good. Is it not enough for you that all the evil should be theirs and all the good your own? But if you yield up yourselves to the power of a vindictive mind, you take effectual measures to rob yourselves of the good that you might derive from what is evil to them, and you share with them in their sin, and in its just consequences. The far worst thing they have done is not what they have done against you, but what they have done against God. And you wish to follow the same example, as if God had not been sufficiently provoked by their behaviour, unless you likewise take your share in kindling His fierce anger.

"God meant it, as it is this day, to save much people alive." The Egyptians were saved alive; the house of Jacob was saved alive; the seed that should spring from Joseph was preserved from extinction in the loins of their progenitors. Plain facts, obvious both to Joseph and to his brethren, clearly illustrate the wisdom and goodness of Divine Providence in overruling the bad intentions of Joseph's brethren to excellent ends.

Although their sin was not lessened by its happy consequences, they were more than sufficient to preserve the mind of Joseph from irritation, and to set the minds of his brethren at rest from any fears of his resentment. If God meant that event for good to themselves, He would take care that Joseph should not frustrate His purpose. Their business was, not to give place to groundless fears, but to humble themselves for their iniquity, and to adore that kind Providence which brought so much good to themselves, to their children, and to the world, out of their sins. Have we not likewise reason to be amazed at the depths of the Divine counsels in overruling the wickedness of Jacob's house for the preservation of that family out of which the Redeemer of mankind was to spring? The Christ was to come out of Judah and Pharez, and therefore it was necessary that they should not perish by hunger; and that to save them alive Joseph should be sent into Egypt.

Perhaps we would stretch the meaning of Joseph's words beyond his intention if we should use them as an argument that his brethren, in his apprehensions, had truly repented, and found mercy with God. This, however, is certain, that the good brought to them out of their sin did not to themselves counterbalance the evil of it, if they did not obtain forgiveness from God. No outward advantages that may be the consequences of any unpardoned sin are to be compared with the misery to which it exposes the sinner. What will it avail us to have our lives protracted to the utmost period of human life and to be furnished, during the whole space of our existence, with all the delights of the sons of men, if we must at last be consigned to perdition? The punishment of but one of our sins in hell will bring infinitely more pain than all of our sins together could ever bring of pleasure or advantage.

VER. 21. *Now therefore fear ye not: I will nourish you, and your little ones. And he comforted them, and spake kindly unto them.*

Again Joseph kindly entreated and exhorted them to confide in his love, and to banish their fear. He was vexed to see them unhappy. He wished them to be as happy as himself, and at the same time exempted from those cares which were inseparable from his station. "Fear ye not : I will nourish you and your little ones." Do you say that you forgive those who have offended you? You say well; but how do you verify your words? Are you ready to perform offices of charity and kindness to them, as you have opportunity to comfort them when they are oppressed with grief; to supply their necessities when they are indigent; to assist them in whatever thing they have need of you? Such were the ways by which Joseph assured his brethren of his goodwill to them after their offences. Hypocrisy is not well-pleasing to God, and when it is detected it is abhorred by men.

There are some who are very forward in promising, but slow in performing. There are others who will not promise when they intend to perform; although the half, or more than the half, of the intended benefit is lost by the uncertainty in which the persons are placed for whom it is intended. Joseph was equally ready at promising and performing, and both his promises and performances were evidences of the goodness of his heart. Although he intended to deal kindly and generously with his brethren, yet, if he had concealed his purpose in his own mind, that very concealment would have been ungenerous and unkind.

"And he comforted them, and spake kindly unto them." Although words without deeds are but wind, yet words of kindness to which deeds correspond are of great use. Job did as much good by the words of his mouth as by the liberality of his hands. He instructed many, and strengthened the weak hands. His words upheld him that was falling, and strengthened the feeble knees. His friends brake him in pieces with their cruel words; but if they had been in his place, he would have consoled them by his words, and the moving of his lips would have assuaged their griefs.

Is it your wish to walk in the good old path wherein all the holy men of old walked? Forgive injuries, not only with the mouth, but from the heart. What sort of pardon do you wish from God for your manifold transgressions? Is it your desire that your sins should be entirely blotted out of the book of God, and that you may hear His loving-kindness, and enjoy the riches of His liberality, notwithstanding of all that you have done to provoke His displeasure? Will you not be satisfied with the mere ungrounded hope of pardon, or with a temporary forbearance of deserved punishment? Then learn to forgive your offending brethren from your hearts. If you do not, beware of the fifth petition of that prayer which Christ taught His disciples. In your mouths it would be a curse to yourselves, and a horrible profanation of the name of God. The atheist or infidel, who makes no scruple of profaning the glorious and fearful name of God by needless oaths, is not more wicked than the false Christian who retains rancour in his heart against his brother, and yet presumes to say to the Lord, " Forgive us our debts, as we forgive our debtors."

Seek the knowledge, the faith, the assurance of pardoning mercy from God, and you will be able to say of the commandment to forgive your enemies, as well as of all the commandments of the Lord, that they are not grievous, that they are sweeter to your taste than honey from the comb.

LECTURE 36
The dying words and death of Joseph.
l 22–26

VER. 22. *And Joseph dwelt in Egypt, he, and his father's house : and Joseph lived an hundred and ten years.*

PAUL says of Abraham that by faith he sojourned in the Land of Promise as in a strange country, dwelling in tabernacles with Isaac and Jacob, the heirs with him of the same promise. The life of Joseph was very different from that of his progenitors. He lived in a sumptuous palace, and was honoured by the whole nation of Egypt, and by the surrounding nations as the wisest and one of the greatest of men. Yet he lived in his palace by faith, as his fathers had done in their tents. Amidst all his honour and affluence, he valued the promise of Canaan more than all the treasures of Egypt ; and looked forward with pleasure to the time when the tribes that sprung from him should count it their chief glory to be numbered amongst the tribes of Israel, as Joseph himself accounted it a greater glory to be the son of Jacob and an heir of the inheritance promised to Abraham, than to be the favourite of Pharaoh and the lord of Egypt.

"And Joseph dwelt in Egypt." Why did he dwell in Egypt, he and his father's house ? Not for the sake of the honours and pleasures which the court of Egypt could afford him, but because it was the will of God that he should dwell there, to be a father to Pharaoh, and to be the shepherd of Israel. His father's house dwelt there with him, probably by the direction of their father, or of Joseph himself, who knew the mind of God. The people of Canaan were probably by this time multiplied to such a degree that the family of Jacob would not easily have found a place to live together a pastoral life as one great family. The report that the whole land was expected by Abraham, and Isaac, and Jacob, to be the inheritance of their seed, was perhaps now current in Canaan, and therefore it might have been unsafe for them to dwell in it, both because they would have been exposed to the jealousy of the Canaanites, and because they might have been under too strong temptations to use unhallowed means to gain possession of it before the time appointed. When the Jews, whose hearts were set upon the good things of this present world, thought that Jesus was the Christ, the King of Israel, who was to save His people from their enemies, they endeavoured to make Him a secular king, for they thought that the power of God attending Him would easily give Him the victory over all the enemies of Israel. Thus the brethren of Joseph, or their children after them, might have formed premature designs to possess themselves by force of the promised inheritance. What desperate boldness of enterprise might not have been expected from such men as Simeon and Levi? There is some reason to think that some of the descendants of Ephraim did actually form the design, or indulge the hope, before the time appointed by God, of seizing on the property of some of the people who dwelt in the land, which was one day to be the inheritance of Israel. The men of Gath, we are told, slew the sons of Ephraim, because they came against them to take away their cattle, 1 Chron. vii.

Whatever were the motives which determined the children of Israel to dwell in Egypt, we know that their abode in that land had been fore-appointed for them by God, for His own glory, and for their good. It was not hid from Abraham, when God promised him the land of Canaan for his seed, that he and his seed should be sojourners in a land that was not theirs, for the space of four hundred and fifty years. The one-half of their time they abode in the land of Canaan, as in a strange land, the other half of it in the land of Egypt. " Now," says Moses, " the sojourning of the children of Israel in Egypt (observe he does not say their sojourning in Egypt, but the sojourning of the children of Israel who dwelt in Egypt) was four hundred and thirty years ; and it came to pass at the end of the four hundred and thirty years, even the selfsame day it came to pass, that all the hosts of the Lord went out from the land of Egypt."

" He and his father's house," of which he was now the head, for Reuben had forfeited his birthright. When heads of families die it is happy when a member of the family is able and willing to discharge the offices of a head in it. The elder brother, if he is of proper age, ought to be a father to the younger, and the younger ought to pay that deference which is due to his age, his qualifications, and his endeavours to promote the common benefit.

It was a great benefit to the sons of Jacob that, when their father was taken from their head, Joseph was left. Little did they know when they went about to kill him in his early years that they were forming a scheme for their own destruction. Surely they blessed God a hundred and a hundred times that his valuable life was preserved from their own hands, and that the government of Joseph, which they dreaded as a curse and an intolerable degradation, was made a blessing to them, and to their seed after them.

" And Joseph lived an hundred and ten years." He was shorter lived than his father Jacob, whose days had been fewer than those of any of his progenitors from the days of Adam. But if men's lives were to be measured by their good works, or by their usefulness, Joseph had lived longer than the greater part of them. Julius Cæsar, at the age of fifty-six, said that he had lived long enough for nature and for glory. Joseph, at near double that age, had lived long enough, and not longer than enough, to serve his generation according to the will of God. Although he might still have been very useful if he had lived as long as Abraham, Isaac, or Jacob, yet all the glorious works allotted to him were already finished, and the set time was come, when he died, that he should go to a better world to receive his reward.

Some, even after the time of Joseph, lived much longer. Job very probably lived after Joseph, and seems not to have been much less than two hundred years old when he died. Levi, Kohath, Amram, Moses, and Aaron lived longer than Joseph ; but his days were many compared with the days we may expect to live on earth. Do you wish to live as long as those good men of ancient times, whose names are so famous in history ? Be sober, be temperate, be cheerful, that you may not shorten your own days by the indulgence of your appetites or passions. Learn and keep the commandments of the Lord. Think not that the Scripture says in vain, " My son, forget not my law, but let thine heart keep my commandments ; for length of days, and long life and peace, shall they add to thee." You may not live as many days as Joseph, because God has not occasion for your service so long in this world ; but what though the number of your years be cut off in the midst, if the residue of them is made up in the better country.

VER. 23. *And Joseph saw Ephraim's children of the third generation : the children also of Machir the son of Manasseh were brought up upon Joseph's knees.*

Although Joseph was displeased when he saw Ephraim put before Manasseh, yet, when he knew the mind of God, he was well pleased with the preference given to his younger son ; and it was one part of his happiness, that he saw the children of Ephraim to the third generation. He could not expect to see with his own eyes the full accomplishment of a promise relating to the latter days, yet he saw steps towards it. Race unto race grew up under his eye to praise the Lord, and to enjoy the privileges of the Church. Of what incalculable use is length of days to a man so well qualified, so well inclined, and furnished with such opportunities to be useful. Joseph lived at a time when there were no Bibles, but he had the opportunity of learning the mind of God from a living Bible, and was himself a living Bible to four generations of the people of God. It was not necessary to tell us that Joseph was careful to transmit the knowledge and love of religion to the generations that followed him. His faith of the promise, and his desire of a rich share in the inheritance of Jacob, leave us no room to doubt of his care to train up his children, and his children's children, in the way that they should go.

Whether Joseph lived to see the sad disaster that befell the family of Ephraim, before Ephraim himself died, we are not informed; but we may observe that, on the whole, there was a great difference between the first and the last part of Joseph's life. He was torn in early youth from his father's family, and lived in slavery, or in a dungeon, during that period of life which is esteemed the most pleasant. Through the last part of his life he enjoyed a prosperity nearly, if not altogether, unmixed in the bosom of his family. His own posterity greatly increased in number. The care of all his father's family occupied much of his time and care. This time was pleasantly employed, and his care was attended with the consciousness that he was doing eminent services to the interests of religion, that he was showing his reverence and gratitude to his father, after he had laid him in the grave, and that he was the instrument of Providence to prepare the way for the accomplishment of all the great things which had been promised to Abraham, Isaac, and Jacob, and to the sons of Jacob.

Whilst Joseph had the pleasure of beholding the multiplication of his family by Ephraim, he found no reason to fear that Manasseh would be forgotten by God. The children of Machir, the son of Manasseh, were at their birth laid upon his knees, as if they had been his own children, and brought up under his paternal eye. What he saw with his eyes was a confirmation of what he had heard with his ears, that though Ephraim was to be greater than Manasseh, yet Manasseh also was to be great. Joseph enjoyed not merely the pleasure of a father, but the pleasure of faith and hope in those descendants that were trained up under his care to be an ornament to his house. If children's children are the glory of old men, they were so in a very eminent degree to Joseph, who was assured that the blessings of Divine goodness should descend upon his head in the persons of his descendants.

Many are miserable in their descendants, because they are a disgrace to their parents, or because the wrath of God distresses them in the persons of their seed. To have children of the promise for our children is delightful. If we train up our children for good, and trust the promises made to the seed of the righteous, we shall enjoy pleasure in our families of which the men who have their portion in this life cannot taste.

We do not find that Joseph had any more children by Asenath than Ephraim and Manasseh, nor did he marry another wife to increase the number of his children. He did not pretend to be a wiser or better man than his father, but he had seen and felt the miseries which the marriage of more wives than one brings into a house. He was content with two sons of his own body, in the prospect of thousands and millions of descendants in the latter days. He walked by faith, and not by sight.

VER. 24. *And Joseph said unto his brethren, I die : and God will surely visit you, and bring you out of this land unto the land which he sware to Abraham, to Isaac, and to Jacob.*

Levi was alive at this time, and probably some others of his eleven brethren ; but he accounted all the persons of his father's house his brethren or sons. His heart was not lifted up above his brethren. He was better pleased with his place in the family of Israel than in the kingdom of Egypt.

" I die." Dying men are often very unwilling to believe what all by-standers see. They take hold of every shadow of appearance to flatter themselves with vain hopes that they may live sometime longer in this world. But Joseph was not afraid to die, or to observe the symptoms of his approaching dissolution. He had lived in such a manner as, when death came, he wished to have lived, and he held fast in death that hope in God which had animated his soul amidst all the afflictions of life.

When he was dying, his thoughts were not engrossed by his own concerns, although he was on the borders of the everlasting world. His mind was at perfect ease concerning his own state. But he did what he could to console the hearts of his brethren, and of all his father's house, whom his death was depriving of their best earthly friend. He let them know that they had a far better Friend in heaven, who could not die, and who would surely visit them, and bring them again out of Egypt. Thus Jesus, in the view of His own death, administered strong consolation to His disciples whom He left behind Him in the world. He assured them that they should not be left orphans, and that they should be brought safe through all the tribulations of the present life to the possession of the everlasting kingdom.

"I die ; and God will surely visit you." The death of our worthy friends is just cause for sorrow, but not for despondency. They were but brittle cisterns at the best. They are now broken cisterns, in which no water is left ; but the fountain of living water can never be exhausted ; with God is the fountain of life—" In his light we shall see light."

"God will surely visit you." He takes it for granted that they would not always enjoy sensible discoveries of the Divine favour. God may, to the apprehension of His people, stand at a distance from them in a time of trouble, but He cannot forget them. He hath promised, and He will fulfil His promise, that though for a small moment He may forsake them, yet with everlasting kindness He will have mercy upon them. "He will regard the prayer of the destitute, and He will not despise their prayer."

"God will surely visit you, and bring you out of this land." Egypt had hitherto been kind to the house of Israel, but it was not the Land of Promise ; and every true Israelite in Egypt considered himself as a stranger in it, and looked forward with vehement desire to the time of entering on the possession of Canaan.

Joseph probably foresaw that after his death the situation of his brethren would become unpleasant. It was not to be expected that seventy-three years would pass from the time of Jacob's coming down to Egypt without discovering some symptoms of jealousy or envy in the Egyptians. Shepherds still continued to be an abomination to them. Besides, Joseph had heard the prediction handed down from Abraham, that his seed were to undergo great oppression from a nation amongst whom they were to sojourn for a long course of years. It now appeared morally certain that this nation must be the Egyptian. But with the prediction of oppression was joined a prediction of deliverance, and Joseph firmly believed, and wished his brethren to believe, that it would be most certainly fulfilled in its season, Gen. xv.

How precious are the promises of support under trouble, and deliverance from it! How carefully ought they to be treasured up in our minds, that we may be fitted to live and die with comfort, and to comfort one another! Joseph not only died in faith, but in his last hours of life endeavoured that his friends should have in remembrance what was spoken to them by God, that they might never despair of Divine help, but look forward, through every affliction, to that relief which was secured to them by the covenant of God. When he says, "God will surely visit you, and bring you out of this land," he does not refer them to any new discoveries made to himself, but to the well-known promise made to Abraham, and Isaac, and Jacob. When there was no written word of God, His afflicted people found a sufficient ground for their faith and hope in the sure promises that were handed down from father to son. What rich sources of joy under the darkest dispensations of Providence might we find in that precious book, which is as full of exceeding great and precious promises as the heaven is full of stars! We will perish in the day of our affliction unless the law of God be our delight. But if we remember the words which God hath given us for the ground of our hope, death in its most terrible form will appear a conquered enemy, a serpent that has lost its sting, although its teeth are still left. We cannot hope for exemption from those evils which appear intolerable to the greatest part of men, but we shall be able to say, "Yea, though we walk through the valley of the shadow of death, yet will we fear no evil; for thou art with us; thy rod and thy staff shall comfort us."

" Unto the land which he sware to Abraham, to Isaac, and to Jacob." How wonderful is the condescension of God, in confirming His promise by His oath ! and how inexcusable is our unbelief if we distrust God, when He confirms His promises by an obligation so sacred laid upon Himself to fulfil them ! He swears by Himself to Abraham, saying, "Surely blessing I will bless thee, and multiplying I will multiply thee." Joseph taught the Israelites in his time what improvement they ought to make of this oath for the establishment of their faith and hope. Paul teaches us what improvement we all ought to make of it, Heb. vi.

If God had merely promised, without sealing His word by His oath, ought He not to have been trusted ? But when, to silence all the whispers of our unbelieving hearts, He swears that He will do what He has said, we cannot refuse our assent to His word without making Him not only a liar, but something still worse, too bad to be named. The Lord will not hold the man guiltless who takes His name in vain, and can the man hope to be held guiltless who by his behaviour ascribes a crime to the Almighty which He will not leave unpunished in men ?

If God had sworn but once, ought not all His creatures that are capable of knowing anything of His nature to have given Him the glory of His faithfulness by an unshaken assent ? But He hath confirmed His word, not once or twice only, by His oath. What he sware to Abraham was confirmed to Isaac, and again to Jacob, Gen. xxvi. 4 ; Ps. cv. How often must God not only speak, but swear, and yet be disbelieved by men ! How often do we find God in the Bible interposing His oath to confirm both His promises and His threatenings, that no pretexts might be left for doubt ! Why are not the hearts of stubborn sinners terrified when they hear God swearing that He will never forget any of their works, and that they shall not enter into His rest ? Why are not the hearts of trembling sinners emboldened to flee for refuge, to lay hold on the hope set before them, when they hear the Lord saying, "As I live, saith the Lord God, I have no pleasure in the death of the wicked, but that he should turn and live," Ezek. xxxiii. 11 ; Ps. lxxxix. 35.

The promise was confirmed by oath, not to the individual persons to whom Joseph was speaking, but, what was still better, to their fathers who were now with God. Surely the Lord would not lie to Abraham, Isaac, and Israel, His chosen servants. Surely He would not forget those promises to their seed, in the faith of which they had lived and died. Ought not our faith to derive strength and boldness from the still more important consideration, that the promises of mercy to us were originally made, and confirmed by oath, to our Lord Jesus Christ ? The Lord hath sworn to our Redeemer, and will not repent, "Thou art a priest for ever after the order of Melchisedec." The Lord hath sworn by His holiness, that He will not lie unto David.

Ver. 25. *And Joseph took an oath of the children of Israel, saying, God will surely visit you, and ye shall carry up my bones from hence.*

How readily do we imitate the example of men whom we revere ! Parents, set a good example before your children. It is probable that if you gain their esteem they will follow it. Jacob expressed his faith in God's promise by taking an oath from Joseph that he would carry up his dead body to the land of Canaan, and bury it there. Joseph, before he died, took a like oath of the sons of Jacob. He did not expect that any of his brethren then living would live long enough to carry up his bones at the departure of the children of Israel from Egypt to Canaan, and he did not expect to be buried in Canaan before that time ; yet he took an oath from them, when that happy period should come, that his bones should not be left behind. He hoped that such a sense of the sacred obligations of an oath would remain amongst them that none would pretend to an exemption from the performance of what he had enjoined, on the pretence that they had never taken the obligation on themselves. "God hath sworn," said Joseph, "that he will visit you, and bring you up to the land which he promised to your fathers." "I require an oath from you, that when God performs his oath, you will carry up my bones." When God performed His word they would learn from His faithfulness to perform their own word. When He regarded them in mercy, and established His covenant with them, a grateful sense of His goodness would preserve them from forgetting the promise which their fathers had ratified by His glorious and fearful name. Whoever they be that pour contempt upon the name of the Lord, it may be expected that the redeemed of the Lord will fear Him, and will perform their vows.

Joseph had lived but a short time in Canaan. He had received great favours from the king and people of Egypt. He had spent the greatest part of his life in that country, enjoying all the pleasures which it could afford, and receiving all the honour which a higher-minded man than Joseph would have wished. Yet he never considered Egypt but Canaan as his home; he desired that his bones should lie, not with the dust of the princes of Egypt, but in the land which God sware to Abraham, Isaac, and Jacob. By that faith by which he was persuaded of the truth of the promise, and of its goodness, he gave a commandment concerning his bones.

" God shall visit you, and ye shall carry up my bones hence." Why were they not required to carry up his bones when he died? Because, when he died, there was not another Joseph to obtain leave from the King of Egypt to carry up his bones, and perhaps he knew that the king of Egypt would not so easily give leave for carrying up his dead body, as a former king had given to carry up his father's body. Or what if he thought it inexpedient at this time to make the attempt? The jealousy of the Egyptians might have been awakened if the proposal had been made, or the children of Israel might have been tempted to use premature means for carrying off their property and their little ones to such a permanent settlement as Canaan, when the iniquity of the Amorites was not full, and the time not yet come when God was to make room for them by the destruction of the nations of His wrath. A wise man's heart discerneth both time and judgment.

It may likewise be observed that Joseph was to be embalmed

as his father had been. Joseph caused this ceremony to be performed for his father, not merely because he wished to do all the honour to his father's body which was usually paid to the remains of great men in the country which he governed, but because it was necessary to use the proper means to preserve it from corruption, till it could be carried to the place of sepulture. Joseph knew that his own body would be kept from corruption till the time appointed by God for the departure of the children of Israel from Egypt ; and it was not unusual for the Egyptians to preserve in their houses the embalmed bodies of their fathers and friends.

The impression made by the oath which Joseph took from his brethren would have a happy tendency to turn their thoughts to the promised land, and to the period of their deliverance. Dying saints may do much good to their survivors by requests or speeches, which will give a useful direction to their thoughts.

VER. 26. *So Joseph died, being an hundred and ten years old : and they embalmed him, and he was put in a coffin in Egypt.*

"So Joseph died." All his grandeur, and riches, and goodness could not save him from the hands of the last enemy. And yet it is a certain truth that righteousness delivereth from death. His death was not his destruction. He died that he might live a better life than he could live on earth. He left the Egyptians that he might live with angels. He left his brethren on earth that he might dwell with his fathers in heaven. We did not need to be informed of him as we are informed of the poor man Lazarus, that he was carried by angels into Abraham's bosom. Was it not an addition to the happiness of Abraham, and Isaac, and Jacob to receive Joseph into their celestial society? We can form some idea of the joyful transports of Jacob's heart, when he saw Joseph descend from his chariot in Goshen to throw himself upon his neck ; but we cannot conceive the delight that he must have felt when Joseph was brought by angels into the heavenly regions. "Blessed are the dead who die in the Lord." The pleasures they receive, and the pleasures they give at their entrance into the world of blessedness are far beyond anything which the heart of man can conceive in his present state.

"Joseph died, being an hundred and ten years old." Some of these years were spent in grief; more of them in joy! But when he entered into the everlasting world he found that the years spent in grief had been as necessary for him, and were as productive of benefit, as the years in which he had seen good.

He had not lived so many years as his father, but he had lived to bring forth much fruit unto holiness. What would all his years have availed him if he had lived as long as Methuselah, and spent them all in the enjoyment of every earthly delight, without minding the one thing needful! In another world a thousand years will appear even to us as one day. Yet if no day has been passed without doing good, however short our lives may have been, we may bless God through endless ages that so many days of life have been allowed us; but we will feel no regret that we have not lived so long as many of our friends or progenitors have done.

"And they embalmed him." Those parts of his body which were most liable to putrefaction were extracted. Fragrant herbs supplied their places, and such operations were performed as tended to preserve the carcass from those changes offensive to the eyes, or nostrils, which are incident to the human race, when the dust returns to the earth as it was. Dearly as Abraham loved Sarah, he sought for a place where he might bury her out of his sight, for she could no longer be the desire of his eyes when she became a prey to corruption. Joseph's sons and brethren were under no necessity of burying him out of their sight. His countenance still retained its former features. He was put into a coffin in Egypt, but not buried. Where his body was kept till the departure of the children of Israel we are not told; nor do we know whether the custom was yet introduced into Egypt, of passing judgment upon dead bodies before they were interred. If it was, Joseph had no reason to be afraid of the trial. His memory must have been blessed and praised by the Egyptians as well as by the Israelites. But he had already enjoyed more honour than he desired. His chief desire was, living or dead, to be accepted of God, and to do good to men. When he was dead, he yet spake to the Israelites. His dead body, waiting for the time of its removal to Canaan, cried aloud to his kinsman—"Here is not your rest, you are in a strange land; but God will surely visit you, and bring you into the land which he sware to your fathers to give you." Let us endeavour to be useful all the days of our life; and if we can reasonably indulge the hope of being useful when our life is at an end, let us rejoice, and give thanks to God.

Joseph's dying hopes were not disappointed. When Moses left Egypt with haste, the hurry of the departure, and the immense load of business and care which then lay upon his mind, did not make him forget the bones of Joseph. He would have thought himself guilty of the basest ingratitude, and even of perjury, if the oath made to this dying patriarch had not been observed. Moses took the bones of Joseph with him, for he had straitly sworn to the children of Israel, saying, "God shall surely visit you, and ye shall carry up my bones hence with you." Not one, it may be presumed, of those persons to whom the oath had been administered were then in the land of the living. But the oath which they had sworn was not dead with them.

It is natural to inquire what became of the bodies of the other eleven patriarchs. But how shall our curiosity be satisfied? God did not think it necessary to give us their history, any farther than it was connected with that of their father and brother. Whether their bodies were left in Egypt, or embalmed and carried into Canaan by their descendants, they shall arise and stand in their lot at the end of the days.

It will be more useful for us to know what is to become of our own bodies when our spirits return to God who gave them; and it is possible for us to know everything that we can reasonably desire to know concerning their future destination. We cannot say with our Lord, "Thou wilt not leave our bodies to see corruption." Our souls must be, for a long course of ages perhaps, in a state of separation from our bodies, yet not so long as those holy men of ancient times, whose memories are so highly venerated by us. But if Christ be in us, when they are separated from our bodies, they will be with Christ, which is far better, and our bodies too shall rest in hope, for we shall sleep in Jesus; and " He that raised up Christ from the dead shall also quicken our mortal bodies by His Spirit which dwelleth in us."

The discoveries now made to us by the Gospel are richer and more consoling than those which were made to the ancient patriarchs. Make your calling and election sure, and you will be able to say, " O death! where is thy sting? O grave! where is thy victory?" Jesus hath died and risen again, and He who raised up Jesus will raise up us also by Jesus.

Why should we look forward with such reluctance and terror to an event which will place us in the company of men whom we so greatly admire? We need not be afraid that Abraham, or Isaac, or Israel, or Joseph will refuse to acknowledge us as children, and members of the same body with themselves, if the Spirit of Christ who dwelt in them dwells in us. " Stand in the ways, and see, and ask for the old paths, where is the good way, and walk therein, and ye shall find rest for your souls."

LECTURES ON THE BLESSINGS PRONOUNCED BY JACOB ON HIS TWELVE CHILDREN

LECTURES

ON

THE BLESSINGS PRONOUNCED BY JACOB
ON HIS TWELVE CHILDREN

LECTURE 1

Jacob's solemn call to his children to attend
to his dying words. Prediction
concerning Reuben.

xlix 1–4

VER. 1. *And Jacob called unto his sons, and said, Gather yourselves together, that I may tell you that which shall befall you in the last days.*

NO characters of the very ancient times appear more venerable to us than those of the three great patriarchs of the chosen nation. We are highly entertained and edified by their history. If they had left any writings behind them they would have been read with great avidity. God was not pleased to honour them with a name amongst the list of the holy writers. We have reason, however, to think that some of the sacred histories of the most ancient times given us by Moses were received from them by tradition, if not also by writing. The use of writing appears to have been known before any of the books of Moses were composed, Job xix. And Abraham undoubtedly was anxious to transmit the knowledge of his God to posterity by the most effectual methods, Gen. xix. It is at least certain that many of the words of the patriarchs are recorded in the inspired volumes. This chapter consists chiefly of the words of Jacob, although Moses was the writer of them.   It might be called the book of the prophecies of Jacob; and it contains as large a portion of the oracles of God as the book of the prophecies of Obadiah, or the epistle of Jude.

Abraham, Isaac, and Jacob are called prophets, Ps. cv.   The word of the Lord came unto Jacob at divers times of his life. But his dying words are the most memorable of his prophecies; all his sons were summoned to hear him, he was full of hope that his last sayings would make a happy impression on all his children.   Living and dying, it was his earnest wish to be useful to them; and in his death, as well as in his life, he set us an example which we should endeavour to imitate.   God grant that when our time comes that we must die we may be enabled to say something to surviving friends that will be remembered by them with advantage.   We do not expect the prophetic *afflatus* on our death-bed.   But if we die in faith, we may leave a useful testimony behind us of the pleasantness and peace of the ways of wisdom.

" Gather yourselves together, that I may tell you that which shall befall you in the last (or latter) days."   Although he was now almost blind, yet he might have called himself the man whose eyes were opened.   No man on earth saw like him the interesting events which were to befall his posterity.   Things to come are as clearly seen as things present by the all-seeing God; and He revealed them with what degree of plainness He saw fit to His prophets, for the benefit of the Church.

It would not have been good, either for Jacob or for his sons, to have known the events that were to befall their posterity as distinctly as we know them from the Bible.   They might have been overwhelmed with excess of sorrow at the foresight of the tremendous judgments to be inflicted in some distant periods on their posterity, when the Lord rejected and forsook the generations of His wrath.   Do not wonder that we cannot learn with certainty from the Scripture prophecies all the successive events of future times.   The great Author of prophecy best knew how far it was fit to open to our view the sealed book of His purposes.

The latter days, in the prophetical writings, do not necessarily signify the times posterior to the appearance of Christ in human flesh. The days that followed the time of Moses might very well be called in Jacob's time the latter days. One of the prophecies of this chapter plainly relates to the days of Messiah. Perhaps others of them may receive a new accomplishment in days yet to come; for any period of time, long after the death of Jacob, might with propriety be called the latter days. Yet the known accomplishment of many of them in times long since past affords us an undeniable proof that Jacob spake, and that Moses wrote, by Divine inspiration; and doubtless the tribes of Israel, after their settlement in the land promised to Abraham, had more abundant evidence from what they saw, than we can expect from a compendious history, that the Spirit of the Lord spake by their venerable ancestor, and that the word of God was in his tongue. And it deserves remark, that Moses inserted the prophecies of Jacob in the sacred canon when the accomplishment of them was not yet seen. He was well assured that the time was approaching when they would be fully accomplished, and when the accomplishment of what had been spoken and written before-time would be a clear proof of the Divine original of his own books.

"I will tell you what shall befall you in the latter days." They were all to be in their graves before the last days, and yet the things foretold were to befall them. They reckoned themselves deeply interested in the fortunes of their children at the distance of many generations, and were bound to give thanks to God for all the good and great things which He promised to do to the latest of their posterity. "What am I," said David, when he received precious promises from God concerning his seed, "what am I, and what is my father's house, that thou hast brought me hitherto? And this was but a small thing in thine eyes, but thou hast also spoken of thy servant's house for a great while to come."

We cannot know what will happen in the last days to our posterity, or whether we shall have a posterity in the earth at the distance of a hundred years, or of one year. But let us fix our attention on those more interesting events which we may know, and leave uncertainties to that God who gives us sufficient grounds to trust all our distant concerns in His hands. We may know, and ought to know, what shall be our own future state. And if we can commit our own souls and bodies with confidence to God, we may likewise look for good things in every generation to the Church of Christ, in which we hope our own seed will be included, if a seed is left to us in the earth. If such hopes enable us to look forward with cheerfulness to future times, it will be our heart's desire, and our earnest endeavour, to communicate the knowledge and love of pure and undefiled religion to the children whom God is pleased to give us, that they may perform the same office of love to their children after them, that our most remote descendants, if God leave us a name and remnant among men, may praise the God of their fathers.

VER. 2. *Gather yourselves together, and hear, ye sons of Jacob ; and hearken unto Israel your father.*

If all parents are entitled to respect from their children, such a man as Jacob, who received from God the glorious name of ISRAEL for himself and his seed, might expect a very high degree of reverence from the men who had the honour to call themselves his children. When the esteem due to eminent piety meets with the honour due to the parental relation, children should reckon themselves bound to give double honour to their fathers and mothers ; but no man, since the time of Noah, was entitled to greater honour from his children according to the flesh than Jacob, who had been through a great part of his life labouring and wrestling for blessings to his seed, and by his power with God and with the Angel of His presence, had obtained for them exceeding great and precious promises.

"Hearken unto Israel your father." At all times such a father deserved to be heard with attention by his sons, but most of all at this time. He was going from them to God. He spake by Divine inspiration of things most deeply interesting to them. He was about to leave them his dying benedictions. They would have been more stupid than the ox and the ass if they had not given the most earnest heed at this time to the things that were to be spoken by their father Israel. We have no reason to doubt of their treasuring up in their minds all the words which now proceeded from his mouth, and communicating them to their children's children. Moses knew all these blessings by tradition from his fathers before he was authorised by the Spirit of God to record them in the Scriptures for our instruction, on whom the ends of the world are come, as well as for the instruction of the tribes of Israel.

The sons of Jacob were called to hearken, not only to the Divine doctrines and precepts which they heard from their father, but likewise to the prophecies concerning future events which he published in their ears. And ought not we likewise to attend to what is revealed in the prophecies of Scripture concerning events in which the Church of God, and in which probably our own offspring, will be deeply interested. We may indeed allege that there are many things in them dark and hard to be understood. But the sons of Jacob would also find it difficult to understand some of their father's predictions. Yet they learned so much from what he said as tended greatly to establish their faith and hope in their father's God, and to assist them in preparing their children after them to meet those happy or disastrous events of which they had some obscure view afar off, although they could not form a distinct apprehension of them. Beware of thinking that those parts of Scripture are useless of which you cannot fully comprehend the meaning. The prophecies concerning the Messiah were but imperfectly understood by the ancient Church. Yet many thousands in Israel were saved by the faith of them. Surely the sons of Jacob could not be under more sacred obligations to attend to the predictions of their father, although he was dignified with the name of Israel, than we are to attend to the revelation made to us by the Lamb in the midst of the throne, who prevailed to open the sealed book, and to loose its seven seals, because He was slain, and redeemed us to God by His blood, and made us kings and priests to God, Matt. xxiv; Rev. i. 3-22.

VER. 3. *Reuben, thou art my first-born, my might, and the beginning of my strength, the excellency of dignity, and the excellency of power.*

We reckon ourselves honoured by our extraction if we are the descendants of illustrious men. The first-born sons of the great reckon themselves entitled to peculiar honour in their families. The privileges attached to the progenitors in the very ancient ages were a temptation to Jacob to use means very unworthy of his character to obtain them. Reuben had the honour to be the first-born in Jacob's family—"Thou art my first-born, and my might, the excellency of dignity, and the excellency of power." These honours were his by the course of nature. But by his folly and wickedness he turned his glory into shame.

"Thou art my first-born, my might, and the beginning of strength." In that state of society, when nations were very small, men derived great consequence and power from a numerous family. Even in our days children are the strength and ornament of their parents, when they behave virtuously. But miserable are those children who, instead of proving a comfort and a blessing to their parents, are their shame and reproach. Their unnatural conduct blasts their reputation among men, and brings down judgments from Heaven. "Thou art my might, the beginning of my sorrow" (so the words have been read, without any force on the original). It was true in fact, whatever way the words are rendered, that Reuben was the cause of most bitter and lasting grief to that venerable father, whose support and defence he might have been.

The excellency of dignity and the excellency of power belonged to the birthright. Jacob seemed to begin the contest for the birthright in the womb, when he took his brother by the heel. Although his behaviour to Esau in the purchase of the birthright is quite unjustifiable, yet his earnest desire of it was a sign of his wisdom. And as it was an evidence of Esau's profaneness that for one morsel of meat he sold his birthright, it was no less a proof of the folly of Reuben that to a most abominable lust he sacrificed the dignity and power attached to the birthright in that glorious family of which he was the first-born. Jacob does not mean that the enjoyment of the privileges of the birthright had been actually possessed by Reuben, or that he could have looked forward to them with an assured hope in case of his good behaviour. Manasseh did not forfeit the birthright, and yet it was given to Ephraim. But Reuben's exclusion from this honour was his punishment for his grievous offence against his father ; and he was expressly informed by his father's dying words what glory his posterity might have enjoyed if his transgression had not robbed them of the privileges which they might have expected to enjoy. Reuben was probably pardoned by God. But for his own humiliation, and for a warning to other men, it was expedient to give him this solemn rebuke; and to put him in mind of what he had forfeited, not to himself only, but to his seed after him.

VER. 4. *Unstable as water, thou shalt not excel, because thou wentest up to thy father's bed ; then defiledst thou it : he went up to my couch.*

The word which we render unstable, when applied to men, signifies licentious or dissolute. Such were the men whom Abimelech the son of Gideon hired to be his followers, and to assist him in the murder of his brethren, Judges ix. 4. Such were the false prophets in the days of Zephaniah, chap. iii. 4 ; Jer. xxiii. 32. The passage before us is the only place besides the passage mentioned where the word occurs, and seems to signify that property in water which is analogous to an unrestrained licentiousness in the characters of men. The force of a great current of water, when the barriers that restrained it are removed, is irresistible. Such is the force of corruption in men destitute of religious principle. Yet nothing is weaker than water in small quantities. It has no principle of stability. Such is the weakness of men who walk after their own lusts. They have no power to resist the most pernicious temptations, or the most inordinate and detestable impulses of their own corrupt minds.

Whether the instability or the impetuosity of water are here alluded to, it is perhaps impossible and not very necessary to determine. Reuben's wickedness was a plain evidence of his own lamentable weakness, and of the dreadful power of corruption within him. He had as little power to restrain his lusts as water has to preserve itself from falling to the ground when it is poured from the vessel that contained it. He rushed on to the commission of a crime that was to load him with guilt and infamy, with the irresistible impetuosity of a mighty river when it comes up over all its channels, and goes up over all its banks, Isa. viii. 7. To gratify a momentary inclination, he violated all the laws of honour, of natural affection, of God and man. He might have seen, if his eyes had not been blinded by the deceitfulness of sin, that by going up to his father's couch he would purchase a moment's pleasure at the expense of everlasting disgrace to himself, of lasting anguish to a venerable father, of a grievous stain to his posterity, and of the vengeance of Heaven upon his immortal soul, if sovereign mercy was not pleased to interpose.

" Unstable as water, thou shalt not excel." Thou hast forfeited the excellency of dignity and the excellency of power. Thou shalt not enjoy that high respect, those peculiar honours, those distinguished privileges, which are annexed to the birthright.

" Because thou wentest up to my bed." He ought, above all his brethren, to have been a defence to his father against every invader of his honour or property. But there was not one of the thirteen children of Jacob that inflicted more painful wounds on their father's heart. The injury done to Joseph was not so irreparable. The murder of the Shechemites was indeed not less but more criminal, and yet it was not such a direct outrage against the man whom of all others on earth he was most bound to honour. It was a violent assault upon the tenderest part of his honour. It was an outrageous attempt to tear away from him a part of his own flesh, and make it the fuel of everlasting burning. He corrupted Bilhah, whom Jacob was bound to love as a part of himself, and involved her in such wickedness as that which brought down fire and brimstone on Sodom and Gomorrah, and the other cities of the plain. Could

Reuben, then, expect the first place of honour in his father's family? He had reason to wonder that he was not turned out of it with disgrace, and set up, like the sinners of Sodom, a monument of wrath to all generations.

"Thou shalt not excel." We never find that any one of the tribe of Reuben was distinguished by peculiar honours; neither the priesthood nor the royalty was given to the tribe of the first-born of Jacob. None of the ancient heroes, whose names are yet famous, belonged to this tribe. There were kings of different tribes, but none, as far as we know, of the tribe of Reuben. There were doubtless many of the sons of Reuben who found favour with God, 1 Chron. v. But none of them ever obtained such glory in this world as many of the other tribes obtained.

If the sentence depriving Reuben of the glory of the birth-right had been a mere act of the Divine sovereignty, it needed not to have excited a blush in his countenance, or awakened sorrow in his heart. But it was a just sentence pronounced in God's displeasure against his sin. He was the first-born, but forasmuch as he defiled his father's bed, his birthright was given unto the sons of Joseph, the son of Israel: and the genealogy is not to be reckoned after the birthright, for Judah prevailed above his brethren, and of him came the chief ruler, but the birthright was Joseph's, 1 Chron. v. 1, 2.

"Because thou wentest up to my bed; then defiledst thou it: he went up to my couch." Jacob spoke in the language of indignation concerning the shameful conduct of Reuben, not because he hated, but rather because he still loved this unnatural son. "Whom Christ loves, he rebukes and chastens;" and those offending sons, who are loved by wise parents, will not only be admonished by them, but rebuked with a severity proportioned to the offence. Eli rebuked his sons, but with too much lenity to do them any good. He was their enemy and his own, when he thought he was treating them with the kindness of a parent. Jacob acted the part of a wise father and a faithful friend to Reuben when, with his dying breath, he endeavoured to pierce his heart with a just sense of the enormity of his guilt.   He was certainly struck with bitter remorse long before this time.   It is to be hoped that he had obtained repentance unto life.   But after such a transgression, it became him all the days of his life to remember with shame how he had disgraced himself, how he had lacerated the heart of his father, and especially how presumptuously he had sinned against the God of his father, that he might watch and pray against temptation, and bring forth fruits meet for repentance. The mourning of the true penitent is not at an end when he has obtained good hope through grace that iniquity shall not be his ruin.   Nor is the permanency of holy sorrow inconsistent with the joy of the Lord.   When Reuben thought with horror of his great transgression, and looked forward with sorrow to its consequences amongst his children's children, he would admire and praise that mercy which left him a place and a name in Israel, although he had so justly forfeited the excellency of dignity and the excellency of power.   " Good is the word of the Lord concerning me," said Hezekiah, " for there shall be peace and truth in my days."   He was not angry with the prophet, who reproved him for his pride of heart, and told him that his children should be eunuchs in the palace of the King of Babylon ; but he magnified that mercy which punished him less than his iniquities deserved.

Reuben did a very great kindness to his father in contributing to the preservation of his favourite son.   But his exertions in the cause of virtue made no atonement for his transgressions. Think not that you can compensate your vices by your virtues. No doubt, when Jacob was informed of the particular circumstances of Joseph's exile, he was highly pleased with Reuben's interposition in his favour.   Still, however, the iniquity of Reuben was remembered with detestation, and it must have been punished with eternal vengeance, if it had not been blotted out by the sovereign mercy of God.   Do not imagine that your Judge will weigh your good deeds against your bad, and give sentence for or against you as the scale of virtue or vice preponderates.   Nothing can procure the pardon of any of your sins but that blood which cleanseth from all sin.

Oh! do not that abominable thing which God hates! Beware of bringing the displeasure of God upon yourselves. Beware of bringing dishonour and misery upon your children yet unborn. Do you say that God is too righteous to punish the iniquities of the fathers upon the children? Without doubt, the Lord is righteous in all His ways, and holy in all His works. He will not lay upon man more than is right, that he should enter into judgment with God. But was God unjust because the birthright was given to Joseph, and the dominion to Judah, rather than to the family of Reuben? Would He not have been righteous although Reuben had been as completely banished from the family of Jacob as Ishmael was from the family of Abraham? Is He unrighteous because the House of Hanover sits upon the throne which was forfeited by a prince of the House of Stuart? Is He unrighteous because the natural seed of Abraham and Israel have long been exiles and wanderers among the nations, and stript of all the glorious privileges which their fathers long enjoyed.

Flee from fornication and all uncleanness. Make not the members of Christ the members of a harlot. What disgrace did fleshly impurities bring on Jacob's eldest son, and on another of the wisest of them, and on his only daughter! Prov. v. ; 2 Pet. ii.

LECTURE 2
Prophecy concerning Simeon and Levi.
xlix 5–7

VER. 5. *Simeon and Levi are brethren ; instruments of cruelty are in their habitations* [*or, their swords are instruments of cruelty*].

REUBEN was not the only great offender in Jacob's family ; his two next sons were guilty of a crime still worse, if possible, than Reuben's. If it did not wound his father in a part so tender, it gave him not less pain, and exposed him to greater mischief. If a merciful Providence had not wonderfully preserved him, he and all his family must have been destroyed in the consequences to be apprehended from the revenge of the enraged Canaanites.

"Simeon and Levi are brethren." Moses and Aaron were brethren, but in a very different sense. They were brethren not only in the flesh, but in the Lord, and in the noblest virtues ; Simeon and Levi were brethren in wickedness. Seldom have two children of the wicked one perpetrated actions more horrible than these two sons of Jacob did ; and their relation to Jacob was a very great aggravation of their wickedness. They were trained up in the knowledge of God ; they were circumcised in the flesh of their foreskin ; yet they were brothers in fraud and violence, in treachery and murder.

Let all associates in sin consider the detestation which Jacob, and which the Spirit of God, expresses against confederacies in evil. You probably think that you cannot be singular in wickedness whilst you behave no worse than your companions. It is true that there are other persons capable of as great wickedness as you. But will it be any comfort to the damned that they have associates in torment? Are the devils to be excused for their infernal wickedness because there are many legions of wicked spirits employed in the same works of darkness? You are perhaps seduced by your companions; but why do you choose rather to hearken to the voice of wicked men, of Satan's agents, than to the voice of God? Adam hearkened to the voice of his wife; but was he excused for eating the fruit of the forbidden tree because his wife persuaded him to eat of it?

When you suffer yourself to be seduced you harden your seducer. If he must bear a part of the blame of your transgression, must not you in return share in his guilt? He drew you into the way of sin, and you encouraged him to hold on in that path of destruction on which he entered before you.

Evil men make one another worse. Ought not good men to improve one another in goodness? Why should bad men be more active in the accursed service of the devil than good men in the service of God?

"Instruments of cruelty are in their habitations." How shameful is it to have any instrument of iniquity in those habitations where a kind Providence places us, and where the voice of prayer and praise is heard? But the original words seem to be more justly rendered, "Their swords are instruments of cruelty." With what reason may this be said of the swords of those men who employ them to execute their intemperate rage against those who have offended them. Can those men be followers of Christ who, instead of forgiving offences, endeavour to return a mortal blow for a slight injury, or perhaps for an imaginary affront? O my soul, come not thou into the secret of such barbarous men! The fifth petition of the Lord's prayer in their mouths would be a petition for damnation.

VER. 6. *O my soul, come not thou into their secret; unto their assembly, mine honour, be not thou united: for in their anger they slew a man, and in their self-will they digged down a wall.*

David frequently calls his tongue his glory; perhaps this is what Jacob means in this place by his honour or his glory, as it might with equal propriety be rendered. Jacob abhorred the crime of his sons. He would not for a world have suffered his tongue to justify or to excuse their abominable wickedness. It is too ordinary with parents to excuse the faults of their children. It is too ordinary for men to excuse the bad actions of their friends in language that makes them partners in the guilt. He who justifies, or even excuses, a bad action encourages other men to follow a bad example, and hardens those who are already guilty, instead of endeavouring to bring them to repentance.

But the word, in its ordinary sense, affords us a meaning sufficiently plain. " O my soul, come not thou into their secret meetings." Let me never associate myself with the plotters of such execrable wickedness. " Unto their assembly, mine honour, be not thou united." Let not my name suffer by my paternal relation to those assassins. Let it never be supposed that I could approve of such infernal confederacies as theirs.

Parents, beware of bringing the guilt and dishonour of your children's faults upon yourselves. Will you plead for sin? Will you say that a conduct evidently wicked is either justifiable or excusable, because your children are chargeable with it? Your children ought to be dear to you, but the law of God ought to be far dearer. If they are dear to you, endeavour to make them sensible of all the evil of their conduct, that they may confess before God the sinfulness of their ways. If they confess their sins, and implore the mercy of God in Christ, God is faithful and just to forgive their sins. But you are unfaithful to their souls if by frivolous excuses you make them believe that they stand in little need of forgiveness.

When parents discover a becoming detestation of the offences of their children, they redeem at least their own credit. Why should any man be charged with a share in that guilt which he detests! We justly complain of Adam for eating the forbidden fruit; but is the memory of our first father to be loaded also with the guilt of the first murder because he had the unhappiness to call Cain his son? Or was Jacob the less venerable that he was the father of Reuben, and Simeon, and Levi? On the contrary, he deserves praise for his behaviour to his offending children, for expressing a just indignation against their crimes, tempered with that paternal love which he still retained for their persons.

"O my soul, come not thou into their secret; unto their assembly, mine honour, be not thou united." It may be supposed that Simeon and Levi held several secret consultations between themselves, or with other persons whom they took into partnership in their guilt, for they could not perpetrate their daring enterprise without many other hands besides their own. It is not to be doubted that some, perhaps the greater part of their brethren, were drawn into the horrid conspiracy. Those were indeed less guilty than the contrivers of the wickedness, but they were very far from being blameless. Beware of imagining that you are clear from the blame of a bad action because you were tempted by other men to do what you would not otherwise have done. Perhaps Adam might not have eaten of the forbidden fruit if Eve had not tempted him; and Eve might have retained her innocence if she had not been seduced by the serpent. Yet neither Adam nor Eve were suffered to remain in paradise. Simeon and Levi did not call their father to their consultations; they knew that he would have abhorred and disconcerted them. He sharply reproved his guilty sons when the action was committed; he retained his detestation of it to the last, and did not go out of the world without leaving his dying testimony against it.

"For in their anger they slew a man." They slew a great number of men, and they did an irreparable injury to the women and to the little ones. The singular number is here used for the plural, as in many other places. Or if one man is meant, it must be the lord of the country, who was the principal object of their rage. After entering into sacred engagements with him, they treacherously killed him. They were at once bloody and deceitful men. But in executing their revenge they could not stop short at one man; it was necessary, in their view, to destroy the whole city, that they might not leave avengers to retaliate their atrocities.

" In their anger they slew a man, and in their self-will they digged down a wall." Some make the expression to signify, they hewed down an ox. The patriarch's meaning evidently is, that in their fury they spread ravage and desolation throughout the city of Shechem. Whether he intended to say that they laid the walls level with the dust, or that they butchered the cattle with their owners, the instruction to us is the same—we are taught how dreadful a thing it is to act under the impulse of ungoverned rage. These furious sons of Jacob spared neither man nor beast. Everthing that came in their way was destroyed in their rage. And what greatly aggravated their wickedness was the deliberation and obstinacy with which it was perpetrated. They held consultations, and strengthened one another in mischief. Three days did not cool the rage of their spirits ; so long time had they to think of their plan of vengeance before it was carried into execution. Yet still their anger burned so hot that they slew all the men of Shechem, as if they had been but one man. In their deliberate malice they destroyed the dwellings of the people, against whom they had no quarrel, but that their prince had put an affront upon their family, which he was very willing to repair, and which he was actually preparing to repair, according to an agreement made with themselves, in which he showed all readiness to comply with their desires.

In the heat of passion a man is not his own master, he is the slave of an infernal lust. He is worse than a madman, because he has no more command of himself than a madman, and what understanding is left to him only serves to fit him for doing the greater mischief.

VER. 7. *Cursed be their anger, for it was fierce ; and their wrath, for it was cruel: I will divide them in Jacob, and scatter them in Israel.*

There is a kind of anger which deserves not to be cursed, but blessed. Such was the anger of Moses when he saw the idolatries of the children of Israel, and broke the tables of the law. Such was the anger of Phinehas when he pierced the hearts of Zimri and Cozbi with his javelin, in his jealousy for the Lord. He executed judgment, and it was accounted to him for righteousness in all generations, for ever and ever.

There is an anger which, though not fierce, is sinful, and brings down judgments from Heaven. "Whoso," says our Lord, "is angry against his brother without cause shall be in danger of the judgment." Moses was angry at the waters of Meribah; and although his anger was kindled by the sin of the people, yet he sinned in his anger. The consequence was, that he was debarred from entering into the pleasant land.

If the anger of Moses, which was kindled by intolerable provocations, and the unadvised words which it drew from his lips, excluded him from the Land of Promise, what curses were merited by the fierce rage of Simeon and Levi, which involved them in the guilt of so many massacres of innocent persons! If they had gone down quick to hell they would have deserved no more pity than Dathan and Abiram. They might be thankful to hear their father, as the messenger of Heaven, cursing only their fierce anger, and not their persons. He entertained no hatred against them; he loved their souls, and therefore declared their anger to be execrable, that they might think of it with remorse, and implore that mercy which alone could free them from the guilt of such horrible enormities.

It is to be hoped that at this time Simeon and Levi were sensible of the extreme wickedness of their conduct, yet it might be useful for themselves to be warned against any new indulgence of their furious tempers. Still they might have brought upon themselves new guilt by giving an unhallowed license to that pride which, though subdued, was not eradicated. The remembrance of the guilt of blood, and the impressions which their father's abhorrence of their conduct was fitted to make, would be a strong guard upon their tempers. The reproofs that humble us are far better than the commendations that foment our pride. And sharp rebuke is necessary for those who have greatly offended.

2 K

But punishment is likewise threatened, though great mercy is remembered in the midst of wrath. " I will divide them in Jacob, and scatter them in Israel." These are the words of God by the mouth of Jacob. God hath determined the times before appointed, and the bounds of our habitation. In His great mercy He assigned the posterity of Simeon and Levi their dwelling in Israel ; but to testify His abhorrence of the iniquity of these patriarchs, their descendants were to be divided and scattered through the land. The other tribes were to have their dwelling in a chosen spot sufficient to contain their whole number, that they might live commodiously together, and be ready to give mutual assistance to their brethren when it should be necessary. But the tribes of Simeon and Levi were to be dispersed into different parts of the country, and their friends and brethren might live at such a distance as to be incapable to unite for their general benefit.

The tribe of Simeon had a portion of land given them on the west of Judah, but it appears to have been insufficient to contain the whole tribe after they had continued some time in the possession of it, and therefore they are supposed to have been under the necessity of frequently emigrating from their own part of the country, to seek a residence, and bread for their families, amongst their brethren of the other tribes. A great body of them were forced to seek distant settlements in the days of Hezekiah, 1 Chron. iv.

The children of Levi were excluded from any particular allotment in the land of Canaan. The offerings of the Lord made by fire, the tithes, and first-fruits, and other holy things, were their inheritance. This, it may be said, was no hardship, but a blessing. And certainly that tribe was happy above the other tribes which the Lord chose for His own special service. The priests and Levites were made in some measure dependent on the justice and generosity of the other tribes. When the people of Israel revolted, as they too often did, from the God of their fathers, the tribe of Levi were exposed to great danger of losing that which stood in the place of an inheritance to them, or of being drawn along with the body of the people into those courses of defection which it would have cost them their livings to oppose; yet, on the whole, it may be said that what seemed to be a curse was turned to them into a blessing. But the words of Jacob were true—" They were divided in Jacob, and scattered in Israel," still more than the children of Simeon. And Levi, for aught we know, was denied the comfort of knowing that his children should be happy and honourable in their dispersion, that he might all his days mourn for the evils that might come upon his posterity for his own fault. It is just that bad men, or even good men that have provoked the Lord by bad behaviour, should be punished with the sight or with the knowledge of the calamities which they have brought upon those whom they most dearly love; and it is not less just that they should not be suffered to see or know the good which Divine Providence may bring out of these evils. Hezekiah knew that his descendants should be eunuchs in the palace of the King of Babylon; but he did not know that some of the seed-royal were to be more honoured, and do more good in Babylon than they could have done in Jerusalem. Levi could easily foresee the inconveniences to which his seed would be subjected, but it is not likely that he foresaw the shining glory of his race.

We may observe by the way one answer that may be made to those presumptuous intermeddlers with the Divine government, who allege that it is inconsistent with the righteousness of the Most High to visit the iniquities of the children upon the parents, because the children may be holy although the parents are wicked. It is very true that the children of wicked parents may be holy, and eminent in holiness, and yet suffer under the effects of the guilt of their parents. Zerubbabel suffered the effects of the wickedness of his progenitors when he rose to no higher a station in Judah than that of governor under the kings of Persia. But who will say that God was unrighteous because He did not give to that prince the throne of his father David in all its ancient splendour? Many of the sons of Levi were holy men in an eminent degree. Was the Lord under any obligation on that account to set them free from all the inconveniences which attended the dispersion of that tribe in Israel? He did what was far better, He made their dispersion a blessing to themselves and to all the people. They taught Jacob God's statutes, and Israel His laws, through all the provinces of the Holy Land. Although they had not inheritances of the same kind with those of the other tribes, the Lord was their inheritance; and they could say, " The Lord is the portion of our inheritance and of our cup, he maintaineth our lot."

When the people revolted from the house of David, it was a great hardship on this tribe that they were stripped of those privileges which were intended to indemnify them for the want of a share in the division of the land. Jeroboam made priests of the lowest of the people, because he found that many of the former priests and of the Levites would not willingly walk after his commandment. But it was the advantage of this tribe, in that time of apostacy, that they were divided in Jacob. Many of the sons of Levi had their dwelling within the boundaries of Judah and Benjamin. And others who were deprived of their privileges and property, in the territories of other tribes, found a welcome reception amongst those tribes that still clave to the house of David, and to the service of the Lord.

The Simeonites, in their dispersion, did not enjoy the same privileges with the tribe of Levi, but such of them as feared God were happy, for they enjoyed a share in all the felicities of the chosen people of God. They were closely connected with the tribe of Judah, and many of them, in the bad days of Jeroboam and his successors, were kept from the general apostacy. As for the children of Israel that dwelt in the cities of Judah, Rehoboam reigned over them, 1 Kings xii. Many of these children of Israel who are distinguished from the people of Judah were doubtless Simeonites.

Let not those men who smart under the losses or afflictions brought upon them by the bad behaviour of their parents think that they are excluded from the favour of God any more than the happy children of the godly, who enjoy the honour and advantages left them by their pious ancestors. It is to be hoped that Simeon and Levi are at this day blessing God for the methods taken to work a sound repentance in their souls. It is certain that some of the ancients of the family of Levi were eminently pious, and that they left the blessing of God to their descendants. " My covenant," says God by Malachi, " was with him of life and peace ; and I gave them to him for the fear wherewith he feared me, and was afraid before my name. The law of truth was in his mouth, and iniquity was not found in his lips ; he walked with me in peace and equity, and did turn many away from iniquity," Mal. ii.

Some will perhaps allege that other tribes met with the same fate as Simeon and Levi, and therefore it was no great discovery of foresight in Jacob to foretell that they were to be dispersed in Israel. It is true that the tribe of Manasseh was divided from itself by its own choice ; yet the individuals of the half tribe lived in the neighbourhood of their brethren of the same tribe. There were but a few hundreds of the Danites who went to seek out new possessions ; and the reason why they found their former possessions too strait was because they had not sufficiently exerted their force in driving the Canaanites out of the possessions given them by lot. But the words of the inspired patriarch by no means implied that none except the descendants of Simeon and Levi should be scattered in Israel. What was in their case the consequence of the behaviour of the fathers of the tribes might in other cases result from causes of a different kind.

It is well worthy of our observation that the inspired historian who records the sentence pronounced on Simeon and Levi was himself a great-grandson of Levi by the mother's side, and removed only one degree farther from him in descent by his father's side. Why does Moses record a sentence so dishonourable to his progenitor, and so likely to expose the family of Moses, with the other families of his tribe, to the reproach of their enemies ? Because Moses was an honest man, and his pen was that of a ready writer, employed by the Holy Ghost to record everything that seemed good to him for the use of edifying.

Ordinary writers take pleasure in magnifying their ancestors. They are strongly disposed to entertain a too favourable opinion of persons entitled to their veneration, and to conceal or to soften anything in their character that deserved to be reprobated. Moses was preserved by the Spirit, who enlightened his mind, from all false judgments concerning persons or actions; and he had no wish to spread false colours over any bad action, by whomsoever it was committed. When we read his history of Abraham, Isaac, and Jacob, we find that he draws not the character of perfect men; yet we find only human frailties in any part of their behaviour that does not meet our approbation. But in his account of Levi, who was nearer to himself in the line of genealogy than any of them, we find almost nothing that is not execrable. Although we hope to find Levi at last amongst the number of those great criminals who will be eternal monuments of the glory of divine grace, yet Moses gives us no account of his repentance, or of its fruits. He finishes the life of this ancestor in this place, where his behaviour is so severely censured by his own father; sure evidence that he wrote it not under the influence of such motives as those by which the generality of men are governed.

Moses was no less eminent for meekness than this ancestor for the contrary vice. It is possible that his knowledge of this piece of history was one motive to that wonderful government of his temper for which he was so justly renowned. And he wished all the sons of Levi to remember what infamy and rebuke the father of their tribe had brought upon himself, that they might learn to be meek and gentle towards all men.

When Moses himself blessed the tribes of Israel he took no notice of the tribe of Simeon. The children of that patriarch in the wilderness appear to have been too like their father. But his benediction of the tribe of Levi was very different from Jacob's. Jacob blesses the tribe so far as to leave it a place in Israel; but Moses foretells that the Thummim and the Urim should be with God's Holy One, that family which He had set apart for His own immediate service. Whatever our ancestors have been, or whatever we ourselves have been or done, there is mercy and forgiveness with the Lord. If we have a place and a name amongst His people, we enjoy inestimable privileges and advantages. " A day in God's courts is better than a thousand. It were better to be door-keepers in the house of our God, than to dwell in the tents of wickedness ; for the Lord God is a sun and shield. He will bless the house of Aaron, he will bless the house of Levi. He will bless all that fear the Lord, both small and great." He will curse the blessings of those that will not turn at the voice of His reproof. He will turn into blessings the curses of sinners that forsake their ways and their thoughts, and turn unto the Lord, and seek His favour through the great atonement. " Although their sins be as scarlet, they shall be as white as snow ; although they be red like crimson, they shall be as wool."

LECTURE 3
The blessing of Judah.
xlix 8–12

VER. 8. *Judah, thou art he whom thy brethren shall praise: thy hand shall be in the neck of thine enemies; thy father's children shall bow down before thee.*

ONE would almost say that Leah prophesied when she gave the name of Judah to the fourth of her children. It signifies praise; she expressed by this name her gratitude to the God of her mercies. But Jacob makes use of the word from which the name is taken to express the future glory of the sons of this patriarch—" Judah, thou art he whom thy brethren shall praise." We are most likely to obtain comfort and credit in those children for whom we gave praise to God, or whom by ardent devotions we commit to His care.

" Judah, thou art he whom thy brethren shall praise." To Reuben the venerable patriarch had said, Thou shalt not excel. To Judah he promises the most distinguished rank amongst all the tribes of Israel. Judah had sinned like Reuben, but his guilt was not so aggravated. He had not gone up to his father's bed. His crime was intentionally fornication. This, indeed, was sufficient to have procured him sharp rebuke from his dying father, and curses from God, who abhors all impurity of heart and conduct. What shall we say, then? Is there partiality with God, who gives to one sinner the honours of which He divests another for his iniquity? God forbid. He will not lay upon any man more than is just, but He will give to some men what they had no ground to expect. The incestuous Reuben is bereaved of the excellency of dignity and the excellency of power; but it is given to Judah, who, by the unbridled indulgence of his fleshly desires, exposed himself to the stain of incest, as well as Reuben. The shame of such execrable lewdness was attached to his name. The guilt of a shameful impurity was really contracted, but the Lord will have mercy on whom He will have mercy.

"Thou art he whom thy brethren shall praise: thy hand shall be in the neck of thine enemies." The intrepid and successful bravery of the men of Judah was often the subject of admiration. As soon as the tribes of Israel sent forth separate armies against the Canaanites that were left in their land, the tribe of Judah gained high renown, which was well maintained in succeeding generations. The fiercest giants could not stand before Caleb and his brave associates. David was of the tribe of Judah. By him was the kingdom of Israel raised to a power and glory which made his name great in distant lands; and his valiant exploits, as well as his eminent piety, will never be forgotten.

Valour exerted in a bad cause deserves not praise, but execration. Valour in the service of one's country, or in the defence of the oppressed, has always been praised, and it well deserves a very high degree of praise. It is glorious to risk one's life for what ought to be valued far above life. It is shameful to be so anxious about the safety of our persons, as to decline the bearing of our part in the defence of our country, or our religion.

"Thy father's children shall bow down before thee." Israel continued hundreds of years without a king. The first lawful king was of the tribe of Benjamin; Abimelech had been chosen to the regal office only by a small part of his people, but the covenant of royalty was made with David. The Lord gave the kingdom of Israel to him by a covenant of salt. He did indeed rend a great part of the kingdom from David's grand-son, and gave it to a man of the house of Ephraim; but He still gave David a light in Jerusalem. Besides Judah and

Benjamin, a great part of the tribe of Levi, many of the tribe of Simeon, and probably some pious refugees or exiles of all the tribes continued under the government of the family of David. His throne was overturned by the righteous judgment of God, when the people were carried to Babylon. It is not, however, to be doubted but the government was in a great measure vested in rulers of the tribe of Judah after the people returned to their own land. But in Christ Jesus this part of the blessing of Judah has its principal verification. " The Lord God hath given him the throne of his father David, that he may rule over the house of Jacob for ever; and of his kingdom there shall be no end."

VER. 9. *Judah is a lion's whelp: from the prey, my son, thou art gone up. He stooped down, he couched as a lion, and as an old lion; who shall rouse him up ?*

The lion is the strongest among beasts, and turneth not away for any. Yet this noble animal is not ashamed of artifices to make sure of its prey. " They have now compassed us in our steps," says David, speaking of his enemies, " like as a lion that is greedy of its prey, and as it were a young lion lurking in secret places." When Judah is compared to a lion stooping and couching down to watch for his prey, that he may spring upon it, and seize it, before it perceives the danger, the holy patriarch might possibly intend to signify that union of artifice with valour by which success is ensured in military operations. Yet it seems more suitable to the character here given of this valiant tribe to suppose that this image points out that fearless confidence which set their enemies at defiance. As the lion rends his prey, and then lies down to devour it at his ease; so the men of Judah spoiled their enemies, and enjoyed the fruits of their victory, without any fear of retaliation, or of losing what they had gained.

Judah was like a lion's whelp, who goes up from tearing his prey to his den, and fears no pursuer. If a multitude of shepherds should go forth against him, he will not turn back at their voice, nor abase himself for the noise of them. Judah was like an old lion come to its maturity of vigour, who couches

down, and lies at his ease : none dare stir him up ; or if any
should undertake such a perilous enterprise, his life is the
penalty of his rashness.

This character of the tribe of Judah was abundantly verified
in the exploits of David and of his champions and armies, as
well as in many lion-like exploits of this tribe both before and
after the time of David. The hands of Judah were through
the help of God sufficient for him, and the Lord was his
defence from the enemy.

Christ is, in the book of the Revelation, in allusion to this
part of the blessing of Judah, called the Lion of the tribe of
Judah. The glorious things spoken of Judah were still more
eminently verified in Him than in Caleb or David, whose
exploits and successes seem to have prefigured the glorious
actions and acquisitions of the great King, in whom the
covenant of royalty with David has its full accomplishment.
" He hath done excellent things : this is known in all the
earth." He will still perform marvellous things in the defence
of His people, and in the destruction of their enemies. As the
lion roaring upon his prey, when the multitude of shepherds is
called forth against him, he will not regard their voice, nor
abase himself for the noise of them ; so will the Lord of hosts
come down to fight for mount Zion, and for the hill thereof,"
Isa. xxxi. 4, 5.

VER. 10. *The sceptre shall not depart from Judah, nor a law-*
giver from between his feet, until Shiloh come, and unto him shall
the gathering of the people be.

Although very different meanings are given by translators to
some words in this famous prophecy, yet the general sense of
the whole is so plain that it furnishes us one of the most
convincing and unexceptionable proofs against the Jews that
the Messiah is already come, and that it is vain to look for
another.

The word which we render *sceptre* frequently signifies a
tribe ; and some take the meaning of the first part of the
verse to be, that Judah should continue a separate tribe till the
Shiloh came. Whilst most of the other tribes were to lose

their separate existence, the tribe of Judah was to make a figure as a distinct tribe of Israel.

The word for lawgiver does not always, if ever, mean the supreme magistrate in the nation. David says, "Judah is my lawgiver," Ps. lx. 7. "Out of Machir came down governors," Judges v. 14. The same word is here used to denote governors which we render lawgiver in the passage before us.

When it is said, "The lawgiver or governor shall not depart from between his feet," the meaning plainly is, that the tribe of Judah should have governors proceeding from itself.

There is a difference of opinion concerning the Messiah being called the Shiloh, although there does not seem to be any good reason for it. There is no doubt that Messiah must be meant. Those who mean anything else by this word can neither give a tolerable reason for it, nor a good sense to the passage. The peaceful one, or he that is the giver of tranquillity, appears to be the true meaning of the name. And what fitter name can be given to Him who hath reconciled us to God by His blood, and who gives us that peace which passeth all understanding ! He is expressly called the Prince of Peace.

"The sceptre shall not depart from Judah, and the lawgiver from between his feet." So the first part of the verse may be literally rendered—that is, they shall not both depart. If the sceptre, the emblem of royal power, should fail, yet there shall be governors proceeding from the Jews themselves, to rule over them, until Shiloh come.

The word *shall* may, without violating the sense of the original, be left out of the last part of the verse, and then the meaning will be, that the Shiloh shall not only come, but the gathering of the people shall be to Him, before the sceptre and the governors proceeding from Judah fail.

It is abundantly evident that both the sceptre and what is called the lawgiver are long since lost in Judah ; that the tribe of Judah has lost the records of its genealogies ; and that none can discriminate the true descendants of the patriarch Judah from the descendants of Benjamin, or of the other patriarchs. Either this word of promise to Judah has failed for evermore, or Shiloh is come, and it is vain to look for another Messiah.

It is no less evident, on the other side, that the registers of the tribe of Judah contained an authentic account of their genealogies, at least till the reign of Herod, under whom Jesus of Nazareth was born; and that the Jews either gave kings to all Israel, or to a great part of the nation, or furnished governors, in whom a great part of the public authority was vested, till Jesus appeared amongst men, and till the Gentiles were gathered to Him to be His subjects. The word which we render "gathering of the people," occurs only in one other passage, where it is justly rendered *obey*, Prov. xxx. 17. Now, not only many of the Jews, but great multitudes of Gentiles yielded obedience to Jesus before the time of the destruction of the Jewish commonwealth. The Gospel, according to our Lord's prediction, was first preached to all nations, and then the end came.

We now see the excellency of the blessing given to Judah. He was to be the father of the Shiloh ; and till the Shiloh came, this tribe was to be the most glorious of all the tribes of Israel. The word *sceptre*, in the beginning of the verse, seems to be the true meaning of the original word in this place ; for Israel had already said that Judah's brethren were to bow down to him. A king, in Scripture language, does not always mean a supreme or independent ruler; we read of kings being subject to other kings. Herod was King of the Jews in our Lord's time, and yet he was a slave to the Romans. A sceptre, therefore, the emblem of royal power, may be used to denote those rulers who have a superior on earth, if their own nation acknowledge their authority. In this sense of the word, even after the diadem fell from the heads of David's family, the sceptre might still be said, in some inferior sense, to continue in Judah. Daniel probably ruled over the Jews during a great part of the Babylonian captivity. The power given him by Nebuchadnezzar would enable him to be their protector. Even Jehoiachin, who had formerly been their king in the middle of the years of captivity, seems to have recovered some portion of his former authority under the patronage of Evil-Merodach.

Zerubbabel, who long held the government under the kings of Persia, was the great-grandson of this prince. Nehemiah is supposed, likewise, to have been of the stock of David. The Maccabean princes were of the tribe of Levi, but it is probable that, in a certain sense, they might be ranked amongst the descendants of Judah, for in the long and friendly intercourse between these two tribes, the posterity of the two patriarchs were frequently intermingled by marriage. Jehoiada the priest, in Ahaziah's time, was married to his sister; Zacharias, the father of John the Baptist, was married to a cousin of Mary the mother of our Lord, who was certainly of the tribe of Judah, and of the family of David. The Jews reckoned their genealogies for the most part by the fathers, yet sometimes, as amongst ourselves, they seem to have been reckoned from the mothers, when these were more eminent in rank. Our present race of kings are not reckoned strangers, although their right to the throne of Britain, as far as it depends on birth, is derived from a princess of the ancient blood of our kings. Some of the ancient priests were called the children of Barzillai, who was not of the family of Aaron, or of the tribe of Levi, but a descendant of Manasseh, Ezra ii. 61. When Judah was told that the sceptre should not depart from his line, he would not have thought that God's word of promise merited the less return of gratitude, although he was not informed whether he was to be the father by the male or female line of those kings that should proceed from him. Some of the progenitors of Joseph, in the lists given us by Matthew or Luke, must have obtained their place in that glorious register, not by a natural but by a legal relation to him; and yet who will say that the honour done to them was a false gift, like clouds or wind without rain? All God's promises are good and true, although they are not all fulfilled in the manner which might have occurred to the mind when they were first published.

But although there had been no relation between the Maccabean princes and the descendants of Judah, except the common relation of the Israelites to one another, yet the word of God to Judah did not fail, when a great part of the power of government was vested in the elders of the house of Judah, by whose cheerful consent the supreme power was lodged in a family that had been the saviours of the nation. When Herod obtained the crown, a great part of the power still remained with the Sanhedrim. If the sceptre departed, the lawgiver did not depart from Judah either during his reign or during the administration of the Roman governors. It was, indeed, wisely ordered in the Divine councils that the sceptre should depart from Judah, and yet the power of the council of Judah should be left, when Shiloh came. He was to appear, not as a secular prince, but as a servant. He was to be a servant of princes, and to suffer the worst of indignities and outrages, both from Jews and Gentiles, that He might lay the foundations of His widely extended dominion in the blood of His cross.

But did this glorious blessing of Judah terminate in the coming of the Shiloh? It was expected that the Messiah would bring with Him the richest blessings to men, and in particular to His own people. The name here given Him is in effect a promise of the most precious blessings. Were the seed of Judah, then, to lose their glory and felicity when the great Son of Judah rose up to reign over the Gentiles, and to bless them with His salvation? Far from it; Judah was still to be blessed, Israel was to be saved by the Messiah with a more glorious salvation than had ever been bestowed on the chosen people in ancient times. But the distinction between Jews and Gentiles was to be set aside. In Christ there was to be neither Jew nor Greek, Barbarian, Scythian, bond nor free, but Christ was to be all in all. The obedience of the nations was to be yielded unto Shiloh. He was to reign over the house of Jacob for ever; but the house of Jacob was to consist of all that in every place called on the name of the Lord Jesus Christ. Judah was to have the distinguishing glory of giving a Saviour to the world, and of spreading the light of the Gospel to the uttermost parts of the earth. The seed of Jacob was to be from the Lord of hosts like a dew to the nations, that waiteth not for man, nor tarrieth for the sons of man. They were to be like a lion among the beasts of the forest, to subdue the nations to the obedience of Christ; but the nations subjugated to Christ were to be the Lord's free men, and to enjoy all the privileges of their conquerors.

It was the joy of the ancient patriarchs that the Shiloh was to proceed from them. It was their joy that a large part of their natural seed should be blessed in him; but it was the completion of their joy that to him the gathering or the obedience of the people should be. Abraham and his seed were the heirs of the world, and then they were put in possession of the inheritance when the Gentiles were made to rejoice with His people in the administration of the same Lord, whose dominion was to extend from sea to sea, and from the river to the ends of the earth.

Do you think that Judah was a happy man when he heard his father's prophetical blessing? Do you think that the tribe of Judah was happy because they were heirs of the blessing? But are not we too happy when the blessing of Jacob and Abraham comes upon us Gentiles through Jesus Christ? Have we yielded the obedience of faith to the great Redeemer? He came unto His own, and His own received Him not; but to as many as receive Him to them, whether Jews or Gentiles, He gives power to become the sons of God. The same Lord over all is rich to all that call upon Him, whether Jews or Gentiles; for it is written—"Whosoever shall call upon the name of the Lord shall be saved, and to him shall the obedience of the people (not of one people only) be."

The whole blessing of Judah had a favourable aspect toward us when it was predicted that the tribe should be preserved and blessed with distinguishing honours till the Shiloh came. The Lord had in view not only the honour and advantage of His highly favoured people of Israel, and of the tribe of Judah in particular, but the salvation of the Gentiles who were to be gathered in to Shiloh. For our sakes Israel and Judah enjoyed the Divine protection till the Christ came, that we might be saved by His obedience to the death. The whole train of providential administration in the world, and especially towards the chosen nation, was directed towards the redemption and salvation of men as its object. David's family was preserved from destruction when it was threatened by its most implacable enemies, because Immanuel was to be born by a virgin of that family.

It is a senseless objection which some have made to this prophecy, or to the use which Christians have made of it, that the sceptre did not come into the hands of Judah till several hundreds of years had elapsed after this prophecy was published. Can it be thought that this objection proceeds from mere inattention? or have the objectors wilfully forgotten that Jacob was professing to speak only of those things that should befall his children in the latter days?

VER. 11. *Binding his foal unto the vine, and his ass's colt unto the choice vine: he washed his garments in wine, and his clothes in the blood of grapes.*

Why do not those who take pleasure in cavilling at the Word of God tell us that this prediction also was found false? The plain meaning of it is, that the country of Judah was to abound in vines, and yet Judah, like the other tribes of Israel, was left in Egypt almost two hundred years after this time, and did not obtain possession of the land of vineyards till about half a century after they came out of Egypt. But it is evident that even a child could answer such an objection as this, and therefore it was perhaps never started.

That part of the land of Canaan which was allotted to the tribe of Judah was to be so fertile in vines that it would not be unusual for men to bind their young asses to vines, as they do in other countries to any kind of barren timber. Wine was to be produced in so rich abundance that the people might have washed their garments in wine, and their clothes in the blood of the grape. Job uses a like figure of speech when he says "that he washed his steps with butter, and the rock poured him out rivers of oil."

We cannot say that Divine Providence has bestowed on us a country like this which was given to Judah. But we have no reason either to complain of our own condition, or to envy those whose lines are fallen in a land of vineyards. If we are to be numbered amongst those who walk righteously and speak uprightly our bread shall be given us, and our water shall be sure.   If our dwelling is not of the fatness of the earth, we shall dwell on high, and the place of our defence shall be the munition of rocks.   If we are truly obedient to Shiloh, although we drink not of the produce of the wine, we are refreshed by that new wine which goeth down sweetly, causing even the lips of them that are asleep to speak.

The Lord does not grudge the comforts of life, any more than the blessings of eternity, to His people.   But we must leave it to His kindness and wisdom to judge what portion of these good things is fit for us.   Let us ever trust in God, who giveth us all things richly to enjoy.

VER. 12. *His eyes shall be red with wine, and his teeth white with milk.*

Would it have been a blessing to Judah to have his eyes in the literal sense of the expression red with wine?   Very far from it; but it was a blessing to him to have a land so rich that he might drink wine in as much plenty as the laws of temperance would give him leave.   When it is said that he should wash his garments in wine it certainly is not meant that he would actually make use of wine instead of water to wash his clothes.   This would have been a very grievous abuse of the goodness of God.   But would it not be a more grievous abuse of Divine goodness to make use of it to destroy our own under-standings, and to disfigure our faces?

The same word which is here used to denote redness is used in Prov. xxiii. 29, and, I believe, nowhere else in Scripture. In that passage Solomon speaks of redness of eyes as one of the detestable effects of drunkenness: "Who hath woe? who hath sorrow? who hath contentions? who hath babblings? who hath redness of eyes? who hath wounds without cause?   They that tarry long at the wine, they that go to seek mixed wine.   Look not upon the wine when it is red, when it giveth its colour in the cup, when it moveth itself aright; at the last it biteth like a serpent, and stingeth like an adder."

Yet, when the patriarch says his eyes are red with wine, he perhaps intended to show what use would too often be made of the goodness of God by the favoured tribe of Judah. If the words be considered as a blessing, they can only signify that wine should abound so much as to give occasion for intemperance to men whose appetites were not restrained by piety. But if we consider them as a prediction that many would abuse the plenty of their soil, they can by no means be pleaded as a justification, but may rather be considered as a censure of the crime. God's foresight of the wickedness of men does not turn it into righteousness.

Those who must drink water, whilst others drink wine in bowls, may learn from these words not to envy those who are richer than themselves, and who can command at pleasure the best productions of the earth. Wealth is a blessing, but a blessing that may be greatly abused, and often is abused to the worst purposes. If you were lords of a rich estate, are you sure you would make a good use of it? You see a rich man faring sumptuously every day, and swallowing down the delicious draughts which, by his intemperate indulgences, are converted into poison. You think that if you were in his place you would rather throw your wealth into the sea than use it to the destruction of your own bodies and souls. But how do you know that if you were in his place more grace would be given you than he has received. God only knows how you would have used anything that has been withheld from you ; leave it, therefore, to His wisdom to choose the lot of your inheritance.

" His eyes shall be red with wine, and his teeth white with milk." In our own country we enjoy the richest part of this blessing ; milk is better than wine. There is a great difference between the price and nature of commodities. Those which are lowest in price are often highest in value. What reason have we to thank God that those good things which are most necessary for our subsistence and comfort are most easily procured ! We have still greater reason to be thankful that blessings infinitely more precious than the wine and milk of Canaan are set before us in the Gospel, to be bought without money and without price, Isa. lv. 1, 2.

LECTURE 4

The blessings of Zebulun, Issachar, and Dan.

xlix 13–18

VER. 13. *Zebulun shall dwell at the haven of the sea ; and he shall be for an haven of ships ; and his border shall be unto Zidon [or, towards Zidon].*

IT is plain that the bounds of our habitations are allotted to us by God ; it was by lot that all the tribes of Israel had their inheritances assigned to them. How, then, did Jacob know, so long before his seed obtained possession of Canaan, what portion should be assigned unto any one of them ? He says concerning the inheritance of the tribe of Zebulun what would not have been true if it had been said of any other of the inheritances of the twelve tribes except Asher, and yet was strictly true concerning theirs, that they should dwell at the haven of the sea, and enjoy the advantages of commodious harbours in the neighbourhood of the ancient city of Zidon. How could Moses, when he committed this prophecy to writing, know that it would be verified ? No other way but by his faith in the word of God. There could be no artifice used to effect an agreement between the lots used in the division of the land and the prophecies of Jacob or Moses. But the whole disposing of lots is of the Lord.

All the tribes of Israel were to possess a good land which the Lord had spied out for them, yet some of them were to enjoy a richer or a more commodious portion than others. The land of Judah was to be more fertile in vines than the inheritances of most, if not all, of the other tribes. But Zebulun was to have this great advantage of dwelling near to the sea, where he should be a haven for ships, and enjoy the riches which commerce affords to maritime countries. They were to suck of the abundance of the seas, and of treasures hid in the sands.

Let those who are furnished with every facility for acquiring riches consider to whom they are indebted for this benefit. It is God that gives us power to become rich. If we obtain a large portion of His earthly blessings, let us use them for His glory, and be watchful against the temptations that accompany them. Tyrus, in her days of Pagan darkness, acquired prodigious riches by trade, which swelled her with pride to her destruction, Ezek. xxviii. The same city, when she received the Gospel, learned how to make herself friends of the Mammon of unrighteousness, Isa. xxiii. 18.

"And his border shall be unto Zidon." This famous city was situated in the vicinity of the land of Israel, and yet never learned the religion of Israel before the days of the Gospel. The nations would not change their gods, which yet were no gods. And yet the nation which was taught the knowledge of the only living God borrowed strange gods from its neighbours. The neighbourhood of Zidon was often a snare to Israel; Jezebel was a princess of that country, and brought her idols with her, which were the destruction of her husband's house, and of many thousands in Israel. If you have wicked neighbours, be on your guard. Those who would rob you of your innocence or of your faith are the most dangerous of all thieves.

From the account of the inheritances of the tribes (Josh. xix.), it appears that Asher bordered on great Zidon, and that the tribe of Zebulun was separated by Asher from that famous city; yet we have no reason to doubt that the blessing of Zebulun was more distinctive of that tribe than it could have been of that of Asher, which probably did not avail itself so much of its maritime situation, or of the neighbourhood of Zidon. Those who lived in the days of the judges and kings of Israel knew better than we can do how exactly the ancient predictions concerning the natural seed of Abraham were accomplished. But we know enough of their accomplishment to fill us with wonder and praise, and to banish all doubts concerning the Divine original of the word of prophecy.

Zebulun bordered not only on the great sea, which we now call the Mediterranean, but on another sea frequently spoken of in the Gospels, the Sea of Tiberias, where our Lord found several of those holy men whom He called to the glorious office of apostleship. It is probable that some of the apostles were sons of Zebulun.

VER. 14. *Issachar is a strong ass couching down between two burdens [or borders].*

Asses were not so contemptible animals in the eyes of the Jews as they are amongst us. In the blessing of Judah it is said that he should bind his young ass to the vine, and his ass's colt to the choice vine. Rich as this tribe was to be in vine-yards and pastures, asses were to be in common use. When Ziba wished to make his court to David by a present, asses for the king's household to ride on were a part of it. We ought not, therefore, to think that Issachar was vilified when he was compared to a strong ass any more than Dan when he was called a serpent, or Benjamin when he was likened to a wolf. Homer compares Ajax, one of his most illustrious heroes, to an ass that could bear the strokes of the driver without moving from his place.

Yet when Issachar is compared to a strong ass, lying down between two burdens, an idea seems to be conveyed of a mean and cowardly spirit that dares not assert its own rights. But perhaps this idea of the tribe of Issachar is given us not so much in these words as in our translation of the next verse. The word which we render burdens seems to signify borders. Issachar is like a strong-boned ass lying down between the two borders or extremities of his inheritance.

VER. 15. *And he saw that rest was good, and the land that it was pleasant ; and bowed his shoulder to bear, and became a servant unto tribute.*

He was to be very unlike the lion-like tribe of Judah ; Judah's hand was to be in the neck of his enemies, but Issachar was, like the tame ass, rather to suffer blows with patience than to exert his great strength for redressing his own wrongs. It is certainly good to delight in peace, and to bear much for its sake ; but there are extremes to which even the love of peace ought not to be carried. Some of the tribes of Israel suffered much from their cowardice when they obtained possession of Canaan. They preferred their ease of pleasure to the toils of war, in driving out their implacable enemies, the Canaanites, and the consequences were fatal, both to their outward and to their spiritual welfare.

" He saw that rest was good," or that his place of rest was good, " and the land that it was pleasant." What, then, ought he to have done ? He ought to have exerted a noble spirit to secure the enjoyment of his rich inheritance. " Wilt thou not possess," said Jephthah to the king of the children of Ammon, " what Chemosh the god giveth thee to possess ? and shall I not possess that which the Lord my God giveth me to possess ? " Deborah highly praised those governors and common people of Israel who jeoparded their lives in the high places of the field for the liberty and safety of their people, but pronounced a curse upon those cowards that came not forth to the help of the Lord against the mighty.

If we are not lovers of peace and justice, we are enemies to God and man. We ought to bear much for the sake of peace. But sloth and cowardice often have sheltered themselves under a fair name, and, under pretence of aversion to strife and variance, have brought on those evils which they sought by foolish methods to avoid. Our fathers deserve high commendation for the efforts which they often made to repel the invaders of their liberty.

Our Lord tells us that when men give us a blow on one cheek we ought to turn to them the other ; and that when they compel us to go one mile with them we should rather go two miles than stir up strife, which may be attended with bad consequences that we cannot foresee. Our Lord's admonitions are all full of truth and wisdom, but they do not bind even private persons to part with their rights without using such means to vindicate them as are warranted by justice and charity. Far less ought nations to crouch under the insolence of oppressors when they have power to vindicate their liberties. Civil, and especially religious liberty, is a very precious blessing, which ought to be maintained at the risk of life, though not with the loss of a good conscience, which is infinitely more valuable than life itself. Nations, as well as individuals, ought above all things to follow after righteousness. It is not every act of oppression that will justify a war amongst nations, any more than an insurrection of subjects against their rulers. That aversion to war which is founded in the sincere love of peace and justice is highly to be praised. That dislike of trouble, and toil, and danger, which is purely the effect of cowardice, and disqualifies men from bearing their part in the defence of liberty, just government, or religion, is unworthy of men or Christians.

These observations occur to us in reading this part of Scripture prophecy, yet it may be questioned whether Jacob intended a censure on the posterity of Issachar. The words are very differently translated by the Seventy. Issachar desired that which is excellent, resting in the midst of the lots; and having seen the rest that it is excellent, and the land that it is fat, he subjected his shoulder to labour, and became a husbandman. Issachar was surrounded by other tribes, and seeing his portion of the good land to be very fertile, he devoted himself to husbandry. Husbandmen are ordinarily as virtuous a part of public communities as any whatsoever. Their business exposes them to fewer temptations than many others. There is, however, no condition of life entirely exempted from temptations. When men are so entirely occupied with their own affairs that they have no spirit for engaging in hazardous enterprises when the public interest requires their exertions, their industry, which at other times is praiseworthy, exposes them to just censure, and may be attended with bad consequences, both to themselves and to the communities of which they make a part. How the tribe of Issachar behaved on other occasions we know not; but we are

informed that in the war with Jabin their princes behaved
nobly, when some of the other tribes disgraced themselves by
their cowardice. Asher abode in his breaches, Gilead abode
beyond Jordan, Dan remained in his ships, Reuben abode among
the sheepfolds to hear the bleating of the sheep, whilst the
princes of Issachar were with Barak and Deborah, to fight the
battles of the Lord and of Israel.

In the days of David a good character is given of the men
of Issachar. They were men that had knowledge of the times
to know what Israel ought to do. All the tribes of Israel were
then blamable, except that of Judah, in submitting to the
usurpation of Ishbosheth, or Abner, who reigned in the name
of Ishbosheth. Perhaps the men of Issachar were more
blamable than the other tribes, because their rulers better
knew their duty, and were induced by prudential considerations
to decline it till Ishbosheth was dead.

Let us all be lovers of peace, and as far as possible live
peaceably with all men; but let us not seek peace with other
men by means that would deprive us of the peace of our own
minds. Let us all cultivate a warm zeal for liberty, civil and
religious, and for civil liberty, chiefly because of its tendency
to promote virtue, and to secure our religious liberty. The
most precious of all kinds of liberty is that wherewith Christ
hath made His people free. In this we ought to stand fast,
whatever may be the consequence. Although we should be
bereaved of other kinds of liberty, we are still the Lord's free
men.

VER. 16. *Dan shall judge his people, as one of the tribes of
Israel.*

Already Jacob in spirit saw his seed distributed into tribes,
and forming together one great people. Abraham found it
necessary to send away the son of the bond woman from the
house, for he was not to share the inheritance with the son of
the free woman. But Jacob had the pleasure of knowing that
in his seed there was to be no distinction made between the
sons of the free woman and the sons of the concubines.
Divinely authorised, he declared to his sons assembled to hear

his last words, that Dan, the oldest of the sons of the bond woman, was to judge his people like any of the other tribes. Their judgment and their dignity was to proceed as much from themselves as if they had sprung from Rachel or Leah.

Such was the will of God concerning the ancient Israel, and none in the spiritual Israel must be excluded from any of the privileges obtained for us by Christ on account of their extraction. In Jesus Christ there is neither Jew nor Greek, Barbarian, Scythian, bond man, nor free. All are one in Christ.

VER. 17. *Dan shall be a serpent by the way, an adder in the path, that biteth the horse heels, so that his rider shall fall backwards.*

Courage in different persons or nations has its different characters. The character of Judah's courage is, that it resembles the courage of the generous lion, the strongest amongst beasts, that turneth not away for any. Dan was to give eminent instances of courage, but he was to resemble the serpent rather than the lion. The adder and other serpents cannot confide in their strength or speed, but lie hid in the paths, or amongst the grass, and, by a sudden spring upon the traveller, wound or destroy him, when he is not apprehensive of danger. Thus the Danites, by sudden and unexpected attacks, were to destroy their enemies. This was eminently verified in Samson ; never was a man of Judah more intrepid than he. He could tear a lion as if it had been a kid, yet he was placed in circumstances that compelled him to attack his enemies like a serpent, springing upon them when they were in no dread of any enemy. Little did they expect, when the men of Judah delivered him into their hands, that he would destroy a thousand of them with his single arm. As little did they fear, when they had put out his eyes, that he would make a greater slaughter amongst them than he had made through the whole course of his life.

How uncertain is human life ! How many adversaries have our sins raised up against us, and how soon may we be brought down to destruction by unforeseen attacks ! We who live in the island of Great Britain are in little danger from the serpents of the dust, and in none at all from the lions of the forest. Yet our lives are little more secure than the lives of men who live in the regions infested by the most venomous, or the most ferocious beasts. A slate from the roof of the house, a fall from a horse, the accidental firing of a musket, or a fit of laughter, may bring us to our graves. Men, too, are armed against one another. They are become lions and serpents to their fellow-men. All the lions and serpents that ever existed have destroyed fewer of our race in a thousand years than they have often destroyed of one another in the space of a few years.

Yet men do not always sin in destroying their fellow-creatures. The mighty men of Judah and Dan, who destroyed the enemies of their country, are praised in the book of God. And we ought to bless God for raising up heroes, who, partly by their intrepid courage, and partly by their military and naval skill and stratagems, have wrought deliverances for our king and country. It was the Lord that wrought deliverance for Syria by Naaman at a time when Naaman knew not the Lord. It is God that wrought deliverance for Britain by Nelson and other illustrious heroes, whose names will live for ever in history.

But there is an infinitely greater salvation, for which, living or dying, we are bound to give thanks to the Lord, that great salvation to which Jacob turned his eyes in his dying moments.

Ver. 18. *I have waited for thy salvation, O Lord.*

What are we to understand by this salvation? or why does Jacob express his longings after God's salvation at this time when he had blessed only a part of his sons, and was about to bless the rest of them?

What can be more properly meant by God's salvation than He who is frequently called by this name in Scripture, whose day Jacob, no less earnestly than Abraham, desired to see? When Jesus was about to come into the world, Zacharias praised the Lord God of Israel for raising up a horn of salvation to His people, according to the promise made to their fathers.. When Simeon saw the child Jesus in the Temple, he took Him up in his arms, and blessed God, saying, "Lord, now lettest thou thy servant depart in peace, according to thy word, for mine eyes have seen thy salvation, the glory of thy people Israel."

For this salvation Jacob waited all his lifelong. He believed the promise to Abraham and to himself, that in his seed all the nations of the earth should be blessed. Above all blessings, he desired the blessings that were to be procured for men by the Christ whose day he saw in the light of the promise. What could all the good things of the land of Canaan do for him or his seed without the salvation to be wrought by the Shiloh, to whom the gathering of the people was to be? Few and evil had the days of the years of Israel's pilgrimage been, and he knew not that the days of the greater part of his seed in this evil world would be better than the days which himself had seen. He sought not for a city on earth, but for a city that hath foundations; not so much for the earthly Canaan as for the better country, for that incorruptible, undefiled, and unfading inheritance, which was to be obtained for men by the blessed seed.

The reason why Jacob expresses his longing desire after God's salvation in the midst of the blessings which he had pronounced on his children may easily be given. His heart was set on this salvation. It had been the object of his most delightful contemplations, and his most ardent desires, through the course of his life. It was all his desire, and all his joy, in his last hours. His mind turned to it as the mind of a miser is ever turning to his gold.

It is probable that the predictions he published concerning his sons put him in mind of the great Saviour. He foresaw that God would raise up many saviours for Israel, but that all those salvations which any other of his descendants might accomplish would be but transient and partial salvations, salvations from particular distresses, which might leave the body of the people still in a miserable condition through the tyranny of sin. The great salvation to be accomplished by the Messiah was that deliverance on which he placed all his own hope, and to which he directed the hope of his seed. An ancient Jewish paraphrast gives this comment on the words : "I do not expect the salvation of Gideon, the son of Joash, whose salvation is temporal; nor the salvation of Samson, the son of Manoah, which is a transitory salvation; but I expect the redemption of the Christ, the Son of David, who shall come to gather to Himself the sons of Israel, whose redemption my soul desires."

The Saviour for whom the ancient patriarchs waited and longed has long since come into our world, and obtained eternal redemption for us. Blessed be the Lord, who hath accomplished the desire of His ancient servants, and hath provided better things for us than for them, that they without us should not be made perfect. Still, however, we must wait for the Son of God from heaven, who is our deliverer from the wrath to come; whilst we live, and when we die, let us wait for Him, and our hope shall not be in vain. "It is a good thing that a man should both hope, and quietly wait for the salvation of the Lord."

It is good for dying saints to tell what the Lord has done for their souls, and what dependence they place in their dying hours on the great Redeemer. All the ancient saints died in faith, not having received the promises, but were persuaded of them, and embraced them, and expressed their hope of a blessed immortality. "Let me die the death of the righteous, and let my last end be like his." But, that my last end may be like his, let my life, like his, be a life of faith on the Son of God, and on the promises of His grace.

LECTURE 5
The blessings of Gad, Asher, and Naphtali.
xlix 19–21

VER. 19. *Gad, a troop shall overcome him, but he shall overcome at the last.*

THE tribes of Reuben and Gad, and the half tribe of Manasseh, desired to have the portion of their inheritance on the east side of Jordan, and obtained their wish. But let us never imagine that the possession of any earthly object, however desirable in our eyes, will ensure our tranquillity. The Gadites had rich and large pastures for their cattle, but they bordered on some of those nations that were deadly enemies to the Israel of God from generation to generation. Their coast was Jazer, and all the cities of Gilead, and half the land of the children of Ammon, and Aroer, that is before Rabbah (the chief city of the children of Ammon). What kind of enemies the Ammonites were we may judge from their religion, which taught them that their own children would be acceptable sacrifices to Moloch, their god.

Thus said the Lord by Amos, " For three transgressions of the children of Ammon, and for four, I will not turn away the punishment thereof; because they have ripped up the women with child of Gilead, that they might enlarge their border."

Although the Israelites were the people of God, they were not assured of constant peace, or of constant victory, when they were attacked by enemies. Too often they provoked God to sell them into the hands of cruel enemies. The Gadites, in the neighbourhood of several fierce nations, were peculiarly exposed to incursions from the armies of the aliens. Gad signifies a troop, and the prediction of Jacob alludes to his name. He was often overcome by a troop, yet he was not to be forsaken. He was by his troops to overcome at the last. When, in the days of their distress, they humbled themselves before the Lord, they were to be blessed with victory and triumph. We find an instance of the completion of this prophecy (1 Chron. v.) in a war carried on with the Hagarites and the men of Jeutar, and Nephish, and Nodab, by the Gadites and the neighbouring tribes. They cried unto the Lord in the battle, and He heard them, and granted them a glorious victory.

" At the last." These words do not mean that the Gadites were to be exempted from the general calamity, when God cast Israel out of His sight, but that they were to be often delivered from their enemies, and blessed with victory in the conclusion of wars, in which at the beginning they were beaten by their enemies. We ought not to despond even under those calamities which we bring upon ourselves by our sins. If the Gadites had not sinned, they would not have been overcome by the troops of their enemies. And yet, when they cried to the Lord, and turned to him from their evil ways, their enemies were made to flee before them.

" He shall overcome at the last." These words would be of great use to the faithful among the children of God, to support their courage in evil days. When they groaned under the oppressions of their enemies, they would be able to say, " Rejoice not against us, O our enemies! when we fall, we shall arise ; when we sit in darkness, the Lord shall be a light unto us.—Our father Jacob, inspired by God, has promised us deliverance and victory, and not aught of any good thing promised by the Lord shall fail of accomplishment. Our God, our father's God, has delivered, and he will yet deliver us ; and at what time we are afraid, we will trust in him."

But did not this blessing fail for evermore when " the Lord stirred up the spirit of Pul, King of Assyria, and the spirit of

Tiglath-pilnezer, King of Assyria, and he carried them away (even the Reubenites, and Gadites, and the half tribe of Manasseh), and brought them unto Halah, and Habor, and Hara, and unto the river Gozan, unto this day ?"

The word of God did not fall to the ground, but was fulfilled, when they were carried out of their own land. The same God who had promised by Jacob that they should overcome at the last, had threatened by other prophets that the Assyrian should be their king, if they refused to return to Him, when they forsook His law. Is the law against the promises, or are the threatenings made void by the promises of God ? He will perform His promises to their utmost extent of meaning. He will give no just occasion to any of His people to say that He has become to them as a liar, or as waters that fail. But He has not bound Himself by any of His promises to turn away oftener than He pleases the punishment of backsliders, who shall be filled with the fruit of their own ways.

It may not, however, be unworthy of remark that when God cast this and the neighbouring tribes out of His sight, He did not forget to be gracious to a remnant of them. His zeal, and the sounding of His bowels, were not altogether restrained by their many iniquities. But in the midst of wrath He remembered His mercy, and promised to resent the wrongs done to them, and to heal the stroke of their wounds. Long after Gad seemed to be irrecoverably ruined by the armies of the Assyrians, we find the Lord saying concerning the Ammonites by Jeremiah, "Had Israel no sons ? Hath he no heir ? Why then doth their king inherit Gad, and his people dwell in his cities ? Therefore behold, the days come, saith the Lord, that I will cause an alarm of war to be heard in Rabbah of the Ammonites, and it shall be a desolate heap, and her daughters shall be burnt with fire ; then shall Israel be heir unto them that were heirs." This prediction seems to have been accomplished (in part at least) in the victories of Judas the Maccabee over the enemies of Israel on the other side Jordan. Some part of that country might be occupied by a remnant of the tribes which had possessed in former times the land of Gilead, for the edict of deliverance published by Cyrus invited the remnant of the ten tribes, as well as of Judah, to return to their own land if they pleased. There was a promise made concerning the land of Zebulun and Naphtali, not long before the destruction of the kingdom of the ten tribes, which received its accomplishment in the time of our Lord's abode on earth, Isa. ix. 1-6 ; Matt. iv. 12-16. Have we not reason to believe that a remnant (though perhaps a very small remnant) of the men of these tribes shared in the happiness predicted to their land ? Blessings to our land would be of little use to us if neither we nor those in whom we have an interest were to share in them.

The days are coming in which it will be again true of Gad, though not more true concerning him than concerning the other sons of Jacob, that he shall be delivered from all his enemies. The Lord is not only faithful, but abundant in goodness and truth, and will set his hand to recover a second time the remnant of His people, which are left in the different countries to which He has driven them. The dispersed of Ephraim, and of the tribes that separated themselves with him from Judah, shall then be blessed with richer testimonies of the favour of the Lord than in the days of old. In these days He will be the God of all the families of Israel, and they shall be His people. He will be a Father to Israel, and Ephraim shall be His first-born, Jer. xxxi. 8-20 ; Rom. xi. 25, 26.

Happy would it have been for the tribes of God's inheritance if they had not forsaken their father's God. The blessings of their father Jacob, and the blessings of his progenitors, would still have been resting upon their heads. But all the spiritual Israel are placed under the protection of a better covenant than that under which the ancient Israel enjoyed the Land of Promise. God has made an everlasting covenant with them, that He will not turn away from them to do them good. And whatever distresses they may suffer from enemies prevailing against them, they will certainly overcome at the last.

Those are truly happy who are assured of being happy at last, although they should suffer a thousand miseries before the

2 M

day of their final triumph.   And this happiness is the portion of none but the true Israel of God ; and it is the portion, not only of every tribe, but of every individual of those whom God hath taken to be His people.   In the midst of persecution, afflictions, reproaches, necessities, and distresses, although they should have no prospect of an end to them whilst they live on earth, they are authorised to say, and they are enabled to say, when their confidence in God is not shaken, "In all things we are more than conquerors through him that loved us," Rom. viii. 37.

The martyrs slain by the dragon overcame him by the blood of the Lamb, and by the word of their testimony, whilst they loved not their lives unto the death, Rev. xii. 11.   John, in the visions of God, saw the souls of those that were beheaded for the witness of Jesus, and for the Word of God, and which had not worshipped the beast, neither his image, neither had received his mark upon their foreheads or in their hands ; and they lived and reigned with Christ a thousand years, Rev. xx.

Although we are not called to resist unto blood, striving against sin, yet we must wrestle against principalities and powers, and against those fleshly and spiritual lusts which war against our souls.   In the contest we may be brought low by the power of our enemies, but we shall overcome at the last. God hath said, "Sin shall not have dominion over you.   The God of peace shall bruise Satan under your feet shortly."   And therefore, when we see a law in our members warring against the law of our minds, and bringing us into captivity to the law of sin, we can still thank God through Christ Jesus.   We may provoke God to sore displeasure by yielding to temptations, and may be left for a time to lament our folly.   "But he will turn again, he will have compassion upon us.   Thou wilt subdue our iniquities ; thou wilt cast all our sins into the depths of the sea," Micah vii. 19, 20 ; Thess. v. 23-29 ; Rom. vii. 23-25.

Ver. 20. *Out of Asher his bread shall be fat, and he shall yield royal dainties.*

It might have been said of Asher, as well as of Zebulun, that he should dwell at the haven of the sea, and his border should reach to Zidon, Josh. xix. 28, 29. But it is probable that he did not avail himself of his maritime situation so much as Zebulun. The extraordinary fertility of his soil might render him careless about the advantages of his situation for trade. When men can easily obtain everything they wish to enjoy, they want that stimulus to exertion which others feel whose needs are a spur to action. It is wisely ordered by Providence that in our present state industry is necessary for the greatest part of mankind.

Asher was to need little from his neighbours, or from foreign countries. Industry in cultivating his own fields might be necessary for him, but these were to supply him abundantly, not only with the means of subsistence, but with materials of very profitable traffic. His land was to afford every luxury that kings could wish to have at their tables. He was to dip his foot in oil, and his shoes were to be iron and brass. The greatest part of the land of Canaan flowed with milk and honey; but the inheritance of Asher was blessed with these, and other precious commodities, more abundantly than most of the other tribes.

Beware of looking with an anxious eye upon those who possess more fruitful fields, or enjoy the comforts of life in richer abundance, than yourselves. God is good unto all, but He is sovereignly free in the distribution of His favours. If He gave to Asher a richer portion in the land of Canaan than He gave to some of the other tribes, had He not a right to do what He would with His own? Remember that Jesus Himself, when He was on earth, did not feed on royal dainties. He would not employ His miraculous power in changing stones into bread, when after a fast of forty days He was an hungered, but waited many hours till a supply of provisions was sent to Him by God, after His temptations were finished. And when, on another occasion, He showed forth His glorious power in feeding the multitudes that came to receive instruction from Him, He fed them not with the finest of the wheat, or with fat things full of marrow, but with barley loaves and fishes, which seem to have been His own common fare when He travelled in Galilee.

If we are true disciples of Christ, having such food and raiment as God is pleased to give us, we will be therewith content. For He requires us to labour, not for the meat that perisheth, but for that which endureth to everlasting life; and He gives to His followers, as He had for Himself, meat to eat that the world knows not of.

Yet if God has blessed you with a rich portion of the good things of this life, you ought to bless His name for your abundance, and for the opportunities which you enjoy of performing services to Him and to your generation which cannot be performed by the indigent. If your riches are the food of pride or luxury, you pervert the gifts of God into instruments of rebellion against your benefactor, and of misery to yourselves. But happy are the men who, whether rich or poor in the world, are rich towards God. They may eat their food, whatever it is, with cheerfulness, and drink their wine (or their water) with merry hearts, for God accepteth their works.

Ver. 21. *Naphtali is a hind let loose: he giveth goodly words.*

The allusion in the beginning of this verse is perhaps to the loving hind, or pleasant roe, which, after being taken in the snare, is tamed, and then suffered to enjoy liberty from confinement. In this view of the words, the image represents an amiable disposition as a characteristic of the tribe of Naphtali— "He giveth goodly words." He is affable and courteous, and engages the affections of his neighbours by those pleasant words, which are like a honey-comb, sweet to the soul, and health to the bones. By an image taken from the loving hind and pleasant roe, Solomon expresses that reciprocity of affection and friendly converse which should take place between a man and his wife.

If we take the words in this sense, they give us a very pleasing character of the descendants of this patriarch. Words of kindness that do not proceed from the heart are to be abhorred. They are like a potsherd covered over with silver dross. Yet it is the duty of all men to express that goodness by their words which ought to be sealed in their hearts.

Mutual love is greatly promoted by affability and pleasing converse, whilst it is checked and damped by asperity of language, or by a morose behaviour. The lips of the wise know what is acceptable. Honey and milk are under the tongue of the spouse of our blessed Redeemer, Song of Sol. v. 1.

But there is another sense which appears equally agreeable to the words. By the "hind let loose," we may understand the hind springing along with unequalled speed. In this view, it gives us an idea of that celerity in action or movement by which ancient warriors often acquired great fame, and performed great exploits. David says that the Lord had made his feet like hinds' feet, to pursue and overtake his enemies, and to overrun their countries. Julius Cæsar thought that he had exceeded himself in his exploits against Pharnace when he could say, "I came, I saw, I conquered." If we take the words in this sense, they seem to have been verified in Barak, the son of Abinoam, who dwelt in Kedesh-Naphtali. His exploits were celebrated by Deborah the prophetess, and he has the honour to have his name inserted amongst those noble champions who obtained a good name through faith, because, depending on the help of God, they waxed valiant in fight, and turned to flight the armies of the aliens.

But the mere English reader will wonder to be told that the blessing of Naphtali is capable of a sense no less agreeable to the original, which some learned expositors take to be its true signification, though totally different from our translation— "Naphtali is a flourishing oak (or turpentine tree), which produceth branches of glory." This reading gives an easy sense. There are many passages in Scripture where prosperous men or prosperous nations are compared to stately trees with spreading branches. Thus the nation of Israel is compared to a vine which spreads forth its branches to the sea, and its boughs to the rivers. That the tribe of Naphtali deserved to be compared to a tree with goodly branches may be inferred from the account of its numbers, which were fifty-three thousand and four hundred when they came out of Egypt, all of whom were the offspring of four sons of Naphtali, who came into Egypt 215 years before.

They decreased considerably in numbers in the wilderness. But the most prosperous families or nations are not in continual progress.   The most luxuriant trees have their winters as well as their summers.

Every man who meditates on the law of God day and night is blessed like Naphtali—" He shall be like a tree planted by the waters, that bringeth forth her fruits in due season." The visible prosperity of Naphtali was blasted by the judgments of God when Israel revolted from the Lord; but the trees of righteousness shall never wither, nor shall their leaves fade. The Lord will be as the dew to their souls, and therefore their branches shall spread, and their beauty shall be as the olive-tree, and their smell as Lebanon.

LECTURE 6
The blessing of Joseph.
xlix 22–26

VER. 22. *Joseph is a fruitful bough, even a fruitful bough by a well; whose branches run over the wall.*

A RICH blessing is given to Joseph. None of the blessings of the sons of Jacob were equal to it, except the blessing of Judah, which far excels, because it was promised to him that he should be the father of Shiloh, the glory of Israel, and of the human race. Joseph had the birthright, and was the best-beloved of his father, and yet his father did not give him the best of his blessings. Why? Because the Spirit of the Lord spake by Jacob. Jacob pronounced not so much the wishes of his own heart as the dictates of the Holy Ghost. He wished well to the posterity of all his sons. He wished best of all to the posterity of Joseph; but God only could tell what was to befall them in the latter days.

"Joseph is a fruitful bough, even a fruitful bough by a well, whose branches run over the wall;" or, Joseph is a fruitful tree, a son of fertility. As Jacob alludes to the names of Judah, Dan, and Gad in the blessings which he pronounces upon them, the readers of the Hebrew text will perceive an allusion to the name of Ephraim in the blessing pronounced on Joseph. Ephraim was the name given to Joseph's second son, because the Lord had made him fruitful in the land of his affliction. And Jacob foresaw that this son would be more fruitful than Manasseh, or most of the other sons of Jacob.

Joseph was in his own person a fruitful bough, growing out of the stock of Jacob. He was like a fruitful bough growing by a river of water, whose branches spread over the wall by which the tree was planted, and from which it received the warm rays of the sun. He was eminently fruitful in every virtue, and became eminently prosperous by the favour of Heaven, so that he covered with his shadow all the branches of that stock from which he derived his origin.

But it seems most proper to consider these words as referring to the ten thousands of Ephraim, and to the thousands of Manasseh. Joseph was fruitful in the land of his affliction, after he was gathered to his fathers. He was fruitful to a still greater degree in the Land of Promise. None of the tribes of Israel, except the tribe of Judah, made a greater figure than that of Ephraim. Under the conduct of a leader of this tribe, Israel was put in possession of the promised land. When the ten tribes revolted from the family of David, the kingdom which they composed was often called by the name of this tribe. And if Jeroboam, who was a descendant of Joseph by Ephraim, would have walked in the ways of God, his house would have been established like the house of David. God saw Ephraim, like Tyrus, planted in a very pleasant place. But Ephraim brought forth his children to the murderer. God had not forgotten His promises to Joseph and Jacob, but Ephraim had forgotten his father's God. Ephraim provoked Him to anger most bitterly, therefore his blood was left upon him, and his reproach did his Lord return unto him.

VER. 23. *The archers have sorely grieved him, and shot at him, and hated him.*

In ancient times the weapons of war were very different from such as are now in use, and therefore the images taken from war in Scripture are quite different from those now borrowed from the military art. Arrows were much used in the very ancient times, and therefore the enemies of Joseph are represented as archers. The archers sorely grieved him, for they shot at him, and their wounds were very painful. They hated him with a cruel hatred. They assaulted him with the sharp arrows of bitter words and injurious deeds. He was reproached as a dreamer, who raised himself unto power and dignity in his own vain imagination. He was cast into a pit, where a miserable death seemed to await him. He was sold into Egypt; he was accused of the basest and blackest crimes; he was cast into a loathsome dungeon, where he dwelt for a time that would appear very long to a man who had a right to expect very different usage. He would be often tempted to say, "How long wilt thou forget me, O Lord; how long shall mine enemies triumph over me!"

His own brethren were the archers that first attacked him, and they brought him very low; but he was brought lower still by other enemies; when he was put into prison by Potiphar, at the instigation of an imperious whorish woman, the irons entered into his soul.

What had poor Joseph done to incur such hatred? He had done nothing amiss. Whatsoever things were pure and lovely, praiseworthy and of good report, on these things he thought from his earliest years. But no innocency, no beneficence, will secure men from the arrows of slander, or the assaults of violence. Jesus Himself was a sign that was spoken against, and He suffered unrelenting persecution from Jews and Gentiles. Joseph's sufferings may be justly considered as a figure of what Christ endured from His brethren according to the flesh, as well as from strangers. Why, then, should the followers of Jesus think it a strange thing if they meet with such treatment as the best men have met with in former ages, and with that treatment to which Christ Himself was exposed for their sins?

VER. 24. *But his bow abode in strength, and the arms of his hands were made strong by the hands of the mighty God of Jacob; (from thence is the shepherd, the stone of Israel).*

When Joseph was sore assaulted and wounded by the archers he seemed to be entirely defenceless. In all human appearance it was impossible he could survive such deadly assaults of so many adversaries. But Joseph, as well as his enemies, had a bow in his hand, and this bow was neither broken, nor unemployed, nor weakened in his hand.   It still abode in its strength, and the arms of his hands were so far from being enfeebled by the sore assaults made upon him, that they waxed stronger and stronger, and his bow was renewed in his hand.   His faith did not utterly fail ; when he felt his soul ready to be overwhelmed he remembered the Lord, and his cry came into the ears of the Almighty, whose strength was made perfect in his weakness. The terrors of an ignominious death could not shake his constancy.   He knew that God was able to perform that which He had promised to him ; and that, in His own time, which was the best time, He would bring all his afflictions to a glorious termination.

A bow is an instrument of offence, and yet it is not here said that his shield or buckler, but that his bow abode in its strength. He not only remained safe under the Divine protection, but overcame all his enemies.   They were more than conquered, for they found all their malice baffled through the grace of God to Joseph.   He was not overcome of evil, but overcame evil with good.   Out of weakness he was made strong, and all that his enemies could do against him tended only to their own confusion, and to the praise and glory of the man they persecuted.

"The arms of his hands were made strong by the hands of the mighty God."   It would not have been in the power of any man to have stood firm against such potent and deadly enemies, unless the Lord had supported him.   There are, indeed, men who, by their natural constitution, or by their acquired habits, are able to encounter the terrors of death.   But Joseph's resolution of soul was the fruit of faith in God, wrought in him by His Divine power.   It was a steadfast continuance in the exercise of those graces which suited his condition.   He was strong, not by opposing a bold and desperate courage to evils that could not be avoided, but by a patient submission to the will of God in those evils which he was appointed to endure ; and this strength came from Heaven.   God is able to make all grace to abound to us, that we always, having His all-sufficiency, may abound in all good works unto His praise, in the worst conditions in which we can be placed.

"The mighty God of Jacob." The power of God is terrible to the wicked. They are the people of His indignation, who shall be punished, if they repent not, with everlasting destruction from the presence of the Lord, and from the glory of His power. But it is a pleasing attribute to His own people, because it is engaged by His covenant for their protection. "There is none like unto the God of Jeshurun, who rideth on the heavens for their help, and in his excellency on the skies." That Power which stretched out the heavens, and created all their hosts, that Power which gave being, and still gives it, to ourselves and to all the creatures in the universe, is under inviolable engagements to preserve us from all evil, and to bless us with all precious blessings in Christ Jesus. This God is our God, and therefore we may safely rest on His almighty arm.

"From thence is the shepherd, the stone of Israel." From the strength of the mighty God of Jacob is the shepherd and stone of Israel; from the help given to Joseph by this Divine Power he was fitted to be the shepherd and the support of Jacob's family. What would have become of Israel in the seven years of famine if a man had not been sent before them to provide food for them in the time of their distress? God would not have suffered them to perish, for His covenant with Abraham, and Isaac, and Jacob could not be broken. But the means prepared by Him for their preservation was the help given to Joseph. God intended that he should be the shepherd and stone of Israel, and therefore preserved him in his integrity, and exalted him to power.

We can easily see why Joseph is called the shepherd, but why is he likewise called the stone of Israel? This image frequently occurs in Scripture. Christ Himself, the foundation of all our hope, is compared to a stone, a precious corner-stone, a sure foundation. Christ called Simon, the son of Jonas, by the new name of Peter, or Cephas, which signifies a stone. David seems to be compared to a stone in these words, "The stone which the builders despised, the same is made the head of the corner." Christ Himself must chiefly be meant by this stone;

but David, who was first humbled very low, and then highly exalted, was a type of Christ in His sufferings and glory. Herein there was a resemblance between Joseph and David. The former, as well as the latter, was exalted from a state of abasement to a state of glory, for which he was prepared by his sufferings. Would it be unreasonable to think that the Spirit, who spake by the mouth of Jacob, had a view to Christ in the words before us, as well as in the 118th Psalm? Joseph was the stone as well as the shepherd of Israel. By his firmness under trial he attained that high condition in which he became the support of his father's family. What was said of Eliakim, who likewise may be considered as a type of Christ, might have been said of Joseph, that he was a glorious throne to his father's house, and a nail fastened in a sure place, on which were hung all the vessels, from those of small quantity even to the vessels of flagons.

It was God that made Joseph the shepherd and stone of Israel. By Divine Providence we are made what we are ; and we have great reason to bless God when He makes us useful to others, especially to His own people.

The Lord often brings His people through fire and water ; but let them wait for the event of His counsels, He is bringing them to a wealthy place. He is preparing them for happiness, and perhaps, too, for the honour of giving happiness to others along with themselves. If Joseph had not been greatly afflicted he would not have attained to such honours.

" The archers have sorely grieved him." The sons of Israel were the first and the most inexcusable of those archers who wounded Joseph. Yet Joseph is prepared by what he suffered from them to be a blessing to them. How amazing is the grace of God ! He will chasten us for our offences, and yet bless us by His chastisements. He will bring good to us out of those evils which we bring on ourselves. Joseph's exaltation might have enabled him to punish his earliest enemies. He might have kept them all in prison for a long time, or found some pretence for taking vengeance on them for their former works; but he knew and rejoiced that God had sent him before them to preserve to them a posterity in the earth, and to save their lives by a great deliverance.

VER. 25. *Even by the God of thy father, who shall help thee; and by the Almighty, who shall bless thee with blessings of heaven above, blessings of the deep that lieth under, blessings of the breast, and of the womb.*

Again Jacob repeats the important truth, that all the glory of Joseph, as the lord of Egypt, and the shepherd and stay of the sons of Jacob, was from the Lord, the God of his fathers. The best and humblest of men need to be often reminded that to God they are indebted for all that they have, and for all that they are.

"Even by the God of thy father." In these words Jacob expressed his warm gratitude to his God for the kindnesses bestowed on his beloved son. Jacob's God promised blessings to his seed along with himself, and remarkably verified His promise in the glorious exaltation and in the illustrious virtues of Joseph. Wise children give pleasure to their parents, and that pleasure ought to be returned to God in thankful acknowledgments. What more fervent petitions do pious parents present to God than those by which they implore His grace to their children. Prayers fulfilled should be the subject of praise, 2 Cor. i. 11.

"Even by the God of thy father, who shall help thee." Experience worketh hope. Joseph obtained signal mercies, and these mercies were bright manifestations of the power and faithfulness of the God whom he trusted. If He has already given us great deliverances from troubles, have we not reason to trust in Him that He will yet deliver us, however hopeless our situation in new troubles may appear to be.

"And by the Almighty." The heathen had no reason to expect anything from their gods. They had no power to deliver their worshippers. They could neither do good nor evil. But the portion of Jacob was not like them, for He was the former of all things. He made Himself known to their fathers by the name of God Almighty, and His works made it apparent that this was no unmeaning title. Could He ever have done such things as He had already done for them if there had been anything too hard for Him?

"And by the Almighty, who shall bless thee." He is no less wonderful in goodness than in power. He delights to bless; He had promised blessings, He had bestowed blessings on Joseph, and the blessings already given him were pledges of blessings to come. He gives liberally, and the more we have received of His bounty, the greater is our encouragement to hope for new and for still richer blessings.

"Who shall bless thee with blessings of the heaven above, blessings of the deep that lieth under." When God destroyed the old world, the windows of heaven were opened to pour down incessant showers of rain for its destruction; and the fountains of the great deep were broken up, that the waters from below, calling to the waters above, might leave no hope of escape for guilty mortals. But when blessings were promised to Joseph, he was assured that the Lord would open the windows of heaven to pour down the rain in its season on his land, and that it should be refreshed and fructified by springs issuing from the bowels of the earth. The earth shall rise up against the wicked, and the heaven shall reveal their iniquity; but heaven, and earth, and the waters below the earth, shall combine, under the superintendence of Divine Providence, to furnish blessings to God's people. He will hear the heavens, and the heavens shall hear the earth, and the earth shall hear the corn, and the wine, and the oil, to supply their wants, and to satisfy their desires.

The blessings here promised, it may be said, are not the best of blessings; they are only such blessings as God often bestows on the objects of his indignation. It is true, that the belly of the wicked man is often filled with the treasures of God; but they are like oxen fed for the slaughter, their prosperity is their destruction. But the blessings even of the present life are delightful when they are expressions of the favour of God. In the good things which Providence was to bestow on the seed of Joseph, Jacob saw the answer of his own prayers, and the accomplishment of his hope in the word of God.

The promises relating to the present life might be very useful to the family of Joseph, in particular to counteract the temptations of prosperity in Egypt, and the prospects which they might form of grandeur, by their connection with the family of Potipherah, priest of On. They might have hoped to be princes in Egypt if they had separated their interests from the family of Jacob ; but they had a surer prospect even of temporal prosperity from the promise of the God of their fathers.

When rich men have no heirs of their own bodies to enjoy their wealth, they are tempted to envy their poor neighbours, who are rich in a kind of prosperity more valuable than their own. But, with the blessing of a fruitful territory the blessings of the breast and of the womb were promised to Joseph. Sin afterwards made a miserable change in the prospects of this tribe, and of the tribes associated with it, when the prophet Hosea prayed that the Lord would give them a miscarrying womb and dry breasts.

Jacob, all his lifelong (from the time, at least, when he knew the grace of God in truth), had been seeking after blessings far more precious than those which descend from the visible heavens, or spring out of the bowels of the earth; yet he blessed God, who had fed him all his lifelong, and who gave him the cheering prospect of a plentiful provision for his numerous seed. If God not only gives us all things richly to enjoy, but enables us also to make a comfortable provision for our children, or to put them in the way of making a comfortable provision for themselves, we ought to abound in thanksgivings to that abundant goodness which loads us with benefits all the days, and beyond the days, of our natural life. Yet certainly the chief desire of our hearts for ourselves and our seed should be, that we and they may be blessed with all spiritual blessings in heavenly places in Christ. It would have given little pleasure to Joseph to have been told that his seed should be great in the land of Egypt; it was his joy that they were to have a rich portion among their brethren in the land where God's name was to be well known, and where God would command the blessing, even life for evermore.

VER. 26. *The blessings of thy father have prevailed above the blessings of my progenitors unto the utmost bounds* of the everlasting hills: they shall be on the head of Joseph, and on the crown of the head of him that was separate from his brethren.*

"Few and evil," said Jacob to Pharaoh, "have the days of the years of my life been, and have not attained to the days of the years of the life of my fathers in the days of their pilgrimage." He had a much more afflicted life, and fewer days allotted to him, than Abraham or Isaac. But let no man measure his happiness by his prosperity, or by his exemption from distress, or by the length of his mortal life. When Jacob was dying, he thought himself happier than either Abraham or Isaac, and he had reason for it. He did not indeed think that he was going to receive a richer portion of the blessedness of heaven; he very probably thought that he was far inferior in spiritual endowments to Abraham, and not equal to Isaac. But through the sovereign goodness of God, his blessings prevailed above the blessings of his progenitors. They had but one blessing to give, but Jacob had blessings for all his sons without exception; for although he administered reproofs to some of them, and denounced against them testimonies of the Divine displeasure, yet he left to them all the glorious hope of a share in the Land of Promise, and in the privileges of God's inheritance. Abraham and Isaac, doubtless, did all they could to train up all their children in the service of God, for the possession of eternal blessings; and, for aught we know, they might be blessed with success in their endeavours to be useful to the souls of all, or the greatest part of their children. But they knew that none of them were to share with Jacob in the inheritance of Canaan. Nor had they the cheering prospect concerning their distant posterity, that those measures were to be taken for preserving the knowledge of God amongst them, by which it was to be preserved amongst the chosen people of the Lord.

* Or termination, or desirable things.

We ought to observe the special kindnesses of the Lord to us, that our thanksgivings may abound to His glory. When we consider God's dealings with ourselves and with our families we will probably find reason to praise God for singular mercies, for mercies not vouchsafed to many better men than ourselves. If we cannot leave to our children rich possessions in the land of promise, we can leave them what neither Abraham, nor Isaac, nor Jacob could leave to their posterity; we leave them in possession of Bibles and of religious institutions, more valuable than those by which the seed of Jacob was distinguished from all the nations around them. Christ told His disciples that many prophets and righteous men had desired to see those things which they saw, and had not seen them, to hear those things which they heard, and had not heard them. We are enemies to our own comfort if we are not careful to observe distinguishing mercies.

"To the utmost bounds of the everlasting hills." It is difficult, among many senses which are given to these words, to determine which is the true. Most of the hills in the world may be called everlasting hills, for the word in the original is applicable to anything of very ancient date, or of very long continuance. "The everlasting mountains were scattered," says Habakkuk. They were so ancient that none knew when they were formed; and in all appearance they were coeval with the earth. The formation of the earth, and the production of the mountains, are spoken of by the Psalmist as contemporary events, Ps. xc. 2. We read of new mountains rising up out of the earth or sea, and of mountains destroyed by convulsions of the earth. But such wonderful changes in the face of nature are rare events. According to the common language of Scripture, and of mankind, these strong foundations of the earth are supposed to have existed from the beginning, and expected to keep their place till the earth itself be destroyed.

Some take the utmost bounds of the everlasting mountains to refer to the extent of the possessions of Jacob's family. Others consider the expression as denoting perpetual duration. In this last sense we expect a glorious accomplishment of the prediction, although it may seem at present to be forgotten. But it is questionable whether our translation expresses the sense of the original. The word which we render the utmost bound usually signifies desire, or desirable things. Moses himself seems to lead us to this meaning; when he blessed the tribes of Israel he prayed for the same blessings to Joseph that Jacob did. After having spoken of the precious things of heaven, and of the deep that coucheth beneath, of the precious fruits brought forth by the sun, and of the precious things put forth by the moon, he adds, the chief things of the ancient mountains, and the precious things of the lasting hills.

There were many precious fruits brought forth in the mountains of Palestine. When Moses expresses his earnest desire that a rich share of these might be granted to the tribes that sprung from Joseph, he seems to repeat Jacob's blessing in a richer variety of expression.

Some think that Jacob had in his view something far more excellent than the figs, or vines, or olives of Canaan. The hills were places where the patriarchs sometimes presented their sacrifices to God. There was one of them in particular where God chose to place His name, the holy hill of Zion, which God promised to establish for ever. The righteous are compared to Mount Zion, which abideth for ever—"There the Lord commanded the blessing, even life for evermore." When the Psalmist directed the views of the people to the hills from whence came their help, he certainly did not mean that their salvation was to be expected from the hills, or from the multitude of mountains, but from the Lord, who dwelt in Zion. The interpreters to whom I allude make the desirable things of the everlasting mountains to signify the blessings given from Zion, which is spoken of in the plural number (Ps. lxxxvii. 1), because Moriah, where the Temple was built, might either be called a part of Mount Zion, or a distinct mountain adjoining to Zion. Not far distant from this famous mountain was the hill of Calvary, where that sacrifice was perfected which was prefigured by the sacrifices on Mount Moriah, and by which eternal redemption was obtained for all the true Israel of God.

It is at least certain that nothing in the land of Canaan was so desirable in Jacob's eyes, for himself or for his beloved children, as those blessings which God bestows upon men through the great atonement. It may likewise be observed, that the service of God in His holy mount, and the privileges of the sanctuary, are frequently spoken of in Scripture as the chief pleasures of the holy land. That land is called the pleasant land (Dan. viii. 9), not so much from its precious productions, in which some other lands were almost if not entirely equal to it, as from the special privileges enjoyed in it from the distinguishing favour of God to His people. When Jerusalem was destroyed, the pious remnant deeply lamented that all their pleasant things were laid waste, Isa. lxix. 8 ; Lam. ii.

" The blessings of thy father have prevailed above the blessings of my progenitors, unto the utmost bound (or termination) of the everlasting hills," or to the desirable things of the everlasting hills. Whatever may be the precise meaning of the last part of these words, there is no doubt that the promise to Joseph was exceeding great and precious, that they should be upon the head of Joseph, and upon the crown of the head of him that was separated from his brethren. All the seed of Jacob were to enjoy rich and singular blessings—" Happy wast thou, O Israel! who was a people like unto thee, O people saved by the Lord ! "—but a distinguished share in these blessings was allotted to Jacob's beloved son. They were to come down from heaven in rich abundance upon Joseph's head, like the showers that water the earth. " Blessings," says Solomon, " shall be upon the head of the just." Here we find them descending so plenteously upon the head of a just man, that his posterity were enriched by them for many generations. Have we not reason to hope that they will yet come down in the last days upon the head of Joseph in richer abundance than ever ? The Lord will yet be the God of all the families of Israel. He will be a father to Israel, and Ephraim shall be His first-born. God will say of him, " Is Ephraim my dear son ? is he a pleasant child? for since I spake against him, I do earnestly remember him still: therefore my bowels are troubled for him; I will surely have mercy upon him, saith the Lord," Jer. xxxi. 20.

"And upon the crown of the head of him that was separated from his brethren." The separation of Joseph from his brethren seemed to cut off not only his hope of eminence amongst them, but even his hope of sharing in their blessings. He became not only a stranger, but an exile and a slave in a strange land. Could any hope remain that he should share in the heritage of Jacob? Yes, his strength and his hope did not perish from the Lord, to whom nothing is impossible. If he did not return to his father's house, his father's house came down to him. In his person he became the shepherd and stone of Israel. In his posterity he enjoyed distinguished honours and blessings in the land of Canaan. Nothing can hinder God from doing what He pleases; and therefore no afflictions or tribulations shall be suffered to obstruct the accomplishment of His gracious purposes. Are you separated from those whom you love? Resign yourselves to the will of God. He is able to turn the valley of Achor into a door of hope. He puts all the tears of His people into His bottle—"Blessed are they that mourn, for they shall be comforted." Blessed are all those sufferers who bear with meekness and patience the evils appointed them. Remember Joseph, remember Job, remember the Captain of our salvation, who, for the joy that was set before Him, endured the cross, despising the shame, and is now set down at the right hand of God. To him that overcometh will He grant to sit with Him on His throne, even as He also overcame, and sat down with His Father on His throne.

"They shall be upon the crown of the head of him that was (crowned among) his brethren." The original word sometimes signifies one who is crowned, or separated to high and distinguishing honours, Neh. iii. 17. Jacob never entertained high notions of the honours of this world. Yet he could not but rejoice in the honours done to his beloved son, after the unworthy treatment with which he had met in his early years. He rejoiced greatly in them, as testimonies of the favour of his

God to his favourite son, and to himself, and to all his family. The delicious pleasure enjoyed by Jacob, when he gave his last blessing to Joseph, was a rich recompense for all the pains he had endured, when Joseph was supposed to have been torn by wild beasts. Happy are the saints of God, even when they sow in tears, for they shall reap in joy. "Let me die the death of the righteous, and let my last end be like his."

LECTURE 7

The blessing of Benjamin.
Jacob dies after giving orders
to all his sons concerning
his burial.
xlix 27–33

VER. 27. *Benjamin shall ravin as a wolf: in the morning he
shall devour the prey, and at night he shall divide the spoil.*

ALTHOUGH Jacob had the pleasure of knowing that his
seed would be powerful and great, yet he foresaw that
they would not always enjoy peace. A constant peace
is not to be expected in this world. All good men are lovers
of peace, but they dwell in a world where there are too many
lovers of war.

Courage is a noble quality where contentions and fightings
are often unavoidable. The Israel of God were to have wars,
but many of them were furnished with heroic virtues, to
encounter the armies of the aliens. Judah was a lion's whelp,
or like a lion in the vigour of his age, whom none could raise
up with impunity. Dan was like a serpent, or an adder, that
bites the horse's heels, and makes his rider to fall backward.
Benjamin was like the fierce and ravening wolf, which in the
morning tears the prey, and in the evening divides the spoil
with its companions.

The enemies of God's people are sometimes compared to
evening wolves when they come forth famished from their dens,
and necessity inflames their courage, Hab. i. 8.

The Benjamites on some occasions discovered too much of the

fierce and savage spirit of evening wolves. Yet it is not probable that their father Jacob intended by this comparison to pass a censure upon them, any more than those other tribes which he compares to beasts of the earth, or serpents of the dust.

God is pleased to compare His own fierce indignation against sinners to that of a bear bereaved of her whelps. The fact is, that Jacob had but a very general and indistinct view of the completion of his own prophecies. He foresaw that Benjamin would display a fierce courage like that of the wolf, when hunger forces him to encounter every danger to supply his craving appetite. We know that this character was verified in the wars of the Benjamites against the eleven tribes, in the wars of Eliud, and Saul, and Abner; in the wars of Judah and Benjamin against the other tribes of Israel; in the vengeance executed, at the instigation of Mordecai and Esther, against the enemies of the Jews in the days of Ahasuerus. Some think that the blessed exploits of Paul the apostle ought to be considered as the accomplishment of the last part of the prediction. He was indeed a warrior, than whom no braver hero ever entered into the field of battle. He did not count his life dear unto him, that he might recover sinners out of the snare of the devil, who had been taken captive by him at his will. The weapons of his warfare were not carnal, but they were mighty through God to the pulling down of strongholds, bringing into captivity every thought to the obedience of Christ. He warred a good warfare, and divided the prey with the strong. Alexander the Great gained but the world when he conquered the world, and held it but a very short time. But many thousands of saints will be a joy and a crown of rejoicing to Paul in the day of Christ.

VER. 28. *All these are the twelve tribes of Israel: and this is it that their father spake unto them, and blessed them; every one according to his blessing he blessed them.*

The twelve tribes of Jacob are here first mentioned. From henceforth we will find them mentioned, or referred to, through every part of the Scripture. The fathers of these tribes were now with their dying father, hearing from his mouth such a portion of the mind of God concerning the future destinies of their seed, as he thought fit to declare.   The last book of the Bible contains such discoveries as God thought fit to make in His Word of the events that were to happen to the New Testament Israel.   Known unto God are all His works from the beginning of the world ; but it is fit that we should know only a part of these ways that will be more fully discovered in God's time.

   " And this is it that their father spake unto them, and blessed them."   How did he bless Reuben, or Simeon, or Levi ?   He gives them a part in the inheritance of Jacob.   Reuben was not to excel, but he was to have a part and a name in Israel ; Simeon and Levi were to be divided and scattered, but not among the Gentiles that knew not God.   We may add that their chastisements under the Divine management were blessings to them.   They were taught more effectually by the denunciations of Divine displeasure than they would have been without them, how evil and bitter their transgressions were, for which their dying father laid them under a censure never to be forgotten.   Those threatenings, and reproofs, and chastisements which do us good are needful blessings, and we ought to receive them with thankfulness.

   " Every one according to his blessing he blessed them."   He did not give them all the same blessing.   He could not have blessed any of them without Divine direction, for it was impossible for him to know, unless God had told him, that any of them would live to inherit the blessing, or that any of them should ever leave the land of Egypt.   But he not only gave them all a common blessing, but he gave each of them his own peculiar blessing ; what he said of any one of them could not be said of all, or could not be said with equal propriety of any other of them.   The scanty materials which we have of the history of the various tribes of Israel puts it out of our power to give a copious illustration of the blessings of each of the tribes from their history.   If it had been as customary three thousand years ago as at present to write histories of particular districts of countries we would have seen greater reason than we can now perceive to admire the foreknowledge of God, as it appears in the prophetical benedictions of Jacob and Moses. God's people in the ancient ages possessed some advantages which we do not now enjoy for understanding some parts of the Bible. Yet their advantages for understanding the most important of the ancient prophecies are not to be compared with ours.

It was a sublime source of joy to Jacob on his death-bed that he could leave blessings to all his seed. The greatest evils that Jacob saw in his life were the wicked actions of some of his children. How rich was the mercy of God to himself as well as to them, that after all that most of them had done to provoke the Lord to anger, he was authorised to bless them !

Parents, mourn over the sins of your children, when you see them despising the instruction which you give them. Yet discontinue not your endeavours to reform them ; what know you whether God may not give you reason for better thoughts of them before you leave the world ? Or if you should leave the world without seeing any good effects of your parental admonitions, or any answer to the prayers you presented to God for your children, you are not sure that they will be lost to them, and you may be sure that they are not lost to yourselves.

If God had given you such a father as Jacob, or promised you such blessings by the mouths of your dying fathers, as those which Jacob promised from God to some of his children, would you not have reckoned yourselves very happy? would you not have lived all your days in the faith of such gracious promises, and in the hope of such precious blessings? But all that believe in Christ are his spiritual seed. He bequeathed to them all the most precious blessings when he was leaving the world. The dying speeches and last words of Jesus may afford us far richer consolation than the best blessings of Jacob could afford to his sons. "Peace," said Jesus, "I give you, my peace I leave with you." With whom did He leave it? Not with the apostles only, but with all that should believe on Him through their word.

VER. 29. *And he charged them, and said unto them, I am to be gathered unto my people: bury me with my fathers, in the cave that is in the field of Ephron the Hittite.*

"I am to be gathered to my people." This expression does not mean that he was to be buried in the same place with his ancestors, for it is plainly implied, that whether he was buried in Egypt or in Canaan, he would be gathered to his people. Ishmael was gathered to his people (Gen. xxv. 17), although he was not buried in the cave of Machpelah, or in a country where any of his ancestors had been buried. The expression seems to signify that Jacob expected to be received again into the society of his departed kindred. Thus David says concerning his deceased child, "I shall go to him." We must all die, but none of us shall sleep for ever in death, nor shall our souls sleep with our bodies. If we belong to the congregation of the just, we are come to the general assembly and Church of the first-born which are written in heaven, and to the spirits of just men made perfect, and when we die, shall rejoin those good men who left us to dwell with Christ.

Jacob's views of death were pleasant; he was well assured that his soul would not be gathered with sinners, but with Abraham, and Isaac, and other holy men who had exchanged this world for a better. We must all soon be gathered to our people; we shall be joined in the other world with many whom we once knew in this world, whose place now knows them no more. We have little reason to doubt but there are some of those whom we once knew on earth at present in heaven; and we have too much reason to fear that others of them are in the place where God's mercy is gone for ever. Do we not know with which of these we shall dwell in the other world? What have we been doing all our days if this point is yet to be determined? O my soul, come thou not into the secret assembly of those men with whom thou wouldst not wish to be joined in the eternal state! What will wishes to die the death of the righteous avail us if we walk in the paths which lead to destruction.

Jacob had given a charge to Joseph, and exacted a solemn

promise from him to bury him, not in Egypt, but in the land of Canaan, and in the cave of Ephron the Hittite. Joseph's promise might have appeared sufficient for the good man. He knew that Joseph was too honest to violate his engagements, too affectionate to neglect his father's dying charge, and too powerful in Egypt to find any great difficulty in performing what he had promised. But the good man wished that all his sons should take part in his funeral, and that all of them should know his earnest desire to be buried in Canaan.

" Bury me with my fathers, in the cave that is in the field of Ephron the Hittite."

VER. 30. *In the cave that is in the field of Machpelah, which is before Mamre, in the land of Canaan, which Abraham bought with the field of Ephron the Hittite for a possession of a burying-place.*

It cannot be supposed that the sons of Jacob were ignorant of the place where the remains of Abraham were deposited, for they had lived for a considerable time in the neighbourhood of it, and they had doubtless assisted their father and uncles to bury Isaac in the same place. Why, then, did Jacob give them such a minute account of particulars relating to a place which they could not but know? He seems in his last moments to have taken some pains to call to their remembrance that affecting account which is given us (Gen. xxiii.) of the purchase of a burying-ground for the family. God gave not to Abraham a foot-breadth of land in the country which his seed was to inherit. He had only one little possession in it, and that was a burying-ground bought with his own money. A plain evidence both of the strength of Abraham's faith in the promise of Canaan, and of his patient submission to the will of God in delaying the accomplishment of the promise beyond the term of his own life upon earth. He was willing to be only a stranger and a sojourner in the Land of Promise all his life-long. But he desired to take possession of it for his seed, as an everlasting inheritance, with his dead body, when he should leave the world. Good men desire to be useful in death as well as in life. Jacob wished to lie in a place which the inhabitants of the country knew to be the property of the family, and expected that his seed after him would still retain their hope and desire of living in a country so much valued by their ancestors, the land which God had promised to give them, and where he was to dwell among them and bless them.

VER. 31. *There they buried Abraham and Sarah his wife; there they buried Isaac and Rebekah his wife; and there I buried Leah.*

"Abraham is dead, and the prophets are dead," said the unbelieving Jews to our Lord, "whom makest thou thyself?" They knew not that Jesus was incomparably more glorious than Abraham or any of the prophets. But certainly we have forgotten our own rank in the creation if we are unwilling to submit to that providence which will bring us to the house appointed for all living. Are we better than Abraham and Isaac, than Sarah and Rebekah? Whom do we make ourselves, if we cannot bear the thought of saying to corruption, Thou art our father; to the worm, Thou art our mother and our sister?

Jacob wished to be buried with his father and mother. The grave lost its horrors to him, when he had the prospect of being buried with persons so dear to his heart, and so venerable in his eyes. The thought that Jesus lay for some time in the grave will have a more powerful effect in reconciling our minds to the land of darkness. Jesus was buried, and continued three days in the grave, and rose again according to the Scriptures; and if we know that Jesus died and rose again, we know that them also who sleep in Jesus God will bring with Him.

VER. 32. *The purchase of the field and of the cave that is therein was from the children of Heth.*

The transaction between Abraham and the sons of Heth was public and well known; it was confirmed by the modes used in the country for ascertaining the transference of property. Jacob's sons had therefore no reason to fear that they would meet with any opposition from the people of the land when they carried their father's body to the place where his forefathers were buried. The field and the burying-place were made sure to Abraham by the sons of Heth for a possession of a burying-place.

Abraham and Jacob knew that the whole land of Canaan was to be theirs, but they claimed no right from that promise to seize upon any part of it as their exclusive property; when they found it proper to secure any spot of ground for themselves, they bargained for it, and paid the price in current money of the merchant. The time was not yet come for possessing the land by the right which the Divine grant of it gave to their posterity. Good men provide for things honest, both in the sight of the Lord and in the sight of all men.

Jacob undoubtedly loved Rachel with warmer affection than his fathers Abraham or Isaac. Yet it was not his wish to be buried with her, but with his fathers in the sepulchre which they had purchased. He hoped to see Rachel as well as Abraham in heaven. But the cave of Machpelah was the unquestionable property of the family, bought to be a burial-place. Abraham had testified his faith of the Divine promise, and his persuasion of its goodness, by the purchase which he made of a burying-place, not to himself only, but to his family. And what Jacob said to all his sons was a public profession that he also had lived and was now dying in the same faith by which his pious progenitors had embraced the promise. What was said by Paul of Joseph may with equal propriety be said of Jacob, that " by faith he gave commandment concerning his bones."

VER. 33. *And when Jacob had made an end of commanding his sons, he gathered up his feet into the bed, and yielded up the ghost, and was gathered unto his people.*

It is surprising that Jacob was able to speak so many and so excellent things, and finish them almost in the moment of his death. It was more wonderful that Jesus on the cross could speak so many words full of grace and wisdom, and should be able to cry out with a loud voice, " Father, into thy hands I commend my spirit."

When the celebrated Addison was dying, he sent for his

son-in-law, the Earl of Warwick, that he might see how a Christian could die. Here we see how a saint could die, long before saints had the name of Christians. Jacob died in faith. By faith he blessed not only the two sons of Joseph, but all his sons, and gave commandment concerning his burial; and then he gathered up his feet into the bed, and cheerfully resigned his spirit into the hand of his Father and his God. He knew that the Angel who had redeemed him out of all evil through the course of his life would not suffer him to be swallowed up by the most terrible of all the evils of affliction.

"He yielded up the ghost, or spirit." His body now turned to its dust, but his spirit returned to God who gave it. Death cannot make an end of our souls: when we die, we must either be carried by devils to the place of everlasting torment, or by angels to Abraham's bosom.

He was gathered to his people, according to his own earnest expectation and his hope, ver. 29. He had lived but fifteen years of his life with Abraham. He had lived with his father a considerable part of his short life on earth; but now he has been living with them in a better world thousands of years, and will live with them through endless ages, and with Christ, which is far better. Live by faith, as the patriarchs did, and you also shall be gathered to them when you die. How wretched will we be if we see millions with Abraham, Isaac, and Jacob in the kingdom of heaven, and ourselves cast into utter darkness! But how excellent will our joys be if we are admitted to those blessed regions, where our fellowship with Abraham, and Isaac, and Jacob, and with an innumerable multitude of saints and angels, will make but a small part of our happiness!